Beyond the sociology of development

International Library of Sociology

Founded by Karl Mannheim

Editor: John Rex, University of Warwick

Arbor Scientiae
Arbor Vitae

A catalogue of the books available in the **International Library of Sociology** and other series of Social Science books published by Routledge & Kegan Paul will be found at the end of this volume.

Beyond the sociology of development

Economy and society
in Latin America and Africa

Edited by

Ivar Oxaal

Department of Sociology and Social Anthropology,
University of Hull

Tony Barnett

School of Development Studies,
University of East Anglia

David Booth

Department of Sociology and Social Anthropology,
University of Hull

Routledge & Kegan Paul

London, Boston and Henley

First published in 1975
by Routledge & Kegan Paul Ltd
39 Store Street
London WC1E 7DD,
Broadway House, Newtown Road
Henley-on-Thames
Oxon, RG9 1EN and
9 Park Street
Boston, Mass. 02108, USA
Reprinted 1976, 1979 and 1982
Set in 10 on 11 Times (327)
Printed in Great Britain by
Unwin Brothers Limited
The Gresham Press, Old Woking, Surrey
A member of the Staples Printing Group

ISBN 0 7100 8049 2 (c)
ISBN 0 7100 8050 6 (p)

Contents

Rural social differentiation and political goals in Tanzania
Rayah Feldman 154

The Gezira Scheme: production of cotton and the reproduction of underdevelopment
Tony Barnett 183

Economic anthropology and the sociology of development: 'liberal' anthropology and its French critics
John Clammer 208

The theory of internal colonialism: the South African case
Harold Wolpe 229

Structural dependency, modes of production and economic brokerage in rural Peru
Norman Long 253

Acknowledgments

Most of the papers in this book were presented in earlier versions at a weekend conference sponsored by the Department of Sociology and Social Anthropology of the University of Hull at the end of November 1973. We should like to thank the Head of the Department, Professor Ian Cunnison, for the support which he gave to the project, and we wish to extend our appreciation to Talal Asad and Ann Zammit, who chaired sessions of the conference. Eileen Lee was, as always, most helpful and efficient in assisting with the preparation of the manuscript.

Professor John Rex encouraged this project at an early stage and we are most grateful to him. Professor Peter Worsley has been an important influence, both personal and professional, in the intellectual development of a number of the contributors to the volume. The publication of his study *The Third World*—which was written in Hull just over a decade ago—broadened the perspectives of a new generation of scholars concerned with the problems of developing countries. We should like, finally, to thank all those friends and colleagues who have offered encouragement and constructive criticism to one or other of us during the gestation of this book, although we bear the entire responsibility for its final form.

We are grateful to the United Nations and to the International Labour Office for allowing us to reproduce some of their official statistics in our tables.

Notes on the contributors

Tony Barnett teaches at the School of Development Studies, University of East Anglia. Among his earlier work, he has conducted research into race relations in Manchester.

David Booth lectures in sociology at the University of Hull. He has conducted research on social change in Cuba.

John Clammer lectures on economic anthropology and anthropological theory at the University of Hull. He has done field work in the South Pacific.

Robin Cohen teaches sociology at the University of Birmingham. Born in South Africa, he has done research in Nigeria.

Rayah Feldman has done fieldwork in Tanzania under the auspices of the Institute of Development Studies, University of Sussex, where she was a Research Officer 1969–72.

Eric Hanley lectures on race relations in the Department of Social Anthropology at the University of Edinburgh.

Caroline Hutton is a member of the sociology department at Brunel University and has conducted research on rural change in Uganda.

Norman Long is Reader in Social Anthropology at the University of Durham. He has conducted research in Zambia and Tanzania as well as Latin America.

Philip O'Brien is an economist attached to the Institute of Latin American Studies, University of Glasgow. He has done research in Latin America and was formerly at the Institute of Development Studies, University of Sussex.

Ivar Oxaal is Senior Lecturer in Sociology at the University of Hull. An American, he has been Professor of Sociology at the University of Guyana and a staff member of the Russell Sage Foundation.

John Weeks teaches in the Department of Economics, Birkbeck College. An American, he has written critiques of economic theory.

Harold Wolpe lectures in sociology at the University of Essex. A South African, he is a founding editor of the journal *Economy and Society*.

Abbreviations

The following abbreviations occur in the text:

APRA Alianza Popular Revolucionaria Americana (Peru)
ECLA United Nations Economic Commission for Latin America
ISER Institute of Social and Economic Research (Jamaica)
KANU Kenya African National Union
OLAS Latin American Solidarity Organization
PNC People's National Congress (Guyana)
PNM People's National Movement (Trinidad–Tobago)
PPP People's Progressive Party (Guyana)
RDC Rice Development Company (Guyana)
RMB Rice Marketing Board (Guyana)
RPA Rice Producers' Association (Guyana)
TANU Tanganyika African National Union
USAID United States Agency for International Development
VDC Village Development Committee (Tanzania)
WFP Workers' and Farmers' Party (Trinidad–Tobago)

1 Editors' introduction: beyond the sociology of development

The implication of our rather provocative title for this collection of new research papers can be simply stated: we believe that as a consequence of their extreme economic naïveté and implicit metropolitan bias many of the studies and theories presented under the rubric of 'the sociology of development' in the 1950s and 1960s were misconceived, intellectually abortive, and in some instances downright pernicious in their influence. We do not feel obliged to document this unavoidably harsh judgment here; it has been sufficiently demonstrated, in our view, by a number of vigorous critiques, the most important of which was supplied by Andre Gunder Frank in his *Sociology of Development and Underdevelopment of Sociology.*[1] In no other field of sociological investigation have the disastrous consequences of the economic illiteracy of professional sociologists been so starkly revealed as in the 'sociology of development'. In retrospect we can understand how this trained professional incapacity made sociologists into so many sitting ducks for the Cold War evolutionary paradigm of economic development epitomized by W. W. Rostow's classic *The Stages of Economic Growth.*[2] Those who suffered less from intellectual parochialism where economics was concerned made up for this, moreover, with a hearty disdain for history. Rostow's master metaphor which saw underdeveloped economies as so many aeroplanes waiting to 'take off' was seductive not least because it seemed to provide an alibi for the disconnected ahistoricism which typified studies of the social 'factor' in economic growth.

It is thus the contention of the editors—one with which we believe all of the contributors to this volume would agree—that the shallow and ultimately nonsensical character of much traditional 'sociology of development' resulted from the separation within academic disciplines of the 'social' and 'psychological' from the concrete historical and 'economic' aspects of change. Rather than issue yet

1

another plea for 'interdisciplinary' and ideologically demystified research, however, the intention of this volume is to provide the reader with actual examples of field studies and theoretical reviews which indicate the directions which we feel a conceptually more adequate study of developing societies should take. The writings of Andre Gunder Frank have proved crucial to us for two major reasons: first, it was principally Frank who provided the definitive dissection of mainstream studies in the sociology of development. His critique was devastating not only because he wrote as a Marxist —but equally as much because he wrote as a trained economist who could pick apart the flimsy assumptions of the economically naïve writers he attacked. Secondly, Frank was not only—or even primarily —a critic of academic sociology; he also provided the outlines of a macro-structural paradigm of the way in which economic under-development in dependent economies is actively maintained in a vicious spiral by the very forces—foreign economic investment and aid—which conventional economic theory held to be necessary for the development of such societies. It is this combination of critique of sociology with an alternative and suggestive theoretical orientation which accounts for the centrality of Frank's contribution for the various studies in this volume.[3] As will be seen, however, we have not adopted a reverential posture toward Frank's work—quite the opposite; the dominant spirit in these papers has been to try to test Frank's ideas scientifically by applying them to new empirical situations, and to pursue alternative or complementary lines of theoretical enquiry where these appear fruitful or challenging.

Three of the papers in this collection—Barnett's on the Sudan, Long's on rural Peru, and Wolpe's on South Africa—make links between the Frankian model and the approaches developed by a number of French-speaking economic anthropologists. Their incor-poration of certain features from this tradition of economic anthro-pology—which Clammer reviews and criticizes in Chapter 10— reflects a concern with two areas insufficiently analysed in Frank's work. One is the problem of the structure and range of variation of the relationships ruling between metropolitan centres and satellites; the other is what Frank calls the problem of 'continuity in change'. The Frankian model of a 'whole chain of metropolises and satellites' is considered to be inadequate by Long and Barnett. This is partic-ularly significant in as much as both are attempting to analyse field-work data in terms of the model. It is apparent that both consider that the model as presented provides no clue to the interpretation of micro-level ethnographic data.

Long's paper grows out of a regional study in Peru, and Barnett's from the analysis of a very large-scale irrigation development in the Sudan. The task which they both faced was that of locating the local level social relations observed in the course of field-work within the regional, and, ultimately, national and international contexts. Here they encountered questions similar to those faced by Hanley in his work in Guyana. If the structure of local social and economic relations is in some way conditioned by the satellite status of the society, as the model predicts, how does this dependence manifest itself in empirical field data? For Long, the work of Meillassoux, Dupré and Rey, and Coquery-Vidrovitch on the articulation of different modes of social production provides the vital link between the local, regional, and national levels. The concepts of 'mode of production' and of 'articulation'—concepts whose intricacies are explored by Clammer—are of central importance to this current. The notion of mode of production refers for them to the combination of material, human and cultural elements, in a systematic relation, through which the exploitation of the environment is possible for a group of human actors. The idea of articulation focuses attention on the social and economic relationships by means of which modes of production with different organizing principles—capitalism, feudalism, patrimonialism, and others which may not so far have been described—are empirically linked one with another. With the aid of these concepts, it becomes possible to describe the benefits which certain actors, or groups, operating in the context of different modes of production obtain from their activities as brokers (in Long's terminology) within and between modes.

For Barnett, the problem is the related one of explaining the continuity of a structure of dependence and underdevelopment. He sees Frank's use of the term 'continuity' as essentially an obfuscation which loses sight of the need to explain continuity in terms of social and economic *processes*. In the field-work situation it was this processual aspect of socio-economic structures which became crucial. Barnett feels that the Frank model does not really help here, whereas the work of the economic anthropologists does, by redefining the question in terms of the concept of reproduction. A mode of production requires for its continuity the provision of the means of subsistence for the human actors within its boundaries. This ensures the supply of personnel and material for the continuation of the social unit through time. Thus the contradictions between actors and groups of actors within one mode of production, and *between* different modes, may be explained through an examination of the common and conflicting interests which they have in common in the production of basic subsistence needs within the context of the wider system of relations (the total social formation). For, as Long says in his paper, 'the reproduction of the social relations of production for one mode is dependent on the continuity of other social relations of production found in other modes'.

3

Consideration of the question of the reproduction of the social relations of production is what directs Wolpe to this literature. For him the singular nature of South African society and politics can only be explained by recourse to an analysis of the articulation of capitalism with non-capitalist modes of production. South African capitalism may be said to be dependent on the reproduction of its relations with other modes of production. By using these terms, Wolpe is able to go beyond the unsatisfactory model of South Africa, derived from the notion of internal colonialism, to a discussion which directs our attention to very specific features of the social and economic structure. Thus he says: 'in order to avoid the abstraction involved in treating racial or ethnic groups as undifferentiated and homogeneous, we must think of each such group as having . . . a specific structure'.

It is clear, then, that for Barnett, Long, and Wolpe the marriage of economic anthropology to the Frank model supplies a theoretical vocabulary which effectively elucidates research problems, and makes possible an understanding of social processes common to three very different underdeveloped societies.

The absence of this theoretical marriage in Hanley's analysis serves as a partial demonstration of some of the inadequacies of the crude Frank model when applied to research data. Nevertheless, Hanley's study provides a wealth of specificity regarding a particular mode of agricultural development in which an embattled Marxist colonial politician attempted to partially outflank the iron grip of metropolitan domination. Moving from the Americas back to Africa, the Feldman paper documents in appropriate detail the gradual, but apparently relentless, emergence of rural capitalism in Tanzania and the conflict between this and the socialist goals of the central government. Hutton and Cohen focus on a continuing orthodoxy in the sociology of development, though they deal with an area largely missed by previous critiques. Despite the time-honoured sociological practice of blaming poverty on its principal victims, they argue, the meaning of peasant resistance to change is far from self-evident. Indeed, in the absence of an exhaustive analysis of the total context—history and contemporary economic structure—to characterize such resistance as 'irrational' is to beg some very big questions indeed. This paper—which was first given at a conference in Addis Ababa—is in fact a critical manifesto directed at the superficial ahistoricism of some contemporary studies of development in Africa.

The major thrust of this book is to suggest that a point has now been reached where theoretical convergences from within economic anthropology, sociology, and economics are making possible an integration of work on development at an advanced level of multidisciplinary sophistication. We are mindful that many readers of the book—especially sociologists and anthropologists—may be alarmed by this prospect in view of the reputed technicalities of economics. We feel none the less that with a little persistence such readers will be adequately rewarded by our first four papers. Two of the contributors to this section of the book—Weeks and O'Brien—are professional economists. Weeks has provided what is probably the most technical —yet, we would urge, lucid and indispensable—example of how a radical economist approaches the problem of underdevelopment. For the non-economist we particularly recommend this paper as an entrée to the level of economic analysis which we think indispensable to serious future students of the sociology of development. O'Brien's paper on the other hand provides a clear, concise, and perceptive introduction to the recent Latin American literature on economic 'dependence', much of which remains otherwise inaccessible to English readers.

Enough has been said to account for the inclusion in this collection of a paper devoted especially to the work of Andre Gunder Frank. Booth's essay takes the form of a retrospective introduction to Frank's work which highlights the contribution to the Frankian 'synthesis' of some of the Latin American intellectual and political currents also discussed by O'Brien. The lacunae in Frank's theory, it is suggested, have to be understood in the context of the specific polemical function which the theory performed in the Latin America of the 1960s.

Since it is really the socio-cultural praxis of economics which forms one of the central problematics of this book, the chapter by Oxaal, a 'layman's introduction' to the language and contexts of the debate over dependency theory and practice in a former British colony, provides an appropriate sequel to O'Brien's. Trinidad does not loom large on the world stage, yet with its growing susceptibility to Latin American influences combined with the juxtaposition of its Afro-West Indian population alongside its Indian, Chinese, and other minorities—'the Third World's Third World' as the novelist Vidia Naipaul has dubbed it—it makes a not inappropriate setting for a close-up look at the universe of discourse concerning economic dependency and its relationship to social change.

But we need not dwell at length on the manifold dimensions of social science thought revealed by the writers of these pages; these largely speak for themselves. This is a work of partial—not final— synthesis. In any event, partial synthesis is all that is practical: the writers represented here form no 'school' but reflect, rather, the crystallizing theoretical understandings of some, mainly young, sociologists, anthropologists and economists working out of Britain in the mid-1970s. We have no combined research programme, or prospects of founding some grandiose global research scheme. Nor do we expect or wish events in the less developed countries of the world to wait upon the creation of a finished Grand Theory of Development. As a modest, but we hope suggestive, introduction to the world of enquiry which lies beyond the 'sociology of development', we commend this book to the reader.

Notes

1 Pluto Press, London, 1971; first published in *Catalyst* (Buffalo, New York) in 1967. Other wide-ranging critical essays include especially Jamil Hilal, 'Sociology and underdevelopment', Sociology Department, Durham University, mimeo, February 1970, and Henry Bernstein, 'Modernization theory and the sociological study of development', *Journal of Development Studies*, vol. 7, no. 2, 1971.
2 Cambridge University Press, 1960.
3 Cf. in this respect the papers presented to the 1972 conference of the British Sociological Association: Emanuel de Kadt and Gavin Williams, eds, *Sociology and Development*, Tavistock Publications, London, 1974.

2 A critique of Latin American theories of dependency
Philip J. O'Brien

Dependency is very much in vogue in Latin America. Much writing on cultural, political, social, and economic matters adopts as a framework for analysis the concept of dependency. Faced with such an overwhelming mass of writing, it is pertinent to raise a number of questions—what is the background of the dependency school, and why did it emerge when it did? What sort of theory is it? How successful is it in establishing a framework for analysing the dynamics of Latin American society? What are the mechanisms involved? Does available empirical evidence seem to support the theory? What policy implications (if any) can be drawn from the theory? And how new, useful, and important really is the concept of dependency?

A. O. Hirschman, in a perceptive essay, 'Ideologies of economic development in Latin America', has traced the main views advanced by Latin Americans to explain the causes of Latin America's underdevelopment and what could be done about it.[1] The theory of dependency is a response to the failure of these explanations and those offered by the advanced countries to give either a convincing explanation of the backwardness of Latin America or a way out of that backwardness. Specifically the theory of dependency is a response to the perceived failure of the previous dominant ideology of development in Latin America, that of 'import substitution' industrialization.

A. Gerschenkron noted in his essay, 'Economic backwardness in historical perspective', that in backward countries certain institutional innovations and the acceptance of specific ideologies in favour of industrialization were necessary to break down the gap between obstacles to industrialization and the promises inherent in such a development.[2] Backward countries had to substitute for some of the factors which were prerequisites for industrialization elsewhere. This

7

substitution process and the drive for industrialization was usually accompanied by an ideology explaining the cause of, and suggesting a cure for, the relative backwardness of the country concerned. Nineteenth-century Latin America, however, evolved few ideas concerning its underdevelopment and it was not until the twentieth century that Latin American writers concentrated on attempting to explain Latin American underdevelopment.

Two themes dominated these early explanations of relative backwardness: philosophical and psychological explanations, and imperialist exploitation. The first was, and still is, very common; Latin Americans, it is argued, have certain character traits or philosophies of life which prevent the determined pursuit of rapid development. These philosophies of life or character traits, the latter often accompanied by racial interpretations, were variously identified as laziness, sadness and arrogance (e.g. C. O. Bunge, *Nuestra América*[3]), or anti-materialist, spiritual qualities as in José Rodó's *Ariel*,[4] or inequality being the result of a collective sense of inferiority as in *Profile of Man and Culture in Mexico* by Samuel Ramos.[5]

The second theme, popularized by the Peruvian leader and founder of APRA (Alianza Popular Revolucionaria Americana), Haya de la Torre, puts the blame for Latin America's underdevelopment squarely on imperialist exploitation. But interestingly and importantly *the blame is not put on capitalism.* Haya de la Torre explicitly argued that the Latin American proletariat was too weak to make a revolution, and that the responsibility for developing Latin America lay with the intellectuals and the middle classes whom Haya de la Torre characterized as being more dynamic than their European counterparts: 'In our countries, the capitalist stage must therefore unfold under the leadership of the anti-imperialist State.'[6] The anti-imperialist and anti-Marxist perspective was to have, and still does have, tremendous sway in Latin America. It was, for example, to be espoused by nearly all the post-Second World War populist leaders. But none of these ideologies—philosophical and psychological or anti-imperialist—amounted to a coherent economic programme.

Until 1929 Latin America had pursued a development strategy which has been called *desarrollo hacia afuera* (an outward-orientated development path), a reference to the fact that exports were the engine of growth of the Latin American economies. The Great Depression dramatically revealed the costs of depending on exports as the engine of growth; for when Latin America suffered a significant decline in her export earnings, the result was economic and political chaos. A new strategy and development path seemed called for; one that emphasized an inward-looking development path, *desarrollo hacia adentro.*

So after the Second World War a coherent ideology and economic programme, explaining both the causes of Latin America's problems and the way forward, and emphasizing *desarrollo hacia adentro*, was advanced. Significantly this ideology and programme came from the newly established United Nations Economic Commission for Latin America (ECLA) whose offices were opened in Santiago de Chile in 1948. It is significant because the new ideology reflected more the frustrations of technocrats and intellectuals than that of a newly emerging powerful social class. Thus unlike, for example, Adam Smith's *The Wealth of Nations* which reflected the ideology of the powerful industrial bourgeoisie of England, ECLA espoused an ideology for a class too weak to implement it—the Latin American industrial bourgeoisie aided by an educated middle class running the State machine. Moreover ECLA's voice reflected the fact that it was a UN agency. The highly-paid officials of ECLA, however radical in an international agency context, nevertheless conformed to the UN style of analysis with its bland, apolitical language of the international bureaucrat. Divorced from contact with the mass of the Latin American poor by his style of life, the international bureaucrat tends to look for compromises and for the lowest common denominator, thus not offending anyone. Not surprisingly ECLA managed to avoid the realities of the class struggle in Latin America and the role of the USA in that struggle.

ECLA's perspective was based on the belief that conventional economic theory as expounded in developed capitalist countries was inadequate for dealing with the problems of underdevelopment. The study of underdevelopment required, it was thought, a 'structuralist' perspective, an appreciation of different historical situations and national contexts. An underdeveloped country is underdeveloped precisely because it consists of different structures each with a specific type of behaviour. It was argued that conventional economic theory, with its emphasis on the theory of prices and general equilibrium, failed to recognize the existence of different structures.

The main tenets of ECLA's early position were those propounded by its first General Secretary, Dr Raúl Prebisch. He argued that Latin American underdevelopment was the result of Latin America's position in the world economy, and its adoption of liberal capitalist economic policies. Prebisch's theory was a continuation of the anti-imperialist, anti-Marxist tradition—although in a much subtler and milder form—substituting, for example, politically stronger and more precise expressions of imperialism with the misleading expression 'centre-periphery relations' (misleading in that the class content of imperialist theory is dissolved).

Prebisch argued that the Latin American engine of growth, primary product exports, was faced with a long-term secular decline in their

9

terms of trade, and that the centre's income elasticity of demand for these exports was declining whilst the periphery's income elasticity of demand for the imports from the centre was increasing. The result was a chronic structural balance of payments crisis. In addition there was an unequal distribution of productivity gains; in the centre productivity gains led to higher wages and other factor prices whilst in the periphery they led to a decline in commodity prices and stagnant wages.[7]

ECLA proposed that Latin America needed to industrialize behind high protective barriers. These barriers would not only assist the 'infant industries', but would also, given structural unemployment and under-utilization of capital, assist the optimal allocation of resources. It was recognized that the industrialization drive had to be assisted by the State, and in particular by State planning. Later, ECLA added the need to create a Latin American Common Market to achieve economies of scale. In these ways Latin America would achieve an inward-orientated development path. This strategy became known as import substitution industrialization because it was based on setting up industries which would satisfy demand previously met by imports. The assumption was that this would lessen the demand for imports and therefore help the balance of payments. The strategy accepted as given the existing demand pattern, i.e. the existing pattern of income distribution, and led to a proliferation of industries producing final consumer demand goods, especially consumer durables.

Varieties of dependency theory

The theory of dependency is the response to the perceived failure of national development through import substitution industrialization and to a growing disillusionment with existing development theory. Dos Santos has summarized the intentions of the post-war model of development in Latin America, as follows:

(1) a change from development *hacia afuera* to one *hacia adentro* would lessen dependence on foreign trade and lead to a more locally controlled economy;

(2) industrialization would lessen the power of traditional oligarchies and lead to a process of political democratization which

(3) would lead to more equal income distribution, and integrate the rural masses into a modern society;

(4) the above three encouraging the emergence of a modern, developmentally-minded State which would in turn further their development;

(5) and all would cause a change of consciousness, the emergence

of a Latin American consciousness, which would help to unite society in the pursuit of national independence.[8]

By the 1960s, it had become obvious that this model was in crisis. Import substitution industrialization had not lessened dependence. Income distribution seemed to be growing more unequal, and a large segment of the population remained marginal. Cultural alienation was widespread, and Latin American societies still continued divided and unstable. National policies for industrialization had succumbed to the multi-national corporations, and industrialization in Latin America was primarily being undertaken by foreign investors. Finally, the military were entrenched in power in many Latin American countries. The theory of dependence emerged as an attempt to explain this failure.

There are, however, a number of different traditions within the theory of dependency: one clearly stems from the ECLA structuralist perspective, and should be seen as a continuation and deepening of that perspective. Another stems from a Marxist perspective, particularly that perspective which broke with the stultifying dogmatism of the Stalinist heritage. Associated with the first are the names of Osvaldo Sunkel and Celso Furtado; and with the second, the names of Ruy Mauro Marini, Theotonio Dos Santos, and A. G. Frank. There is another group of writers, mainly sociologists like Aníbal Quijano, Fernando Cardoso, Octávio Ianni, and Florestan Fernandes, who seem to straddle both the Marxian and structuralist perspectives. The differences between these groups is clearest when it comes to perspectives for political action.

To a social scientist brought up in the dominant positivist hypothetical–deductive methodology, theories of dependency may seem at best trivial or irrelevant and at worst political slogans wrapped up as a theory. Thus it is important to appreciate the methodology behind the dependency theories. This methodology seems very similar to the Marxian one (not surprisingly, for many of the dependency theorists explicitly recognize the theory of dependency as a subordinate field within a general Marxian theory of capitalism, and in particular a complementary part of the theory of imperialism) in that it is not considered possible to study the dynamics of a society merely at an empirical or impressionistic level. Instead, as a prerequisite for understanding reality, abstractions which do not exist in a pure form in the real world have to be made and the concrete approached via 'successive approximations'.[9]

The theory of dependence, therefore, is a higher level or general hypothesis the objective of which is to define the problem or area of interest and to try and show how lower level, more specific *ad hoc* hypotheses fit within this framework. The purpose of a higher level

11

interpretation is to guide and make more coherent at an abstract level, lower level explanations, e.g. explanations of the last Brazilian *coup*. If a sufficient number of *ad hoc* explanations cannot be accommodated within the higher level hypothesis, then the plausibility and usefulness of the framework must be rejected. The theory of dependency therefore represents a framework of reference within which various heterogeneous phenomena are analysed to see how they link and interact with each other to form a total system. The theory must therefore be judged with reference to its adequacy or inadequacy as a framework for the articulation of the dynamics of certain relationships. In brief, it is an attempt to establish a new paradigm.[10]

Obviously in unsophisticated hands the danger with total viewpoints is that dependency can easily become a pseudo-concept which explains everything in general and hence nothing in particular. In the hands of some Latin American writers, the theory of dependency is used as a *deus ex machina* explanation for everything which seems to be wrong with Latin American society. Instead of having a synthesis of the historical process, a descriptive catalogue of different types of dependency is given. But the fact that some or even the majority misuse the concept of dependency should not blind one to the merits of the theory.[11]

The basic hypothesis of the theory of dependency is that development and underdevelopment are partial, interdependent, structures of one global system. Dos Santos puts it as follows:[12]

Dependence is a conditioning situation in which the economies of one group of countries are conditioned by the development and expansion of others. A relationship of interdependence between two or more economies or between such economies and the world trading system becomes a dependent relationship when some countries can expand through self-impulsion while others, being in a dependent position, can only expand as a reflection of the expansion of the dominant countries, which may have positive or negative effects on their immediate development.

Sunkel and Paz put the same point in very similar language; development is a global, structural process of change and underdeveloped countries are those countries which lack an autonomous capacity for change and growth and are dependent for these on the centre.[13] Thus, the objectives, intensity, instruments and efficiency of development policies are limited within certain margins of flexibility.[14] Furtado also emphasizes the necessity to begin with the structure of the world economy as a totality within which underdeveloped countries are sub-systems, and so the theory of underdevelopment turns out to be essentially a theory of dependence'.[15] And finally,

Cardoso and Faletto maintain that development/underdevelopment are not different stages or states of a productive system, but rather are functions or positions within an international system of distribution and production.[16]

The view that underdevelopment can only be understood as part of the world capitalist system is of course not new. All Marxist writers on imperialism emphasize this aspect; but what is new in the theory of dependency is the attempt to start from the world economic structure to then develop the laws of motion of the dependent economies. Clearly as capitalism changes from one phase to another, one would expect these changes to set into motion changes in the structures of the underdeveloped countries. Much of the writing on dependency is in fact an attempt to use a periodization approach to typologize and explain how the changes in capitalism led to changes within Latin America. It is in this historical analysis, and the present-day analysis of the problems of Latin America, that the interest in a theory of dependency lies. For the theories of dependency are trying to show that the internal dynamics of Latin American society and its underdevelopment was and is primarily conditioned by Latin America's position in the international economy, and the resultant ties between the internal and the external structures.

However, each author emphasizes different aspects of how and why the international economy and its changes, condition changes in Latin America. Cardoso is primarily interested in the economic process as a social process. He and Faletto emphasize that dependency is not an external variable, but part of a system of social relations between different social classes within the same broad ambit of dependency. They stress that the social and political aspects of the development process need to be concretely linked with the economic aspects, and not just juxtaposed with them. For the economic process is also a social process in which economic groups establish, or try to establish, a system of social relations which permits them to impose on society an economic form compatible with their interests and objectives. In a dependent economy the dominant economic groups are those which cluster around the interchanges with the metropolitan country, and these groups develop an interest in maintaining or only slightly modifying these interchanges. The dynamics of Latin American society therefore depend on changes in the world economy, and how these changes produce changes in the Latin American economy which in turn spark off political and social processes for change and so on. The emphasis throughout is on the formation of classes, class contradictions, and class alliances, and the interplay between these and changes in the economy. The intention is to try and show in a precise form, the connection between the economic and political spheres, the basic relations between a dependent Latin

America and the hegemonic centres, and the whys and wherefores of particular Latin American socio-economic formations.

Sunkel has summarized his basic approach as follows:[17]

> An analytical scheme appropriate for the study of underdevelopment and for the formulation of strategies of development should be based on the concepts of process, structure and system. It is illegitimate to argue that underdevelopment is a stage in the evolution of a society both autonomous and economically, culturally and politically isolated. On the contrary we postulate that development and underdevelopment are the two faces of the same universal process . . . and that its geographic expression is translated into two great polarizations: on the one hand the polarization of the world between industrial, advanced, developed and metropolitan countries and underdeveloped, backward, poor, peripheral and dependent countries; and on the other hand, a polarization within countries in terms of space, backward, primitive, marginal and dependent groups and activities.

To understand these polarizations, it is necessary to adopt an historical, structural and total approach, which is not arbitrary, but the result of theoretical and empirical reflection about the historical development of Latin America. The approach is also the result of a pre-analytic cognitive act—a 'vision':

> In order to point out the implications of any problem, we must first assess a defined group of coherent phenomena, which should be the object of our analytical efforts . . . efforts which must necessarily be preceded by a cognitive, pre-analytic act . . . which like Schumpeter we might call 'a vision'.[18]

What Sunkel seems to have in mind is that each structure is made up of certain elements which have their own laws, that the complex of structures held together by certain laws makes up a system, and that the system undergoes a process of change. The historical approach allows one to identify the changing structures; the productive and social structures and the power derived from them allows one to identify how these influence economic and social policies; and the total approach allows one to understand the relation of the parts to the whole as facets or dimensions of the process of change of a system—in particular, in the case of dependent countries, how changes in the productive structure and power are the result of changes in the centre countries and of the ties between these countries and the dependent ones. The conclusion derived from this approach is that many of the so-called causes of underdevelopment are really the symptoms or results of the normal functioning of the total

14

system, i.e. underdevelopment with all its generally understood characteristics is a normal part of the process of world capitalist development.

In Dos Santos's view, dependency is a conditioning situation which causes underdeveloped countries to be both backward and exploited. By a conditioning situation, he means a situation which 'determines the limits and possibilities of action and behaviour of men'.[19] The development of capitalism, he argues, led and continues to lead to a combined and unequal development of its constitutive parts: unequal, because development of parts of the system occurs at the expense of other parts; combined, because it is the combination of inequalities plus the transfer of resources from underdeveloped to developed countries which explains inequality, deepens it, and transforms it into a necessary and structural element of the world economy.[20] The conditioning situation of dependency requires an analysis of the economic relations in the capitalist centres, and the centres' expansion outward, and economic relations in the periphery, and the compromises and collusions 'among the various international and national elements which make the dependent situation'.[21]

The precise mechanisms of dependency will of course vary, and there is no substitute for detailed research on the mechanisms. Also, the nature of the foreign ties and their general and specific impact need to be analysed within identifiable historical periods. Dependency theorists generally distinguish three such periods for Latin America: the colonial, the *desarrollo hacia afuera*, and the present-day period. Their analysis of the patterns of dependency during the colonial period adds but little to, e.g., *The Colonial Heritage of Latin America* by S. and B. Stein. However, Cardoso and Faletto do manage to give a welcome social and political analysis to the Prebisch-style approach of the *desarrollo hacia afuera*. They draw an interesting distinction between the patterns of development in countries where a national bourgeoisie controlled internal production for export (although they themselves were controlled in turn by the metropolitan countries' control over commercialization, etc.) and began a process of capital accumulation through their exploitation of cheap labour and abundant land, and those countries whose ruling groups accumulated capital primarily through taxes on a foreign enclave.

The general view is that the incorporation of Latin America into the emerging world capitalist economy, first through a direct colonial administration and then, more subtly, through free trade, ensured that Latin American production was geared towards producing exports for the dominant economies, and the political and social system ensured that the gains from this were divided between a small

15

Latin American class (who used much of their gains for importing luxury consumer goods rather than diversifying investment) and the dominant metropolitan countries. The system was not static, but in general terms both social infrastructure and direct production investment decisions depended on the metropolitan countries. Thus the determinant of the growth and structure of the Latin American socio-economic formations remained largely exogenous to Latin America. By concentrating on primary product exports, Latin America was unable to develop an autonomous capacity for growth and change. Whereas the metropolitan countries, by concentrating on a productive process which had a built-in bias towards technical progress, formed 'poles of command'[22] in which capital accumulation, decisions about capital flows, the formation of prices, technical change, etc., were almost entirely concentrated within their boundaries. The result was growth and development in the dominant countries, and growth and underdevelopment in the dependent countries.

With the collapse of the world capitalist economic order in 1929, Latin America began a process of trying to lessen her external vulnerability on the world markets. This entailed both radical shifts in political alliances and power (Cardoso and Faletto neatly summarize the variety and causes of these shifts), and the use of various policies—direct and indirect foreign commerce controls, fiscal and pricing policies, State investments, and new controls over foreign investment—in the drive for national development. This drive mainly took the form of import substitution industrialization. But instead of national development, the result was but another form of dependency.

The multinational corporation

The identification of the mechanism and consequences of this new dependency has been and still is subject to change. Sunkel once argued that the interconnections of four essential elements—the stagnation of traditional agriculture, the mono-export of a primary product, the type of industrialization policies, and the functions of the State—led to 'an overbearing and implacable necessity to obtain foreign finance'[23]—the crucial mechanism of dependency. But now he argues that the key to present-day dependency is 'the penetration of the underdeveloped countries by the most powerful economic agent in the developed countries'[24]—the multinational corporation. There seems to be a consensus among writers on dependency with this viewpoint.

The thesis is that the multinational corporation (with its basic characteristic of integration of diverse activities with a single firm) is internationalizing the dynamic sectors of the Latin American economy. And so, after a brief spurt of national import substitution, the nature of the structure of production and the system of decision-making, income distribution and patterns of consumption, are becoming increasingly related to the internationalization of capital. But in contrast to previous forms of dependency, it is not trade but production for the internal market which characterizes modern dependency, and this process has taken place alongside increasing State management in the running of a dependent economy.

The key to the power of the multinational corporation is usually considered to be their control over commercial technology. Local industrialists, in order to have access to modern technology, link up with multinational corporations, and thus begin a process of de-nationalization of Latin American industry. This is part of a process whereby, in contrast to past dependency, internal markets now assume special strategic significance. Cardoso quotes from an ECLA study showing that the percentage of US direct investment in manufacturing compared with total US direct investment in Latin America rose from 7 per cent in 1929 to 34 per cent in 1968, and in the more industrialized countries of the continent, Argentina, Brazil and Mexico, from 17 per cent in 1929 to 66 per cent in 1968.[25]

The restructuring of the international economy via the multinational corporation has a number of important implications for Latin America. First, although control over primary materials is still important for the developed countries, the tendency for foreign investment to produce for internal markets means that foreign investment mainly goes to where such markets exist—i.e. developed countries. Thus, Latin America's participation in international trade has declined from 12 per cent in 1948 to 6 per cent in 1968, and her share of US foreign investment from 39 per cent in 1950 to 20 per cent in 1968. Secondly, the tendency to link local capitalists to the multinational corporation has led to an increasing use of local capital to finance the joint ventures. US subsidiaries in Latin America have only a tiny percentage of their investment funds coming from the USA, as is shown in Table 2.1.[26]

The implications of this switch to local sources of capital has been an increase of the net export of capital from Latin America to the dominant economies. The repatriation of capital by multinational corporations (not to mention the capital sent abroad by Latin Americans) can take many forms[27]—repatriation of profits, royalties and other commissions, interest and payments on inter-affiliate debts, and transfer prices. This outflow and the deficits which it implies for the balance of payments of most Latin American countries is replaced by obtaining foreign loans. However, such 'aid' entails a further loss of national powers of decision-making, and adds a new

PHILIP J. O'BRIEN

dimension to dependency. For aid brings with it the right of donors to take part in policy-making, and the necessity for dependent countries to justify constantly their policies in order to keep the flow of foreign loans coming. Loans also have to be repaid with interest, and the consequent spiralling debt of Latin America further adds to the above problems. Thus the 'national development' policies of import substitution industrialization made the balance of payments the Achilles' heel of Latin American economies. To obtain the imports necessary for industrialization and to finance capital outflows, most countries conserved their agrarian/mining export structures (including in many cases, the political power of the oligarchies

TABLE 2.1 *Source of investment funds in Latin America*

Sector:	1957–9 Source of investment			1963–5 Source of investment		
	IF	LF	US	IF	LF	US
Total	0·50	0·17	0·33	0·60	0·31	0·09
Mining	0·46	0·11	0·43	1·04	0·13	−0·17
Oil	0·57	0·09	0·34	0·96	0·14	−0·10
Manufacturing	0·36	0·40	0·24	0·38	0·40	0·22

Key: IF Internal Funds (reinvestment of profits and depreciation).
LF Local Funds, or funds coming from third countries.
US Funds coming from the USA.

which controlled them) and indebted themselves to the USA—the country whose dominance over them they were hoping to lessen.

Nevertheless, the loss of a reinvestable surplus, however considerable, is considered by Cardoso, Sunkel, and Furtado to be of less importance than the restructuring of the internal Latin American structure of production by the multinational corporation, and the subsequent socio-political effects of this change. In contrast to past foreign investment activities, the multinational corporation does industrialize in dependent countries by satisfying or even creating internal market demands. But these internal market demands are those of a small bourgeois and middle class, who, by appropriating for themselves the fruits of technical progress and other sources of high income,[28] maintain consumption patterns and styles of living comparable to their counterparts in developed countries (as *Time* magazine advertisements explicitly recognize). Growth-rates and patterns of growth come to depend on a skewed pattern of income distribution and the allocation of resources in keeping with that distribution.

18

Cardoso argues (in contrast to A. G. Frank's notion of the development of underdevelopment) that 'there occurs a kind of dependent capitalist development in the sectors of the third world integrated into the new forms of monopolistic expansion'.[29] By this he seems to mean that capitalism, albeit foreign capital, can industrialize the more advanced underdeveloped countries: the new dependency has a structural dynamism, rather than stagnation. Nevertheless, the social and economic costs of this industrialization are high. For the technology of the multinational corporation is labour-displacing. Also, many local entrepreneurs who fail to link up successfully with the multinational corporation are being displaced, as are segments of the petty bourgeoisie, e.g. small shopkeepers are being displaced by large supermarkets. The result is massive unemployment and the marginalization of masses of people who engage in low-productivity activities. The differences between the internationalized sector and the non-internationalized or marginal sector are the direct result of capitalist expansion, and become a form of structural dualism.

Cardoso rightly denies that it is possible to derive in a mechanistic way the political and social consequences of the new dependency. But he and Sunkel agree on a number of probable trends. All segments connected with the internationalized sector—agrarian, commercial, financial and industrial local bourgeoisie, much of the middle class, and the working class employed in the internationalized sector—can and probably do prosper from the new developments. The result is a fragmentation of interests—in Sunkel's view, the replacement of the class struggle by a sectorial struggle between those connected with the internationalized sector and those marginal to it. Furthermore, the restructuring of Latin America by the multinational corporation is destabilizing. To overcome the instability and to maintain the process, some Latin American countries (notably Brazil) have fallen into the clutches of a modernizing, authoritarian, military rule.

The empirical evidence offered in support of these hypotheses is admittedly somewhat casual. An historian would probably find the evidence in the historical part rather thin. But then, the theory of dependency is not meant to offer an economic history of Latin America, but rather a perspective within which to analyse that history. The evidence offered in support of the present day analysis of dependency is also scanty. What precisely is happening to income distribution and other features is problematic, but what evidence there is, does seem to support the dependency theorists. Nevertheless, more empirical evidence (especially of a more rigorous kind) would be welcome.

Policy conclusions derived from this analysis of dependency have been couched in very general terms. Furtado argues that the elimination or co-option of the national bourgeoisie rules out the possibility of the classical capitalist path of autonomous development, and that the way out is for the State to create institutions to prevent technical change concentrating income and distorting allocation, to widen the market, and to influence technical development to meet the needs of the masses.[30] To ach eve this kind of State intervention, mobilization of the masses is needed. For Sunkel, to overcome dependency means to transform existing structures in order to create a capacity for autonomous growth.[31] One must be able to manipulate natural, technical and social factors as well as relations with other countries in the pursuit of economic development. To achieve these goals, the participation of marginal groups is essential. Dos Santos makes a similar point: dependency, with all its consequences, cannot be broken by autarkism; to break with dependency, it is necessary 'to change its internal structure—a course which necessarily leads to confrontation with the existing international structure'.[32] And finally, Cardoso asserts that national development—sovereignty, internal cohesion, and progressive social integration—should be posed as an alternative to the dependent capitalist development promoted by the multinational corporation (which is attractive for all those connected with the internationalized sector, including the labour aristocracy). An awareness of social inequalities and national dependency should be promoted. Once again, the organization of the unstructured masses, of the marginal sectors, is necessary.[33]

There can be little doubt that many of the points stressed in the theory of dependency—the very concept of dependency itself, for one—have provided important perspectives for understanding development and underdevelopment. The international economy is likely to prove a more seminal starting point, than, e.g., traditional and modern society, stages of growth, achievement motivation, or even Myrdal's causally interrelated conditions of a social system. A starting point is of course no more than that—a place to begin— but it lays the basis for the direction of the analysis.[34] The new perspective is relevant to a wide range of problems. It also draws on a number of diverse intellectual currents: structuralism, Marxism, nationalism—though this is not necessarily a virtue: the eclecticism of a theory which can straddle petty bourgeois nationalism and socialist revolution should cause concern.

Usually, theorists of dependency emphasize that the classical Marxian theory of imperialism was Eurocentric: i.e. Lenin, Bukharin, Luxemburg, and Hilferding were concerned with analysing the characteristic stage of capitalism which resulted in imperialism, and its effects on the European class struggle, while the imperialized countries were of little concern, and little attempt was made to analyse the dynamics of their situation. Broadly speaking, this is true. A brief analysis was made by Rosa Luxemburg, who predicted that[35]

the imperialist phase of capitalist accumulation, which implies competition, comprises the industrialization and capitalist emancipation of the hinterland. . . . Revolution is an essential for the process of capitalist emancipation. The backward communities must shed their obsolete political organizations, and create a modern State machinery adapted to the purposes of capitalist production.

In this, she followed Marx's view that the colonies would be forced to adopt the capitalist mode of production, and that they would eventually industrialize. However, formal independence was achieved without the industrialization of most of the hinterland, and for fifty-odd years, capitalism, rather than industrializing the under-developed countries, seemed to hinder their industrialization. Bukharin was aware of the problems of imperialism as a problem of the world economy and the necessity to analyse tendencies in the development of the world economy, and probable changes in its inner structure. But although he emphasized the importance of the concentration and centralization of capital, and the rivalry among imperialist capitals for 'increased competition in the sales markets, in the market of raw materials, and for spheres of capital invest-ment',[36] he nowhere analysed what effects these developments would have on dependent economies.

Nevertheless, if one takes into account the Marxist analysis of Russia at the beginning of the twentieth century (when Russia could be seen as a dependent country) then the Marxist approach to the development of capitalism can be seen as more varied than that acknowledged by the Latin American theorists of dependency. Lenin's *The Development of Capitalism in Russia* and Trotsky's *History of the Russian Revolution* both stress the ambiguous role of foreign capital in Russia, and the weak, dependent nature of the Russian bourgeoisie, the extent of unemployment and under-employment, etc. Trotsky of course drew the conclusion that Russia's industrial proletariat (small in relation to the rest of the population but concentrated in large factories) could play the vital political role in a revolutionary situation—a conclusion which dependency theorists seem to doubt can be applied to Latin America. Trotsky also gave a brilliant summary of the law of uneven and com-bined development (a phrase taken up by Dos Santos) which rules out 'a repetition of the forms of development by different nations. . . . The laws of history have nothing in common with a pedantic schematism.'[37]

In some respects, Baran and Frank seem to share the perspective of the dependency theorists. Baran[38] offered a framework of analysis which emphasized an historical perspective and its importance for understanding the existing structures of underdeveloped countries, as well as an analysis of the interactions between underdeveloped and developed countries. He argued that underdevelopment is the result of the subordination by capitalists of pre-capitalist structures. For, although contact accelerated the decomposition of pre-capitalist structures and thus established some of the prerequisites for rapid development, the method of contact extracted an important part of the underdeveloped country's surplus for use in the developed countries, prevented the possibilities of industrialization, conditioned class formations (yielding, e.g., a *comprador* bourgeoisie) and, in general, distorted the development process to suit developed country needs. A. G. Frank[39] takes up and develops this theme: underdevelopment is the result of the process of capitalist development, which led and still leads to a series of metropolis–satellite relations in which the satellized national, regional, and local metropoles are incorporated into a world capitalist process which ensures their development of underdevelopment and their underdevelopment of development. The mechanisms of this process are the metropolis–satellite relationships, the expropriation/appropriation of the economic surplus, and a continuity in change which leaves intact the basic structures.

In many important respects, the theory of dependency adds to and enriches the classical Marxist and *Monthly Review* approach to imperialism and underdevelopment. To the classical Marxist writers, it has added an attempt to formulate the viewpoint and the laws of motion of the dependent countries. It has thus modified substantially the simplistic Marxist views on the likely effects of capitalist expansion in the underdeveloped countries, by stressing the interplay between the internal and external structures, whereas classical Marxists tended to see the expansion of capitalism into underdeveloped countries as simply a process of destruction and replacement of pre-capitalist structures.

Baran's analysis was one of the first sophisticated Marxist writings on the effects of capitalism in the underdeveloped countries. To this, the dependency theorists have added a more sophisticated and realistic analysis of classes, have added to the varieties of historical examples, e.g. the 'independent' pattern of development of countries like Argentina, and have shown that Baran's assumption that capitalism in an underdeveloped country is a framework for economic stagnation, archaic technology, and for social backwardness, is far too simplistic.

Frank has been criticized for not recognizing that the process of

underdevelopment is not one of satellization, but 'one of the formation of a certain type of internal structure conditioned by international relations of dependency'.[40] This criticism is somewhat
unfair as Frank frequently emphasizes the importance of internal
structures and their relationship to the international economy.
Nevertheless, the theorists of dependency offer a more subtle and
convincing analysis of the dynamics of the interrelationship of the
internal and external structures than Frank's rather crude, propa-
gandistic slogans on this matter. Cardoso also explicitly attacks
Frank's famous slogan 'the development of underdevelopment'. He
argues that this phrase ignores the structural dynamism of industrialization now being carried out by the multinational corporation—it
is thus possible to have a 'dependent development'—and that this
process can lead to important reforms in the old oligarchic structures,
e.g. perhaps a reform of land tenure and traditional patterns of
underdevelopment.[41] But it is not clear that Frank denies the
possibility of a dependent industrialization: what he does deny, is
the possibility of an *independent*, autonomous industrialization. He
also denies that any such process would have an effect on the
worsening poverty of the great mass of the population—the process
of underdevelopment necessarily sinks the majority of its people
into even greater poverty.[42] If Cardoso is arguing that reforms in
oligarchic structures would, for example, help the condition of the
rural masses, then he really is questioning Frank's 'development of
underdevelopment' thesis. But it is not at all clear that Cardoso
would disagree with Frank on the increasing immiserization of the
mass of the population. As neither 'the development of underdevelopment' nor 'dependent development' is sufficiently spelt out,
it is not clear what the differences are.

The actual mechanisms of dependency are seldom spelt out in
detail. In the correct desire to avoid illegitimate isolation (a fault
dependency theorists certainly cannot be accused of) they tend to
lose the parts in the totality. Everything is connected to everything
else, but how and why, often remains obscure. For example, Dos
Santos's assertion that the development of parts of the system occurs
at the expense of the other parts is probably true (Myrdal made a
similar point, though somewhat surprisingly, he is never mentioned
by dependency theorists) but the argument would be more convincing
if the precise mechanisms were specified. Moreover, past politics
and policy instruments receive only a cursory treatment, and
usually only to point out that they failed to lead to national development.

In many respects, therefore, the theory of dependency provides a
less useful perspective on underdevelopment than much Marxist
writing. Lenin's definition of imperialism, whether right or wrong,

23

enumerated what he considered to be the essential characteristics of the stage of capitalism which led to imperialism. One looks in vain through the theories of dependency for the essential characteristics of dependency. Instead one is given a circular argument: dependent countries are those which lack the capacity for autonomous growth and they lack this because their structures are dependent ones. But in a world of increasing interdependence it is important to know what makes a dependent country dependent. For clearly many countries have many of the characteristics of dependency. Canada is an obvious example of a dependent country, and yet Canada has also many of the characteristics of a developed country—high *per capita* incomes, and high levels of education, health, welfare and so on. If the concept of dependency is to replace the concept of under-development, as, for example, Celso Furtado has suggested, it is important to answer why some dependent countries are rich and others poor—for the important consideration is still poverty in all its manifestations. Obviously many of Canada's problems—regional inequality, unemployment, Quebec nationalism—can be fruitfully analysed within the dependency framework. Nevertheless, if dependency is taken to be the conditioning structure of poverty, as Dos Santos argues, then one has to explain why some dependent countries are rich and others poor.

The failure to enumerate and analyse the essential characteristics of dependency leads to confusion when it comes to policy. For policy conclusions are also (perhaps deliberately) left very vague. It is never clear whether the multinational corporation is to be national-ized or to be controlled by an Andean Pact-style foreign investment code, nor which specific policies are to be followed with regard to technical transfer and technical development, unemployment and income distribution, etc. The main policy advocated is that of chang-ing the internal structure to obtain national development. Dos Santos seems to view socialism as being a precondition for this change. Cardoso possibly takes this view as well: his analysis of the industrial bourgeoisie of Brazil and Argentina[43] had led him to conclude that they preferred an alliance with foreign capital, and accommodationist political alliances, to preserve their market positions, rather than trying to obtain State power directly for them-selves. Thus 'it is not very realistic to expect the national bourgeoisie to lead resistance against external penetration'.[44] But Cardoso also gives the impression that the industrial proletariat has been bought out, and that the nationalist banner (who is to lead it, and what policies are to be inscribed on it is left unspecified) should be adopted to unite all marginal sectors in a drive for national integrity. Sunkel and Furtado are perhaps more squarely in the reformist ECLA tradition which wants national development without the class struggle and independence without revolution. Much writing on dependency seems to leave one with the vision of the desirability of an anti-imperialist, populist leader uniting his people under a technocratic State. The trend may be in that direction: but is it any more likely to succeed now than it was in the past, or has been elsewhere? Dependency is undoubtedly here to stay. The basic point it makes —that the interplay between the internal Latin American structures and international structures is the critical starting point for an understanding of the process of development in Latin America—is of vital importance. It opens up new possibilities for future work. But was it really necessary to write so many millions of words to establish just this perspective?

Notes

1 A. O. Hirschman, 'Ideologies of economic development in Latin America', in A. O. Hirschman, ed., *Latin American Issues—Essays and Comments*, Twentieth Century Fund, New York, 1961; reprinted in A. O. Hirschman, *A Bias for Hope*, Yale University Press, New Haven and London, 1971.

2 A. Gerschenkron, 'Economic backwardness in historical perspective', in B. Hoselitz, ed., *The Progress of Underdeveloped Areas*, Chicago University Press, 1952.

3 Carlos Octavio Bunge, *Nuestra América*, 1st ed., Buenos Aires, 1903.

4 José Enrique Rodó, *Ariel*, 1st ed., Montevideo, 1900; Cambridge University Press 1967 ed. has notes and introduction in English by G. Brotherston.

5 Samuel Ramos, *El Perfil del Hombre y de la Cultura en México*, 1st ed. Mexico, 1930; English translation, *Profile of Man and Culture in Mexico*, University of Texas Press, 1962.

6 V. R. Haya de la Torre, *El Antiimperialismo y el Apra*, Publicaciones del Partido Aprista Peruana, Lima, 1928.

7 R. Prebisch, *The Economic Development of Latin America and its Principal Problems*, United Nations, New York, 1950.

8 T. Dos Santos, 'The crisis of development theory and the problem of dependence in Latin America', in H. Bernstein, ed., *Underdevelopment and Development*, Penguin, Harmondsworth, 1973.

9 Cf. P. M. Sweezy, *The Theory of Capitalist Development*, Monthly Review Press, New York, 1942, chapter 1.

10 Cf. T. Kuhn, *The Structure of Scientific Revolutions*, Chicago University Press, 1962.

11 J. Hodera, 'La dependencia de la dependencia', *Aportes* (Paris), July 1971.

12 T. Dos Santos, *op. cit.*

13 O. Sunkel and P. Paz, *El Subdesarrollo Latinoamericano y la Teoría del Desarrollo*, Siglo XXI editores, Mexico, 1970.

14 O. Sunkel, 'National development policy and external dependence in Latin America', *Journal of Development Studies*, vol. 6, no. 1, October 1969.

15 C. Furtado, 'Dependencia externa y teoría económica', *El Trimestre Económico*, April–June 1971. Translations from Spanish sources are by the author.

16 F. Cardoso and E. Faletto, *Dependencia y Desarrollo en América Latina*, Siglo XXI editores, Mexico, 1970.

17 O. Sunkel, 'Capitalismo transnacional y desintegración nacional', *El Trimestre Económico*, April–June 1971.

18 O. Sunkel and P. Paz, *op. cit.*

19 T. Dos Santos, *op. cit.*

20 T. Dos Santos, 'The structure of dependence', *American Economic Review*, May 1970.

21 T. Dos Santos, 1973, *op. cit.*

22 C. Furtado, *Economic Development of Latin America: A Survey from Colonial Times to the Cuban Revolution*, Cambridge University Press, 1970.

23 O. Sunkel, 1969, *op. cit.*

24 O. Sunkel, 1971, *op. cit.*

25 F. Cardoso, 'Dependency and development in Latin America', *New Left Review*, no. 74, July–August 1972.

26 Source: *Survey of Current Business*, several numbers: ECLA analysis in F. Fajnzylber, *Estrategia Industrial y Empresas Internacionales*, Rio de Janeiro, UN, 1971, reproduced in Cardoso, *op. cit.*, p. 92.

27 Cf. C. Vaitsos, 'Transfer of resources and preservation of monopoly rents', paper presented at the Dubrovnik Conference of the Development Advisory Service of Harvard University, 2–6 June 1970.

28 O. Sunkel, 1971, *op. cit.*, identifies the sources as '(*a*) high productivity activities; (*b*) transfer of income from high productivity sectors to areas unrelated to them; (*c*) monopolistic exploitation of product or factor markets in sectors of low productivity; (*d*) external transfers of income'.

29 F. Cardoso and E. Faletto, *op. cit.*

30 C. Furtado, 'La concentración del poder económico en los Estados Unidos y sus proyecciones en América Latina', *Estudios Internacionales* (Instituto de Estudios Internacionales, University of Chile), October–March 1968.

31 'Economic independence cannot be the magical consequence of an heroic act', O. Sunkel, 1969, *op. cit.*

32 T. Dos Santos, 1973, *op. cit.*

33 F. Cardoso, 1972, *op. cit.*

34 T. Vasconi argues that dependency is not a causal category but a matrix of relations of a general condition. Thus it offers no specific empirical references, but rather a new perspective. Cf. 'Dependencia y superestructura', *Revista Mexicana de Sociología*, October/December 1969.

35 R. Luxemburg, *The Accumulation of Capital*, Routledge & Kegan Paul, London, 1951.

36 N. Bukharin, *Imperialism and World Economy*, Merlin Press, London, 1972.

37 L. Trotsky, *The History of the Russian Revolution*, Gollancz, London, 1965.

38 P. Baran, *The Political Economy of Growth*, Monthly Review Press, New York, 1957; Penguin, Harmondsworth, 1973.

39 A. G. Frank, *Capitalism and Underdevelopment in Latin America*, revised ed., Monthly Review Press, New York, 1969; Penguin, Harmondsworth, 1972; *Latin America: Underdevelopment or Revolution*, Monthly Review Press, New York, 1969; *Lumpenbourgeoisie: Lumpendevelopment*, Monthly Review Press, New York, 1972.

40 T. Dos Santos, 1973, *op. cit.* Frank has also been criticized from a Marxist standpoint (in E. Laclau, 'Feudalism and capitalism in Latin America', *New Left Review*, no. 67, May–June, 1971) for using capitalism to mean '(a) a system of production for market in which (b) profit constitutes the motive of production and (c) this profit is realized for the benefit of someone other than the direct producer, who is thereby dispossessed of it'. Laclau argues that this definition deals only with the circulation of commodities and ignores relations of production. Frank, it is true, fails to define his key terms—capitalism, metropolis–satellite, exploitation, underdevelopment—clearly or adequately; e.g. he relies on an image of exploitation (a path leading from the Bolivian peasant to the rich New York capitalist) rather than giving an analysis of exploitation. His single unilinear explanation of all imbalances is a way of avoiding an explanation of the mechanism of differentiating imbalances. Nevertheless, Frank's basic point holds: that it was capitalism which implanted slavery in the us South, the latifundio in Latin America, etc. It may be true (as Laclau says) that, e.g., slavery in the us South was a slave mode of production, but the important point is the relationship between this and the dominant mode of production, industrial capitalism. Where the source of the subordinate mode of production was pre-industrial or mercantile capitalism (e.g. in the case of the latifundio in Latin America) the question is obviously more complicated.

41 Cardoso gives few examples.

42 A. G. Frank, 1969, *op. cit.*

43 F. Cardoso, *Ideologías de la Burguesía Industrial en Sociedades Dependientes (Argentina y Brasil)*, Siglo XXI editores, Mexico, 1971.

44 F. Cardoso, 1972, *op. cit.*

3   The dependency economist as grassroots politician in the Caribbean

Ivar Oxaal

Lying a few miles from Latin America, with the hills of Eastern Venezuela visible across the placid Gulf of Paria, is the island of Trinidad. With one million inhabitants it is the major industrial and commercial centre of the islands comprising the Lesser Antilles. Sighted, named and claimed for the Spanish by Columbus on his third voyage, this minor conquest on the fringe of the continent remained undeveloped for centuries. Toward the end of the eighteenth century, however, a more vigorous breed of French Creole planters and their slaves were admitted who opened new land to cultivation and established a picturesque social ascendancy with their balls, fêtes and carnival. In the early nineteenth century the island passed over to the British who instituted Crown Colony rule and greatly expanded the production of slave-grown sugar. With the abolition of slavery in the 1830s the resulting labour shortage on the plantations was resolved by the importation of thousands of indentured labourers from India, thus establishing the island as a conspicuous example of one of those makeshift social and cultural conglomerates which the British Empire created, as needed, throughout the world in the heyday of European direct rule.

The discovery and exploitation of oil amidst the sugar-cane fields in the early years of this century did much to hasten the development of social forces in the island. The traditional colonial social pyramid had consisted basically of the rival English and French white elites at the top, generally socially and occupationally aloof from a developing brown-skinned middle class, who were in turn at a social and cultural distance from the masses of black Afro-Trinidadians. Originally, the new migrants from India were regarded by all as merely 'Coolies' at the foot of the social ladder, but eventually they, too, would rise into middle-class positions and become viewed as a minority rival community which might possibly block the forward progress of the black population. In the 1930s, however, both Indo- and Afro-Trinidadians united in a militant working-class movement, tinged with socialist ideas, which demanded Home Rule for the colony and its diminutive sister island, Tobago.

The evolution of the British Empire after the Second World War conferred on these demands for colonial independence a greater degree of realism. In 1947 the British announced their readiness to leave their old sugar islands and territories, which stretched in a great arc from British Honduras to Jamaica and down the Leeward and Windward islands through Trinidad to British Guiana on the mainland. Nationalist parties, generally with a middle-class leadership, flourished in bewildering profusion throughout the region with the largest of the British islands, Jamaica, leading the way. In 1956 Dr Eric Williams, the dynamic Oxford-educated historian and author of *Capitalism and Slavery*, successfully contested for office in Trinidad with his newly formed People's National Movement. This gave a tremendous fillip to hopes for radical change in the region even though Williams had not been able to enlist the support of the Indian population who now organized themselves into a rival ethnic-based party. He brought back to Trinidad his old tutor, the Marxist writer and Trotskyist revolutionary, C. L. R. James, author of that other Caribbean classic *The Black Jacobins*. After a period of ferment, however, James was dismissed from his position of influence and Dr Williams began, before the attainment of political independence in 1962, to strike a far more accommodative posture toward the very metropolitan powers which some of his followers, inspired by developments in revolutionary Cuba, had hoped he might oppose more persistently. Despite these disappointments, however, even his opponents would concede that Dr Williams with his speeches in 'The University of Woodford Square' in downtown Port of Spain had done much to raise the level of political awareness in Trinidad. Ironically enough, this growing political consciousness had by 1970 resulted in an indigenous Black Power movement, based chiefly on the Afro-Trinidadian unemployed youth and university students, who would see in Dr Williams's own parliamentary regime the chief barrier to social progress.

In response to the problems of political independence there arose a West Indian school of dependency economists who have supplied for the plantation societies of the capitalist Caribbean a critique similar to their Latin American counterparts described above by O'Brien. Here we will trace the unusual career of one of them: a professional economist who has ventured to translate his analysis into direct action.

The Mimic Men

In his 1967 novel, *The Mimic Men*, the Indo-Trinidadian writer Vidia Naipaul describes the misadventures of the colonial politicians who inherit power in the mythical island of 'Isabella', a thinly disguised Trinidad with a dash of Jamaica and Guyana added in. Having thrust themselves forward to fill the vacuum created by the departing colonial establishment, these 'mimic men' find themselves utterly unable to cope with the problems of government. They spout socialist slogans and have themselves photographed cutting ribbons to inaugurate various minor public construction projects which in the past would have gone unheralded. But all is sham; they are made frantic and ultimately overwhelmed by the twin furies of the chronic social distress in Isabella and the cool, olympian control over its economy exercised by the foreign management of the bauxite companies. They are hoodwinked by unscrupulous and incompetent foreign entrepreneurs who take advantage of the lavish tax concessions offered through 'Pioneer Industries' status. For the neo-colonial mimic men life becomes surreal; the mirage of national independence having been exposed, there sets in a psychological disassociation from the environment. Throughout the story Naipaul's Indian participant-narrator projects a sense of hysteria bordering on chaos. In the end disaster comes, and he is forced to flee from Isabella. 'For those who lose, and nearly everyone in the end loses, there is only one course: flight. Flight to the greater disorder, the final emptiness: London and the home counties.'[1]

For Naipaul the West Indies constitute a particularly striking example of the absurdity of the human condition. They seem, indeed, to be virtually the sociological incarnation of the Absurd. Writing in the *New York Review of Books* in 1970, on the occasion of the mass Black Power demonstrations in Trinidad, Naipaul sourly noted:[2]

In the United States Black Power may have its victories.
But they will be American victories. The small islands of the
Caribbean will remain islands, impoverished and unskilled,
ringed as now by a *cordon sanitaire*, their people not needed
anywhere. They may get less innocent or less corrupt politicians;
they will not get less helpless ones. The island blacks will
continue to be dependent on the books, films, and goods of
others; in this important way they will continue to be the half-
made societies of a dependent people, the Third World's
third world. They will forever consume; they will never create.
They are without material resources; they will never develop
the higher skills. Identity depends in the end on achievement;

and achievement here cannot but be small. Again and again the millennium will seem about to come.

In this characteristic passage Naipaul reveals himself as a Frantz Fanon in reverse. Like Fanon—who came from the nearby French West Indies—Naipaul recognizes that the colonial condition is one of extreme degradation and dependency. But according to Naipaul there can be no exit from this condition in the West Indies. Their past history condemns them. There can be no transcendence of these historic limitations. Unlike Fanon, Naipaul is passive and unable to recommend struggle against these conditions.

Although Naipaul's resignation may be extreme, he articulates a definition of the West Indian situation recognized—if not often publicly expressed—by many of its leading politicians. Faith in the viability of the region is still the point around which all analyses and prescriptions for the West Indian future turns. The question of the possible degree of national autonomy was by no means a new one when Naipaul wrote his novel in the 1960s. Dr Eric Williams, the actual Trinidad Prime Minister, had wrestled with it at the time of the struggle for the return of the US naval base at Chaguaramas in the late 1950s. It had been the central animating issue of the Black Power crusade and remained, in the aftermath of that defeat, the first entry on the political agenda for all of the contending groups. Could there really be a new, independent Trinidad free of both middle-class 'Afro-Saxon' mimic men and the disorganization caused by the picaresque 'Quashie'—the average fête-loving, rum-drinking, lower-class Creole man?

Although detached from the West Indian national cause, Naipaul was too great and sensitive an artist to miss much that was essential in the neo-colonial malaise. *The Mimic Men* shows us that he does recognize that the neo-colonial moral situation of absurdity and moral chaos is directly connected with the fact of economic dependency. On the other hand, his depiction of the intellectual concomitants of this situation are fatally superficial—a one-sided burlesque. Its net effect is to further mystify and confuse the situation, and to promote a conservative image of its inevitability. A serious political novel on the contemporary West Indies would have to come to terms with the developments during the 1960s, such as the rise of the New World Group in the region as a whole and the emergence of Lloyd Best and Tapia House in Trinidad. These forces represented a post-mimic men consciousness, and they are absent in any recognizable form from anything which Naipaul has written about the West Indies. Where Naipaul has settled for a vision of West Indian man as destiny's scapegoat, the new generation of West Indian intellectuals who grew up just behind him during the 1950s achieved a major, if

31

still problematical, clarification of the underlying structural reality of the West Indies.

Lloyd Best and the New World Group

Whether or not Lloyd Best ever becomes Prime Minister, or Chief Servant, or whatever title is selected for the titular leader of the new Trinidad, during the 1960s he established a place for himself in West Indies intellectual, if not political, history. With C. L. R. James largely resident back in London during those years, the role of radical critique of the independence dispensation fell on a growing circle of young dons and students at the University of the West Indies campus in Kingston, Jamaica, the New World Group. The UWI campus became the leading centre of West Indian intellectual development and would have on its staff historians like Roy Augier, James Millette, and Walter Rodney; sociologists like Orlando Patterson and M. G. Smith; and a large stable of gifted young economists like Norman Girvan, Owen Jefferson, Havelock Brewster, and Clive Thomas. Among this galaxy of new nationalist scholars Lloyd Best would be a founding and representative figure. The son of a carpenter, Best was born in 1934 and grew up on Orange Grove estate, Tunapuna, yet another product of that fertile region below the Northern Range east of Port of Spain whence sprang Learie Constantine the cricketer, and the black revolutionaries George Padmore and C. L. R. James. The ubiquitous Barbadian influence in the district was also present in the case of Best: both of his grand-fathers had come to Trinidad from 'Little England'—as the island of Barbados is nicknamed. Young Best followed the upward colonial academic path, winning an Island Scholarship from Queen's Royal College and setting off for Cambridge University in 1953.

Best represented an interesting progression among Trinidadian scholars from the example of Eric Williams. In the 1930s Williams had broken with tradition in electing not to study law or medicine. But by choosing to read history at Oxford he remained suited largely for academic pursuits. Lloyd Best, like his predecessor Arthur Lewis from St Lucia—a contemporary of Eric Williams—would choose to read a directly practical subject—economics. At Cambridge he was taught by such famous practitioners as Joan Robinson and Nicholas Kaldor. The path to further advancement opened to him when he was offered a postgraduate fellowship in economics at Oxford where he intended to continue studies for a doctorate. This was in 1956, the year in which Eric Williams had revolutionized politics back home in Trinidad, and a period when West Indian patriotic sentiment over a possible federation was at its highest. When Best received an offer to take up a junior post at the Institute of Social and Economic

Research (ISER) at the University in Kingston he abandoned Oxford, England, and a Ph.D.

Thus, at the age of twenty-three, Lloyd Best was back in the West Indies. He knew next to nothing about the region, but he would dedicate himself to the task of finding out what made it tick. In collaboration with a number of other young scholars he helped to found the West Indian Society for Social Issues in 1961. During this period, 1958–60, while Arthur Lewis was Vice-Chancellor, the University was making a special effort to involve itself in the life of the West Indian community. This was thought to be made necessary by the inauguration of the West Indies federation and a series of background lectures were delivered by such prominent supporters of West Indian nationalism as C. L. R. James and E. R. Waddington. After these lectures drink-and-talk sessions were organized in the flats of young members of the faculty, with the university paying for entertainment costs.

Out of such informal interaction came the activities which eventually produced a semi-formal organization, the so-called New World Group. The Group attracted that name after 1963 when the first issue of its quarterly journal *New World* was published in Georgetown, Guiana, where Best was then working for the government of Dr Cheddi Jagan as a United Nations development planning expert. During this period he acquired close contacts with members of a Guianese radical-socialist group centred on the 'Itabo' coffee-house and cultural centre—a grass-roots operation which later served as a partial inspiration for Tapia house.

In between all this Best had spent seven months in Trinidad during 1960–1 as economic planning adviser to William Demas's Planning Unit. Here he came under the direct influence of C. L. R. James and took a firm position against Williams's domination of the PNM. During these months he also sorted out his ideas about the development strategy being pursued by the Trinidad Government, based largely on the recommendations of Arthur Lewis and Teodoro Moscoso, leading theoreticians of what he would derisively call the 'Industrialization by Invitation' school of West Indian economics. He returned to the UWI campus in Jamaica in 1961, a controversial but increasingly influential teacher of economics, and a recognized intellectual leader.

The *New World Quarterly* was a sophisticated but thoroughly indigenous journal which would contain some of the finest writing on the West Indies during the middle and latter 1960s. With articles on politics, economics, literature, and the arts, *New World* set a steady standard of competence far above that which the Williams generation had attained. (The latter, of course, had not had the advantage of a subsidized university base in the West Indies from which to operate.) Some of the social scientists who contributed to the *Quarterly*, particularly the economists, appear to have had the enviable, if somewhat schizoid, option of publishing their popular analyses in the *Quarterly* while reserving their technical writings for the pages of the *Social and Economic Studies*, the journal of the ISER. Thus professional, technical competence of a high order was developed alongside the practice of aiming for wider communication.

What were the social and political perspectives of Lloyd Best of the growing New World tendency? There was never unanimity on many aspects of outlook, but the official consensus was that it should foster a broadly-based, non-sectarian Caribbean radicalism. In a paper delivered to a conference in Jamaica in October 1965, delegates from the New World Group declared that

> our radicalism was at no point to be identified with any of
> the going political doctrines, be it Socialism or Liberalism,
> Communism or Radicalism, or what have you. Rather we want
> our radicalism to be interpreted as nothing more nor less than
> the sustained application of thought to the matters that
> concern us deeply.

In the context of a society still steeped in colonial myths and prejudices, they stated, social criticism and the simple exercise of reason were in themselves revolutionary. The New World Group was to be an instrument for change in the field of ideas throughout the Caribbean through 'the politics of journalism'. Nothing outside actual politics was a better training for politics than the collaborative effort of putting out an unsubsidized periodical. However, New World would leave it to other organizations to give direct support to political parties or political doctrines.[3] The establishment of the *New World Quarterly* marked a renaissance in the development of West Indian radical thought, a process which had largely fizzled out once the older generation of nationalist leaders and their coteries—who had generated a certain intellectual accompaniment to the claim to office —eventually succeeded in their ambitions.

Among intellectuals there are always ambiguous attitudes toward practical politics, and the West Indian intelligentsia were no exception. Eric Williams had managed to parlay knowledge into power by creating a bridging institution, the University of Woodford Square, between the middle class and the masses in the mid-fifties. Although the New World Group was—despite its attempt to avoid classification—ideologically to the left of Williams, it too would require an organizational method for disseminating its views. This West Indian New Left certainly did not have the degree of social and psychic distance from the masses as had been the norm in the more inhibited days prior to the end of colonial rule, but it was none the less largely the product of the expanded but still elitist, educational system which had produced the scholarship boys of the previous generations. New World, like its precursors which led to the founding of nationalist parties in the preceding generation, was chiefly a middle-class talk shop, without deep or stable roots in working-class organizations. That is to say, the question of political method was not solved for them merely by virtue of opposing the existing neo-colonial regimes from their base in the University of the West Indies or the University of Guyana. What was to be done?

Foundation of Tapia House

The natural impulse of taking one's message to the masses in a great gathering could, of course, still be tried. The UWI history lecturer Walter Rodney attracted large audiences in Jamaica in response to his Black Power lectures, lectures for which he was expelled from the country. But in Trinidad there was the additional complication that the standard 'charismatic' gambit of generating a mass following (although one still in good repute in Castro's Cuba) was locally in ill repute. How could one attack Eric Williams and not at the same time criticize the demagoguery inherent in the University of Woodford Square? The charismatic Hero haranguing the colonial Crowd had been indicted for the mystifying, essentially stabilizing ritual which it was, or could easily become.[4] Thus for a conscientious radical like Lloyd Best who, moreover, had then only a tiny following, that road to notoriety was ruled out. Instead, when he finally returned to Trinidad in the mid-1960s to a permanent post at the St Augustine branch campus of the University of the West Indies he established his so-called Tapia House. This was quite literally a house, or spacious palm-thatched shed, built by Best, his followers and associates, and neighbours in the backyard of Best's house on the Upper Tunapuna Road, not far from the campus. (Tapia is a mixture of mud and cow-dung used as a construction material by the rural poor in Trinidad.) This became a community centre for arts and adult education. Politics by journalism was continued with the publication of *Tapia*, a splendidly literate and informed popular tabloid which surpassed even the standard for political journalism set by C. L. R. James during his days as editor of the PNM *Nation*. Tapia house, group, and paper continued the New World emphasis on rational analysis and non-sectarian ideology.

Lloyd Best had become by this time convinced that passing ideological enthusiasms were a genuine detriment to serious political progress in the West Indies. At a meeting of the emerging opposition groups in 1969 he spoke at length against a premature open conflict with the Williams regime. The movement was at that stage, he argued, too weak and poorly organized to succeed. The yearning for Armageddon could lead to defeat and demoralization and a re-entrenchment of the Doctor's position—a prophecy the correctness of which would not endear him, he later believed, to those who had insisted on carrying on the 'Black Power' struggle in the streets to the fiasco of April 1970. Thus Tapia House members, while active in many of the meetings and marches during the 'February Revolution' of 1970, did not find themselves in sufficient tactical agreement with the Black Power leaders to play an official role on their platform. Non-affiliated critical support of the mass movement became the Tapia posture. Tapia mistrusted the facility with which a spontaneous movement could be mounted in the street of the carnival capital, Port of Spain, a facility which gave a seductive, but false, promise of permanent result. As a bridging institution between the intellectuals and the masses, Tapia House, with its small-scale intimacy and backyard informality, its emphasis on artistic as well as high-powered intellectual labours, its thatched-roof simplicity and do-it-yourself ambience, could claim to avoid the inherent pitfalls of basing a movement on the big show in the square. If this approach could be criticized as an example of virtue based on the necessity of a low budget and limited popular support, it was none the less arguably sound in principle, in so far as an organic rooting in the local community was seen as the indispensable prerequisite of a successful popular revolution, consistent, one might suppose, with the doctrines and anti-vanguardist praxis of the libertarian Marxist C. L. R. James.

But James became, in fact, openly hostile to the Tapia House idea and to the programmes put forward by Lloyd Best and his associates. Their estrangement had begun in 1965 when Best declined to join the so-called Workers' and Farmers' Party which James had formed during a brief return visit to Trinidad, feeling that it was a hasty, opportunistic, and foredoomed attempt to unseat Williams. The WFP, moreover, seemed to violate the very postulates of thorough and careful party organization which James had emphasized a few years before in his critique of the PNM in *Party Politics in the West Indies*, a book which Best had adopted as a virtual bible of sound organizational practice. Best's analysis of the West Indian situation, and his development of a radical reformist programme, differed significantly from the views of James; but no one could deny that they were based on a considerable analysis of West Indian history and political economy.

Dependency theory in the West Indies

The centrepiece of the West Indian critique of political economy produced during the UN's Decade of Development was the paper entitled 'Outlines of a model of pure plantation economy', which Lloyd Best in collaboration with the Canadian economist, Kari Levitt, published in *Social and Economic Studies* in 1968. In this paper (which was locally famous for several years before publication in manuscript form) Best and Levitt trace the stages in the development of underdevelopment and continuing dependency in colonial plantation economies. Rich in insight and historical breadth, it has been criticized for an over-reliance on typological thinking—New World was never wanting in memorable apophthegms—but must be ranked as the nearest thing to an inspired, technical discussion of the development of underdevelopment in the West Indian economies along the lines developed by the Latin American structuralists. In a footnote the authors acknowledge their awareness of the work of structuralist writers, particularly Celso Furtado. On the basis of a detailed analysis of the implicit accounting framework of societies of this type, the authors contend that the pure plantation model has three essential characteristics. The first involves the demonstration that these 'hinterland' societies are structurally part of an 'overseas economy' of the industrial metropole; secondly, that such societies comprise a locus of 'total economic institutions', and, thirdly, that the value flows in such a system are typically incalculable. The authors observe that the third characteristic is in fact derived from the previous ones:[5]

> Summarily, it stems from the processes of provisioning and disposal which are associated with a hinterland economy which is structurally part of an overseas economy and institutionally organized by total economic institutions. Almost all intermediate and final supplies of goods and services are either produced within the complex or advanced by associated merchant bankers. Since the latter also receive the bulk of the staple for sale in the metropole and re-export, the commodity flow from stage to stage does not involve any considerable money flows. Accounting takes the form of imputing prices. There is thus a large measure of price indeterminacy.

These particular characteristics of societies which, like the West Indies, approximate the pure type of the plantation model, mean that the conventional formulations of economic laws and practice cannot be expected to operate in the same way as in the metropolitan country itself. There is a fatal lack of interconnectedness between the internal elements of plantation model economies—the major structural linkages run between the individual local branch firm to its metropolitan headquarters.

Developing this central point in greater contemporary detail, the consequences of this lack of internal linkages have been statistically demonstrated by the Guyanese economist Havelock Brewster. On the basis of a correlation matrix of major economic functions in the Trinidad economy—employment, wage-rates, exports, import ratio, output, consumption, prices, and investment—Brewster showed that no co-variation between these variables occurred over a decade in a manner prescribed by the orthodox wisdom of metropolitan economics. Writes Brewster:[6]

> In orthodox economies it is argued that by repressing wage increases rises in unit cost price are kept down, export demand expands and with this employment. In the dependent system, however, all these relationships break down. Wage rises have little impact on cost–price changes, which in turn have no importance for changing the level of export demand which itself does little to alter the level of employment. Prices cannot be kept down by operating on wages. Suppressing wage rises does not lead to increased exports.

Nor do increased exports make for increased employment. Brewster's correlation matrix for Trinidad shows indeed an *inverse* relationship between them. The nature of the dependent, plantation-descended economy is that, despite all the rhetoric and paraphernalia of economic planning introduced by neo-colonial governments, these bear so little relation to the underlying economic reality that, in most crucial respects, Trinidad and other similar societies can hardly be said to possess an economic *system* in any customary sense at all! Herein lies the source of the absurdity, hysteria, and repressive nature of the West Indian 'nationalist' governments. Mystification reigns supreme as Naipaul had intuitively described in *The Mimic Men* but inadequately understood. Living completely out of touch with the facts of the environment politicians like Dr Williams projected onto the population the failings which they themselves either cannot or do not want to see as lodged in the inherently chaotic economic structure of dependency. Brewster concludes:

> A predictable cluster of institutions develop, whose very physical presence is projected as the living symbols that governments govern. Central Banks, Planning Units, Industrial Courts, Tourist Boards, Marketing Boards, Industrial Development Corporations, State Trading Agencies, etc., flourish but do not function. It is not much of an exaggeration to say that if these were all closed down it would have little

or no real effect upon what actually takes place. There are the corresponding postures, businesslike gait, planes, dictating machines and computerization, and, above all, the big voice from the little country on the World's Stage—Punta del Este Cuban reconciliation, United Nations Human Rights, Lusaka non-alignment. And the GNP, phallic symbol *par excellence*, rises ever upward at the involuntary command of honourable economic ministers.

The critique of Arthur Lewis

How had the West Indian leadership got itself into this morass? In Lloyd Best's view the answer was essentially a variant on Lord Keynes's observation about the propensity of governments to fall prey to the theories of a defunct economist; in this instance, Sir Arthur Lewis, the distinguished St Lucian-born economist who was key adviser to West Indian nationalist regimes during the decisive formative years of the 1950s. The brilliant Sir Arthur could hardly be described as defunct, but in Best's view Professor Lewis's advice had not proved to be sound. The basic fallacy in the Lewis approach, which Trinidad, like other parts of the West Indies, had adopted, was that it was premised, as Best saw it, on an inappropriate application of Ricardian economic theory to the West Indies. That is, Lewis's emphasis on attracting maximum foreign capital investment for the development of 'Pioneer Industries' was based on the assumption that this would in the long run produce increasing profits, savings, and reinvestment out of which the road to self-sustaining industrial growth would follow in due course. This had manifestly not happened. The Williams regime was, fifteen years later, struggling for its life in the face of ever-mounting unemployment. The situation was even more acute in that other showplace of 'industrialization by invitation'—Jamaica.

The problem was not that foreign investment had failed to be seduced by the supine posture of the West Indian governments. The level of foreign investment since the PNM came to office had been high. Between 1957 and 1965 foreign direct investment averaged around $86 million per year, and consistently accounted for over half of the total annual investment by the business sector. During five years in the period it had accounted for more than 75 per cent of total private investment, reaching a staggering 99 per cent in 1963. And, as Eric Williams had envisaged at the time of the sale of the major British oil interest to Texaco in 1955, it was the United States which had taken over the major share of the action. According to one measure, the proportions were running as follows: US $145 million, Britain $25 million, Canada $3 million.

Despite this massive inflow of foreign capital, however, Best would insist that Trinidad's dependence on such investment was largely an illusion. He pointed out that although inflows of capital during the 1957–65 period average $86 million per annum, *outflows* of income from the country, not counting management and licensing fees, averaged $111 million—more than 30 per cent higher. In 1966 and 1967 the situation was even worse: *outflows were running at one and a half times the inflows.*[7]

> The grim fact is that we have ourselves been generating the capital with which the firms have been getting more control of our economy. Between 1964 and 1968, 71 cents out of every dollar invested by foreigners came out of profits made in Trinidad and Tobago. And the figure was perhaps higher in the earlier period.

It was becoming clear where the policies derived from Arthur Lewis's original analysis of developing economies had gone wrong. He had expected that the increase in income which foreign investment would generate could lead to the rise of a local, national takeover of business. That policy had not worked because the local share of total profits had simply not been high enough to permit a higher contribution of local savings to investment. 'In most countries savings come mainly from profits not from wages', Best noted. 'The most damaging result of the fact that nationals work mainly as wage earners is that *even a high and rising national income does not lead to more national ownership of business.*'

This was not to say, however, that the traditional elite sections of the society had not done well under the neo-colonial dispensation. Citing a survey by Acton Camejo, a Trinidadian sociologist, Best noted that nearly 80 per cent of the Trinidadian business elite were still phenotypically white or off-white. Out of the 230 business respondents to the survey only 9 per cent were Indians—a surprisingly low figure—while a mere 4 per cent were of African descent. Herein lay the cause of yet another myth-based grievance in the competition between the two major groups: 'The impression that Indians are doing well', Best shrewdly noted, 'is an African impression, but the Indians cannot be excited by their position in the whole picture. So we can see why both groups must feel "We are second class citizens".'[8]

One major cause of the continuing disparity between the status of the numerically small but privileged European elite and that of other groups, was to be found in the data on levels of educational attainment. At the time of the 1960 census fully a quarter of the European working population had obtained the equivalent of a university education, and 53 per cent of that group had some kind of higher school certificates. The tiny Chinese and Syrian ethnic communities had only 3 per cent with university education and 12 per cent with school certificates. 'Mixed' races had figures of 1 per cent university and 10 per cent school certificate. Africans and Indians both had under 4 per cent of their number with school certificates or above, and an insignificant proportion with university education. A quarter of the Indian workers had no education at all. Although educational expansion and reforms during the sixties undoubtedly produced changes in these proportions in a more democratic direction the official belief that educational mobility was the key to general social mobility was an assumption open to question. As the British sociologist Malcolm Cross had warned from a survey of the Trinidad school system in 1967,[9]

> Clearly this assumption is only valid if there is a change in the requirements for the filling of many occupational roles which currently appear dependent on ascriptive criteria. If this does not occur then expansion will only result in the 'devaluation' of educational qualification.

In the meantime it was evident that such expansion as had taken place was in any case far from being a panacea for the growth of youthful unemployment. Youth, even educated youth, were highly redundant in the economy. As Lloyd Best observed, noting the origin of the Black Power protests in the alienation of youth during the post-independence period,[10]

> In 1966 32 per cent of the age group 15–19 and 20 per cent of the age group 20–24 were wholly unemployed. And *62 per cent of the country were under 25*, conscious of the PNM government only in the discredited phase of its history.

Anti-imperialism without Marxism

So the plantation model economy was in its essential respects still very much a going concern in Trinidad. Best now moved from analysis to prescription. The original Tapia proposals were published in 1968 and later formed the basis for the Tapia manifesto of March 1970, *Black Power and National Reconstruction*. Even those who tended to dismiss Best as a politician would concede that the concepts put forward by Tapia during this period had a great influence on the language and policies of Williams and his key advisers. The Tapia perspective, as it developed between 1968 and 1971, comprised both economic and sociological aspects. First, and most important, a scheme for the economic reorganization of Trinidad was outlined, representing in political terms a well-thought radical-reformist

41

programme for the economy. From the analysis of the main features of the plantation economy, and the critique of the Lewis development policy, Best and his colleagues proposed as the key economic reform what they termed 'localization'. This meant that, for a start, the multinational companies which dominated the economy—Texaco, Shell, Grace and Tate and Lyle, banking, advertising, the media— would be required to transform themselves into recognizable and bona fide legal persons of Trinidad and Tobago:

> They must not merely be formally separate from their
> international affiliates as some of them are now; they must be
> actually so. We are invoking anti-trust legislation against
> them on our definition of what constitutes a combination
> harmful to the public interest. Shares must be traded on
> the local market in denominations and forms which provide
> access to every man in the street of Brasso Caparo or Port
> of Spain.

Localization, it was emphasized, was not to be understood as the same thing as nationalization or expropriation. The latter concepts were viewed as inappropriate borrowings by colonial radicals from 'the North Atlantic experience'. It simply did not matter whether the major industries in Trinidad were foreign companies or not so long as they performed in the way dictated by local people. In some cases obtaining ownership might be necessary in order to acquire control, but the key factor was to domesticate the multinationals, and this could be achieved without outright nationalization. To take one example of how the job would be tackled: Texaco ran approximately thirteen companies in Trinidad, but their accounts were conveniently entangled among themselves and with the transactions of Texaco International to hide the true nature of pricing sales and purchases. Such convenient methods of book-keeping—handed down from 'plantation economy'—would have to be disentangled in order to establish radical alterations in methods of tax auditing. A special task force of accountants, economists, and engineers would be set up as a 'Technetariat' to deal with such problems.[11]

> The ultimate aim of all these measures is to clear the field
> for a different kind of collaboration between ourselves and the
> external world. Foreign investment and technology etc. are
> sometimes useful. It is direct metropolitan investment that
> is anathema. Once we have redefined the terms of collaboration
> and broken the psychological and material barriers to advance
> by Caribbean decision-makers there will be plenty of room for
> play. In fact, some of the restraints which are now being
> proposed will become obsolete. Fortunately, they will also

bring into being a class of independent-minded local entrepreneurs and managers holding positions from which they can change the rules again.

In the middle of the 19th century, all sorts of banks were started in Jamaica by local people. But the charters given them by the colonial office and the currency arrangements favoured the British and later, the Canadian banks. These banks then systematically frustrated the emergence of local industrialists including planters and merchants who wanted to stake their future on the West Indies. Recently they have modified their policies but too late to save us from plantation economy.

The historical inability of the West Indies to produce just such a stratum of local entrepreneurs was for Best precisely where the emphasis on the savings and reinvestment model had been premature. In writing about early industrial England classical economists like Adam Smith and David Ricardo could take as an assumption both the existence of a national economy and an entrepreneurial ethos. Arthur Lewis had erred, Best and his colleagues argued, in not realizing that this assumption would not hold in the West Indies. Not that this had been an uncommon failing among economists addressing themselves to the problems of underdevelopment in the post-war period. It was not until 1963 that the developmental economist Dudley Seers 'embarrassed everyone', as one writer has put it, with the publication of his article 'The limitations of the special case'.[12] In this article Seers crystallized the already emergent conviction on the part of many Third World economists, particularly the Latin American theorists, that Western 'economic theory' was not a general theory of economic growth, but related to a *special case* of the already developed capitalist economy. This was the point which the West Indian economists had seized upon, not only attempting to explicate it historically—as in the Best–Levitt plantation model article—but also to apply it to the solution of current economic problems.

Thus for Best one of the major elements of the localization programme would be to create structural inducements for the emergence of local, private entrepreneurial initiative. To this extent his outlook did not imply a radical break from capitalism, but rather its reverse: localization would create the prerequisites for this vital engine of the capitalist dynamic to operate within Trinidad for the first time in its history. In this regard, the economic doctrines of Schumpeter rather than those of Ricardo or Marx were the key theoretical insights. At the same time, however, the Tapia programme clearly envisaged collectivization or stringent controls of the commanding heights of the economy. The net result would apparently be the creation of a mixed economy combining elements of 'peoples' capitalism' with socialization of major industries, and a radical break with the reliance on private investment inputs from abroad. Trinidad was already generating a great deal of profits for potential investment; the problem was to gain control over and divert those processes to producing local growth, to harness local initiative, and thus achieve greater mastery over the urgent problems of social planning, while at the same time working toward a larger vision of an integrated Caribbean community.

These were the outlines of the grand strategy of the Best–Tapia perspective for dealing with the impasse of Trinidad misdevelopment. The programme itself was far more detailed and rich in provocative, original points of concrete detail. Yet it by no means represented a blueprint for future change. Aside from the basic propositions about the chief structural contradictions in the economy, the spirit of the Tapia approach was a free-wheeling, open-ended one. Who could really say, Lloyd Best might ask, in advance of the particular political contingencies which might develop, just what degree of direct state takeover of foreign enterprises might be required? It was not for the Tapia leadership to foreclose decisions on policies—these could only flow out of the popular movement itself during a period of political struggle which had not yet firmly crystallized. A change in regime might come about in one of several ways: the government might collapse in a crisis; it might even be voted out of office. By 1973 Tapia was not yet a political party; but it was very close to becoming one. The mystifications of the condition of dependency had been rigorously examined and cleared away without relying on either the emotive nationalist slogan which Williams had employed, nor by descending to the well-meant but misguided appeals to social solidarity issued by the Black Power movement.

The split between Tapia, C. L. R. James, and other West Indian Marxists can now be readily understood. Tapia could be criticized as a reformist movement which, far from destroying capitalism in Trinidad, was actually proposing to do what Eric Williams had failed to do—*strengthen it through the creation of a national bourgeoisie*. Under neo-colonial rule capitalism had been vulnerable to attack through appeals to patriotic sentiment, and was in its weakest form. The contradictions which had Williams and his regime reeling from crisis to crisis signalled that the time was ripe to smash capitalism—not to resuscitate it by strengthening the weak-to-non-existent local bourgeoisie. Best and his colleagues had provided a brilliant analysis of what was wrong with the West Indian economy, but rather than prescribe the obvious Marxist cure of thoroughgoing socialization of the means of production and the elimination of the profit system, he could be seen as having launched an opportunist campaign aimed at calming the worst fears of foreign companies by preaching 'localization' and by directly appealing to the avaricious energies of both the established business interests and the aspiring petty entrepreneurs among the Africans and Indians.

In Lloyd Best's view, however, such a critique represented merely the latest instalment in the stale and paternalistic theorizing of European Marxism which was as puritanical, obsessional, and irrelevant to the West Indies as were the misleading assumptions of bourgeois economic theory. The first step in mobilizing the intelligence and dedication of the masses was to get out from under the rigid formulas of both liberal capitalism *and* Marxist socialism. Moreover, the social structure of West Indian society in any case made the latter inappropriate:[13]

> There is no 'bourgeoisie' here because we have had no 'bourgs'.
> Nor have we had feudalism or any dynamic class of national
> capitalists so there need not be any 'socialists' or
> 'communists'. What is the meaning of 'middle class'? In
> almost every family we can find represented the full spectrum
> from professional through artisan to labourer. Tapia rejects
> all of these imported categories and we seek to understand what
> is going on here in terms of *Caribbean* definitions. When we
> do that, we see all kinds of very rich possibilities for
> national integration and economic transformation. And we
> make all kinds of fresh interpretations.

Among these fresh interpretations would be the ingenuous claim that, despite its 'middle-class' leadership, Tapia was as 'working class as any in the country: we are working class because we are working!'.

The refusal of Lloyd Best to recognize the importance of making a class analysis of Trinidadian and West Indian society is one of the peculiarities and, in the present writer's opinion, the major weaknesses in Best's ideology. It is consistent with one of the cardinal tenets of the earlier New World Group which may be called the assumption of *Caribbean exceptionalism*. Since Tapia bids fair to represent an important salient in West Indian politics in the seventies, this crucial doctrine requires a brief discussion and critique.

To begin with, it is clear that the analysis of the peculiar, special character of the Caribbean experience was a necessary and powerful line of attack. M. G. Smith had shown this in his sociological studies of the West Indies as 'plural societies'. The critique of the traditional economics of the region provided, as we have seen, further vindication for this approach. But there was always the danger that the

45

adherents of this line of reasoning might fall into the trap of exaggerating the degree of exemption which the Caribbean did in fact have from the structural characteristics of other societies. This, it seems to me, was the basic error of the West Indian New Left.

How could one accept the chief heresy propounded by Best: that the notion of social class was merely an 'imported category' without relevance in a society where nearly every family contains representatives of various social strata? It must be admitted that there is possible support for this proposition in recent work on social stratification in Trinidad and Guyana.[14] These data do show substantial social mobility, both upward *and* downward, between parents and offspring, thus tending to produce some degree of scatter, as Best would have it, across the full spectrum of occupational groups. But a great many families apparently do not experience any very dramatic change from the situation of the parents. And even if they do, this does not by itself indicate that links of kinship with relatives placed lower down the social scale are actively maintained. In any event, there is certainly nothing whatever exceptional in the West Indian tendency for inter-generational social mobility to reduce the individual's subjective perception of class differences: all developing and developed societies show mobility patterns and social relations of the same order, if varying in degree.

To take this criticism one step further: even if it were true—which it is almost certainly not—that the typical relationship of a West Indian manual labourer to the better-off elements in the society was mediated by close and meaningful kinship links, this would not contradict the evidence for the existence of a class or status hierarchy incorporating great discrepancies in the objective distribution of private wealth, social prestige, and power. All that would be proven in such a case would be that one dimension of social stratification would be relatively weak, namely that of social distance. Visitors have often found that the small-scale, post-agrarian ambience of Trinidad does in fact tend to produce more intimate and casual social relations across formal status lines. The tendency to practise a degree of fluidity with respect to the maintenance of social distance should not, however, be allowed to obscure the central fact of structural inequalities which, although mitigated by various personal bonds, formed the backbone of the Trinidad social hierarchy. Quite apart from the white elite, large disparities in income, power, and life styles characterized the vertical status order of the neo-colonial society.

Moreover, the barriers to a more inclusive national solidarity represented by the horizontal plural social divisions between blacks and Indians could also not be ignored in a serious analysis. Here a contemporary study of the Trinidad city of San Fernando by Colin G. Clarke is most illuminating. Although the spatial relationships between various groups showed a considerable degree of racial and religious integration, this did not entail an equally high degree of intermarriage. Mixed unions were not clandestine nor typically extra-legal, but they were far from representing the norm. Among some 143 Creole households sampled fully 88 per cent had spouses of the same race as that of the head of the household. The figure was about the same among Christian East Indians where 89 per cent of the parents were both of East Indian descent. Among the Hindus and Muslims the rate of racial endogamy was even higher: 97 and 98 per cent respectively.[15] Thus, from these data obtained in a town which has traditionally boasted of its high degree of racial integration, it can be seen that the kinship-based links on which Best had laid great stress were not only of doubtful value in undermining the hardening of class divisions, but were still virtually non-existent in forging bonds between the two major ethnic groups.

Conclusion

From the foregoing case study of the debate over developmental economic theory in the West Indies several points of general relevance stand out. First, we observe that a radical critique of a neo-imperialist economic system does not automatically lead, as one might expect, to a conventional Marxist analysis of the exploitative character of internal social class relationships. In this respect Lloyd Best closely resembles certain Latin American dependency theorists presented by O'Brien in the preceding chapter. The West Indian radical academic economists occupy an elite position not totally dissimilar from the social science technicians in Latin America described by O'Brien; their policies may appear revolutionary in their external aspects, but reformist with respect to internal social changes. In the West Indian case, however, there are also other influences at work to undermine a more revolutionary direction for economic analysis. Despite its often feeble—and sometimes even fraudulent—nature the political legacy of British parliamentarianism still wields a powerful influence. In addition, an Anglo-Saxon, Oxbridge dislike of metaphysics seems deeply ingrained in the West Indian educated elite. Marxism in its deeper theoretical aspects is scarcely read, let alone understood, in these former colonies. It is an alien tradition, and even a popularizer of genius like C. L. R. James has had scant success in communicating its deeper subtleties.

A second point which I have attempted to demonstrate—particularly for the benefit of readers who may have had no previous exposure to developmental economics reasoning—is the elementary point that economic theory is inevitably political and social in its consequences. The maintenance of old or creation of new channels and mechanisms of economic activity affects the lives of different categories of persons in different ways. Thus the study of sociology cannot be divorced from the study of economics. This is, I believe, quite clearly revealed in the case we have just been considering—and it is to the credit of Lloyd Best and his colleagues that they have themselves made this connection quite explicit and public.

The West Indian school of political economy is more diverse than I have been able to suggest in this brief account. Although the major works of Andre Gunder Frank appear to have been published—or, at any rate, read—too late in the 1960s to have had much effect on the formation of their key assumptions, the Frankian–Marxist influence is clearly present in Walter Rodney's 1972 work of exile in Africa entitled *How Europe Underdeveloped Africa*.[16] The Cuban model will possibly become more significant in future West Indian discussion of alternative policies as diplomatic and cultural relations are progressively consolidated between these two major Caribbean societies. The work on the structure of multinational corporations conducted by Norman Girvan played a direct role in the decision taken by the Guyana government in 1971 to totally nationalize its major foreign-owned bauxite mine. With Guyana leading the way, and with William Demas as architect of the Caribbean Free Trade Area, a partial official co-optation of dependency theory is under way. Perhaps a period of 'dependent development' is in store for the region. Meanwhile these and other economic doctrines connected with development theory should be scrutinized by the sociologist of knowledge bearing in mind that Marx's question of 'who educates the educator?' is always in season.[17]

Notes

1 V. Naipaul, *The Mimic Men*, André Deutsch, London, 1967.
2 V. Naipaul, *New York Review of Books*, 3 September 1970, pp. 32–3.
3 New World Pamphlet, *The Withdrawal of Dr Beckford's Passport*, Jamaica, 1966.
4 For an important discussion of this problem, based on a study of Eric Gairy in Grenada, see A. W. Singham, *The Hero and the Crowd in a Colonial Polity*, Yale University Press, New Haven, 1968.
5 L. Best and K. Levitt, 'Outlines of a model of pure plantation economy', *Social and Economic Studies*, vol. 17, no. 3, September 1968, pp. 283–326.
6 'Economic dependence', paper delivered by Havelock Brewster to seminar at Institute of Commonwealth Studies, London University, 4 May 1971. Quoted by permission of the author.
7 'Who owns Trinidad and Tobago?', *Tapia* (91, Tunapuna Road, Tunapuna, Trinidad), Independence Special and Economic Bulletin, 29 August 1971.

8 *Ibid.*
9 M. Cross and A. M. Schwartzbaum, 'Social mobility and secondary school selection in Trinidad and Tobago', *Social and Economic Studies*, vol. 18, no. 2, June 1969, pp. 189–207.
10 'A short biography of the labour market in the Caribbean', paper presented by Lloyd Best to a conference on The Political Economy of British Racialism, London, December 1971. The present writer was able to interview Mr Best during breaks in this conference and these discussions were the source of the other quotations and views I have attributed to Lloyd Best without citation.
11 *Tapia*, 29 August 1971.
12 See 'Introduction' by I. Livingstone, ed., *Economic Policy for Development*, Penguin, Harmondsworth, 1971, p. 10; D. Seers, 'The limitations of the special case', *Bulletin of the Oxford Institute of Economics and Statistics*, May 1963.
13 *Tapia*, 29 August 1971.
14 Unpublished studies by Malcolm Cross, forthcoming.
15 'Residential segregation and intermarriage in San Fernando, Trinidad', *Geographical Review*, vol. 61, no. 2, 1971, pp. 198–218.
16 W. Rodney, *How Europe Underdeveloped Africa*, Bogle-L'Ouverture Publications, London, 1972.
17 A major attempt at self-analysis by the West Indian dependency school has been essayed by Norman Girvan in 'The development of dependency economics in the Caribbean and Latin America: Review and comparison', *Social and Economic Studies*, vol. 22, no. 1, pp. 2–33. See also Adlith Brown and Havelock Brewster, 'Review of the study of economics in the English-speaking Caribbean', *Social and Economic Studies*, vol. 23, no. 1, pp. 48–57. For an excellent collection of popular economics papers see Norman Girvan and Owen Jefferson, *Readings in the Political Economy of the Caribbean*, New World Group, Jamaica, 1971. The present writer has conducted interviews with William Demas, Dudley Seers, Havelock Brewster and others with a view to further elucidation of the development of economic thought in the West Indies, forthcoming. For the general intellectual background to recent developments in Trinidad see my earlier studies, *Black Intellectuals Come to Power*, Schenkman, Cambridge, Mass., 1968, and *Race and Revolutionary Consciousness: A Documentary Interpretation of the 1970 Black Power in Trinidad*, Schenkman, Cambridge, Mass., 1971.

4 Andre Gunder Frank:
an introduction and appreciation
David Booth

A little over a decade ago Dudley Seers concluded his well known essay on the future of development economics by proposing the 'modest but revolutionary' slogan that Economics is the study of Economies.[1] Too many economists, Seers contended, still insisted on writing and teaching as if their discipline consisted of a body of theory which was universally valid and capable of application with a similar measure of success in the industrialized and the unindustrialized countries of the world. The fact was that conventional economics was based almost exclusively upon the 'special case' of a handful of industrially developed economies. When applied elsewhere it tended to focus on the wrong factors and to yield models which did not fit at all closely the way in which economies actually operated.

This being the case, Seers suggested, teachers of economics should consider the wisdom of encouraging the belief among their graduate students (particularly those from overseas) that the technical sophistication, formal elegance, and abstractness of the latest mathematical models was the measure of their scientific rigour and usefulness. More attention should be given to studies carried out in nonindustrial settings with specific reference to the problems actually faced there. A good example was the work of the Latin American 'structuralist' school. The structuralists had already prepared the basic framework for a relevant and realistic development economics, basing itself upon the experience of a number of economies in the Latin American region but remaining flexible enough to be extended to other parts of the underdeveloped world. A great deal remained to be done, however.[2]

Since the publication of Seers' paper, significant progress has undoubtedly been made in the study of the economies of the less developed capitalist countries, even if little of the knowledge gained thereby has trickled down to the level of undergraduate courses in economics, and though the supremacy of highly abstract growth models in the academic economist's prestige-rating remains as secure as ever. An important element in this progress has been the diffusion into the English-speaking world of some of the Latin American economic ideas to which Seers drew attention. As far as the specialist is concerned, the major influence here has been the official and semi-official publications of the United Nations Economic Commission for Latin America (ECLA)—the common *pied-à-terre* and reference point of the structuralist school.[3] On a more popular level and for the non-economist, however, nobody has done more to advance the cause of economics as the study of economies among English readers than Andre Gunder Frank.[4] Whereas today the typical development economist may be expected with some degree of confidence to be familiar with the theories of Raúl Prebisch and Celso Furtado, the general reader or mere sociologist concerned with the 'Third World' is far more likely to have encountered some of Frank's leading ideas.

This has resulted in a somewhat curious situation, and not only because Frank writes as a Marxist, a contributor to *Monthly Review* rather than to the *Economic Journal*, and with the avowed intention of aiding 'the Revolution in Latin America and the world'.[5] The latter consideration, together with Frank's insistent refusal to concede any ground at all to the orthodox universe of discourse, has provided a convenient cover for treatises on the economics of development which ignore Frank's very existence.[6] Equally, though, Frank's studies have reached and influenced an audience which has received by and large no prior schooling in the critique of orthodox doctrine which was conducted by Latin Americans in and around ECLA in the immediate post-war decades.

Does this matter? This paper stems from the belief that it does. In Chapter 2 above, O'Brien has shown how the recent literature on economic 'dependence' in Latin America grew up in response to the perceived inadequacies of the post-war development model whose principal academic protagonists were the ECLA economists. From this point of view I believe it is correct and illuminating to regard Frank as a special case of a general intellectual phenomenon in the region. Like the dependency theorists, that is to say, Frank took as his theoretical point of departure the doctrines of ECLA rather than those of established 'Anglo-Saxon' economics, and the general drift of his concerns cannot be understood apart from this fact. For instance, it is this which explains the apparent asymmetry in the observation that although Frank has provided the most systematic and devastating critique to date of post-war *sociological* theories of development he has paid scant attention to the corresponding economic literature.[7] ECLA's critique of orthodox theory is central to the background to Frank's studies, and yet the latter themselves provide few guide-lines as to the nature of this critique for the reader who is unfamiliar with the Latin American intellectual scene. The object of the first section of this chapter, therefore, is to offer a partial remedy for this state of affairs, in the form of a brief survey of ECLA's principal theories.

Considered in its proper context, Frank's contribution nevertheless remains a special case. On the view I wish to advance here it is useful to regard the Frankian account of capitalist underdevelopment as a *synthesis* of the ideas of the ECLA/structuralist current and those of Marxism, or, to be more precise, those of a Marxism rooted on the one hand in the Cuban revolution and on the other in the economics of *Monthly Review*. The middle sections of the chapter identify the major strands which have contributed to Frank's creative synthesis, locating the corresponding continuities and points of rupture.

To suggest that Frank's studies are synthetic in character is by no means to denigrate the influence they have had on the rest of us. On the contrary my main purpose is to create the conditions for a better appreciation of the extremely positive and significant stimulus that they have given to the scientific study of dependent capitalist societies. At the same time, certain notable lacunae and ambiguities *are* to be found among Frank's formulations, and these are not unrelated to the theoretical and polemical functions which the theory was originally designed to fulfil. In addition to focusing upon some of the drawbacks of the Frankian scheme, the discussion in the final sections of the chapter thus attempts to explain the source of these difficulties in the light of the preceding analysis.

The new nationalism and the ECLA school[8]

Andre Gunder Frank is probably most widely known for what is certainly one of the least distinctive elements in his theoretical framework: the vision of a world in which the development of a handful of 'metropoli' onomies governs, hinders and distorts the development of a rather larger number of 'satellite' economies. Although Frank's concept introduces a new emphasis, its parentage is not in doubt. It is the direct offspring of the image of a world consisting of a developed 'centre' and an underdeveloped 'periphery' which was employed by ECLA in its earliest studies.[9] That this should come as a surprise to some readers is the measure of the continued parochialism of the higher learning in the English-speaking world. For in a real sense there was no development economics before ECLA and few, if any, centres of social science research in the developed capitalist world can boast the combination of theoretical audacity and 'policy-relevance' which the Commission sustained throughout the immediate post-war years.

In retrospect it is clear that in the decade or so following the Second World War bourgeois social science in the metropolitan countries was presented with an intellectual challenge of unprecedented human significance. The events which filled these years—the foundation of the United Nations, the Chinese revolution, the Cold War, and the rise of nationalist movements throughout the colonial world—combined to produce the recognition of a new problem at the level of world consciousness: the problem of *under*development. In retrospect it is also plain that, straightforward ideological barriers aside, these years found the various social-science disciplines singularly ill-equipped to meet the challenge of providing a factually exact and theoretically adequate account of the sources of underdevelopment and the conditions for its definitive suppression. Economics continued to bear the heavy weight of the neo-classical tradition of the late nineteenth century, with its systematic neglect of long-run evolutionary trends and bias in favour of the micro-economics of allocative efficiency. Although under the direct influence of Keynes economists had once again begun to concern themselves with the process of economic growth, the dominant tendency was towards the restriction of economics to the refined business of constructing models which, whatever their relevance to advanced capitalism (or on the other hand to the ideal construct of the fully planned economy), were characterized by a rigorous expulsion from their focal concerns of anything which smacked of history, let alone the history of ex-colonial territories on the other side of the world.[10] Theoretical sociology, in the meantime, was undergoing a revival of that tradition of social thought spanning the careers of Emile Durkheim and Max Weber which had formed the core of the conservative European reaction to the social tensions of early monopoly capitalism. A distinguishing feature of this tradition was that it placed at the centre of the stage not the study of societies but the theoretical analysis of Society and Social Action as such.[11] This was the nature of the dominant intellectual climate on a world level when ECLA began to develop a series of arguments with the modest aim of accounting for aspects of the recent economic history of the Latin American region.

It is a fact which is of crucial importance for an understanding of ECLA's contribution to the foundation of an adequate theory of underdevelopment that by 1945 a number of the larger Latin American countries had undergone an appreciable degree of industrialization. Like Hegel's owl of Minerva, economic science seldom experiences autonomous theoretical revolutions and the most significant advances are invariably the result of *ex post facto* inter-pretations of a recent turn of economic events. ECLA is no exception in this respect. The situation which presented itself in Latin America in the second half of the 1940s was one in which, in the words of the Commission itself, 'a contradiction—or at least a lack of har-mony' had grown up 'between the behavior and aims of what are now the economically more advanced countries of the region and the prevailing body of ideas, theories, and doctrines'.[12] Under the peculiar economic circumstances created by the Depression of the 1930s and subsequently by the Second World War, a number of countries—including most notably Argentina, Brazil, and Mexico—had in effect abandoned the 'outward-directed' export-led growth model which had prevailed in the region for more than a century. Force of circumstance and in some instances the more or less for-tuitous play of economic interests at the level of the state had dictated new policies which for the most part still lacked any theoretical rationale. In the absence of the necessary ideological adjustments, concepts and theories associated with 'growth towards the outside' continued to dominate the intellectual scene.

The ending of Latin America's relative economic isolation and the reactivation of the traditional export sectors following the Second World War contributed to the prevailing confusion in the sense that it tended to revive the corpse of the outward-directed model:[13]

> Both inside and outside the region, a basis in fact was found
> for maintaining that the past fifteen years or so had been merely
> an unfortunate interregnum produced by exceptional factors,
> and that the 'normal' condition—that is to say, the
> advantageous division-of-labor model of the past—would
> resume its place.

For reasons about which ECLA continues to be studiously vague,[14] moreover, the political backing for the further diversification of nearly all those Latin American economies which had so far achieved a measure of industrialization significantly weakened during the first post-war decade. These circumstances helped to give a militant tone to ECLA's analyses and policy-prescriptions even where these stemmed directly from 'what most countries of the region . . . had been doing since the depression'.[15]

In point of fact the first landmark in ECLA's career was a frontal assault upon the intellectual bases of the 'outward-directed' develop-ment model. 'Orthodox' international trade theory, upon which ECLA published a devastating attack in 1949,[16] had shown that, given free trade and certain other conditions, the benefits deriving from trends in productivity in the world economy as a whole would be distributed towards the primary-producing 'periphery', since technical progress was more vigorous and widespread in the production of industrial goods. ECLA prepared its offensive by producing statistics showing long-term movements in the terms of trade between primary and industrial producers which appeared to suggest that over a long period quite the opposite had been happening. The next step was to suggest why the model proved to have such misleading results, and to examine possible explanations of the actual trend.

In the first place, it was pointed out, the model made the wildly unrealistic assumption of perfect mobility of the factors of production—labour and capital—between trading countries. The falsity of this assumption as applied to the real world made it impossible to draw *any* definite conclusions from the model.[17] An alternative view was that the sharply contrasting labour conditions obtaining in the industrial countries of the 'centre' and the primary-producing countries of the 'periphery'—on the one hand a relatively well-organized workforce and relatively full employment, on the other a permanent pool of unemployed and underemployed labour—were among the causes of the movement of the terms of trade against primary producers in that they permitted the gains from productivity increases in the centre to be retained there in the form of higher wages and allowed some of the gains from productivity increases in the periphery to be 'exported' in the form of cheaper commodities.[18] A second dubious assumption usually made in discussions of the benefits of trade was that the centre's demand for primary products would grow at least as fast as income, and 'perhaps even faster if consideration was given to the possibility of a depletion in the supply of those goods and increases in their costs and prices'.[19] To be sure, from the vantage point of 1974 these ideas appear less wide of the mark than they did ten or even five years ago. None the less it should be remembered that what became known as the 'Prebisch thesis' was first advanced in commodity–export conditions not altogether unlike those obtaining today and that nothing has changed which could conceivably detract from ECLA's core contention: that there is no natural law which decrees that the income elasticities of demand for a country's imports and exports remain constant. The ghost of an in-built and inevitable tendency for the evolution of industrial and non-industrial economies to lead to a deterioration in the latter's terms of trade is still very far from being laid.

From ECLA's new view of international trade there flowed the realization that an increase in the traditional exports of the typical Latin American country might well produce *no* increase in national income. This meant that a given increment of investment might be more profitably employed in import substituting industries, even if the latter operated at a lower level of productivity than their counterparts in the economies of the 'centre'.[20] Thus the conclusions of ECLA's trade theory gave direct sustenance to its well-known advocacy of industrialization and industrial protectionism in Third World countries.

It has been suggested that ECLA's early concentration upon trade stemmed in part from the need to dwell upon what clearly constituted the common denominator of the development problems of the Latin American region.[21] Whether or not this interpretation is correct, it is certainly the case that the most important of its subsequent analyses focused upon the *contrasting* experiences of those countries which had experienced a significant degree of 'inward-directed' growth and of those which had not. It was by examining this contrast that ECLA arrived at a balance-sheet of the experience of 'inward-directed' growth which contained the germs of a thorough-going critique.

For practical purposes, development 'towards the inside' meant industrialization, but industrialization of a specific type. Whereas during the industrial development of the countries of the 'centre' it had proved to a greater or lesser degree possible to sell the same manufactured goods on the domestic and foreign markets, the structure of the world economy now forced industrialization into the path of import substitution, at least in its initial stages. The industrial growth which had occurred in Argentina, Brazil and elsewhere during the First World War and on a greater scale in the 1930s and 1940s had resulted from the region's reduced capacity to import manufactures in circumstances which maintained the level of domestic demand. For reasons which were not intrinsic to import substitution industrialization as such, however, the growth process had suffered from serious limitations. Because not only the level but also the structure of the demand previously satisfied by imports had remained unchanged since the export-orientated phase and because the latter had created a highly unequal distribution of national incomes, the new industries had tended to produce consumer goods of a luxury sort. This tendency had been reinforced by the natural inclination of governments to 'save on foreign exchange' in the first instance by means of restrictions on the import of non-essential goods. Where such measures were applied they had served in practice to channel import substituting efforts into precisely those sectors judged to be of low priority—hardly the course that would have been recommended by a rational development strategy.[22]

Because of the circumstances indicated in the preceding paragraph, industrial growth along import substitution lines had had another contradictory result: it had increased rather than reduced the pressure on the balance of payments. Domestic production of 'non-essential' manufactured goods which had formerly been imported had stimulated the demand for inputs and equipment from abroad. In the early stages this had not mattered too much. However, the logic of the import substitution process was such that each new step in the business of replacing non-essential imports with imports required for this very act of substitution increased the proportion of relatively indispensable or 'strategic' goods in the total import package. This had progressively reduced the 'room for manoeuvre' of the industrially more advanced economies of the region—or, if we may be permitted to use a term of more recent vintage, it had *increased their economic dependence.*[23]

Was the only possible form of industrial growth in Latin America one which led to increased dependency and hence to the eventual strangulation of the initial developmental impulse? Had this outcome been inevitable or was it simply the product of a fortuitous and therefore unforeseen combination of circumstances? On questions such as these ECLA reserved judgment, sometimes suggesting one interpretation, sometimes the other. In retrospect, however, the Commission has expressed the official opinion that 'it is not easy to devise other economic policy options that would have been feasible in the original conditions under which the problem was posed', adding that such options would have involved 'considerable changes' in the income distribution and in 'the whole institutional framework' of the societies in question.[24] It is only necessary to lift the veil of diplomatic language which enshrouds statements of this type to understand why it is that ECLA's studies have influenced revolutionaries as well as reformers.

If most Latin American revolutionaries, and a good many reformists besides, eventually turned their back on ECLA's perspective, this was due in large measure to the issue of foreign investment. From the middle of the 1950s ECLA's publications began to give increasing attention to what they referred to as 'external cooperation'.[25] The timing was not fortuitous nor was it just a result of the fact that by this date the task of dissecting the import substitution experience had been completed in its main outlines, thus permitting ECLA's resident economists to turn their attention to new problems. As we have seen, the progress which had been made by some Latin American countries towards industrialization of a certain sort had led to an increase in their national incomes but at the same time to a disproportionate expansion and growing inflexibility in their demand for imports. To a large extent, however, the problems created by this new economic pattern had been masked during the immediate post-war years by an unusually favourable set of conditions. Initially, even the most industrially advanced countries retained a certain capacity to alter the composition of their imports in such a way as to allow growth to continue unabated. For several years most countries were also able to draw upon substantial reserves of foreign exchange which they had accumulated during the war. In addition the post-war boom in the region's traditional export items helped indirectly to finance continued capital accumulation in industry, but only for a time. Changes in the international economic situation coinciding with the end of the Korean War brought the export boom to an abrupt end, opening a long period in which the region's terms of trade steadily deteriorated. The combination of this conjunctional shift with the long-term trends inherent in the industrialization process brought severe balance-of-payments crises (and corresponding political shocks) to one country after another.[26] For most of the preceding quarter of a century capital formation had been sustained preponderantly by means of domestic savings. Now, however, government after government turned to the encouragement of foreign sources of investment to finance its external deficit.

Contrary to what has sometimes been claimed, ECLA looked favourably upon foreign investment as a means of escape from the Latin American dilemma of the 1950s. Indeed it argued with some force that 'foreign cooperation' would enable countries to maintain a high rate of development whilst at the same time closing the gap between the new demand for imports thus generated and the region's depleted export earnings. In other words, an inflow of foreign funds would relieve the 'built-in disequilibrium' to which ECLA had drawn attention. It would also reduce the pressure on Latin American governments in a number of secondary but by no means negligible ways. Foreign investment would supplement in a particularly decisive fashion the region's capacity to import capital goods, thus reducing the need to restrict consumer imports unduly, and a 'timely and adequate' inflow of funds from abroad would cushion the depressive impact of an energetic effort to correct a balance-of-payments deficit or control inflation (on which more presently). Finally, direct private investment would have the particular merit of serving as an agent for the transfer to Latin America of the new industrial techniques and organizational patterns which the region required.[27]

Did it occur to ECLA that the large quantities of foreign capital which were welcomed into Latin America from the mid-1950s onwards, a substantial and growing proportion of which consisted of direct investments in the manufacturing sector, might solve the short-run problems which faced the governments of the day only at a significant cost to the region's future prosperity and social well-being? It is certainly true that ECLA took care to spell out the conditions which would have to be fulfilled if external cooperation was to discharge the functions ascribed to it. 'It was not overlooked', we have been informed,[28]

> that such cooperation might bypass the purposes and functions for which it was intended and become yet another factor making for disequilibrium and yet another obstacle to self-sustained development, in so far as the requirements stipulated were not complied with in full.

In the present context we need pay attention to only three of these preconditions. First, and most obviously, the funds involved had to be sufficient in quantity to have appreciable effects on the development process. Second—a weighty condition in the light of the subsequent turn of events—the terms upon which loans were obtained needed to be sufficiently favourable and the rate of return on investments sufficiently low to permit the net inflow of funds—inflow of external funds less repayments, interest and repatriated profits—to remain at a constant level throughout the period to be covered. Third, the inflow of funds should have sufficient continuity to enable internal investment and programming to be conducted with a measure of security and stability.[29]

What assurances, if any, could ECLA give that foreign capital, public or private, would be prepared to accept terms such as these in the first place and that it could be trusted not to renegue on the bargain once it had been struck? In point of fact not even ECLA was in a position to make reliable predictions about such things. We have to admit that in relative terms very little was known at this juncture about the impact upon semi-industrialized economies of direct foreign investment in manufacturing. The vertically- and horizontally-integrated 'multinational' corporation, which was to become the principal vehicle of such investment in the second half of the twentieth century, remained to a considerable extent a mystery. It fell to others to probe these topics in the 1960s. Nevertheless, ECLA might have been expected to have shown rather more concern about these lacunae in its theory than it actually did. A significant influence here was no doubt the absence of politically acceptable alternatives to foreign investment. Another was ECLA's view that in any case it would only be required for a relatively brief transitional stage of Latin America's development.

The assumptions upon which this optimistic prognosis was based were not spelt out in detail or specified with precision. In at least four respects, however, it was expected that an inflow of foreign capital in the medium term would facilitate Latin America's evolution to economic independence in the long term. First and secondly, it would promote the internal diversification of the economies and thus widen the margin of domestic savings; thirdly and fourthly, it would open up new export opportunities and thus increase foreign exchange earnings.[30] It was partly the poor performance of foreign firms according to these very criteria which drew many young economists, among them Andre Gunder Frank, to place a question-mark over the ECLA model.

To be sure, foreign investment was not the only remedy which ECLA recommended for the ills of the Latin American economy in the 1950s. A number of new policy proposals as well as some important theoretical advances flowed out of the ECLA school's participation in the debate which raged throughout the late 1950s and early 1960s around the issue of inflation. For some years a number of economies in the region had experienced extremely high rates of inflation, whereas others had with equal consistency only suffered from 'normal' rates of inflation. How was the difference to be explained? The answer which ECLA, together with other independent 'structuralist' economists, was led to give to this question contains a simple but invaluable lesson for those of us who are still inclined to think of underdeveloped economies as an undifferentiated group and of underdevelopment as a state of affairs subject only to quantitative variations. The analysis began with the observation that high rates of inflation were invariably found in those countries which had acquired the instruments of an autonomous monetary policy and which had employed these instruments along 'unorthodox' lines. On the other hand those economies which lacked monetary autonomy and had perforce pursued 'orthodox' policies were invariably characterized by normal inflation rates. Rejecting the alternative of concentrating upon the purely monetary side of the matter, the structuralists drew particular attention to the fact that the first group of countries (dubbed 'Group U' by ECLA) had the additional characteristics of being relatively large and partially industrialized. In general, exports accounted for a relatively small proportion of their gross production. The other group ('Group O') on the other hand consisted mostly of small, largely unindustrialized economies which still relied heavily on their traditional exports.[31]

By deliberately searching for the causes of inflation in the process of 'inward-directed' growth experienced by Group U countries the ECLA economists were able to place their fingers upon a variety of potential or actual 'bottlenecks' liable to affect any economy at a comparable stage of import substituting industrialization. By adopting a wide-ranging comparative perspective they laid the bases of a development economics rooted in the diversity as well as the commonality of the experience of underdevelopment, a point to which I shall return. ECLA's probing of the inflationary spiral also contributed (assisted by the growing social crisis which manifested itself in the cities and countryside of Latin America in the 1960s) to the conversion of the Commission into a champion of income redistribution, land reform and (finally?) regional economic integration.[32] But as far as policy was concerned the course of events in the 1960s increasingly passed ECLA by.

From ECLA to Frank

Andre Gunder Frank was brought up in middle-class North America and trained as an economist at the University of Chicago under the influence, as he puts it, of 'the most reactionary wing of the American bourgeoisie'. This social and professional background had inclined him to think of Latin America's development problems[33]

in terms of largely domestic problems of capital scarcity, feudal and traditional institutions which impede saving and investment, concentration of political power in the hands of rural oligarchies, and many of the universally known supposed obstacles to the economic development of supposedly traditionally underdeveloped societies.

A brief spell of teaching and research in Latin America in the early 1960s sufficed to convey to Frank the largely fictional character of what he had been taught, and what he had himself written, about underdevelopment, and to convince him of the importance of familiarity with the actual structure and, still more important, the *history* of underdeveloped economies.[34]

Although Frank himself is not given to praising ECLA, there can be little doubt that the fact that the Commission had already established a working body of theory based precisely upon an historical analysis of the Latin American economic experience of the previous half-century, was a powerful stimulus to new creative endeavours and facilitated a radical rejection of the ideas which still prevailed at the University of Chicago. In Latin America ECLA's thinking was now the conventional economic wisdom in numerous academic institutions. Nevertheless certain of its ideas, notably its optimistic prognoses regarding the role which would be played by foreign investment in Latin America's development during the second post-war decade, were beginning to be taken up and subjected to further critical scrutiny. By the time Frank arrived in Latin America, moreover, there were already palpable indications that the region's economic history in the 1960s was not going to conform to the pattern expected and hoped for by ECLA. In retrospect it is possible to perceive the major underlying trends quite clearly and it will be useful to begin by enumerating them briefly, drawing upon Frank's own summary of statistics derived from ECLA's empirical studies for this purpose. The major thrust of ECLA's analysis in the 1950s had been to provide an explanation of the observed tendency for the region's annual growth rate of *per capita* income to decline. In the 1960s, first of all, this tendency continued to make itself felt. Comparing average figures for successive five-year periods since the war, we get a decline from 4·8 per cent in 1945–9 to 1·9 per cent in 1950–5, 1·4 per cent in 1955–60, and 1·2 per cent in 1960–6. A particularly significant decline was observable over the whole period in the growth rate of industrial output—once the dynamic sector *par excellence* of the region's economies.[35]

On the other hand, foreign investment did not seem to be serving to counteract the causes of slower growth, at any rate not in the way that ECLA had said it might. As a proportion of gross investment in Latin America, the net contribution of external financing, as computed by ECLA and *including the reinvestment of earnings* retained in the region by foreign capital, *fell* from an average of 10·3 per cent in 1955–9 to an average of 7·4 per cent in 1960–4 and 4·3 per cent in 1965–6.[36] This was partly a reflection of the fact that the outflow of funds in the form of profits, interest, and amortization payments directly attributable to foreign investment and 'aid' represented a sharply rising proportion of Latin America's total foreign exchange income from exports—18·4 per cent in 1950–4, 25·4 per cent in 1955–9, and 36·1 per cent in 1965–6.[37] More significantly, *if reinvested earnings are excluded from the calculation*, the net contribution of external funds was beginning to become negative, that is, to be transformed into a net outflow of financial capital. In 1963, 1965, and again in 1967–9, this became the situation for the region as a whole, and for several individual countries the tide turned in this respect somewhat earlier.[38] And this was assuming that these statistics adequately reflected the true drain of funds out of Latin America due to the presence of foreign capital, which in several respects they almost certainly did not.[39]

A number of typical characteristics of the economic growth that was occurring in the region drew attention in their own right. First, Latin America's terms of trade were continuing to deteriorate in spite of the growing contribution that industry was making to gross domestic production and the increasing proportion of new foreign investment which had been attracted to manufacturing.[40] The possibilities of Latin America moving rapidly into the industrial exporting stage seemed as distant as ever. Second, industrial growth was not helping to eliminate a major source of the region's social crisis, a combination of widespread unemployment with that fathomless 'underemployment' which lay concealed under the low productivity of agriculture and the artificially swollen 'services' sector. Thus, whereas the share of industrial production in the regional gross domestic product increased from 11 per cent in 1925 to 19 per cent in 1950, 22 per cent in 1960, and 23 per cent in 1967, the proportion of the total labour force employed by industry remained constant at around 14 per cent over the whole period.[41] Third, patterns of social inequality showed few signs of responding to the spread of modern industry in such a way as to ameliorate the lot of the broad masses of inhabitants of Latin American countries. Despite partial industrialization or because of its character, estimates for 1965 suggested that 20 per cent of the regional population received only 3 per cent of all incomes, or an average of $60 per year in 1960 prices. Even the poorest 50 per cent received only 13 per cent, or an average of $100 per year. On the other hand the richest 20 per cent of the population accounted for 63 per cent of national incomes, the richest 5 per cent for as much as 33 per cent, and the richest 1 per cent for no less than 17 per cent.[42]

It was in response to the first signs of findings such as these that some Latin American economists, among them Frank, began to question in a systematic way the viability and the desirability of a model of development based upon an association with foreign capital and permitting only the most rudimentary, and needless to say non-socialist, forms of 'planning' at the national level. A series of studies began to shed light upon the interconnections between the various global trends we have just recalled, to investigate the actual mode of operation of foreign capital in its Latin American environment and to dwell upon the limitations of what began to be seen as a new colonial relationship as an engine of growth and harbinger of social progress.[43] The individuality of Frank's contribution rested upon the fact that he was among the first to go beyond a merely empirical reinterpretation of the latest phase of Latin American economic history and to try to spell out its implications in the context of a longer view of the character and sources of underdevelopment in the region.

ECLA, it will be remembered, had argued against the ideologies of the old nineteenth-century neo-colonial 'pact' that the import substitution industrialization of the 1930s and 1940s was no mere transitory phenomenon but had permanent consequences. It now fell to Frank to turn ECLA on its head and to submit that the experience of the 1930s and 1940s could indeed be regarded as a mere incident in the long history of Latin America's underdevelopment. Adopting and lightly modifying ECLA's concept of a world consisting of a developed 'centre' and an underdeveloped 'periphery', Frank pointed to a constant in the region's economic development since the Conquest. That was that, although it had taken a variety of forms, it had always been *satellite*-development. Not only did Latin America have a specific history which rendered virtually useless interpretations and prescriptions based on the experience of the now developed countries—a point of view which, among non-Marxists, ECLA itself had done much to advance—but this specificity affected the possibility as well as the form of progress under capitalism.

The debate within Marxism

Up to a point it makes sense to regard Frank as a radical critic of ECLA who was led by the force of his own argument to adopt anti-capitalist and ultimately Marxist positions. Intellectual history is seldom so simple, however, and from the outset Frank addressed himself directly to a question at issue within Marxist theory and brought into prominence by the most significant political event of post-war Latin American history—the Cuban revolution.

There are several senses in which we can say that without Fidel Castro, Andre Gunder Frank would not have been possible. The specific issue to which it is necessary to draw attention here concerns one of the lesser known but most significant features of the impact of the Cuban revolution upon the rest of Latin America. Marxists who are already familiar with the problems in question will excuse a brief and therefore necessarily superficial digression here.

Since the war, bourgeois development theory has been involved in a somewhat anaemic debate, which is only just beginning to peter out, about the possibility of constructing a scheme of universal developmental 'stages'.[44] In all its essentials, this phenomenon was anticipated by the vigorous debate which was initiated more than half a century before within Russian radical thought. Notwithstanding the views of stages–theorists such as Rostow who think that, in this respect, they can find in Marx a companion spirit, it is not impossible to perceive the germs of all the positions advanced subsequently in Marx's own writings on India, Russia, and Germany respectively.[45] Without discussing the various points of view in detail, we may note that the October Revolution took place because and only because the view came to prevail among the Bolsheviks and their supporters that Russia could not be expected to undergo a repetition of that Western European historical experience generally known as the bourgeois-democratic revolution.[46] Although the Russian ruling class might, for its own reasons, *initiate* progressive innovations— land reform, political democratization, industrial development—this social revolution could only be completed under the leadership of the proletariat. In Russia's economic and social development a decisive turning point would be reached from which there would be no turning back and at this point socialists would be presented with the option of taking the necessary steps to ensure the 'continuation' of the bourgeois-democratic revolution under socialist auspices or of seeing the entire process brought to a halt by the reactionary forces that it would inevitably unleash. In this sense the only possible type of social revolution would be an 'uninterrupted', or, to use Trotsky's more famous formulation, a 'permanent' revolution.

After 1917 the concept of the uninterrupted revolution was recommended by the Bolsheviks to the Communist International as a rule-of-thumb applicable to backward countries generally. Far from being a case of illegitimate generalization from Soviet experience, this was correct to the extent that it had been shown that the major 'peculiarity' of Russia's socio-economic development—its extreme 'unevenness' by comparison with that of the West—was rooted not in specifically Russian conditions but in the manner of the country's insertion into the world capitalist system.[47] Nevertheless, the rejection of stages–theories of development and the revolution in colonial and semi-colonial countries did not outlive the first five years of the International. A political theory and practice which, in the context just indicated, may be characterized as a new 'Menshevism' acquired a grip on Communist parties throughout the world which, brief phases of equally disastrous and 'ultra-left' insurrectionism aside, it has not relinquished to this day.

Against this backdrop it is possible and correct to see in the Cuban revolution, much less importantly than a vindication of armed struggle and less still of the tactics of rural guerrilla warfare, a reassertion of the actuality of the theory of permanent revolution. The important 'Castroist' revolutionary current which grew up in Latin America during the 1960s failed by and large to make the 'theoretical' connections necessary for the complete regeneration of the Leninist tradition in the region. None the less, one important 'lesson' of the Cuban experience was not lost on the Latin American left. It was no secret inside Cuba or abroad that a sharp political battle had had to be fought against the leadership of the old Communist *Partido Socialista Popular* not merely to get it to take up arms against the dictator Batista but also to obtain its support for anything more sweeping than a 'democratic and anti-imperialist' revolution on the morrow of the collapse of the old order.[48] Though overshadowed to some extent by the question of armed struggle, the strategic message of both the 1962 Second Declaration of Havana[49] and the resolutions and declarations of the first conference of OLAS (Latin American Solidarity Organization) held in Havana in 1967, was that the democratic and anti-imperialist revolution which the continent required could only take a *socialist* form. The Latin American bourgeoisie, the OLAS resolution explained, was structurally incapable of performing its supposed historic tasks:[50]

The so-called Latin American bourgeoisie, because of its origins and because of its economic connections and even kinship-links

65

with landowners, forms a part of the oligarchies which rule
our America and is in consequence incapable of acting
independently.

By the same token,

> It would be absurd to suppose that . . . the so-called Latin
> American bourgeoisie is capable of developing a political line
> independent . . . of imperialism, in defence of the interests and
> aspirations of the nation. The contradiction within which it is
> objectively trapped is, by its nature, insuperable.

It was with the theoretical elaboration and documentation of this
proposition that Frank's work was very largely concerned.

The idiom in which Frank advanced his critique of the Stalinist
orthodoxy was not of course Trotsky's. In fact references which
indicate an awareness of the antecedents of his views are as rare in
Frank's writings as they are in the appropriate speeches of Fidel
Castro. It is not the case, however, that the theoretical apparatus
which Frank adopted was entirely his own or that he is generally
remiss about conceding credit where it is due. In particular Frank
has acknowledged profusely his debt to Paul Baran's *The Political
Economy of Growth*[51] and in more ways than one he has been
powerfully influenced by the particular brand of Marxist thought
associated with the American journal *Monthly Review*.

Frank's first book, *Capitalism and Underdevelopment in Latin
America*,[52] introduced two theoretical innovations of importance in
this context. The first was expressed in the proposition which constituted the core of the book: that, contrary to the claims made by
the theory of the 'dual society' (as well as by 'orthodox' Marxism),[53]
most of Latin America had been thoroughly incorporated into world
capitalism during the very first phase of its colonial history. 'A
mounting body of evidence suggests', as Frank put it elsewhere,
'. . . that the expansion of the capitalist system over past centuries
effectively and entirely penetrated even the apparently most isolated
sectors of the underdeveloped world.'[54] Hence it made no sense to
speak of feudal, 'semi-feudal' or 'archaic' elements in Latin American society—elements which would give meaning to the idea of a
'bourgeois-democratic' revolution. There were only *seemingly* feudal
or archaic formations thrown up by the capitalist development of
underdevelopment. As one of Frank's most penetrating critics has
pointed out, and as we shall see in more detail presently, the conception implicit in these statements of what it means to characterize
a given social relationship or institution as 'capitalist' or 'feudal',
departs radically not only from the usage of latter-day stages-
theorists but also from that of Marx. Before considering the difficulties

attendant upon the use of a concept of capitalism so inclusive as to permit Frank to argue in the way he does, however, it is worth saying something about its origins. Latin American precursors of this view are not impossible to find (the Argentine economic historian Sergio Bagú, upon whose work Frank draws, is a case in point)[55] but the only vigorous and consistent defence of the position is that which Paul Sweezy, the editor of *Monthly Review*, wrote in the pages of *Science and Society* in the early 1950s.[56]

The second theoretical innovation to which we must make reference is as follows. In the study of Chile with which Frank opened his first book, he enumerated three 'contradictions' of capitalism to which it was proposed to trace the causes of underdevelopment. The first, 'the contradiction of expropriation/appropriation of economic surplus', was introduced in a way which merits quotation in full.[57]

It was Marx's analysis of capitalism which identified and emphasized the expropriation of the surplus value created by producers and its appropriation by capitalists. A century later, Paul Baran emphasized the role of economic surplus in the generation of economic development and also of underdevelopment. What Baran called 'actual' economic surplus is that part of current production which is saved and in fact invested (and thus is merely one part of surplus value). Baran also distinguished and placed greater emphasis on 'potential' or potentially investible economic surplus which is not available to society because its [society's] monopoly structure prevents its production or (if it is produced) it is appropriated and wasted through luxury consumption. The income differential between high and low income recipients and much of the failure of the former to channel their income into productive investment may also be traced to monopoly. Therefore, the non-realization and unavailability for investment of 'potential' economic surplus is due essentially to the monopoly structure of capitalism

Frank went on to argue (*a*) that a high degree of 'external and internal monopoly' has characterized Chile's insertion into the world economy since the beginning, (*b*) that external monopoly 'has always resulted in the expropriation (and consequent unavailability to Chile) of a significant part of the economic surplus produced in Chile and its appropriation by another part of the world capitalist system', but (*c*) that[58]

this exploitative relation . . . in chain-like fashion extends the capitalist link between the capitalist world and national metropolises to the regional centers (part of whose surplus they appropriate), and from these to local centers, and so on to large landowners or merchants who expropriate surplus from small peasants or tenants, and sometimes even from these latter to landless laborers exploited by them in turn.

Finally (*d*), the result is 'economic development for the few and underdevelopment for the many'.

I have quoted extensively in the preceding paragraph not only because the summary of Baran is competent and the style of Frank's own statement inimitable, but also because the ideas contained in this passage will call for particular critical attention later on. At this point, however, I wish only to give emphasis to the warning issued in passing by Frank that each of Baran's concepts of 'actual' and 'potential' economic surplus has a content which differs decisively from that normally given by Marxists to the concept of surplus value. Attempts to apply the former concepts to the solution of a problem posed in rigorous Marxian terms—a mistake which Frank himself does not actually make—are liable to end in confusion.[59]

The second contradiction of capitalism to which Frank attributed Chilean underdevelopment was what he termed 'metropolis–satellite polarization', and this, for Frank, was the most important. It was in the discussion of this notion that the general proposition was introduced that 'one and the same historical process of the expansion and development of capitalism throughout the world has simultaneously generated—and continues to generate—both economic development and structural underdevelopment'. In this sense, development and underdevelopment are opposite faces of the same coin rather than sequentially related stages of growth.[60] Frank also insisted that capitalism introduces a similar pattern of polarization between regions *within* the underdeveloped society itself and that[61]

for the generation of structural underdevelopment, more important still than the drain of economic surplus from the satellite after its incorporation as such into the world capitalist system, is the impregnation of the satellite's domestic economy with the same capitalist structure and its fundamental contradictions.

However, the reader who expected to be told at this point *what* it is about capitalism that generates international and inter-regional uneven development—other, that is, than the previously mentioned contradiction of surplus-appropriation—was disappointed. With a singularly brief remark Frank associated the contradiction of polarization with Marx's analysis of the 'imminent [*sic*] *centralization* of the capitalist system'.[62] Thereafter 'polarization' was discussed in such a way as to suggest that, from a causal point of view, it was regarded as the most important of the *effects* of 'surplus-appro-priation'. In other words, this contradiction was a characteristic rather than a cause of structural underdevelopment.[63]

In spite of its confused presentation, this passage none the less yielded the 'subsidiary thesis' which permitted Frank to integrate his theoretical discussion with the wealth of historical material on Chile, Brazil, and Latin America as a whole which he was able to array in the body of his work: 'If it is satellite status which generates underdevelopment, then a weaker or lesser degree of metropolis-satellite relations may generate less deep structural underdevelop-ment and/or allow for more possibility of local development.'[64] As Frank has stated in the form of a global hypothesis elsewhere, 'the satellites experience their greatest economic development and especially their most classically capitalist industrial development if and when their ties to their metropolis are weakest.'[65] The examina-tion of two types of relative isolation experienced by Latin America in the course of its history—forms of isolation caused respectively by metropolitan wars or depressions and by the relatively weak in-tegration of specific regions into the world economy—served Frank as the means of confirming this hypothesis. In the present writer's view, it was above all the manner in which Frank was able to bring historical research to bear upon what was, after all, his central con-tention—that for Latin America capitalism has precluded and con-tinues to preclude development—that accounted for the power and obvious importance of his first studies.

We shall return to this point. It remains here, however, to in-dicate the nature of the third and final 'contradiction' to which Frank initially attributed development and underdevelopment in Chile. Once again the reader who expected the pin-pointing of causally decisive processes was disappointed. However, the basic idea of the 'contradiction of continuity in change' was simple. It is time we drew attention, Frank was urging, to 'the continuity and ubiquity of the structural essentials of economic development and underdevelopment throughout the expansion and development of the capitalist system at all times and places'.[66] In his study of Chile, correspondingly, emphasis was placed on 'the continuity of capitalist structure and its generation of underdevelopment rather than on the many undoubtedly important historical changes and transforma-tions that Chile has undergone within this structure'.[67] This, in a sense, is precisely the point at which we came in. It was Frank's view of the normality and inevitability of the sorts of obstacles to further economic development which overtook post-war Latin America that constituted the initial cause of his break with the ECLA school.

Frank and his critics: the initial phase

The proposition which forms the core of all Frank's books is that it was world capitalism which created the condition of underdevelopment and which maintains it in existence to this day. Certainly the most frequent, but probably not the most damaging, form of criticism to which this proposition has been subject, concerns the relationship allegedly established by it between what we may term 'external dependence' on the one hand and the 'internal' structures of underdevelopment on the other. Already in the preface to the revised edition (1969) of *Capitalism and Underdevelopment in Latin America* Frank felt constrained to answer unnamed critics by stressing that the thesis of the book, summarized in the chapter on Chile, 'is precisely that in chainlike fashion the contradictions of expropriation/appropriation and metropolis/satellite polarization totally penetrate the underdeveloped world creating an "internal" structure of underdevelopment'. As Fidel Castro had once said, the imperialists would be welcome to the dollars they drain out of Latin America if they would only let the Latin American people use the remaining resources for their own development. Were it the case that underdevelopment was merely a problem of Latin America's external economic relations and manifested primarily in a capital drain through trade and aid, as some argued, then the simple 'nationalist' solutions criticized in the book might indeed be held to be adequate.[68]

The message seems not to have reached those for whom it was intended, for in the study which he first published in Latin America in 1970, Frank was obliged to renew his defence in a prefatory note entitled 'Mea Culpa'.[69] Indeed the new volume as a whole was addressed very largely to this question, introducing a number of terminological innovations designed to clear up what Frank seems to have recognized as insufficiently explicit arguments in his earlier work. Thus in answer to the charge of a group of Mexican critics that the metropolis–satellite formulation was over-schematic and his historical analysis lacking in that kind of depth which would have been provided by a careful analysis of the relations of exploitation between the domestic social classes, Frank reaffirmed that it *was* most important to define and understand underdevelopment in terms of classes. The point was underlined by the very title of his new book: *Lumpenbourgeoisie: Lumpendevelopment.*[70]

In reality the argument presented by the Mexican collective did rather more than merely draw attention to the importance of domestic class relations. As is clear from the passage of their critique quoted by Frank, they pointed to what I shall suggest at the end was one of the theoretical sources of the ambiguity in the original Frankian thesis. As for the issue of 'external' dependence *versus* 'internal' structures more narrowly posed, it is impossible to avoid the sensation that Frank has served more than one of his critics as an intellectual punch-bag or, to change the metaphor, as a sounding-board for ideas which the authors wish to advance for some extraneous reason. We should not be surprised that this happens; few book reviews are immune from such a tendency and it may not be entirely absent from these pages. None the less some of Frank's critics have indulged themselves to excess.

The Brazilian Marxist and dependency theorist, Theotonio Dos Santos, is a case in point. Contrary to Frank's account of the matter, Dos Santos has asserted, the process which generates underdevelopment cannot be understood simply in terms of the drainage of a large proportion of the available economic surplus: 'The process under consideration, rather than being one of satellization as Frank believes, is a case of the formation of a certain type of internal structure conditioned by international relationships of dependence.'[71]

F. Stirton Weaver, a student of the Chilean economy, has argued along similar lines that[72]

> although inter-nation transfers of economic surplus is useful for understanding the benefits accruing to the developed capitalist trading and investing nations, it is too fragile to bear so much of the burden of explanation for the more complex 'development of underdevelopment'.

For Weaver, 'the *use* of economic surplus, not merely its quantity, must be the center of attention, and this necessitates class analysis'.[73]

Important as it undoubtedly is for students of development to recognize the theoretical and practical deficiencies of what could be called the pure trade-and-aid critique of the contemporary world situation, Frank can hardly be regarded as a member of this school of thought. Were Dos Santos and Weaver to have directed their shafts at, say, Emmanuel[74] or even perhaps Amin[75] they would have been nearer their target. As for Frank, Palloix has pointed out an apparent evolution in his early thinking, reflected within the covers of *Capitalism and Underdevelopment* itself.[76] Thus it is quite true, as I have already suggested, that the chapter on Chile which opens the book has as its central explanatory device—and perhaps its only one —an appropriation of economic surplus resulting from an omnipresent (if somewhat ill-defined) monopoly-power. On the other hand the less formally theoretical study of Brazil, which appears later in the book and perhaps represents, with Palloix, a more advanced stage in the formalization of the Frankian model, seems to herald an abandonment of the concept of the surplus as the key to the explanation of underdevelopment.

In his discussion of the case of Brazil, Frank focuses on the 'strangulation and misdirection' of the development process which has occurred as a result of multi-faceted forms of metropolitan domination to which that country has been subject since its early settlement and due to the species of internal colonialism which has occurred within its borders. Here the appropriation of surplus appears less as a cause and more as a consequence of unequal levels of international and inter-regional development, which stem in turn from a systematic *misdirection* of economic resources.[77] Put differently, the emphasis is upon the potential rather than the actual surplus lost in Baran's terms.

In short, then, Frank's analysis is not so unsophisticated as to be seriously impaired by criticisms of the above type. In what follows I shall comment upon two further lines of attack taken so far by critics of the Frankian model before making a concluding plea of my own. Each, I suggest, has serious implications for the viability of the model as it stands.

Stages of dependence and the question of theory

As was suggested earlier, Frank has formulated some of his major theses in terms of a concept of capitalism as a system which bears more than a family resemblance to Sweezy's. This is what accounts for the otherwise surprising proposition that Latin American societies contain no non-capitalist elements nor have done since the days of Cortés and Pizarro. Working within a conceptually more rigorous tradition of Marxist theory, Laclau[78] has drawn together some of the more serious theoretical consequences of this approach.

If I may be permitted to codify the findings of Laclau's incisive essay in order of importance, the position is now as follows:

(1) By defining capitalism and feudalism not as *modes of production* but as social systems characterized by particular sorts of *exchange* relationship, Frank departs from Marxist theory.

(2) This approach renders virtually impossible a consistent account of the different forms of the transition between feudalism and capitalism.

(3) In Marxist terms, *to affirm the feudal character of relations of production in the agrarian sector does not necessarily involve maintaining a dualist thesis.* (Supporters of the 'dual society' idea have not infrequently employed definitions of feudalism and capitalism similar to Frank's own.) Both protagonists in the debate have confused the two concepts of the *capitalist mode of production* and *participation in a world capitalist economic system*.

(4) The existence of various different modes of production within the world capitalist system is the basis of an important set

of *explanatory hypotheses* relating to the *specifically capitalist epoch* of European expansion.[79]

It is upon this last point that I wish to dwell. Later on I shall argue that Laclau places his finger upon a rather more general failing of Frank's work than that with which he, Laclau, is explicitly concerned.

The explanatory hypotheses in question are the implicit core of the Lenin-Bukharin theory of imperialism, whose function it is to furnish an explanation, by reference to the dynamics of capital accumulation in the metropolitan centres of capitalism, of the process of imperialist expansion and capital-export initiated by the major powers in the 1870s. Frank, I would submit, is at liberty not to place himself on the terrain of the theory of imperialism proper, and he would not be alone if he argued (which to my knowledge he does not) that the 'classical' theory is essentially Eurocentric and hence of little use to revolutionaries on the periphery.[80] Laclau is wrong if, as appears to be the case, he is arguing not merely that in explaining underdevelopment one is sooner or later led back to ask about the causes of capital exports, but also, or rather, that this is the only scientifically valid point of departure.[81] What is completely to the point, however, is that even at the level of analysis with which he is concerned, that of the relatively immediate causes of underdevelopment, Frank is singularly insensitive to the variations to be observed as between the major epochs of world history.

The most important single gap in Frank's scheme of analysis relates to the delineation of the specific characteristics of underdevelopment in the various 'long' periods[82] of modern world history, and it results from the absence of a discussion (for such a discussion is precluded by Frank's initial conceptual *prise de position*) of the interconnections between different modes of production combined in a single, national or international, economic system. Since the problems of investigating empirically, and refining the theoretical vocabulary specific to, 'articulations' of this type are examined in a useful fashion elsewhere in this book,[83] I shall not dwell on them here. It will suffice to suggest that from *this* point of view Frank's most recent work represents if anything a step backwards. In *Lumpenbourgeoisie: Lumpendevelopment* Frank's powers of analysis are directed towards the validation of three theses, which he summarizes as follows:[84]

I. The Conquest placed all of Latin America in a situation of growing subjection and *economic dependence*, both colonial and neocolonial, in the single world system of expanding commercial capitalism.

II. This colonial and neocolonial relationship to the capitalist

73

metropolis has formed and transformed the economic and *class structure*, as well as the culture, of Latin American society. These changes in national structures have occurred as a result of periodic changes in the forms of colonial dependence.

III. This colonial and class structure establishes very well defined class interests for the dominant sector of the bourgeoisie. Using government cabinets and other instruments of the State, the bourgeoisie produces a *policy of underdevelopment* in the economic, social, and political life of the 'nation' and the people of Latin America.

The problem with this scheme from the present point of view is that it systematically directs attention *away* from a specification of the internal coherence of any given stage in the history of economic dependence in terms of the articulations between elements distinguished at the level of *production*. Thus for the purpose of conveying a receptivity (if only that) to this mode of analysis both the key terms are inadequate; that of 'class structure' because it is insufficiently nuanced and dynamic, that of 'policies of underdevelopment' because it is too voluntaristic.

Growth and development: once again stages of dependence

Frank has more than once staked his reputation on the assertion that so long as it remains integrated into the world capitalist system Latin America, and by extension the rest of the 'Third World', will not undergo development. It will only experience the 'development of underdevelopment' or—to use his more recent formulation—a process which can only be conveyed by the use of the pejorative prefix beloved of Marx and Engels: *lumpen-development*. The partial industrialization which has taken place in Latin America is viewed as strengthening rather than weakening the argument to the extent that the corresponding growth process received its dynamic impulse in precisely a period in which the region was weakly linked with the centres of world capitalism.

Stimulated in part by the recovery of Brazil and other Latin American countries from the tendency towards industrial stagnation which they experienced in the 1960s, more than one voice has been raised recently to query the realism of this view of the prospects of the peripheral economies. In one of his unfortunately rare contributions in the English language, Fernando Henrique Cardoso[85] has suggested that the terms *dependency, monopoly capitalism* and *development* are not contradictory. Aside from emphasizing the politically crucial point that imperialist domination in Latin America today rests upon foreign control of the manufacturing sectors rather than the 'traditional' primary-export sectors, Cardoso's article urges us to recognize that as a consequence of such changes 'foreign investment no longer remains a simple zero-sum game of exploitation as was the pattern in classical imperialism'. To the extent that today monopoly capital does promote a form of industrial growth (even if the latter increases the internal structural fragmentation of the dependent economies and possesses other inherent limitations) it makes more sense to speak of a process of *dependent development* than of a 'development of underdevelopment'.[86]

Is this, as philosophers say, an empirical question or a conceptual question? Warren[87] has recently argued to the effect that, from the point of view of the image which the European left at large has of today's Third World, the issue is very much an empirical one. On the basis of a wealth of carefully assembled statistics, Warren is able to demolish what he takes as the current view, showing not only that industrial growth has taken place in the Third World since the war (contrary to a widespread belief in the ubiquity of stagnation) but also that this growth-process has had characteristics frequently thought of as beyond the reach of capitalism in underdeveloped countries. That is, (*a*) it has been based predominantly on the home market; (*b*) it has involved the creation of significant intermediate and capital goods sectors in many countries; (*c*) it has typically come to rely on a quantitatively small net foreign capital input whose qualitative effects have tended to weaken recently for a combination of reasons; and finally (*d*) it has rendered a degree of independent technological progress in the Third World not only possible but inevitable. It is Warren's contention that, in view of these findings and by the criteria of at least one other student of Third World industrialization,[88] we have to say not merely that 'dependent development' is occurring but that *in*dependent industrialization has begun to take place 'rather rapidly'.[89]

My concern with these arguments is restricted to an assessment of the *character* of their implications for the Frankian theoretical framework. I want to suggest first of all that, as far as Frank is concerned (leaving aside for now the alleged preconceptions of the left at large) the issue cannot be resolved *simply* by the production of new empirical evidence. Frank can scarcely be accused of ignorance of the major trends picked out by Warren's statistics, for it was precisely a careful critique of this post-war process of industrial growth in Latin America (where it was most advanced) which led Frank and others to begin to speak of 'neoimperialism' and 'neo-dependence'.[90] On the other hand I do not want to imply that conceptual issues of the sort involved here can usefully be resolved completely without reference to the 'facts'. The role of such concepts as 'development', 'dependence', 'development of underdevelopment', and the rest is quite clearly to *sensitize* us to certain features of a process of economic change and at the same time (and this perhaps is one of the things Warren is saying) to *anaesthetize* us to other features. There can come a point when the latter effect becomes the more significant of the two, especially if relatively new and unfamiliar changes are involved.

Could it be that, the author's intentions aside, the popularization of Frank's insistent refusal to grace what is currently occurring in Latin America with the unqualified title of economic development has had the objective impact of obscuring the real changes which have taken place in the region? It seems to me that we may have to answer this question in the affirmative but also that this question is not separate, as far as a global assessment of Frank's approach is concerned, from two issues which have been no more than hinted at so far. Some further reflections on the conceptual vocabulary which stems from the notion of the 'development of underdevelopment' will help to clarify the nature and scope of the problem.

In an interesting footnote to *Lumpenbourgeoisie: Lumpendevelopment*,[91] Frank has himself indicated an inconsistency in the armoury of neologisms he deployed in his earlier studies. In these studies he had introduced the adjective 'ultra-underdeveloped' to characterize regions of the contemporary Third World such as the Brazilian north-east whose once flourishing primary-export economies went into decline, leaving a permanent inheritance of extreme poverty and social degradation.[92] This usage, we may note, is one which conforms readily to common parlance. On the other hand Frank has insisted all along that, rather than a merely quantitative state of affairs, underdevelopment is a structural ailment created simultaneously with the *development* of the metropolitan economies by the *incorporation* of the satellites into the process of world capitalist expansion. It follows that 'ultra-underdevelopment' must be the product of the 'ultra-incorporation' of a satellite into the metropolitan sphere. To this it has been objected that, by this criterion, the most ultra-underdeveloped part of today's Latin America is not the north-east of Brazil, but rather 'booming' oil-exporting Venezuela, 'where contemporary rather than past colonialism assumes its most extreme forms'.[93] The objection is valid in Frank's terms. Consequently, he has agreed 'very provisionally' to designate the Venezuelan oil boom as an example of the 'active' development of ultra-underdevelopment and to find another term for the 'passive' state of ultra-underdevelopment in the exporting regions of earlier periods in the development of world capitalism.[94]

Where does this leave us? I think we have to admit that it leaves us in a mess. I do not wish to dispute the basic point that, as Frank puts it, the etymological origins and current usage of the word 'underdevelopment' represent 'the most shameless negation—ideological, political, economic, social, cultural, and psychological—of an accurate conception of reality'.[95] On the other hand it is by no means clear that the illumination of reality is well served by a redefinition of terms which treats etymology and current usage in so cavalier a fashion as to render the arid *sertão* less underdeveloped than Venezuela! Rather than twist the concept of underdevelopment out of recognition, would it not be better to abandon it altogether? To be fair, this is precisely what Frank has attempted to do in his latest work by introducing the less confusing term 'lumpendevelopment'. Here too though a problem remains: whether, conceptually speaking, the end product of a process of lumpendevelopment is the *sertão,* or Venezuela.

This problem is compounded by another. It has been suggested that the terminology upon which Frank has chosen to rely fails to serve as an unambiguous and internally-consistent scheme for classifying the varied historical processes and states of affairs identified by him. But it also obliges him to skate over real and important variations in dimensions which he largely neglects. To be sure, the sorts of variations which a given analysis may be expected to identify depends entirely upon the purpose of that analysis. This being the case, what I want to say may be reformulated as follows: the usefulness of Frank's analysis (from a political as well as from a scientific point of view) is curtailed by his conceptual apparatus, which in turn reflects *the relative narrowness of the purpose for which it was created.*

To be specific, the various sorts of weakness in the characterization of different 'stages' and varieties of dependence which have been attributed to Frank so far (together with one which I will now add) stem ultimately from the character of his critique of the post-war ECLA model. As we saw at the beginning, Frank developed his analysis partly as a critical response to ECLA's stress upon the *novelty* of the development situation faced in the post-war period by those countries which had undergone 'development toward the inside' in the decades after 1929. An index of this tendency in his thought was his elevation to the rank of a 'contradiction' of capitalist development of the principle of 'continuity in change' which meant in effect that, where underdevelopment is concerned, *plus ça change, plus c'est la même chose.* 'Contemporary underdevelopment', Frank has argued in his latest book, 'is simply a continuation of the same fundamental processes of dependence, transformation of economic and class structure, and lumpenbourgeois policies of underdevelopment which have been in operation throughout our [Latin America's] history.'[96] Perhaps. But a lot hinges on the meaning of 'fundamental'. Perhaps, too, this is still the most important point to make. But need an insistence on underlying continuities result in the suppression of so much else?

One thing which has been lost, as it were, in the course of Frank's pursuit of a general interpretation of underdevelopment, is the richness of ECLA's comparative analysis of the Latin American economies. I am thinking particularly of the contrast ECLA drew between respective dynamics of the semi-industrial, but dependent, economies of Group U and the 'open' and dependent economies of Group O. Frank insists that he has attempted an interpretation rather than a history of Latin America.[97] None the less it is characteristic of his interpretation that, notably by means of the concept of the 'satellite' economy, it obliterates the marked differences between the mode of operation of type U underdevelopment and that of type O. Moreover, whereas the planetary metaphor applies quite well to open economies, it suggests a somewhat simplistic interpretation of the closed or semi-closed variant. This is important, I would submit, not least for revolutionaries, since a simplist economic analysis is scarcely a good guide to political strategy.[98]

Exploitation and uneven development: from spatial relations to social relations?

The issue which I propose to ventilate briefly in this final section arises from Frank's earliest theoretical formulations. But it also transcends the scope of Frank's studies and touches upon questions which remain a topic of heated if not always very lucid debate among Marxist students of capitalist development. What I shall present, therefore, will be more of an agenda for future discussion than an attempted solution.

The two leading 'contradictions' of capitalist underdevelopment suggested initially by Frank—surplus expropriation/appropriation (sometimes simply 'exploitation') and metropolis–satellite polarization—had a distinctive property to which I have not drawn attention so far but whose significance will be appreciated in the light of some of the foregoing remarks. In short, they could be employed, and were employed, with equal facility to refer to relations between spatial (national or regional) entities and relations between social groups or classes. Use of the Baranian concept of surplus in place of the Marxian concept of surplus value permitted such interchangeability in the case of 'exploitation', whilst 'polarization' conveniently bridged what Marxists have usually termed uneven development and what sociologists call social inequality. The only absurd inconsistency which this scheme contained was that which made it possible and necessary to characterize a big landowner as a 'metropolis' (from the point of view of a peasant or landless labourer).[99] Difficulties such as this aside, though, does it matter if we have an array of theoretical categories which are neutral in this sense with respect to their content?

Critics of the Marxist approach to this question are apt to attribute the 'orthodox' resistance to such concepts as the 'exploitation of countries by countries' to sheer intellectual pigheadedness, the blind faith of converts to the industrial proletariat, or a combination of the two.[100] The reality of the matter is simpler and less dramatic. Frank's Mexican critics, to whom we referred at the beginning complained that 'exploitation is a social phenomenon too complex to be explained exclusively in terms of the metropolis–satellite structure [that is, in context, in terms of spatial relationships]'. 'Would it not be more accurate to state the relations of exploitation in terms of social classes?'[101] More accurate, no. More *concrete*, yes. The collapsing of social relations and spatial relations into the same vocabulary denotes a lack of *concreteness*, or in other words that a substantial residue remains to be properly explained.

The fact is that Frank's own studies, to go no further, contain a wealth of examples of *different* ways in which relations of exploitation (between classes) produce the effect of inter-regional transfers of capital which in turn contribute to uneven development within Latin American countries.[102] The chapter by Long included in this collection indicates something of the range of the empirical literature on the economic and class structures of such highly regionally-stratified societies as Peru. On the inter-national level, Frank's own studies are similarly suggestive regarding the mechanisms which have been used at different points in Latin America's history to effect substantial financial and other transfers. *Pace* Emmanuel, therefore, it is not the case that we lack the empirical bases for the further elucidation of spatial transfers in general or unequal exchange in particular.

Nor are the necessary theoretical tools entirely lacking. Marxist economic theory has created the possibility of a rigorous theoretical formulation of several aspects of the problem. The classical argument about the origins of colonial surplus-profits suggests a number of explanatory hypotheses, as Laclau and others have pointed out. Theoretical discussion of those unequal exchanges and surplus profits which result from the inherent tendency of capitalism towards monopolization has also made more progress than Frank's cursory reference to Marx would suggest.[103] What is needed as much as anything else, therefore, is a *codification*, a systematic restatement in theoretically adequate terms, of existing knowledge relating to the twin themes, exploitation and uneven development. The absence of such a codification in Frank's work to date need not detain us for long. For this is a task for the future. Doubtless in its completion Frank will himself play a major part.[104]

Notes

1 Dudley Seers, 'The limitations of the special case', *Bulletin of the Oxford Institute of Economics and Statistics*, vol. 25, no. 2, 1963, pp. 77–98.

2 *Ibid.*

3 A convenient anthology of ECLA's official publications from 1949 to 1969 is ECLA, *Development Problems in Latin America*, University of Texas Press, Austin and London, 1969. In the semi-official category an influential collection of papers was Werner Baer and Isaac Kerstenetzky, eds, *Inflation and Growth in Latin America*, Richard D. Irwin, Homewood, Illinois, 1964. For Seers's own contribution to the diffusion of structuralist ideas, see for instance 'A theory of inflation and growth in under-developed economies based on the experience of Latin America', *Oxford Economic Papers*, June 1962, pp. 173–95.

4 Andre Gunder Frank, *Capitalism and Underdevelopment in Latin America: Historical Studies of Chile and Brazil*, Monthly Review Press, New York and London, 1967; *Latin America: Underdevelopment or Revolution*, Monthly Review Press, New York and London, 1969; *Lumpenbourgeoisie:Lumpendevelopment—Dependence, Class and Politics in Latin America*, Monthly Review Press, New York and London, 1972; and James D. Cockcroft, Andre Gunder Frank and Dale L. Johnson, *Dependence and Underdevelopment: Latin America's Political Economy*, Doubleday, New York, 1972.

5 Frank, 1969, *op. cit.*, p. ix.

6 The following widely used recent additions to the textbook market are cases in point: Gerald M. Meier, ed., *Leading Issues in Development Economics*, 2nd ed., Oxford University Press, New York, 1970; Bo Södersten, *International Economics*, Macmillan, London, 1970; A. P. Thirlwall, *Growth and Development: with Special Reference to Developing Economies*, Macmillan, London, 1972; Matthew McQueen, *The Economics of Development: Problems and Policies*, Weidenfeld & Nicolson, London, 1973.

7 'Sociology of development and underdevelopment of sociology', in Frank, 1969, *op. cit.*; reprinted as *Sociology of Development and Underdevelopment of Sociology*, Pluto Press, London, 1971.

8 The following section draws very heavily from the above-mentioned anthology (ECLA, *op. cit.*) and its useful introduction.

9 For example, United Nations, *Economic Survey of Latin America, 1949*, E/CN.12/164/Rev. 1, New York, 1951.

10 Cf. Claudio Napoleoni, *Economic Thought of the Twentieth Century*, Martin Robertson, London, 1972.

11 The major landmark was Talcott Parsons and Edward Shils, eds, *Toward a General Theory of Action*, Harvard University Press, Cambridge, Massachusetts, 1951.

12 ECLA, *op. cit.*, p. xiii.

13 *Ibid.*
14 Probably for the reasons suggested by O'Brien above.
15 *Ibid.*, p. xiv.
16 United Nations, 1951, *op. cit.*
17 *Ibid.*, pp. 13–14, 46–61; ECLA, *op. cit.*, pp. xv–xviii.
18 United Nations, 1951, *loc. cit.*
19 ECLA, *op. cit.*, p. xv; see also United Nations, *The Economic Development of Latin America and its Principal Problems* (by Raúl Prebisch), E/CN.12/89/Rev. 1, New York, 1950.
20 United Nations, *Theoretical and Practical Problems of Economic Growth*, E/CN.12/221, New York, 1951.
21 ECLA, *op. cit.*, p. xiv.
22 *Ibid.*, pp. xix–xxv; cf. United Nations, *The Process of Industrial Development in Latin America*, E/CN.12/716/Rev. 1, New York, 1966.
23 *Ibid.*; cf. 'The growth and decline of import substitution in Brazil', *Economic Bulletin for Latin America*, vol. IX, no. 1, 1964.
24 *Ibid.*, pp. xxiv–xxv.
25 e.g. United Nations, *International Cooperation in a Latin American Development Policy*, E/CN.12/359, New York, 1954.
26 ECLA, *op. cit.*, pp. xxi–xxxiii.
27 *Ibid.*, pp. xxxiii–xxxiv.
28 *Ibid.*, p. xxxv.
29 *Ibid.*
30 *Ibid.*, p. xxxiv.
31 Raúl Prebisch, 'Economic development and monetary stability: the false dilemma', *Economic Bulletin for Latin America*, vol. VI, no. 1, 1961; 'Inflation and growth: a summary of the experience of Latin America', *Economic Bulletin for Latin America*, vol. VII, no. 1, 1962. See also International Economic Association, *Economic Development for Latin America* (ed. H. S. Ellis), Macmillan, London, 1961; Baer and Kerstenetzky, *op. cit.*; Werner Baer, 'The inflation controversy in Latin America: a survey', *Latin American Research Review*, vol. II, no. 2, 1967, pp. 3–25; Celso Furtado, *Economic Development of Latin America: A Survey from Colonial Times to the Cuban Revolution*, Cambridge University Press, 1970, pp. 93–104, and bibliography, p. 99.
32 United Nations, *Toward a Dynamic Development Policy for Latin America* (by Raúl Prebisch), E/CN.12/680/Rev. 1, New York, 1963; *The Economic Development of Latin America in the Post-War Period*, E/CN. 12/659/Rev. 1, New York, 1964.
33 Frank, 1967, *op. cit.*; revised ed., 1969, p. xvii.
34 See particularly 'The development of underdevelopment', in Frank, 1969, *op. cit.*, which was written in 1965–6 and first published in the September 1966 number of *Monthly Review*. Keith Griffin, another English-speaking economist who has spent considerable time working in Latin America, has noted in this connection that: 'Most of the theorizing on economic development has been done by economists who live and were trained in the industrial west. Some economists, in fact, have written about the underdeveloped countries before they

have seen them. . . . Almost all . . . are ignorant of much of the economic history of the countries about which they are theorizing.' (K. Griffin, *Underdevelopment in Spanish America*, Allen & Unwin, London, 1969, p. 19.)

35 Frank, 1972, *op. cit.*, p. 93. For further details see United Nations, 1964, *op. cit.*

36 Frank, 1972, *op. cit.*, p. 95.

37 *Ibid.*

38 See the tables on pp. 174–5 of Teresa Hayter, *Aid as Imperialism*, Penguin, Harmondsworth, 1971.

39 Frank, 1972, *op. cit.*, pp. 95–8; and 'Aid or exploitation?' in Frank, 1969, *op. cit.*

40 Frank, 1972, *op. cit.*, pp. 98–100. Cf. United Nations, 1964, *op. cit.*

41 *Ibid.*, pp. 111–15.

42 *Ibid.*, p. 116.

43 Notably Ricardo Lagos, *La Concentración del Poder Económico en Chile*, Editorial de Pacífico, Santiago, 1962; Anibal Pinto Santa Cruz, *Chile: Un Caso de Desarrollo Frustrado*, Editorial Universitaria, Santiago, 1962; José Luis Ceceña, *El Capital Monopolista y la Economía de México*, Cuadernos Americanos, Mexico, 1963; Keith B. Griffin and Ricardo Ffrench-Davis, 'El capital extranjero y el desarrollo', *Revista de Economía* (Santiago), vols 83–4, 1964; Ruy Mauro Marini, 'Brazilian interdependence and imperialist integration', *Monthly Review*, vol. 17, no. 7, December 1964; Celso Furtado, 'us hegemony and the future of Latin America', *The World Today*, Royal Institute of International Affairs, London, September 1966, and *Les États-Unis et le Sous-développement de L'Amérique Latine*, Calmann-Levy, Paris, 1970 (a book based on articles published somewhat earlier in Brazil; it has been published in English by Doubleday under the significantly different title *Obstacles to Development in Latin America*); also Alonso Aguilar *et al.*, *Desarrollo y Desarrollismo*, Editorial Galerna, Buenos Aires, 1969.

44 For discussion and bibliography on the economic and sociological literatures respectively, see Meier, *op. cit.*, chapter 2b, and Frank, 'Sociology of development', *op. cit.*

45 That is, the inevitability of 'modernization', the possibility of 'leaping stages', and the 'Revolution in Permanence'. Karl Marx, 'The British rule in India', in Marx, *Surveys from Exile* (political writings, vol. 2), Penguin, Harmondsworth, 1973; K. Marx, 'Letters to Vera Zasulich', quoted by D. Bensaid, 'Révolution socialiste et contre-révolution bureaucratique' in *Critiques de l'Économie Politique*, nos 7–8, April–September 1972, pp. 116–19; and K. Marx, *Revolution and Counter-Revolution in Germany*, Allen & Unwin, London, 1971.

46 See Livio Maitan, 'The theory of permanent revolution', in Ernest Mandel, ed., *50 Years of World Revolution*, Merit Publishers, New York, 1968; and Jacques Valier, 'Impérialisme et révolution permanente', *Critiques de l'Économie Politique*, nos 4–5, July–December 1971.

47 An excellent discussion of this point may be found in John Robens,

Imperialism, Stalinism and Permanent Revolution, IMG Publications, London, 1973.

48 A useful account may be found in Andrés Suárez, *Cuba: Castroism and Communism, 1959–1966*, MIT Press, Cambridge, Massachusetts, 1967.

49 *The Second Declaration of Havana, with the First Declaration of Havana*, Merit Pamphlets, New York, 1962.

50 *Documentos Aprobados par la Primera Conferencia de la Organización Latinoamericana de Solidardad* (OLAS), Ediciones OR, Havana, no. 23, n.d., pp. 17, 71.

51 Monthly Review Press, New York, 1957, and Penguin, Harmondsworth, 1973.

52 1967, *op. cit.*

53 In fact Frank found a wide spectrum of offenders, including Salvador Allende and Fidel Castro, *ibid.*, p. 4.

54 'The development of underdevelopment', *op. cit.*, p. 5.

55 Sergio Bagú, *Economía de la Sociedad Colonial*, El Ateneo, Buenos Aires, 1949. A long extract from this work was published in *Pensamiento Crítico* (Havana), no. 27, April 1969. Not all the Latin American writers who launched an attack similar to Frank's, and at about the same time, on the dualist conceptions of the Stalinist left appear, in my judgment, to have fallen into this trap—for example, Rodolfo Stavenhagen, 'Seven erroneous theses about Latin America', in Irving Louis Horowitz, ed., *Latin American Radicalism*, Random House, New York, 1969; and Luis Vitale, 'España antes y despues de la conquista de américa', *Pensamiento Crítico*, no. 27, April 1969.

56 'The transition from feudalism to capitalism', *Science and Society*, vol. XIV, no. 2, 1950, and 'Comments on Professor H. K. Takahashi's "Transition from feudalism to capitalism" ', *Science and Society*, vol. XVII, no. 2, 1953.

57 Frank, 1967, *op. cit.*, pp. 6–7.

58 *Ibid.*, pp. 7–8.

59 For example Paul A. Baran and Paul M. Sweezy, *Monopoly Capital: An Essay on the American Economic Order*, Penguin, Harmondsworth, 1968. For a critique of *Monopoly Capital* along these lines, see Ernest Mandel, 'La théorie de la valeur-travail et le capitalisme monopolistique', *Critiques de l'Économie Politique*, no. 1, September–December 1970.

60 Frank, 1967, *op. cit.*, pp. 8–12.

61 *Ibid.*, p. 10.

62 *Ibid.*, p. 8.

63 *Ibid.*, pp. 9–11.

64 *Ibid.*, p. 11.

65 'The development of underdevelopment', *op. cit.*, pp. 9–10.

66 Frank, 1967, *op. cit.*, p. 12.

67 *Ibid.*, p. 13.

68 Frank, 1967, *op. cit.*, revised ed., pp. xxi–xxii.

69 Frank, 1972, *op. cit.*, pp. 1–12.

70 *Ibid.*

71 T. Dos Santos, 'The crisis of development theory and the problem of dependence in Latin America', in Henry Bernstein, ed., *Underdevelopment and Development*, Penguin, Harmondsworth, 1973. Cf. T. Dos Santos, 'La estructura de la dependencia', in Paul M. Sweezy *et al.*, *Economía Política del Imperialismo*, Ediciones Periferia, Buenos Aires, 1971.

72 F. Stirton Weaver, 'Positive economics, comparative advantage, and underdevelopment', *Science and Society*, vol. XXXV, no. 2, 1971, p. 176.

73 *Ibid.*

74 Arghiri Emmanuel, *Unequal Exchange: A Study of the Imperialism of Trade*, New Left Books, London, 1972.

75 Samir Amin, *L'Accumulation à l'Échelle Mondiale*, IFAN/Anthropos, Paris, 1970, forthcoming from Monthly Review Press; and *Neo-Colonialism in West Africa*, Penguin, Harmondsworth, 1973.

76 Christian Palloix, *L'Économie Mondiale Capitaliste*, 2 vols, Maspero, Paris, 1971, vol. II, p. 201.

77 *Ibid.*, pp. 201–4.

78 Ernesto Laclau, 'Feudalism and capitalism in Latin America', *New Left Review*, no. 67, May–June 1971.

79 *Ibid.*

80 See O'Brien, Chapter 2, in the present volume.

81 Laclau, *op. cit.*, p. 34.

82 Amin, 1970, *op. cit.*, and Harry Magdoff, 'Imperialism: A historical survey', *Monthly Review*, vol. 24, no. 1, May 1972; both contain proposed periodizations of this sort.

83 In the chapters by Clammer, Wolpe, and Long.

84 Frank, 1972, *op. cit.*, p. 13.

85 'Dependency and development in Latin America', *New Left Review*, no. 74, July–August 1972.

86 *Ibid.*, pp. 89, 94.

87 Bill Warren, 'Imperialism and capitalist industrialization', *New Left Review*, no. 81, September–October, 1973.

88 Bob Sutcliffe, 'Imperialism and industrialization in the Third World', in Roger Owen and Bob Sutcliffe, eds, *Studies in the Theory of Imperialism*, Longman, London, 1972.

89 Warren, *op. cit.*, p. 34. But cf. *NLR*, no. 85, May–June 1974.

90 Frank, 1972, *op. cit.*, chapter 8, and references by O'Brien; also T. Dos Santos, 'El nuevo caracter de la dependencia', *Cuadernos de CESO* (Santiago), no. 10, 1968, and J. Petras and M. Zeitlin, eds, *Latin America: Reform or Revolution?* Fawcett, New York, 1968.

91 Frank, 1972, *op. cit.*, p. 22.

92 Frank, 1967, *op. cit.*, p. 148.

93 Frank, 1972, *loc. cit.*

94 *Ibid.*

95 *Ibid.*, p. 9.

96 *Ibid.*, p. 92.

97 *Ibid.*, p. 8.

98 Big steps towards an analysis of the shifting parameters of twentieth-

century Latin American politics which takes as its starting point a nuanced comprehension of the changing and varied character of dependency in the region have been taken by Ruy Mauro Marini (*Sous-développement et Révolution en Amérique Latine*, Maspero, Paris, 1972) and Cardoso and Faletto (F. H. Cardoso e Enzo Faletto, *Dependência e Desenvolvimento na América Latina: Ensaio de Interpretaç̃ão Sociológica*, Zahar Editores, Rio de Janeiro, 1970).

99 Frank, 1967, *op. cit.*, p. 7. Aidan Foster-Carter first drew my attention to this difficulty.

100 e.g. Emmanuel, *op. cit.*; and Aidan Foster-Carter, 'Neo-Marxist approaches to development and underdevelopment', paper presented to the 1972 B.S.A. Conference and first published in the *Journal of Contemporary Asia*, vol. 3, no. 1, 1973. This is not the place to go into the continuing debate around Emmanuel's thesis but see particularly Patrick Florian, 'Emmanuel chez les Philistins', and Eugène Chatelain, 'Où mène la thèse de l'échange inégal', *Critiques de l'Économie Politique*, no. 3, April–June 1971; and Geoffrey Pilling, 'Imperialism, trade and "unequal exchange": the work of Arghiri Emmanuel', *Economy and Society*, vol. 2, no. 2, 1973.

101 Quoted by Frank, 1972, *op. cit.*, p. 1.

102 Especially Frank, 1967, *op. cit.*, but see also, for example, Griffin, *op. cit.*, chapter 1.

103 See Ernest Mandel, *Marxist Economic Theory*, Merlin Press, London, 1968, and 'The driving force of imperialism in our era', in Bertrand Russell Peace Foundation, *Spheres of Influence in the Age of Imperialism*, Spokesman Books, London, 1972; and Pierre Salama, *Le Procès de 'Sous-développement'*, Maspero, Paris, 1972.

104 Frank has indicated recently that he now regards his last book, *Lumpenbourgeoisie: Lumpendevelopment*, as a swan song of 'neo-dependency' writing, and hence as the culmination of a phase in his own development. The world crisis of the 1970s has already brought a renewal of interest among revolutionary scholars in the, increasingly problematic, process of capital accumulation, and it is within this perspective that Frank hopes to conduct his studies in the future. A. G. Frank, 'Dependence is dead, long live dependence and the class struggle: an answer to critics', Department of Sociology, University of Dar es Salaam, mimeo, 1972, and 'Additional note', 1974.

5 Imbalance between the centre and periphery and the 'employment crisis' in Kenya
John Weeks

For geographical and historical reasons Kenya in the early part of this century was the only African country north of the Zambezi to be a strong candidate for extensive white settlement. While only a small part of Kenya—in a belt running roughly from just south-east of Nairobi to Lake Victoria—consists of high-potential land, this fertile portion lies at elevations favourable for the growth of cash crops such as tea, coffee, and even wheat. Equally important, when the first white settlers such as Lord Delamere arrived, they found themselves blessed with a stroke of historical luck. During the nineteenth century, the militarily powerful Masai herdsmen came to control large expanses of the fertile highlands and Rift Valley. Thus, the settlers looked across great expanses of valuable land, sparsely populated by a nomadic people immeasurably inferior to themselves in military technology. In the 1930s, the land seizure by Europeans, largely from the Masai, but also from the sedentary Kikuyu, received validation from the British Colonial Office. The Carter Commission set aside just less than 17,000 square miles of Kenya's best land for exclusive white settlement. It appeared for all practical purposes that Lord Delamere's dream of a little Australia in East Africa had moved from *de facto* to *de jure* status.[1]

White political control of Kenya was complete, or so it seemed. A mild attempt by the Colonial Office to spread economic privilege to the Indian population led the 9,651 Europeans in Kenya to threaten armed revolt in 1922. Thus challenged, the Colonial Office capitulated, and for almost thirty years the white population would rest secure in its privileges. Through their political domination, the local white settlers constructed an economy for their almost exclusive benefit; in the late 1950s and early 1960s, the cash economy of Kenya was overwhelming white settler dominated. In 1957, the agricultural sector constituted £25 million to cash Gross Domestic Product, of which £20 million came from non-African farms and plantations. In the same year, 75 per cent of marketed livestock came from a few hundred European ranches.[2]

This was not an economic domination based on productive efficiency. The control of the cash economy did not arise from the greater technical knowledge of the European, nor from their greater propensity to innovate, nor even from their exclusive access to sophisticated techniques of production. Their dominance was the consequence of the prohibition by force of African competition. In 1922, Lord Lugard observed:[3]

> The requirements of the settlers, to put it bluntly, are
> incompatible with the interests of the agricultural tribes,
> nor could they be otherwise than impatient of native
> development as a rival in the growing of coffee, flax, and sisal.

European settlers correctly recognized that African peasant farmers, with lower labour costs, lower personal consumption demands, and more labour-using techniques, could produce and sell at lower prices. If allowed to compete freely, African production would undercut European production in the product market, and by offering an alternative source of cash income, drive up wage rates on European farms, ranches, and plantations.[4] To forestall and permanently prevent this competition, Africans were prohibited from growing coffee and other cash crops upon which Europeans depended.

Thus, early on, Kenya was characterized by a regulated and controlled economy. Far from operating in an open, competitive frontier economy where riches were to be seized by the bold and adventuresome, settlers entered a political economy in which through their control of the power of state coercion they were protected, nurtured, and fostered. Without access to resources being restricted, they had no hope of survival. This restriction of access, formalization of privilege, remains the principle of economic organization in Kenya. The continued racial domination of the Kenyan economy required not only settler control of political power in Kenya, but a commitment by the metropolitan government to maintain white rule, if necessary by military intervention. In the early 1950s, the Mau Mau insurrection forced armed intervention, and the white settlers discovered that the British Government's commitment was not open ended.

Faced with an uprising which could only be suppressed—if at all—at tremendous expense, the Colonial Office changed its strategy, abandoning a white-dominated model for a Kenya controlled by the conservative elements of the nationalist movement. The Royal Commission Report of 1955 sought to establish the economic foundation of black conservative rule in Kenya.[5] This shift represented an extension of privilege,[6] without fundamental change in the system of restriction of access to privilege. It is the dynamics of this system of privilege in colonial and post-colonial times and the pattern of inequality generated in the process of capital accumulation, to which I turn in the following sections.

The dynamics of inequality

One cannot seriously analyse the employment problem in Kenya without understanding how the gross income inequalities were generated. Here we will attempt such an analysis, identifying the mechanisms which in a dynamic context channel the flow of wealth into a few areas and hands.

The usual explanation for the income inequalities generated in the process of economic development is in terms of a traditional–modern division of the economy. The Westernized modern sector, because of its universalistic attitudes and other 'modern' attributes, is the source of dynamism and change.[7] Growth is centred here, and the traditional sector, with all its enervating institutions, is left far behind. At worst, the traditional sector slowly withers away; at best, the dynamism of the modern sector overflows into the traditional sector, and the latter is slowly transformed into hesitant modernity.[8] This simple-minded view does not correspond to the reality of Kenya (or, perhaps, of any other country). It focuses only on the 'spillover' (positive) effects, and ignores the 'backwash' (negative) effects.[9] Specifically the analysis ignores inter-sectorial dynamics. The growth of wealth in the modern sector, which is not 'natural', but the consequence of the political power concentrated in the sector, generates an impoverished and economically deprived modern sub-sector, larger than the sub-sector benefiting from the new wealth. To be concrete, the slums of Nairobi are not part of the traditional sector, but are completely *modern*[10]—the consequence of the gap between the wealth level in the modern and traditional sectors.

In broadest terms, the economy is divided between traditional and modern sectors, where 'traditional' carries no behavioural connotation necessarily, but refers to the pre-colonial social and economic system. The term does not imply a static society, but a society in which the major mode of production was subsistence agriculture, settled or pastoral. Similarly, 'modern' describes a different mode of production, without suggesting that the values of that sector are necessarily more progressive.[11] The 'modern' sector, in turn, is divided between the *formal* and *informal* sectors,[12] with the unemployed existing in a limbo state between the two.

88

The basis of the formal–informal division lies in the relationship of economic activity to the state.[13] The formal sector corresponds to what most authors call the 'modern' sector, and includes both capitalist and state enterprises and institutions. Formal sector capitalist enterprise is large scale, uses capital-intensive and imported techniques, and is organized on the basis of the wage labour system. The informal sector is small scale, uses labour-intensive and local or locally adapted techniques, and is organized on the basis of family labour, clientage, and apprenticeship. These characteristics are the consequence, as said, of the relationship of enterprise to the State. Through tariffs and quotas, the State protects producers of certain products from foreign competition. The internal market is rendered still less competitive because access is not free, but in many cases requires State approval. Capital is administratively cheapened by the State allowing capital goods to be imported duty-free, providing investment credits and other fiscal favours.[14] Thus those firms or individuals lucky enough to obtain State favours operate in a world of factor prices favourable to capital-intensive techniques and in non-competitive markets. As a consequence, such enterprises are large scale, capital-intensive and highly profitable. Since the protected commodities are those originating from the industrial countries, it is foreign enterprise which has the expertise and access to technology to exploit the protected markets. Thus a consequence of this form of import substitution is the ownership of the industrial sector by foreigners. It must be stressed that it is not necessary to attribute any inherent superiority to capital-intensive techniques to explain their predominance in certain lines of production; the competitive advantages bestowed by the State leave little scope for competition from indigenous entrepreneurs using techniques appropriate to the unregulated factor market.

[Margin note: FOREIGN INVESTMENT "SUBSIDIZED" BY THE PERIPHERAL CAP. STATE]

The informal sector in Kenya is defined by more than merely the absence of State favours. In many cases it is actively suppressed and discouraged. For example, the small-scale carpenter not only is limited in his ability to expand by lack of access to cheap credit, foreign exchange, and technical expertise. He may also be unable to obtain a licence to operate, and work in the constant apprehension that he may be closed down by the police. If he wishes to bid for a government furniture contract, he will find that payment may be delayed months after delivery, that the standards of workmanship imposed are based on United Kingdom specifications and beyond possibility given his tools and training. Should he wish to embark upon a major expansion and acquire sophisticated equipment, he will discover that the municipal building code requires his workshop to be of a standard beyond his resources. Such restrictions apply in rural areas as well. Permits or licences are required to transport merchandise, grow coffee and tea, the breeding of beef cattle is controlled, and so on. These regulations cannot, of course, be effectively enforced in all cases. Thus a significant proportion of informal sector economic activity is illegal.[15]

Thus there exists a duality in the economic structure of the society, a duality which is the consequence of access to resources being restricted. This restriction originated in the colonial period, when the intention was to create a colour bar in economic life. Today in Kenya the colour bar has been removed, but the restrictions on access to resources are as pervasive as before, particularly in urban areas.

With these definitions in mind, we can see that the growth of the formal modern sector, by its concentration of wealth, transformed progressively almost all of the economy into 'modernity'. Migration to urban areas by income seekers, because the formal sector was (and is) incapable of absorbing all migrants, led to the growth of a low income urban periphery. This urban informal economy is peripheral both figuratively and literally. In Nairobi it sprang up just outside the borders of the wealthy zone, to supply the goods and services of the fortunate few inside that zone and of its own population as well. Figuratively, it is peripheral in that it has but limited and fortuitous access to the sources of wealth that generated the wealthy zone. The barriers to these sources are discussed below. The fundamental point is that the urban squalor and concentrated poverty in Kenya is not the continuation of traditional forms, but the consequence of, and part of, modernity.[16] Thus the term 'traditional urban sector', coined by numerous economists,[17] is an absurdity. There were no urban areas in Kenya 'traditionally', and this sector grows as part of the modern sector.

In rural areas there is a similar formal–informal, centre–periphery division, with small farmers growing cash crops or raising livestock alongside large-scale enterprise. But here the tension is less acute; because the rural wealth zones provide access to outsiders at lower wage rates than in urban areas, and because the wealth zones are more scattered. Most of the subsequent analysis will concentrate on urban areas, but it is illustrative of the inequalities that characterize the Kenyan economy to show the distribution of land and the imputed cash income to land, and this is done in Table 5.1. It shows clearly that the concentration of wealth in land which was on a racial basis during the colonial period remains after independence.

We can give a first approximation at an explanation of how wealth became concentrated in Kenya. This initial version does not identify the dynamics of concentration, only the dynamics of economic transformation. This simple model divides the economy into two sectors, rural and urban, and characterizes economic flows up to the middle 1950s, when the Kenya economy was still white-dominated in both sectors. The fly-wheel of transformation is the European agricultural sector,[18] with the urban sector providing administrative and marketing services. The European agricultural sector provides the economy's foreign exchange, but generates little transformation of the rural traditional economy (other than land seizure), because (a) there is no spill over of techniques,[19] and (b) wages are too low to induce migration to the rural wealth zones.[20] Colonial trade policy (free trade with the UK) was favourable to the European agricultural sector. The urban centre administered the foreign exchange to provide the settlers with elite consumption goods and agricultural equipment, and collected taxes to finance administration (control of

TABLE 5.1 *Size distribution of registered small holdings in Kenya, 1969*

Size (in hectares)	Number (absolute figures in thousands)	Percentages	Total area (absolute figures in thousand hectares)	Percentages
0·0–0·49	91	11·7	28	1·1
0·5–0·99	121	15·5	89	3·4
1·0–1·9	192	24·6	274	10·3
2·0–2·9	128	16·4	303	11·4
3·0–4·9	104	13·3	404	15·1
5·0–9·9	88	11·3	629	23·8
10 and over	54	7·0	923	34·9
All sizes*	777	100·0	2,646	100·0

*Column totals may not add up exactly owing to rounding.
Source: *Statistical Abstract*, 1970, table 79(a), in *Employment, Incomes and Equality: Productive Employment in Kenya*, ILO, Geneva, 1972.

local population) and infrastructure. Even in the early period of colonial rule Nairobi's growth stimulated a modern informal economy, and administrators complained of labour surplus conditions in towns. This 'surplus' resulted from the possibilities of wealth accumulation created by the urban centre. There existed a labour surplus in the sense that income opportunities in the urban wealth zone were more attractive than outside it. Thus an indigenous community grew up outside the walls of the zone, plying a variety of trades that took advantage of spill-over effects which the administrators of the wealth zone could not prevent. The extensive health and other standards of the colonial period in Nairobi represent ineffectual attempts to eliminate the spill-over effects. As with the present government, the colonial authorities made repeated raids into the informal sector of the periphery to 'clean it out'. Then, as now, police action could only disrupt, not eliminate, the periphery. The only long-term solution to the problem would have been one of apartheid which the colonial government rejected as too expensive.[21]

This flow of resources, biased in favour of European agriculture, was dramatically changed in the 1960s with the policy of industrialization through import substitution.[22] In this second approximation of the dynamics of wealth concentration, foreign exchange arises out of both African and European agriculture, but is used to finance the importation of elite consumer goods primarily for the urban population in the wealth zone, and capital equipment for the urban formal sector. This shift in use of foreign exchange generates the elements necessary and sufficient for a sudden acceleration of wealth concentration, which is the source of the employment problem.[23]

Superficially, one would consider the shift in use of foreign exchange as desirable, for economic development has historically been characterized by the growth in relative importance in Gross Domestic Product of the manufacturing sector. Yet in the Kenya context, the shift has resulted in deepening the crisis of underdevelopment.[24] The shift generated the crisis because of the dynamics of product choice, technological transfer, and external economies. These dynamic effects result in creating a system by which resources are continually drained from the periphery to the centre. The centre can be likened to a whirlpool into which resources are inexorably drawn, and the whirlpool does not broaden out, but only grows deeper. The dynamics are complex, and the following model is necessarily an over-simplification, seeking to identify the most important elements.

Product choice derived from Hirschman's famous strategy of substituting domestic production for imported consumer goods.[25] Since consumer imports were heavily biased toward the elite, it followed that the import substitution industries would be also; similarly, once a decision was made to produce goods domestically, the method of producing them had to be obtained from the rich countries.[26] Whether or not these techniques might have been radically adapted to Kenyan factor prices, such adaptation proved unnecessary because of the extravagant tariff protection granted foreign firms (and still granted).[27]

This syndrome might be called the elite consumption development strategy. The dynamics can be summarized as follows: an unequal distribution of income biases consumption towards products requiring capital intensive methods; a policy decision is made to produce these products domestically; the technology to produce such products can only be obtained through international companies; in order for the products to be profitable at existing factor prices a range of enabling fiscal, monetary, and foreign trade policies must be adopted to reduce the relative price of capital; the importation of capital and intermediate goods generates an overvalued exchange rate as the policy builds up speed.[28] Thus it is not surprising that Kenya should now be facing a deteriorating balance of payments position.[29] One can safely predict that if the elite consumption development strategy continues, the balance of payments will become critical. Indeed, the only significant constraint on this strategy is the balance of payments. When the economy matures into this pattern of underdevelopment, it is characterized by cyclical foreign exchange crises, along with structural inflation and economic stagnation, as in the case of Latin American countries.[30]

The model is incomplete, particularly in that it does not show direct or indirect effects on the rural sector. Nor does it explicitly deal with the extraction of surplus from the periphery by the centre. Both of these are dealt with below; even as an analysis of the centre it is inadequate, for it does not show the feedback from the symptoms generated to policy, which, as I shall argue below, lead to action which aggravates the problem.

It is important to understand the strategy as a feedback system, not an equilibrium system. Other than the balance of payments (which has not proved sufficient to arrest this form of underdevelopment in Latin America) and political constraints arising from the gross income inequalities generated, there are no forces to prevent such dynamics from generating full economic stagnation, given enough time.

There are several important feedback mechanisms. The capital intensive methods of production at the centre generate factor shares characterized by high profits, a relatively small wage bill, and high average wages. The high profits and the international character of enterprise lead to a highly-paid salariat, which feeds back upon the structure of demand, accentuating its elite nature. Perhaps even more important, high average wages create a second tier of elite consumption which broadens the base of the elite demand structure. The broadening is temporary in relative terms, however, for employment grows very slowly, or not at all (this is discussed below). The second tier of elite goods, or 'intermediate' elite goods, is in some ways more pernicious, for it is here that one gets the introduction of goods which replace production by local small enterprises and artisans—plastic sandals, bread, made-up clothing. This wage-earning elite is a more relevant source of comparison for those not in the wealthy zone, and consumption patterns may spread through a 'demonstration effect'. It must be repeated that the broadening of the elite consumption pattern is temporary. In Kenya wage employment in the urban formal sector or wealthy zone has grown by only

33,000 or about 12 per cent between 1963 and 1970. Average earnings of Africans, on the other hand, doubled.[31]

The slow growth of employment in the formal sector is a consequence of the interaction of internal and external forces. Internally, the distribution of income (plus the emphasis on high-income tourists) generates a demand for Western elite production, which requires the importation of technology. This technology is not only capital-intensive but over time exhibits a labour-saving bias. This makes a discussion of the trade-off between current and future employment irrelevant.[32] While at any moment, the techniques used in the formal sector may generate a larger surplus than alternative more labour-using techniques, and even if re-investment rates were high (which

FORMAl
SECTOR'S
USE OF
TECHNOLOGY:
A BIAS AGAINST
HIGH EMPloy.
CREATING
JOBS.

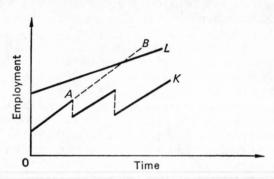

FIGURE 5.1   *Growth of employment over time, capital- and labour-intensive techniques*

they are not), this will not lead to a more rapid growth of employment. The point is demonstrated in Figure 5.1, where K is the more capital-intensive technique with the larger surplus and L is the more labour-intensive technique with the smaller surplus. At any moment the rate of growth of employment is faster in K, but technical change repeatedly shifts the K line downwards, creating a ratchet effect. Were there not this repeated labour-saving innovation and were investment rates high, the more capital-intensive technique might well generate more employment over time than the labour-intensive alternative (shown by line B). But research and development on new techniques occurs in the rich countries, where capital is relatively cheap and labour relatively dear.[33] RIGHT: SEE BRAVERMAN 1974
NOBLE 1984

Feed-back effects

We can now turn to a detailed consideration of the most important feed-back effects.

Terms of trade effects

The tariff protection and other favourable trade policies create a series of feed-back disincentives and incentives. First, by cheapening imports of capital and intermediate goods, they discourage the development of linkages in the economy. This is particularly ironic, since one of the criteria suggested by the Ministry of Commerce and Industry for selection of new industries is the use of Kenyan raw materials and domestically processed inputs. The negative rate of effective protection on capital goods ensures that existing industry will continue to rely on foreign technology, with its dynamic labour-saving bias. It must be stressed that this is not the consequence of misguided policy, but the logical imperative of the industrialization strategy chosen. Indeed, policy exhibits a remarkable consistency. Second, the protection structure discourages the growth of exports, both directly by raising the price of imports relative to exports, and indirectly by raising the prices of items farmers buy relative to prices at which they sell. Third, and related to the second, a balance of payments crisis is built into the growth process. This feeds back on policy, prompting import restrictions which further bias the terms of trade towards the centre.

Infrastructure

Success of the elite consumption strategy requires public investment in roads, water, electricity, etc., to facilitate the growth of industry. The wealth generated at the centre is insufficient to finance such infrastructure, requiring a redistribution of income from the periphery to the centre, through taxation. The growth in depth of the wealthy zone affects virtually all government outlays. The civil service and private sector elite generate a concentration of health, educational, and administrative services in the centre. In 1966, just under 4,000 persons were engaged in health services in 252 hospitals, clinics, and dispensaries in Kenya, 1,554 of whom worked in 91 establishments in Nairobi. Of 380 welfare workers in Kenya in the same year, 352 were in Nairobi.[34] The starvation of social services in the periphery is demonstrated graphically by the district of Kajiado, with a population of 90,000 people spread over 21,000 square kilometres, where in 1972 there was *one* social worker, based in the district headquarters without even a bicycle.[35] The concentration of infrastructure is equally striking. In 1970, Kenya possessed an electrical capacity of 153,000 kilowatts of which the Nairobi, Mount Kenya, and Mombasa areas accounted for all but 11,000. Isiolo District, with 30,000 people, had not a single electric generator in 1972, except for one at the district headquarters compound.[36]

95

These inequities arise from the centralizing and surplus-draining mechanisms inherent in the elite consumption strategy of development. The concentration of infrastructure in Nairobi and Mombasa creates economies external to the firm, thus encouraging new firms to set up operations in these cities rather than elsewhere. This creates a dynamic in which the demand for infrastructure grows where political power to obtain it is greatest.

Formal sector concentration

Implicit or explicit in the above is the fact of extreme geographical concentration of formal sector production. This concentration is

TABLE 5.2　*Sectoral shares of monetary* GDP *and employment arising in Nairobi, in percentages*

	Nairobi's share (1970)	
	GDP	*Employment*
Mining and quarrying	20·0	31
Manufacturing and repairs	56·4	46
Construction	66·9	56
Electricity and water	54·0	40
Transport communications	41·6	49
Commerce	55·4	54
Services	41·8	38

Source: A.-M. Vukovitch, 'Industry', Nairobi Urban Study Group Working Paper, Nairobi, xerox, 1971.

obvious from casual observation, but the numbers are staggering, indicating that Nairobi's position in the economy of Kenya is analogous to that of the rich countries with regard to the poor. According to the 1969 census, Nairobi accounted for just less than 50 per cent of the urban population and about 5 per cent of the total population.[37] In 1970 it produced an overwhelming share of monetary GDP and employment as shown in Table 5.2.

Further, 80 per cent of urban formal sector wage employment is concentrated in four towns. Of these four towns, Nairobi has 58 per cent of total population and 67 per cent of total employment. But most striking is the fact that in four out of the six sectors of monetary GDP for which natural resources do not determine location over 50 per cent of output is produced in Nairobi. It is not surprising, therefore, that from 1968 to 1970, Nairobi claimed 67 per cent of the total urban wage bill. Further, Nairobi's share of Kenyan monetary GDP is growing faster than total GDP.[38]

Within the urban sector, Nairobi is growing much faster than other urban centres. Despite European and Asian out-migration, Nairobi's population grew at 9·7 per cent between 1962 and 1969. Only Mombasa also exceeded 4·0 per cent, and of the other eight major towns, five grew slower than the overall rate of population increase.[39] Thus we are not dealing with general urbanization, but urban growth concentrated at the economic centre—Nairobi. If Nairobi is excluded, Kenya's rate of urban growth for 1962–9 would have been only slightly above the natural rate of population increase.[40] The wage-employed portion of Nairobi's expanding population has benefited *on average* much more than other wage earners from Kenya's geographically concentrated growth. Between 1964 and 1970, average real wages in formal sector employment rose 29 per cent in Nairobi, and 5 per cent in other towns.[41] Thus migration to Nairobi does not seem to have any dampening effect on the growth of wage levels; on the contrary, spread effects seem completely outweighed by backwash effects—those urban areas which have had the slowest rates of population growth have also had the slowest growth of wage incomes. This seems inherent in the dynamics of concentrated growth, and there is no reason to assume that trends will change so long as present development strategy is followed.

Dynamics within the centre

I have outlined above the dynamics which generate a centralization of growth in Nairobi. Within Nairobi itself there are also forces tending to generate an unequal distribution of income and wealth. The city's population grew at almost 10 per cent per annum between 1962 and 1969, yet formal wage employment grew only 14 per cent from 1963 to 1969, while average wages rose twice this amount. This, of course, implies that income distribution worsened, unless the incomes of those in the informal sector rose faster. Vukovitch, making quite reasonable assumptions, estimates that 22·7 per cent of Nairobi's labour force earned less than 200 shillings a month in 1971.[42] Further, she projects that if past trends in the composition of output continue, in 1974, 24·8 per cent of the labour force will be earning less than this amount. Thus on the basis of our analysis and available predictions, it appears that present development strategy will lead to a *worsening* distribution of income in Nairobi. This, of course, will feed back upon the structure of demand, increasing the tendency towards a capital-intensive product mix, centralization of social services, and a deteriorating balance of payments. Further, the slow growth of formal wage employment will increase labour absorption in the informal sector, aggravating tendencies towards involutionary development.[43]

Thus we see both logically and empirically, the present strategy of development seems to drain resources both public and private towards the centre, accentuating and rigidifying geographical inequalities, and within the centre creates an increasingly unequal distribution of income and wealth. It would seem safe to predict that the present strategy incorporates the necessary and sufficient conditions for the following structural characteristics, which might be called 'the Latin American syndrome', to emerge within the next 25 years:

(1) agricultural stagnation resulting from adverse terms of trade, urban migration, and low rates of surplus and reinvestment, leading to urban food shortage and structural inflation;

(2) continual balance of payments crises requiring dependence upon foreign finance to a growing degree, and perhaps repeated devaluation;

(3) non-competitive domestic industrial sector with powerful trade unions, resulting in employers and unions forcing up urban wages and prices to protect against rising import and food prices, further feeding inflationary tendencies; and

(4) increased urban migration as agricultural terms of trade deteriorate, resulting in explosive growth of shanty-towns around Nairobi.

The Kenyan economy has experienced a relatively rapid rate of growth of real monetary GDP, well over 6 per cent per annum for 1964–70.[44] Even given the operation of the dynamic mechanisms discussed in the second section, it is possible to maintain such a rate of growth if foreign exchange is not a constraint. Problems of employment and income distribution would worsen, of course, as they have during the past period of rapid growth. But as we have seen, a foreign exchange crisis is imminent. Despite the generally optimistic view of a recent ILO report,[45] the possibility of a quick solution to the foreign exchange problem that is consistent with a high rate of growth of GDP is remote. Kenya's major exports are unlikely to increase dramatically in the foreseeable future.

Conclusion: economic solutions and political realities

We have sought in the previous section to describe the dynamics of the Kenyan economy, and in doing so to identify the contradictions within those dynamics. An argument has been that the present 'unemployment crisis', the rapid urban migration resulting in appalling slums such as Mathare Valley,[46] and (more immediate from the State's point of view) the emergent balance of payments crisis are all symptoms of these inherent contradictions. Further, the contradictions arise from the unequal distribution of income and wealth, which leads to an underdevelopment process that drains the periphery and enriches the centre. While our analysis is no doubt controversial, much of it is implicit in the report of the recent mission of experts to Kenya sponsored by the International Labour Office.[47] If it is accepted that part or all of the analysis has validity, we can ask the question, what is the possibility of averting underdevelopment and stagnation in Kenya?

The most likely answer to this question is negative, for in every country, rich or poor, the pattern of development or economic growth chosen arises from the economic interests of the politically powerful. The fact that a pattern of development generates intractable social problems is not sufficient to stimulate redress of the situation; this will occur only if the politically powerful see their interests being served as well in some alternative arrangement as in the existing one, or if the problems deepen into a crisis which fundamentally alters the concentration of power. The latter, which implies revolutionary change, is historically unusual, and the former unlikely if, as has been suggested here, a solution to the social problems requires an effective redistribution of income and wealth.

It is relevant here to consider the solution suggested by the ILO mission to Kenya in 1972: 'redistribution from growth'.[48] Such a policy has an appealing ring, for it would seem to suggest that the redistribution required to solve the employment problem is possible without anyone becoming worse off absolutely. In fact, it is no more politically viable than redistribution from existing income and wealth, for in practice the two cannot be separated. In short, 'redistribution from growth' is a will-o'-the-wisp, which exists only as an academic abstraction. But before turning to this point, let us take 'redistribution from growth' at face value. The beneficiaries of the present pattern of growth in Kenya would not take kindly to a policy which denied them in future their disproportionate share of gains, even if such a policy were possible to carry out. The authors of the report recognize this and counter by the observation that a policy of directing growth towards the poor would not lack the support of the poor themselves.[49] This obviously is intended to suggest that while the State may be creating enemies on the one hand, it will be creating a much more numerous set of friends on the other. The important question for governments, however, is not whether friends are being created, but whether or not this can lead to concrete and effective political support. In the Kenyan case this would seem highly unlikely. First, a flow of information must occur which informs the poor that the government is championing their cause. However, the information channels—newspapers, radio and television, and other State propaganda organs—are in the control

99

of and administered by precisely those interests in the private and public sectors which are opposed to the redistributive policies. Second, if the poor were aware of the power struggle within the elite to change the pattern of development, they would have to somehow be mobilized into effective political action. This, in effect, is a suggestion that the entire basis of the political support of the present Kenyan Government and the grass-roots organization of the KANU party structure be changed. Such a fundamental shift is unlikely, and it is open to serious question whether an international mission, made up primarily of non-Kenyans, is at liberty to suggest it, even by implication.

In any case, 'redistribution from growth' is a practical absurdity. It suggests that next year's GDP can magically be divided between GDP this year and the subsequent increase. While one can write, $\text{GDP}_t + \Delta\text{GDP} = \text{GDP}_{t+1}$, this bit of definitional algebra should not be interpreted as referring to any actual division of GDP in period $t + 1$, for the increase in GDP is generated in the same factories and on the same farms as was the total for period t. In short, the increase in GDP is not identifiable as a separate component of national income once it is realized—it is not a growth 'bonus' or 'dividend' that magically comes into the hands of governments for redistribution. The increase accrues, of course, to the same groups and without a change in the productive structure and ownership pattern in much the same proportion (or disproportion) as the previous level of GDP did. Further, redistribution can only take place once the growth has occurred—it is nonsensical to talk of redistributing unrealized output. But once the growth has occurred, the redistribution *by definition* is out of existing income. The effect of the 'redistribution from growth' strategy is nothing more than postponing redistribution from *current* income to the future. This might be justifiable if there were persuasive arguments to indicate that redistribution from current income will be easier in the future than the present. No such arguments are made in the Kenya ILO report and it is difficult to imagine what they might be.

It might be argued that the above is merely a logical exercise, and in no way undermines the point that greater equality can be achieved without making anyone *worse* off. While the political justification—that the rich will be significantly less aroused to opposition by a standstill in incomes than a reduction—is at best dubious,[50] changing future distribution without altering present distribution is simply not possible. In order for the State to significantly affect future distribution, it will have to alter the way in which it spends and taxes. Alterations which would drastically affect the future, but have no impact on the present, would be clever indeed, and no rich country has been successful in discovering them.

To be concrete, an employment-generating policy for Kenya would have to change substantially the system of protection in order to move away from the policy of import substitution. It would be very difficult to argue that a major change in the system of tariffs and quotas would not affect the current distribution of income at any time quite seriously. Similarly, encouraging more labour-intensive methods of production would require drastic changes in incomes policy, industrial licensing, and exchange rate policy. Changes in any of these would necessarily affect current distribution of income.

Finally, 'redistribution from growth' ignores the crucial role of the distribution of *wealth* in determining the distribution of income. If all redistribution is to occur from increases in GDP (which is logically and practically impossible) it follows that the distribution of wealth in period t is to be unchanged. Experience in rich countries indicates clearly that redistributive steps that leave the ownership of property unchanged have little or no long-term impact. If there are economic laws, a fundamental one is that wealth generates income, and if it is desired to generate a different pattern of income flows, it is necessary to alter the pattern of wealth-holding. This is particularly true in poor countries such as Kenya. When the tools of fiscal policy have proved inadequate to alter income distribution in virtually all industrial countries, it is difficult to imagine achieving more success in countries where the range of fiscal instruments is much narrower and their flexibility drastically reduced.

If redistribution from current income is judged politically unpalatable and 'redistribution from growth' nonsensical, then a solution to Kenya's employment problem is elusive indeed.

Notes

1 A. J. Hughes, *East Africa*, Penguin, Harmondsworth, 1963, pp. 87 ff.
2 D. Walker, 'Problems of economic development of East Africa', in E. A. G. Robinson, ed., *Economic Development of Africa South of the Sahara*, Macmillan, London, 1965, p. 92; and B. Van Arkadie and D. Ghai, 'The East Africa economies', in P. Robson and D. Lury, eds, *The Economies of Africa*, Allen & Unwin, London, 1969, pp. 317 ff.
3 Lord Lugard, *The Dual Mandate in British Tropical Africa*, Blackwood, London, 1922, p. 397.
4 'One of the reasons why Kenya . . . European farmers tended to oppose the introduction of coffee into African farming was because they feared the effects of a lucrative cash crop on the supply of labour to non-African farms.' Walker, *op. cit.*, p. 123.
5 *East African Royal Commission 1953–1955 Report*, HMSO, London, Cmd 9475, June 1955.
6 Very important conservative 'reforms' at the same time as the Royal

Commission report were the steps to create a highly-paid proletariat. See John Weeks, 'Wage policy and the colonial legacy—a comparative study', *Journal of Modern African Studies*, vol. 9, no. 3, 1971.

7 Henry Bernstein, 'Modernisation theory and the sociological study of development', *Journal of Development Studies*, vol. 7, no. 2, January 1971; A. G. Frank, 'The sociology of development and the underdevelopment of sociology', *Catalyst*, No. 3, University of New York; and Jamil Hilal, 'Sociology and underdevelopment', Department of Social Theory, University of Durham, mimeo, 1970.

8 John C. F. Fei and Gustav Ranis, *Development of the Labor Surplus Economy: Theory and Policy*, Irwin, Homewood, 1964.

9 Gunnar Myrdal, *Rich Countries and Poor*, Harper & Row, New York, 1957.

10 See P. C. W. Guttkind, 'Tradition, urbanisation, modernity and unemployment in Africa: the roots of instability', *Canadian Journal of African Studies*, vol. 3, no. 2, Spring 1969.

11 See Marx's discussion of modes of production, which does not rest on values of the economic agents in Karl Marx, *Pre-Capitalist Economic Formations*, Lawrence & Wishart, London, 1964, particularly pp. 111 ff.

12 Keith Hart, 'Informal income opportunities and the structure of urban employment in Ghana', published in *Journal of Modern African Studies*, March 1973, paper presented to the Conference on Urban Unemployment in Africa, 12–16 September 1971, Institute of Development Studies, Brighton; John Weeks, 'Urbanisation, ideology and African underdevelopment', unpublished MS 1973; and Dorothy Remy and John Weeks, 'Employment and inequality in a non-industrial city', in Karl Wohlmuth, ed., *Employment in Emerging Societies*, Praeger, New York, 1974.

13 Weeks, 1973, *op. cit.*, and Remy and Weeks, *op. cit.*

14 ILO, *Employment, Incomes and Equality: A Programme for Expanding Productive Employment in Kenya*, ILO, Geneva, 1972.

15 *Ibid.*, chapter 13 and Technical Paper 22.

16 Roger van Zwanenburg, 'History and theory of urban poverty in Nairobi: the problem of slum development', Institute of Development Studies, University of Nairobi, Discussion Paper no. 26, mimeo, 1972.

17 M. P. Todaro, 'A model of labour migration and urban unemployment in less developed countries', *American Economic Review*, vol. LIX, no. 1, March 1969, p. 139; and Charles R. Frank, jr, 'The problem of urban unemployment in Africa', in R. G. Ridker and Harold Lubell, eds, *Employment and Unemployment Problems of the Near East and South Asia*, Vikas, Delhi, 1971, pp. 785–6.

18 In the middle 1950s, non-African production accounted for about 80 per cent of cash GDP from the agricultural sector in Kenya. See D. Walker, 'Problems of economic development of East Africa', in E. A. G. Robinson, ed., *Economic Development of Africa South of the Sahara*, Macmillan, London, 1965, p. 52.

19 One reason for the lack of 'spill over' was the prohibition against Africans growing certain cash crops.

20 John Weeks, 'Wage policy and the colonial legacy—a comparative study', *The Journal of Modern African Studies*, vol. 9, no. 3, 1971, pp. 367–71.
21 Van Zwanenburg, *op. cit.*
22 ILO, *op. cit.*, chapters 6 and 11.
23 John Weeks, 'Employment, growth and foreign domination in underdeveloped countries', *Review of Radical Political Economics*, vol. 4, no. 1, Spring 1972.
24 For a general discussion of this process, see Celso Furtado, *Development and Underdevelopment*, University of California Press, Berkeley, 1964, chapter 4.
25 Albert Hirschman, *The Strategy of Economic Development*, Yale University Press, New Haven, 1958, chapter 6.
26 Frances Stewart, 'Choice of technique in developing countries', *Journal of Development Studies*, vol. 9, no. 1, October 1972; and Charles Cooper (with Francisco Sercovitch), 'The mechanisms for transfer of technology from advanced to developing countries', Science Policy Research Unit, the University of Sussex, unpublished MS 1970.
27 ILO, *op. cit.*, chapters 9 and 11.
28 Weeks, 1971, *op. cit.*
29 ILO, *op. cit.*, chapter 17.
30 See, for example, Werner Baer and Andrea Maneschi, 'Import substitution, stagnation and structural change: an interpretation of the Brazilian case', *Journal of Developing Areas*, vol. 5, no. 2, January 1971; and Celso Furtado, 'Development and stagnation in Latin America: a structuralist approach', Economic Growth Center, Yale University, Paper no. 95, New Haven, 1966.
31 Republic of Kenya, *Statistical Abstract, 1971*, Ministry of Finance and Economic Planning, Nairobi, 1972.
32 It may be irrelevant in any case. See Frances Stewart and Paul Streeten, 'Conflicts between output and employment objectives in developing countries', *Oxford Economic Papers*, vol. 23, no. 2, July 1971.
33 'The Sussex Manifesto', *Science and Technology for Development*, UN Advisory Committee on the Application of Science and Technology to Development, UN/ST/ECA/133, 1971, Annex II.
34 Republic of Kenya, *Survey of Services, 1966*, Ministry of Finance and Economic Planning, Nairobi, 1971.
35 Author's field notes, April 1972.
36 Field notes, April 1972.
37 *Statistical Abstract*, 1970.
38 *Statistical Abstract*, 1971.
39 UNDP/ILO, Employment Policy Mission, *Basic Statistical Tables*, mimeo, 1972, section B.
40 *Ibid.*, table II—2.1.
41 *Statistical Abstract 1971*, and ILO 'data book'.
42 A. M. Vukovich, 'Nairobi: earnings and wages, distribution, 1971 and 1974', draft paper, Nairobi Urban Study Group, July 1971.
43 That is, adaptation and dynamic change in a context of declining

average incomes. Such a situation is described in C. Geertz, *Agricultural Involution*, University of California Press, Berkeley, 1968.

44 *Statistical Abstract, 1971.*

45 ILO, *op. cit.*, chapter 16.

46 Donna Haldane (for the Nairobi Urban Study Group and the National Christian Council of Kenya), *Survey of Temporary Structures*, Nairobi, photocopy, 1971.

47 *Ibid.*, chapter 6.

48 *Ibid.*, pp. 109 ff., Technical Paper no. 6.

49 *Ibid.*

50 It could easily be argued on *a priori* grounds that such a policy is doomed to failure because it arouses the opposition of the rich without reducing their power to resist.

6 African peasants and resistance to change: a reconsideration of sociological approaches[1]

Caroline Hutton and Robin Cohen

Conservative and innovative behaviour occurs in all societies, but there appears to be no uniform pattern of resistance to change or acceptance of the new which enables us to say who will resist particular technological, scientific, and cultural changes. Given this circumstance, the sociologist of development is faced with a set of theoretical problems. One common source of difficulty, which comes under the view of the sociologist is the reluctance or refusal of peasant cultivators[2] or rural workers to co-operate in the achievement of development goals—goals which are either implicitly held as universal goods or are specifically promoted by the planners or politicians in the underdeveloped countries. It would seem to be a pattern of peasant life to evade, impede or ignore many kinds of economic change which are considered likely to benefit those who most vigorously resist them. If sociologists of development have any effective part to play in facilitating economic development, one useful contribution would lie in making clear what factors are involved in resistance behaviour, and how such behaviour comes about.

The general themes of resistance to change in rural areas and peasant conservatism have been widely discussed by sociologists of different kinds and three different approaches to the question may be distinguished:

(1) In the tradition of structural–functionalism and Parsonian sociology are those authors who assume that peasant conservatism is a product of a particular type of traditional rural value system. Familistic and other collectively-orientated norms, superstition, hide-bound habit, and other related elements in the value system, are seen in this perspective as fundamentally impeding socioeconomic progress and modernization.[3]

(2) Other authors have taken less for granted, and have shown, often through detailed empirical work, that peasants far from

105

being in some primeval state of traditionalism have good reasons to resist specific economic developments. These reasons may well come from peasants forming their own economic judgments, or from defining goals in terms of socially-desirable goods and rewards rather than material ones. Where judgments of alternative economic strategies are made by the peasant, it need not be assumed that these are less 'modern' than those of the planner, whose views may indeed be as traditional as anybody else's.[4]

(3) Diverse studies also exist which show that peasants frequently respond to economic opportunities in a profit-orientated and calculating manner but that these responses are set in actual situations that are themselves rather complex both for the actor and the social scientist, and not easily classified as either impeding progress or facilitating it.[5]

If these differing approaches are considered together, we are faced with widely contrasting interpretations of the reality of peasant behaviour. We need to look again at what has previously been taken for granted and to account for both the enormous variation in responses to economic changes which can be documented, and for the diverse explanations that have been advanced to explain such conduct.

A useful starting point is Raymond Apthorpe's critique of 'social values' theory in which he raises the question of how some people come to be labelled as peculiarly resistant to change. Once this labelling process is brought into focus, we need not accept in an *a priori* manner that anyone is especially resistant to change. Rather we should ask: who is resisting whom? What is the content of this resistance? Who defines the behaviour in question as resistant? These questions will have different answers in different situations, but in general it may be assumed that one set of actors (planners, researchers, agricultural officers) is designing changes for another set of actors (peasants, farmers). As Apthorpe argues, development studies of Africa in the 1960s[6]

laid emphasis on a lop-sided interchange, whether co-operation or competitive or both, between what in practice were regarded as two distinct sets of persons. The 'diffusion of innovations' studies that were characteristic . . . called one set of persons 'planners', 'initiators', or 'change agents', depending on the level of reference. The other set was known rather as 'receivers' who, potentially or actually, were supposed to accept gratefully the well-intentioned ministrations of the former.

Where they did not, resistance to change was discovered. But how sensible was the plan? Whose interests did it serve? Did resistant behaviour follow, after a genuine trial, the discovery of error or impracticability on the part of the initiators? Resistance to change cannot, if these issues are raised, be seen simply as opposition to progress by a readily identifiable group of actors.

Instead of assuming that peasants are conservative and then asking why, we need to ask why do conservatism, tradition, fear of witchcraft, religious beliefs, or other associated factors sometimes inhibit, and sometimes present no apparent hindrance, to change? The peculiarities and varieties of resistant behaviour cannot be explained unless we understand peasant economic strategies more generally, and in different situations. Kusum Nair's account of her conversations with peasants all over village India, for example, gives a vivid account of widely differing attitudes and strategies towards economic change. She can, however, find no general explanation for these variations.[7] Peasant behaviour appears to vary from extreme resistance to economic change which comes from outside their group, through partial resistance to selected changes, to innovatory economic behaviour and conformity to the expectations of the government planners. We believe that sociologists do have a contribution to make to the explanation of these variations and even that their explanations can have some practical application, but sociologists have, to a very great extent, sought their explanations within too limited a framework. In this chapter we try to show first, why traditional sociological explanations of resistance to change have persistently been based on asking inappropriate questions, and second, we indicate where explanations might more fruitfully be sought.

As this opens up an enormous field of study we have, for the purpose of this chapter, narrowed our focus in two respects. First, in so far as we have been able to cite supporting studies we have had the African situation in mind, although the arguments used are applicable elsewhere. Second, we have limited our concept of change, referring in this context principally to the economic changes brought about by the gradual incorporation of African economies into a world capitalist economy. We are fully aware that African economies have not been subject to any simple 'before' and 'after' contact situation, and follow Samir Amin's view that the creation of 'dependent peripheral societies' in Africa was an outcome of a 'dialectic . . . between the major colonial policies and the structures inherited from the past'.[8] The terms 'contact' and 'incorporation' are used to draw attention to the fact that the changes which peasants are supposedly resistant to, are themselves outcomes of a gradual involvement of African societies in a world economy, an involvement which was accelerated during the colonial period.

Sociological accounts of resistance to change

Those sociologists who, until recently, have paid particular attention to problems of economic development tend to have been those reared more or less in the functionalist tradition of sociology. Apart from the general criticisms of functionalism that are now current, this school of sociology has two serious weaknesses which affect the study of economic development. In the first place, it is an ahistorical sociology. This has meant that its proponents could talk of concepts such as 'traditional society' as if such societies existed in equilibrium and need not themselves be considered as changing historical products. Many striking features of so-called traditional societies in fact emerged during the nineteenth century as a result of the widespread social, political, and economic changes following colonialism. In the second place, functionalist sociology treated economy as a separate subsystem of society, and this effectively isolated sociology from economics. Although economy was not ignored in functionalist analyses, the development over time of changing relationships between economic and social factors was not emphasized. It is striking that economic anthropologists in general were trained in the ahistorical structural–functional tradition.[9] The result of these two limitations of their discipline has been that sociologists who asked why peasants were resistant to changes brought about by contact and incorporation were hamstrung in two ways: first, their lack of interest in history allowed them to think in terms of two polar types of society, the traditional and modern. Second, they saw 'tradition' as the major source of resistance and thus treated cultural variables as independent variables in explaining why members of traditional types of society failed to become modern. As Apthorpe has noted this meant that sociologists concentrated on social barriers to economic development while ignoring economic barriers to social development.[10]

We would like to suggest that what has happened in the sociology of development is that the explanations offered for peasants' economic strategies have been derived not from explanatory variables, but from a selection of dependent variables. Table 6.1 shows the ways in which sociological observations of peasants' responses to contact and incorporation can be classified. This classification seeks to demonstrate that the explanations which have been given for peasant behaviour should properly be seen as dependent variables, and that frequently, descriptions of attitudes and values illegitimately acquire the status of causal statements. The classification of observers'

TABLE 6.1 *Sociological categories for responses to contact and incorporation*

I   Observers' categories for actors' responses to contact and incorporation

	Response A	Response B*	Response C
Attitudes towards Western economic values	adoption of 'rational' economic values	*need limitation*	extreme resistance
Aspirations	'revolution' of rising expectations	*image of limited good*	*status quo*
Response to gap between needs and achievements	attempts to reach rising ceiling	*attempts to fix or to lower ceiling*	no gap perceived
Style of economic behaviour	individual competition, high *n* achievement	*no dominant style, unexplained variations*	communal defence of economy

II   Observers' models of actors' behaviour

Observers' model of man	maximizing man	*obstacle man*	noble savage
Observers' model of society	modernizing	*traditional*	primitive
Disciplinary bias	sociology and economics of development, urban anthropology	*social psychology acculturation studies, peasant studies*	ethnography

III   Planners' responses to observers' models of actors' behaviour

Planners' strategies	aid and support to increase productivity amongst favoured groups	(*i*) *attempts to change values and cognitive orientations amongst 'obstacle man'*; (*ii*) *provision of information and opportunity to corrigible groups*	(i) preservation or isolation in 'natural' condition; (ii) destruction of the community's means of survival

*Response B indicates identification of the problem area.

109

categories and models contained in the table also serves to highlight the particular problem area (shown as Response B) which requires investigation. The somewhat cryptic references to the work of David McClelland and George Foster, whose views are discussed later, suggest that their work too can usefully be set in a more general context. The work of these authors has been extensively criticized by other sociologists, as has the work of functionalists in general, but so far these criticisms have not been clearly put together to indicate in a general way what has gone wrong. It is not only those who have proposed 'tradition' as an independent variable, but also their critics, who have been looking for answers in too limited a field.[11]

Observers' categories for actors' responses to contact and incorporation

The somewhat laborious heading for the first section of Table 6.1 reflects a complex reality. When we came to look at the accounts which have been given for what might generally be termed resistance to economic development, we found in the literature, studies dealing with three main kinds of response. At one extreme were the classic cases of extreme resistance to economic change. These were usually cases of physical confrontation between simple societies of non-agricultural peoples such as hunters and gatherers or pastoralists, and western or westernized invaders. At the other extreme we found a high degree of commitment to economic development, characterized by the model progressive farmer. In between these two extremes, however, lie the bulk of the peasant population, and numerous studies reveal a situation which is far from clear. It is in attempting to account for this large middle category of actors' responses that the problems of sociological approaches to resistance to change became highlighted.

Extreme resistance to change

When we first became interested in looking again at resistance to change it was these extreme examples of resistance which we felt would pose the hardest problems of explanation, but in considering the many studies of such situations, a pattern emerged which made such resistance perhaps the easiest to account for, and the labelling of such resistance the easiest to understand. Indigenous peoples like the bushmen or pygmies in Africa (and the Amerindians, Esquimaux, and Aborigines in other continents) simply did not have the physical or technological capacity to combat the diseases or guns of the invaders, and put up desperate and often pathetic attempts to resist their onslaught. Resistance was a matter of sheer survival in the face of overwhelming odds. The foreign intruders could offer nothing that the indigenous societies wanted and indeed contrived only (where genocide was not the explicit intent) to disrupt the precariously achieved balance between a local society and its environment. The pygmies were driven into the shrinking forests, those bushmen who were not exterminated into remote areas of the Kalahari, habitats which alone could support the culture and social relationships within which survival was a possibility. Where contact was enforced, dissimilation and mimicry provided a symbolic comfort for the subjected societies, while the dominant societies harboured such gross miscomprehensions of the peoples they vanquished, that they frequently deemed them subhuman. Explanations for the extreme resistance to change shown by these varied peoples, however, do not seem hard to find. First, in all cases there is an absence of a settled agricultural economy (some of these peoples, including nomadic and semi-nomadic pastoralists, have also been crop-growers, but settled agriculture has never been the dominant mode of production). Secondly, in each case the agents of change have posed a direct and dramatic threat to the form of economy and the culture and social structure that is dependent on their way of life. Cattle peoples, hunters and gatherers, and other nomadic peoples, cannot easily adapt their economies to the processes of incorporation into a capitalist market economy. Extreme resistance to change by such peoples has also, it should be added, posed serious social problems to socialist societies, where nomadic reindeer hunters, or the East European gypsies resist incorporation into planned economies. By contrast, settled agriculturalists can adopt new crops or new methods of growing existing crops, new breeds of seed and so on without immediately feeling that their way of life is at risk. Threats to their way of life may in fact gradually accumulate over the years, for example when young men are able to become independent of their fathers by growing their own cash crops, but the initial changes are likely to be partial and relatively gradual so that by the time major changes are put into effect minor changes are already well accepted. Universal primary school education for both sexes, for example, is preceded by years of limited education for small numbers of children, or for boys only. A small cultivator can give one child a couple of years at school without too much anxiety, to see what happens, but for a Mbuti pygmy, for example, to decide to send a child to school a way of life must change not only for the child's immediate family but for a larger group, or else the individuals

111

concerned must opt out of their own society. As Colin Turnbull's poignant study of the Mbuti shows, they have everything to lose by coming out of the forest.[12]

Extreme resistance to change also occurs in those situations in which peoples who are apparently offered a reasonable chance to participate in a Western way of life, and to benefit themselves materially, actually reject the benefits which are offered. A classic case of this sort of behaviour is presented by the Masai people of Kenya and Tanzania. P. H. Gulliver has suggested how such behaviour might be explained.[13] He asks why peoples like the Masai have been so much more committed to their own social and cultural identity than have the other peoples around them. He is not willing to accept innate 'conservatism' as an adequate explanation for this difference and so he investigates Masai conservatism further. He suggests that their conservative commitment is based first on the safeguarding of rites, privileges, and interests which are important to the people concerned, and secondly their desire to preserve established ethical stands, values, and attitudes. His argument takes him further than this, however, at least by implication, as he has to explain why people such as the Masai should have been more concerned about these issues than their neighbours.

The Masai are a people who, before the colonial period, were successful pastoralists in a difficult and uncertain environment. They were wealthy in cattle and heartily despised their neighbours who were cultivators. They were strongly committed to a cultural tradition which differed from that of their agricultural neighbours, and which emphasized their superiority and separation. Masai pastoralism was very well adapted to the harsh environment and European technology, particularly in its early period of contact, had nothing to offer them economically. Change was fraught with potential disaster in an area where the risks of altering tried and tested patterns were very high. In spite of their extreme conservatism the Masai did accept what Gulliver terms 'safe' changes, that is, changes which did not bring risk to the balance of the cattle economy, nor to the culture which depended on this economy. Water supplies, cattle medicines, and the use of bus services for individual journeys were accepted. Education and health services were not offered on a nomadic basis and so acceptance of these would have meant a major change in the Masai way of life without any corresponding reorganization being made in the economy. Masai superiority and apartness was the symbolic representation of essential defensiveness. Gulliver argues that there is no mystical conservatism in the Masai personality, but that their behaviour was a response to threats against their interests which were always at risk in a harsh environment. The Masai could not easily accept change as the settled agricultural peoples could, because their economy was not susceptible to change in the same way. They could only respond to Western contact and incorporation either by defending the economy and the culture dependent on it, or by changing totally; abandoning their culture and way of life and entering on an alien one. The gradual pattern of change brought by Europeans to settled agriculturalists was not an available alternative for the Masai and other pastoralists like them. Opportunities for change were actually available to them, but these opportunities appeared as total threats to their existence, and not surprisingly were met by extreme resistance. The Masai have now accepted, although reluctantly, the necessity of change, as have their neighbours, the Arusha, but this change of attitude has been brought about by the extent to which the outside world has encroached upon the actual land which is the basis of their respective economies. The delicate balance of the pastoral economy is dependent on having large areas of land available to avoid overstocking and overgrazing. Sudden or gradual loss of this land area still threatens to undermine an essential basis of the pastoral economy.

'Rational' acceptance of change

If the conservatism of those who have shown extreme resistance to change can be shown to be a coherent and consistent pattern of behaviour, then it seemed equally likely that acceptance of change would turn out to be a different but comparable pattern. The column of Table 6.1 which is headed 'Response A' lists a set of responses to contact and incorporation which fits well with the observers' model of a rational, modernizing, calculating man; the stuff of which economic development must be made. On closer inspection, however, things become less simple than they seem. It has been assumed that the maximizing man exhibits a rational set of responses to the new economic opportunities which contact with 'modern' societies must bring him, but at this point multiple questions and confusions arise.

The confusions come partly from the nature of the evidence with which we are dealing, that is, the behaviour of the actors in question, but also partly from the way in which we have presented the data in Table 6.1. When we were looking at the C responses, section I of Table 6.1 seemed to be a tabulation of empirical responses. The corresponding section of A responses, however, is more clearly a mixture of actors' responses and the way Western observers and administrators have interpreted these responses. The confusions which are inherent in Table 6.1 are, therefore, confusions which arise from the impossibility of disentangling objective 'facts' from the subjective processes involved in the recording of these 'facts'. In all sections of the table, actors' definitions of the situations are themselves part of these situations. The purpose of separating section I of Table 6.1 from section II is to show how far the models of man and society held by Western observers have limited the way in which evidence is identified as relevant. The B responses show this pattern of confusion much more clearly, but in spite of the apparent coherence and consistency of the A responses, the nature of the evidence is open to question.

The major problem arising from the evidence itself is that of the nature of rationality. The question of what constitutes rational behaviour has proved problematical in the context of Western economic development, and the problems are perhaps more acute in the area of peasant agriculture, when the peasant has relatively little certain information about his expected environment on which he can base rational decisions. Michael Lipton has suggested that economists themselves are unsure of what rational behaviour in this situation might be:[14]

> Last year's rainfall, last year's prices, do not help to guess this year's. What exactly, then, do those who (on the one hand) exhort the peasant to respond to relative prices, and those who (on the other) insist that he already does, seek to achieve?
> In an environment of such uncertainty, is not insurance a more rational policy than profit maximization?

While economists and others continue to debate the problem, peasants must continue to work the answer out for themselves, and planners will continue to offer the strategies they see as appropriate to the situation. One begins to wonder how far the 'rational', maximizing peasant turns out to be simply the peasant who adopts official strategies, in situations where these are relatively successful. The many situations where official strategies do not actually aid increases in productivity make peasant responses more difficult to interpret. The available studies suggest that there are many cases where the peasant's calculations are conducted in much the same manner as those of the planner, balancing expected profit against the risks and inputs involved, but that their calculations are based on different sources of information and consideration of different factors which results in different conclusions and, therefore, different strategies.[15] On occasion such indigenous strategies are strikingly superior to official policies simply in terms of profit maximization.[16] But how is the observer (or indeed the peasant) to know how to interpret cases where peasant strategies are counter to official policies (i.e. resistant to change) and are also unsuccessful in terms of the return to the peasant? Do we have here a typical example of 'obstacle man' or of a frustrated maximizing man? Alternatively should we question, with certain economic anthropologists, whether or not peasant economies can be analysed in term of 'rational' models derived from Western economics?

We do not particularly wish to raise the spectre of economic man here,[17] but it is at least plausible to argue that neither Western wage earners nor African peasants are likely to be consistently rational in pure economic terms, because 'rational' economic values are only part of an individual's total value system. Sociologists not infrequently rate job satisfaction or academic status as a higher value, for the moment, than increased net income. High-status universities have often been able to attract staff to lower salary scales than those of less prestigious institutions. Calculations concerning next year's strategy must involve the weighing of long- and short-term gains, the lessons of experience, the balance of social, economic, political, or more personal rewards. A young man with little to lose and no responsibilities may be willing to take new risks, but equally well, lack of experience, lack of accumulated resources to fall back on, and lack of social support may make him more cautious than his father. The mixed categories of Table 6.1, therefore, reflect a mixed reality. Any real sense in which the 'rational' responses of the maximizing man can consistently be distinguished from the defective responses of the obstacle man, now appears doubtful.

Varied responses to change

The B column of actors' responses to change could at first sight be considered a residual category, but in fact it becomes clear that the great majority of actors will be found in this category rather than either of the others. If we manage successfully to explain both patterns of extreme resistance to change, and also patterns of successful profit maximization, we shall have accounted for only a tiny portion of peasant economic behaviour. The responses of column B do not leave us, therefore, with a small area of behaviour which can be simply cleared up, rather we are thrown back to our starting point, and the need to find adequate explanations for the varied ways in which African peasants, like peasants elsewhere, have responded to changing economic opportunities.

The concept of obstacle man is at root a concept of irrational man. Man as obstacle is one standing in the way of economic advancement which would be to his own advantage. The idea of labelling sections of populations as irrational is, however, antithetical to thinking in social science and so obstacle man is redefined not as irrational but as either ignorant of where his true advantage lies, or as having defined his advantage in his own way. This is the essence of the way in which obstacle man's behaviour has been interpreted. If people consistently fail to grasp opportunities which will work to their own economic advantage, then obviously economic advance is not something which they value highly. Planners' strategies have been divided, as a result of such interpretations, between attempts to counter ignorance, and to make it possible for economic opportunities to be grasped (for example by providing feeder roads) and attempts to work on values which are 'wrong' in terms of national development goals. Sociologists have not been very much concerned with the practical problems of ignorance and opportunity (except at the level of community development) but they have devoted considerable attention to the problems of values which are inadequately 'modern'.

We have now arrived at the heart of the matter. The twin weaknesses of the sociologist's conception of development—ahistoricism and separation from economics—allowed the continuation of an implicit evolutionary model of history, long after evolutionism in sociology had itself declined. The observers' models of man which are identified in Table 6.1 can be seen to fit with corresponding models of society which pass from the primitive through the traditional to the modern. Although theorists such as Redfield, Foster, and McClelland did not share a worked out view of human history in these terms, the temptation to take for granted that traditional society existed as a transitional stage between the primitive and the modern was strong. In line with such an assumption, obstacle man could be seen, not only as a form of irrational man, but also as a transitional form who could be helped to pass through his traditional stage and on to the benefits of modern society.

In fairness to the theorists concerned it must be emphasized that most of them were not concerned to propound this theory of history as such, but nevertheless the implicit view of society with which they worked profoundly affected the way in which they located explanations for peasants' economic behaviour. Rather than looking to see how peasant producers had become linked to world markets over time, their interest was bounded by attention to peasants' cognitive and value systems. The way the peasant actor defined his situation was seen as far more important than the historical and economic structure of the situation. A recent work by Everett Rogers summarizes the main features of peasant society which came to be taken for granted by writers in this field. The lengthy quotation and discussion of Rogers's work is, we feel, justified in view of the representativeness of the views he recounts:[18]

Peasant communities are characterized by *mutual distrust*, suspicion, and evasiveness in interpersonal relations.
Peasants tend to believe in the notion of *limited good* (that all desirables in life are in fixed supply) and in the related idea that one man's gain is another man's loss. Government

officials are viewed with both dependence and hostility. Villagers are *familistic*—that is, they subordinate their individual goals to those of the family. Peasants generally *lack innovativeness* and have an unfavourable attitude towards change. *Fatalism* is the degree to which an individual perceives a lack of ability to control his future. Fatalistic attitudes are widely reported as characteristic of peasants. Social *aspirations* involve desired future states of being, such as living standards, social status, and occupation. A common observation in most studies of peasantry is that the respondents have relatively limited aspirations. They also lack *deferred gratification*, the postponement of immediate satisfaction in anticipation of future rewards. Peasants are also characterized by a limited view of the world. They are localistic in geographic mobility and in their exposure to mass media and have a limited time perspective. *Localiteness* is the degree to which individuals are oriented within, rather than external to, their social system. Peasants are distinguished by relatively low *empathy*, defined as the ability of an individual to project himself into the role of another. . . . The subculture of peasantry outlined here represents a synthesis of what is known. It suggests that the peasant style of life contains many social–psychological barriers to modernization and change.

Rogers's summary highlights several problems in this kind of thinking. First, he characterizes peasant society primarily in terms of its subculture, while ignoring the possible range of variation in the types of peasant economy which he is considering. Elsewhere, in a note, he goes further and suggests that future research may show that this subculture is typical of all traditional societies, not just of peasants. (If this were true, it is hard to see how evolutionists could account for human society ever having advanced out of the traditional stage.) Because Rogers believes he is simply summarizing accepted knowledge on the subject, he makes no attempt to justify the central role cultural factors play in his analysis. Secondly, having character-ized the special features of peasant society, Rogers is not interested in looking at how such features arose, nor at how they might be related to the economy. The features of peasant society are seen as interdependent parts of a particular kind of social system; they are established by comparative observations and treated as persisting through time. Thirdly, the characteristics of peasant society are treated explicitly as observed facts. Studies have shown that peasants are distrustful, fatalistic, familistic, and so on, and these terms are taken to be definable and measurable. This view might, however, be questionable both with regard to the correctness of the facts themselves, and in terms of the nature of objectivity in any socio-logical observation. Finally, Rogers's summary shows very clearly an assumption, not only that the facts of the case have been clearly established, but also that these 'facts' are important in the explanation of underdevelopment. In his last sentence he moves from description of the features of peasant subcultures to the suggestion that such subcultures inhibit development. The facts, as we have indicated, are not as self-evident as he supposes, but much more importantly the weakness of the sociology of development is shown by this glide from description to causal analysis.

Spurious causality

The example that we have just given is one of what may be deemed spurious causality—which in this area is not simply an occasional aberration, but, on the contrary, is characteristic of much socio-logical explanation. If we refer back to Table 6.1, columns A and B reveal a situation in which just this process has taken place; de-scriptions of peasant behaviour in responding to change are first categorized by the observer, for example as need limitation or high need for achievement, and then these categories are used as ex-planations for the behaviour which has been observed. Peasants resist change because they have limited their needs. Alternatively they accept change because they have a high need achievement. In-dividually these separate explanations have been extensively criti-cized (although they are still widely used and practised) but it helps if we can take them together and see them as a general product of a particular way of viewing society. Table 6.1 reveals confusions of thought because dependent variables have been used as if they were independent variables; the consequences of change have been used to account for change.

To take a simple example, the problems of this kind of thinking can be shown clearly by considering the concept of fatalism. Rogers, drawing on several empirical studies of peasant societies, character-izes peasants as fatalistic, and later suggests that such fatalism is one factor inhibiting acceptance of modernization and change. This approach means that Rogers fails to answer the obvious rebuttal—why are peasants fatalistic? Once this question has been raised a series of other issues intrude. How do we discern the presence or absence of fatalism? Are there not sectors of 'modern' societies which are characterized by fatalism? Are some peasants more fatalistic than others, and if this is the case, how do we account for this within a supposedly uniform peasant subculture? It can be seen from these questions that to assume that fatalism, the image of the limited good, or other such factors are inhibiting economic development, effectively stops us from the investigation of these features in themselves. To merely state simply that fatalistic peasants must resist change, fails to explain either fatalism or resistance to change.

The purpose of Table 6.1 has been to bring us to this point. What we have presented in the figure can now be seen to be not an account of the nature of resistance to change, but a particular kind of categorization of dependent variables. There is no reason why we should not see fatalism as a product of change just as plausibly as a preventor of change. Why should need limitation behaviour not be a reaction to the situations in which peasants find themselves, rather than the explanation of such situations?[19] If the observations which we have to hand are really ways of indicating dependent variables, then logically, we must look elsewhere for the independent variables, and it is here we find that the boundaries of traditional sociology are too narrow for our purpose. In order to make our sociology useful, we must link it much more clearly with something closer to political economy.

The independent variables

If we accept that we have a situation in which some peasants are fatalistic and others are not, or at least a situation in which some are more fatalistic than others, then we have a situation of varied responses to change, rather than uniform patterns of acceptance or resistance. It is these varied responses which we now have to explain. Rather than seeking explanations within peasant subcultures we need to look at the nature of such subcultures, and how they came into existence, and at the ways in which they are linked to economy and social structure. Limiting our perspective to the simplified one of contact and incorporation, we find that independent variables may lie in three main areas. These are shown in Figure 6.1.

Figure 6.1 represents, in highly simplified form, the probable factors to which we should look for more useful understanding of the processes of economic development at the present level. If we are to understand why peasants behave as they do, then we need to study not only the peasants' definitions of their situations, although such definitions are essential parts of any situation, but also the situations themselves. One of the chief weaknesses of the sociological approaches has been a glossing over of the variety of actual circumstances in which different peasants find themselves.

The purpose of Figure 6.1 is not only to suggest where we might look for our independent variables, but also to show how extremely complex any actual configuration of variables is likely to be. We have suggested five basic explanatory variables, but in the first place each of these has many different forms and, in the second place, these basic variables are tied to each other in varied relations of interdependence. We have not laid out any actual combinations of independent variables partly because of the difficulty of obtaining the necessary historical information, but chiefly because of the enormous range of patterns which would result. Whereas sociologists

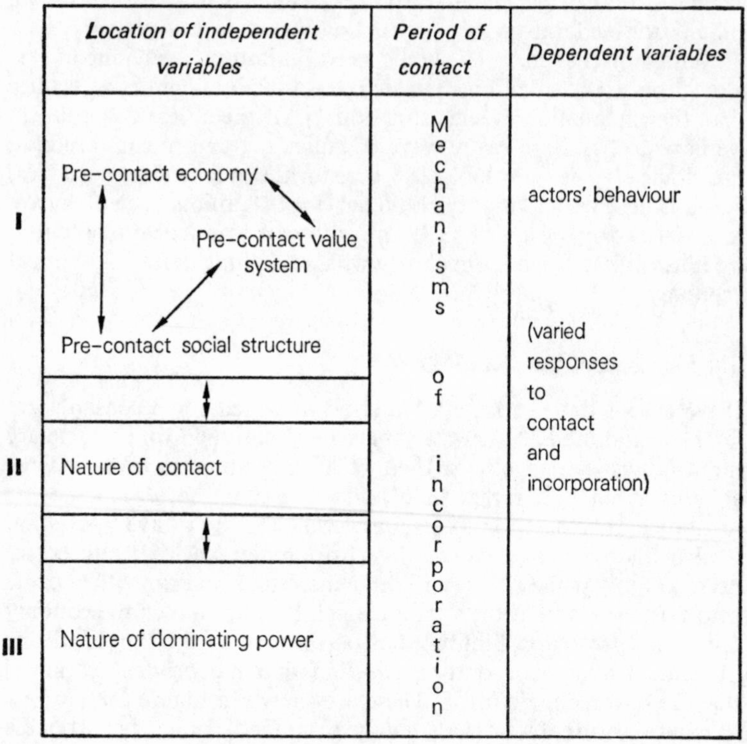

Location of independent variables	Period of contact	Dependent variables
I Pre-contact economy ↕ ↘ Pre-contact value system ↗ Pre-contact social structure	Mechanisms of incorporation	actors' behaviour (varied responses to contact and incorporation)
↕		
II Nature of contact		
↕		
III Nature of dominating power		

Note: the double-headed arrows represent relations of interdependence between the independent variables.

FIGURE 6.1 *Resistance to change—probable explanatory variables*

have tended to treat cultural values as a single independent and explanatory variable, we are suggesting here that values must be seen in relation to the other independent variables with which they are associated. We cannot offer here any quick solution to the sociologists' problems in attempting to understand peasant behaviour once and for all; all we can do is to rephrase the questions which must be asked and the answers which must be looked for in actual

situations where judgments are being made about peasants' behaviour and planning strategies developed on the basis of these
judgments.

In order to treat the variables in Figure 6.1 properly, we should
first establish an appropriate typology for each variable. Rather
than go through this somewhat lengthy process in this chapter, we
will simply suggest the sort of questions which might be asked of
actual situations in order to establish the relevant types.

Economy, values and social structure

The nature of pre-capitalist economies has occupied the attention
both of Marxists and of economic anthropologists, but our knowledge of such economies and of the way they undergo change in
response to both internal and external pressures has remained
limited. In the case of the Marxists the pre-capitalist economy has
until recently not been an area of great theoretical interest, and
concern has been with constructing typologies rather than with the
analysis of the sort that Marx gave us for capitalist societies.[20]
Economic anthropologists have given pre-capitalist economies very
detailed consideration, but their emphasis has tended to be on processes of distribution and exchange, rather than on production and
changes in production.

If we take another look at what we mean by the pre-capitalist
economy what does become clear is that, even within the boundaries
of Africa, we are looking at a long period of human development,
and a variety of economies. When African economies were gradually
incorporated into a changing world capitalist economy, the process
of incorporation was an uneven one, which took place over a
considerable period of history, and was complicated by the diversity
of situations involved. We cannot then envisage situations in which
one form of economy (developed, capitalist, modern) incorporated
another form (underdeveloped, pre-capitalist, traditional) in a single
encounter. It is indeed possible to argue that the articulation of the
dominant mode of production is, and will remain, incomplete, with
certain pre-capitalist structures remaining intact. The processes of
development and underdevelopment in which peasant farmers are
entangled today are the results of the unequal interactions of economies over time. One reason why peasant farmers find themselves in
varying economic circumstances today lies in the variations in the
economic histories of their regions. Agriculture, trade, hunting and
gathering, pastoralism, and the barter of human and natural resources meant that there were considerable variations in early
African economies, and also great variations in the range of contacts
between such economies and the outside world. What African

121

economies have in common through these changing chapters of history is the part they have come to play in the international division of labour, and their peripheral position in relation to the world capitalist market economy; in other words, their shared experience of underdevelopment.[21]

In order to sort this period of history into some kind of order we need to ask the sort of questions suggested by Frankenberg and Meillassoux in their criticisms of economic anthropology.[22] They argue that pre-capitalist economic formations should be typed according to their patterns of, for example:

(1) the social organization of production;

(2) the purposes of production—i.e. whether for use or exchange;

(3) the social control of production surpluses and relations of production;

(4) the processes of reproduction of these formations, both endogenous and exogenous; and

(5) the alternative uses which exist for time which otherwise is given to production.

If we asked questions such as these of African economic history we should get an adequate basis for typology, but we should also arrive at two general conclusions. The first conclusion should be that the relations between economy and society are immensely complicated. This is a point to which we shall return below. The second conclusion, following on from the first, should be that no general propositions hold true for historical processes as such because the patterns in practice are too varied. There is effectively no theory of social change, but only ways of analysing social changes in particular situations.[23] This point becomes even clearer if we attempt to look at particular relations between economy, social structure, and values or culture.

The ways in which African economies have varied from each other and have come together to be incorporated in a world economy is a procedure quite sufficiently complicated for any social scientist to deal with, but these economies cannot be separated in reality from their accompanying social structures and value systems which are of particular relevance to the social organization of production, the social control of surpluses, and the alternative uses to which productive time and energy might be put.[24] The problem is that while it is clear to the sociologists that relationships between these variables must exist, sociologists have not been able to specify with certainty what such relationships are. It is disagreement between sociologists precisely on this issue which has proved a major source of conflict and division within sociology. One of the major bones of contention, for example, between McClelland and Foster and their critics is the debate not over whether McClelland's and Foster's theses are true or false, but over whether it is legitimate to treat values as an independent variable. Debate over this point runs inconclusively through the sociology of religion, and the Marxist–Weberian controversy over the origins of capitalism. The status of sociology as a social science is such that many of its most fundamental propositions are not easily, or at all, testable. We simply cannot say with any certainty whether or not particular sets of values 'cause' particular sorts of social and economic configurations. We can begin to make statements about the sets of values which 'go with' particular social and economic circumstances, but in effect we are saying little more than that interrelations of some sort exist between them. In terms of general historical propositions it seems unlikely that we can advance much beyond this stage, and sociologists should, therefore, be very much more cautious about the sorts of causal or quasi-causal statements which they attempt, particularly when these statements may have adverse effects on the opportunities of other people. But at the same time, in the context of particular situations, sociologists should attempt to put together the possible inter-relations of these major variables which are interwoven in the historical process of incorporation in particular situations.

We are not likely to be helped by attitude surveys and cultural studies designed to test receptivity to modernization. Rather we need some understanding of the ways in which particular economies, social structures, and cultures are tied together, and the impact on these of the experience of colonization and incorporation into a wider economy. Such understanding will not immediately enable us to dispose of the real constraints on economic development, but at least it will enable local planners (if they are disposed to take anything from social science) to adapt their strategies of development to the context of real constraints, rather than to attribute failure to the unco-operative attitudes derived from a stereotype of peasant culture and traditions. We do not want to suggest that peasant attitudes and opinions are irrelevant to the processes of economic development, nor to the success or failure of local projects, but we are arguing that such attitudes are unlikely as such to be important independent variables, and are themselves part of the development situations which require explanation. We should not then ask how we can change peasants' attitudes to more appropriately modern ones before we have answered the question, why do people hold the attitudes towards development which they do have? (And in this process we would find considerable empirical variation both in the social and economic experiences of different peoples and in their attitudes.) In arriving at the answer we would now have to take more

123

factors into account than the most sophisticated concept of traditional peasant society.

The nature of contact and the nature of the dominating power

It is not possible in the space of a single chapter to begin to tackle the historical dramas of the process of contact between African societies and the developing capitalist world. Studies are now appearing which are beginning to deal seriously with the precise nature of contact, but it will take some time to put a general picture together from the detailed pieces. What we do know is that once we are no longer satisfied with the concept of 'tradition' as a sufficient characterization of hundreds of years of African history, we have a great deal of work to do in replacing it with historical alternatives. Not only did contact between African and Arab and Western societies take place over long periods of time, but contact was of several different kinds which also changed over time. Both the time scale of the contact and the nature of the contact are important aspects of the information which we need in order to understand processes of development today.

The chief agents of contact from the Mediterranean and the West were traders, fighters, explorers, settlers, missionaries, grabbers (of land, labour, or loot) and agents of government. Probably two of the most decisive factors were, first, the nature of the slave trade, both Arab and Atlantic; and, second, the change in the terms of trade between African states and the rest of the world as Africa took a steadily more peripheral role in the world capitalist market.[25] Social scientists working in any local area need to be aware not only of the history of their locality, but also of how the local area is situated in relation to general processes of contact, the emergence of a cash economy, the balance of trade, the development of a labour market and the growth of export markets. Peasants today are not isolated either culturally, socially, or economically, however physically remote their villages appear to be, and we can no longer afford to ignore these wider socio-economic relationships, in accounting for variations in behaviour and attitudes.

Identifying the nature of the dominating power throws us back into the hoary debates on the character of imperialism. Was the establishment of political hegemony rooted in 'the imperative necessities of the capitalist mode of production'[26], representing its monopoly stage? Was there, on the other hand, a strong mercantilist element involved? Were political, strategic, or diplomatic factors uppermost in the decision to annex or control territories? How important was the element of local collaboration (by ruling classes, economic interests, etc.) with the imperialist power? How necessary was it for the dominating power to penetrate or replace the administrative and political structures of the country concerned? What was the degree of violence used? What was the significance—numerical and political—of the settler element? Were there conflicts of interest between the various elements of the dominating power—settlers, missionaries, metropolitan government, commercial interests? The variations in pattern that are represented by these questions all critically affect the response of a peasant community to the incorporation of their economies.

Mechanisms of incorporation

The various combinations of the independent variables discussed earlier gave rise to varied forms of incorporation. In discussing this theme separately, we have in mind a somewhat tenuous distinction between the initial conditions that accompanied contact, and the operational conditions of maintenance that perpetuated the hegemony of the metropolis. The colonial powers' domination was exercised through trading, raiding, the extraction of raw materials, new forms of production, and ultimately settlement and government. Though not an exhaustive typology, the mechanisms of incorporation indicated below are those which sociologists tend to leave to other social scientists, but which properly have to be taken into account in any attempt to explain attitudes and behaviour involved in economic change.

First, labour power was expropriated by the introduction of various types of slavery, through forced or contract labour, by the imposition of hut and poll taxes designed to force the sale of labour power and finally through the growth of wage labour itself. Second, surpluses were expropriated by the introduction of a cash economy, the marketing of primary products for a world economy and by the widening and depersonalization of market relations that followed. Third, new modes of production—mines and extractive industries, plantations and manufacturing—were initiated. Fourth, indigenous competition was destroyed by the use of political and legal powers to limit or prohibit local capacity for accumulation, enterprise, innovation or equal competition. Fifth, new commodities in the form of manufactured goods and imported innovations were offered for sale or exchange.

It has been processes such as these in their varied combinations which have helped to shape those societies which we have been taught to call traditional, and it is these processes which we must learn to identify if we want to understand where our explanatory variables are likely to lie.

Conclusions

The general issues which we have raised in this chapter are not going to solve all problems of explaining what is happening to development projects at the local level. We can expect to find great variation and complication in local circumstances, and a general understanding of the relations between history, economy, and social structure will not give us all we need to know. The peculiarities of local co-operatives, the history of disputes between neighbours, the idiosyncratic development of village patterns of gossip, trust and suspicion, the disastrous effects of a drunken extension worker, the example of a devoted school teacher, can all have important consequences for the ways in which actual situations develop on the ground. What our general analysis can do is to make us much more sensitive than perhaps we usually are, to the kinds of statements which we make about development behaviour, and the kinds of explanations on which we draw. If we find a local situation, for example, in which progress is being impeded by fear of witchcraft, or in which the people say that anyone who gets on is in danger of being poisoned by jealous neighbours, we should not take these explanations at their face value without more careful consideration. Why do these people allow fear of witchcraft to inhibit their behaviour in this way, for example, when people not far away have gone ahead with development projects in spite of similar fears? Why do these people fear to compete with each other, when people with similar beliefs have chosen the path of material success and run the risk of poison or worse? In other words we cannot fall back on 'traditional beliefs' or 'the image of limited good' as immediate explanations for such behaviour without also considering how to explain the beliefs themselves, or the reasons for maintaining an image of limited good. Foster himself anticipated the necessity of treating his concept in this way:[27]

> By way of summary I continue to believe that the cognitive orientation of Limited Good goes further than any other model yet advanced to explain peasant behaviour; an astonishingly wide range of phenomena makes sense in the Limited Good context. This is not to say, however, that alternate models of equal or greater explanatory and predictive power may not be adduced. When they appear Limited Good will have to be weighed against them, and if, or the extent that, it is found wanting, it will have to be abandoned or relegated to a second level.

We have not gone so far as to produce an alternative model for Foster, but the relocation of obstacle man in history must push the image of limited good to a secondary level of explanation.

126

Although our criticisms of sociology are not new, it seems important to us to emphasize the way in which sociologists have treated man as obstacle, while the peasant with the 'incorrect' cognitive orientations has tended to become the scapegoat for all the burdens of underdevelopment which he himself suffers. Sociologists can help to alter this situation by altering their analyses, by accepting that the experience of the obstacle man is a product of history and the interrelations of the variables proposed in Figure 6.1, but also by abandoning their predilection for dichotomous models of society.

European sociology passed through its formative stage at a period of history when the overwhelming experience of its genitors was the transformation of society into an advanced industrial stage, accompanied by fears of disorganization, break down of social order, and ultimately world wars. This gave to them a sense of 'before' and 'after' experiences which has bedevilled sociology ever since. Sociologists have taken the contrasts between 'traditional' and 'modern' for granted for so long that they frequently assume these types to be self-evident both in their general characteristics and in their evolutionary relationship to each other. Nowhere, perhaps, have these types done so much damage as when they have been applied to African situations. The European experience of industrialization and the growth of capitalism is simply irrelevant to the current experiences of African society and African sociology. The sociological types derived from European experience have served effectively to obscure what has been happening in Africa. The terms 'traditional' and 'modern' do not have empirical bases in African contexts, and once they are abandoned we shall be much freer to examine the processes which are actually at work in peasant situations.

Once we abandon the dichotomous model of society, and the notion of 'tradition' giving way under the impact of 'modernization', then we are likely to find that we have thrown the baby out with the bath water and lost the sociology of development as well. Sociology of development makes sense as the study of modernizing societies and resistances to modernization; it makes less sense as the historical study of complex interrelations between economy, social structure, and values in particular contexts. Figure 6.1 demonstrates the impossibility of arriving at any one 'theory' of development because even the simplified independent variables which we have selected can appear in a multitude of possible combinations, and thus give rise to many different patterns of development. There is nothing to stop us unravelling and attempting to explain these varied patterns, but we cannot expect an overarching theory based on only part of the picture to help us do it. The sociology of development that continues to be practised, then, must be the pragmatic study of interrelations between structures and processes in particular situations on a limited level of generalization. As Homans has said, distinctions between the boundaries of historical, sociological, and economic approaches disappear when the problem is in control rather than the approach.[28] The only losers from this shift are those whose sociological careers are dependent on the maintenance of academic boundaries. Our gain lies in the freedom to investigate what the real constraints on development are at the local level and to see whether there is anything to be done about them. Local suspicions, jealousies, ignorance, fatalism, passivity, and fears can play their part here, just as they can in any other human situation, but we need no longer use them as general explanations; they can be relegated to their proper place, enabling us to understand why sometimes they impede change and sometimes they do not.

Notes

1 This is a modified version of a paper presented at the Third International Congress of Africanists, Addis Ababa, 9–19 December 1973.
2 We are using 'peasant' here in a loose, general sense to designate the bulk of Africa's small agricultural producers whose production is mainly for household consumption but who also produce for cash. We do not intend this as a universal category applicable to all societies. See John Saul and Roger Woods, 'African peasantries', in Teodor Shanin, ed., *Peasants and Peasant Societies*, Penguin, 1971; and Sutti Ortiz, 'Reflections on the concept of "peasant culture" and peasant "cognitive systems" ', in Teodor Shanin, *op. cit.*
3 See, for example, Bert F. Hoselitz, 'Non-economic barriers to economic growth', *Economic Development and Cultural Change*, vol. I, no. 1, 1952, pp. 8–21; Robert Redfield, *Peasant Society and Culture*, University of Chicago Press, 1960; George M. Foster, 'Interpersonal relations in peasant society', *Human Organisation*, vol. XIX, no. 4, 1960, pp. 174–8; George M. Foster, *Traditional Cultures and the Impact of Technological Change*, Harper & Row, 1962; George M. Foster, 'Peasant society and the image of limited good', *American Anthropologist*, vol. LXVII, 1965, pp. 293–315; David McClelland, *The Achieving Society*, Free Press, 1961. For an example of a study involving fieldwork in Africa see Robert A. LeVine, *Dreams and Deeds: Achievement Motivation in Nigeria*, University of Chicago Press, 1961.
4 See Sutti Ortiz, 'The human factor in social planning in Latin America', and Raymond Apthorpe, 'African rural development planning and conception of the human factor', in R. Apthorpe, ed., *People, Planning and Development Studies*, Cass, 1970; R. Green and S. Hymer, 'Cocoa in the Gold Coast: a study in the relations between African farmers and agricultural experts', *Journal of Economic History*, vol. XXVI, no. 3, 1966, pp. 299–319; Clifton Wharton, 'Risk, uncertainty and the subsistence farmer', in George Dalton, ed., *Economic Development and Social Change*, Natural History Press, 1971; C. Davis Fogg, 'Smallholder agriculture in Eastern Nigeria', in George Dalton, ed.,

1971, *op. cit.*; and Frantz Fanon, *A Dying Colonialism*, Penguin, 1970.

5 See Polly Hill, *Migrant Cocoa Farmers of Southern Ghana*, Cambridge University Press, 1963; Polly Hill, *Studies in Rural Capitalism in West Africa*, Cambridge University Press, 1970; and Edwin Dean, *The Supply Responses of African Farmers*, North-Holland Publishing Co., 1966. We have not included here those anthropologists who have been directly concerned with the transformation of the relations of production.

6 Raymond Apthorpe, 'Peasants and planistrators in eastern Africa 1960–1970', mimeo, Paper to the Conference of the Association of Social Anthropologists, Oxford, June 1973.

7 Kusum Nair, *Blossoms in the Dust*, Duckworth, 1961.

8 Samir Amin, 'Underdevelopment and dependence in Black Africa—origins and contemporary forms', *Journal of Modern African Studies*, vol. X, no. 4, 1972, pp. 503–29.

9 See the discussion in Claude Meillassoux, 'From reproduction to production: a Marxist approach to economic anthropology', *Economy and Society*, vol. I, no. 1, 1972, pp. 93–105, and Ronald Frankenberg, 'Economic anthropology: an anthropologist's view', in Raymond Firth, ed., *Themes in Economic Anthropology*, Tavistock, 1967.

10 Raymond Apthorpe, 'Regional development and social reform', *The Philippine Educational Forum*, December 1973, pp. 5–17.

11 See, for example, Daniel Lerner, *The Passsing of Traditional Society*, Free Press, 1964; S. N. Eisenstadt, 'Social change and modernisation in African societies south of the Sahara', *Cahiers d'Études Africaines*, vol. V, no. 3, 1965, pp. 453–71; Joseph R. Gusfield, 'Tradition and modernity in India: misplaced polarities in the study of social change', *American Journal of Sociology*, vol. LXXII, 1966, pp. 351–62; John G. Kennedy, 'Peasant society and the image of limited good: a critique', *American Anthropologist*, vol. LXVII, no. 5, 1966, pp. 1212–25; Stephen Piker, 'The image of limited good: comments on an exercise in description and interpretation', *American Anthropologist*, vol. LXVIII, no. 5, 1966, pp. 1202–11; and Dov Weintraub, 'Traditions and development: another look at some still unresolved problems', *Rural Sociology*, vol. XXXVII, no. 4, 1972, pp. 578–90. Alternative views derived from setting sociology in a broader context have come, for example, from A. G. Frank, 'Sociology of development and underdevelopment of sociology', in A. G. Frank, *Latin America: Underdevelopment or Revolution*, Monthly Review Press, 1969; and Robert Rhodes, 'The disguised conservatism in evolutionary development theory', *Science and Society*, vol. XXXII, 1968, pp. 383–412.

12 Colin Turnbull, *Wayward Servants: The Two Worlds of the African Pygmies*, Eyre & Spottiswoode, 1966.

13 P. H. Gulliver, 'The conservative commitment in northern Tanzania: The Arusha and Masai', in Gulliver, *Tradition and Transition in East Africa*, Routledge & Kegan Paul, 1969.

14 Michael Lipton, 'Should reasonable farmers respond to price changes?', *Modern Asian Studies*, vol. I, no. 1, 1966, pp. 95–9. For a more

extensive discussion see C. J. Doyle, 'Productivity, technical change and the peasant producer: a profile of the African cultivator', Institute of Agricultural Economics, Oxford, mimeo, 1973.

15 See, for example, Dean, 1966, *op. cit.*; Fogg, 1965, *op. cit.* and Wharton, 1971, *op. cit.*

16 See, for example, Hill, 1963, *op. cit.* and Green and Hymer, 1966, *op. cit.*

17 A particularly clear discussion can be found in Percy Cohen, 'Economic analysis and economic man: some comments on a controversy', in Raymond Firth, ed., 1967, *op. cit.*

18 Everett Rogers, *Modernization Among Peasants*, Holt, Rinehart & Winston, 1969, p. 40. Footnotes to Rogers's quotation indicate the sources from which he derives his generalizations.

19 See, for example, M. A. Jaspan, 'Communal hostility to imposed social changes in South Africa', in George Dalton, ed., 1971, *op. cit.*

20 But see, for an example of contemporary French Marxist writing on this issue, Pierre-Philippe Rey, *Colonialisme, Néo-Colonialisme et Transition au Capitalisme*, Maspero, 1971.

21 For historical accounts see Samir Amin, 1972, *op. cit.*; Basil Davidson, *Old Africa Rediscovered*, Longman, 1970; Walter Rodney, *How Europe Underdeveloped Africa*, Tanzania Publishing House/Bogle-L'Ouverture, 1972; A. G. Hopkins, *An Economic History of West Africa*, Longman, 1973, and their bibliographies.

22 Frankenberg, 1967, *op. cit.*; and Meillassoux, 1972, *op. cit.*

23 George Homans, 'A life of synthesis', in Irving Horowitz, ed., *Sociological Self Images*, Pergamon, 1970.

24 Samir Amin, *Neo-Colonialism in West Africa*, Penguin, 1973.

25 For two recent analyses see Amin, 1972, *op. cit.*, and Arghiri Emmanuel, *Unequal Exchange*, New Left Books, 1972.

26 Tom Kemp, 'The Marxist theory of imperialism', in Roger Owen and Bob Sutcliffe, eds, *Studies in the Theory of Imperialism*, Longman, 1972.

27 George Foster, A second look at limited good', *Anthropological Quarterly*, vol. XLV, no. 2, 1972, pp. 57–64.

28 George Homans, 1970, *op. cit.*

7 Rice, politics and development in Guyana[1]
Eric R. Hanley

Guyana, formerly British Guiana and earlier still the site of Raleigh's El Dorado, lies on the north-east coast of South America between Venezuela and Surinam. It is a country almost exactly the same size as Britain, but with a population of only 750,000 densely settled on the coastal plain. 'The Land of Six Peoples', with its complex ethnic and racial mix of African, East Indian, Chinese, Portuguese, British, and Amerindian, is the outcome of an unsettled colonial history and the continuing search for ways of exploiting its rich potential as a sugar-producing area. It is sugar more than anything else which has made Guyana what it is today, having created the population as a labour supply, completely altered the coastal environment to lay out estates, dominated the country's economy and often had a major and decisive say in political decisions, all of which was aimed at maintaining a convenient supply of cheap labour available for the seasonal tasks of sugar planting. Until the Second World War sugar accounted for some 70 per cent of the country's gross exports and this was still more than 50 per cent by the 1960s.[2]

This domination by 'King Sugar' has had a number of serious consequences for Guyanese society, as for all such 'plantation societies'.[3] It has led to the institutionalization of a system of paternalistic domination, the development of a dependence psychology amongst the population, and the strange combination of cultural assimilation combined with a system of racial and ethnic stratification. The planter class and their latter-day counterparts were able to effectively prevent any serious attempt to exploit the interior, and where this could not be avoided they bought themselves a major stake in the enterprise, as with balata (wild rubber) and cattle ranching. The economy came to be largely controlled by a small number of large firms, and continues to be so today. The most important of these is Bookers, which is itself part of a large international organization with interests throughout the Caribbean and Africa, controlling all but two of the country's sugar estates, the largest store in Georgetown, a shipping line, rum distilleries, a drug house, cattle ranches and several agencies importing agricultural machinery and motor vehicles. From this is derived the old joke about the country being 'Bookers Guiana'. Of this traditional situation Henfrey has recently commented, 'To describe this structure as underdevelopment is an over-simplification. Rather it was a highly developed system of stagnation, tailored to foreign interests.'[4]

In recent years the country's dependence on sugar for most of its export earnings has been reduced by the growth of the bauxite industry. This is centred on Mackenzie some sixty miles up the Demerara River, although there is also a smaller operation on the Berbice River owned by Reynold's Metals of the USA. Until 1971 the Mackenzie operation was owned and controlled by the Demerara Bauxite Company (DEMBA), an offshoot of the Aluminium Company of Canada. In 1971, after an abortive series of discussions over increased government participation, DEMBA was nationalized by the Guyana Government and became GUYBAU. DEMBA's operations had all the characteristics of a company town in the tropics, with a history of strict racial and social segregation and comparatively little interest in the welfare of the mass of its employees.[5] By 1969 bauxite contributed 26 per cent of gross exports and combined with sugar accounted for some 62 per cent of such exports.[6]

In this situation heavy with the domination of foreign multinational organizations, I am here concerned with what is the third major export industry in Guyana, the rice industry. In many ways it is in sharp contrast to the two major ones and yet equally well it is very closely connected with them. Its contribution to exports is much smaller, approximately 10–12 per cent, and is organized on a quite different basis in that it is wholly owned by Guyanese and for the most part relies on small-scale peasant farmers for its production. It has, however, an importance and significance within the society beyond its purely economic one, for it is often claimed to have the largest workforce of any industry, through family labour and rural underemployment. The Rice Producers' Association claim that there are some 45,000 families engaged in the industry.[7] Another estimate puts the number of jobs in the rice industry at 12,000,[8] which compares favourably with the 17,000 or so employed in the sugar industry. The rice industry has also been one of the fastest growing sectors of the economy since the war and has featured prominently in development plans and in the often very heated debates of Guyanese politics.

The Frank model

It is in this situation that the central interest of this paper lies, for the industry has undergone a good deal of 'development' in the past two decades, and yet it has not all been a happy experience and the farmers today do not feel they are much better off. I propose to examine this experience in an attempt to determine the reasons for this disenchantment, and in particular to what extent this is connected with the heavy involvement of large multinational corporations in the Guyanese economy. In this latter respect I should like to consider the applicability of the Andre Gunder Frank model to this situation.[9]

In some ways the Frank model has some difficulty in dealing with situations like the Guyanese rice industry. First of all there are none of the large expatriate firms so often associated with this form of analysis, for the whole of the industry is owned and controlled by Guyanese. Furthermore, the vast majority of the rice exported from the country is sold to the West Indies through agreements and very little is sold on the open market, so that there is not really any question of the viability of the industry being determined on metropolitan commodity markets. During the whole of the post-war period all trading in rice, either for local consumption or for export, has been entirely under the control of the Guyana Rice Marketing Board, who have a legal monopoly of all such trading. This public body is responsible for the regulation of the industry and thus determines in the main what profits are made and by whom, with the result that these have either been made by the farmers in terms of higher purchase prices paid by the Board, or by other government organizations within the industry whose losses have been offset by the Board's profits. The position of peasants and workers under such a system of national regulation is something which is not covered in the Frank model, and is a significant shortcoming since there are many other such systems working in the Third World.

The overall regulation of the industry brings us to another shortcoming in Frank's model: precisely what he means by capitalism and the capitalist mode of production. He has been criticized for not making this clear and has been attacked by Laclau[10] for using a market-orientated definition of capitalism rather than one based on a mode of production. For Laclau, 'the fundamental economic relationship of capitalism is constituted by the free labourer's sale of his labour-power, whose necessary precondition is the loss by the direct producer of ownership of the means of producing.'[11] This is obviously correct if one is using a Marxist interpretation, as both Frank and Laclau claim to be doing. However, it is less so in the case of the Guyana rice industry, where the bulk of the production

133

is obtained from peasant farmers normally using family labour and often owning such major items of productive equipment as tractors and bulls. Land can be rented, leased, or often owned outright by the farmer. In such a situation Laclau's definition makes them non-capitalist, but at the same time they are part of the international commodity-producing system, since they are growing rice almost entirely for export. Furthermore, they are obliged to sell to a monopolistic agency, the Rice Marketing Board, which is interested in maximizing its profits. The fact that the Board sells most of its rice under contract to neighbouring governments does not lessen its interest in profits, for its continued aim since the war has been to balance a protected market in the West Indies with obtaining the highest possible price against the continued complaints of the region's governments.

Guyana is by no means alone in having a situation in which participation in the world capitalist system has taken place without the development of a proletariat, with the labour migration system throughout central, eastern and southern Africa and the seasonal work on New World plantations being but two examples, and there are many others. It would thus seem that Frank's market orientation is in some ways justified, though for the wrong reasons. There is, therefore, an apparent need for more clarification of what we mean by modes of production and in particular of how the capitalist and non-capitalist modes are articulated.

Frank's model has certain other attractions for us in the Guyanese situation. Although the Frank model of metropolitan/satellite re-lationships through the medium of the large capitalist organization is not directly present in the industry, it has made its presence felt indirectly. For, as will be discussed later, the industry has undergone a process of rapid mechanization in the last decade or so, and almost all of this equipment and the spares required to maintain it has been supplied through agencies owned by the two largest sugar com-panies. The cost to the industry for this dependence on imported technology has become very great, and with the official encourage-ment for farmers to be more sophisticated in their use of such things as fertilizers, weedkillers, and pesticides, etc., dependence on the importation of these products will increase. Although the govern-ment agencies offer a subsidized supply of fertilizer and chemicals the supply is often erratic and many farmers prefer to buy from the importing agency where stocks are readily available. Another reason for the attractiveness of the Frank model in this situation is that Guyana was until recently a colony and has less than two decades experience of universal adult suffrage. As will be considered again later, the origins of the industry's recent development had its roots firmly in the imperial system's concept of West Indian development, and most of the significant programmes were implemented under overall colonial supervision. It is in this context that we have to consider the role of local political factors and in particular the scope for political manoeuvre available to the various Jagan administrations during the 1950s and 1960s. I should like to suggest that it is in this area that we can see the relevance of the Frank model, though in a somewhat modified form.

Growth of the rice industry

The coastal plain is flat and low lying, being up to four feet below high water mark in places, which necessitates extensive sea defences if the land is to be farmed. The coast is some 300 miles long and the plain varies in depth from about ten miles in the north-west to some 40 miles in the south-east. Despite the sea defences there is a constant process of erosion, which undermines them, and accretion, which blocks the gravitation drainage outfalls. The plain is cut into several sections by five large rivers, none of which is bridged near the coast, and indeed the Essequibo is so wide as to have several inhabited islands in its mouth. The first Dutch settlements were several miles up the rivers and it was not until the extensive civil engineering works necessary for the draining of the coast lands had been completed that agriculture was possible there.

Adequate water control is essential for successful agriculture on the coast, for not only has the sea water to be kept out but also there has to be protection from the results of rain in the interior which threatens to flood the cultivation from the rear. Despite the adequate annual rainfall of 80–120 inches, there is also the converse problem of drought, for the rainfall can be erratic as well as extreme. It is therefore necessary to have some system of water conservancy if agriculture is to be efficient.

The most adequate solution to these problems has resulted in a system which has a strong sea wall at the front of the cultivation and a 'back dam' at the rear, which also often acts as a retaining wall for a water conservancy. From this the water is led through the cultivated land by a complex system of canals and sluices with cut-offs to distribute the water throughout the cultivation equally. Finally it drains into the sea through a large sluice or 'koker'. All these systems have to be maintained and opened and closed at the appropriate time for the overall system to work.

Effective agriculture in Guyana is therefore heavily dependent on a very expensive system of land preparation, which has been one of the main forces behind the consolidation of the sugar estates into a small number of large units. For the peasant farmer this poses great problems of both expense and organization, so that the history of this activity is one of repeated failures. Even today the situation is not a very satisfactory one, for in many areas there is no proper sea defence and the front lands are constantly washed by the sea, whilst in others there is no proper drainage or irrigation so that farmers have to rely on rainfall for water supplies and hope that this will be neither too little nor too much. In a good year the land will yield a high return, often with little effort and few inputs, but in a bad one there can be sudden disaster.

In general the most critical resource for sugar in the West Indies has been labour and the history of the industry is one of a continuing attempt to ensure its supply. The first real solution was of course slavery, but with the ending of this and the short period of 'apprenticeship' in the British West Indies in 1838 the planters of Guyana were faced with an acute problem, as were those in several of the islands, as the freed slaves refused to work on the plantations and attempted to establish peasant farming communities instead. The effective answer was found by Gladstone's father and other planters in Guyana in indentured labour from India. Between 1838 and 1917 some 239,000 immigrants were brought to Guyana, whilst some 75,000 returned.[12] The descendants of these immigrants now constitute more than half of the country's population.

Although rice has been grown in Guyana since the eighteenth century, it is the East Indians who have done most to develop it into a major industry and they continue to dominate the industry today. As Beckford and Mandle have pointed out[13] it is the aim of the plantation economy to have a large labour force readily available for seasonal work, and thus the planters were for a long time hostile to the idea of labourers planting rice. But with the depression which affected the sugar industry at the end of the nineteenth century the movement off the estates could not be prevented and rice farming became widespread, although it was not until 1917 that the industry was able to supply the needs of the whole country. The first great fillip to the industry came with the First World War, when supplies to the West Indies from the Far East were cut off, and producers and merchants rushed to make profits out of the export of rice. The rush was so frantic that the supply was severely overstrained and local prices shot up, with the result that the Governor temporarily banned the export of rice. After the war the shortages from the Far East continued and the price and output remained high. But in the 1920s the industry in the Far East recovered and the West Indies returned to their traditional suppliers, so that the export price of Guyanese rice plummeted to an all-time low in 1933. Indeed it was not until 1951 that the previous peak price of 1920 was again equalled.

By this time the pattern of the industry had become established and this is basically the way in which it operates today, with small peasant farmers planting one or more plots totalling little more than five acres and with a few farmers planting much larger acreages. In some areas where drainage and irrigation is good it is possible to plant two crops per year, although some 90 per cent of the total output is obtained from the main autumn crop. Most farmers are dependent on unpaid family labour and it has been suggested that this was the crucial element which made rice farming profitable.[14] Until recently equipment was simple, with bulls used for ploughing and dragging, hand tools and perhaps a small punt for travel in the wet season. In most cases seed was initially sown in a small nursery plot on the edge of the rice bed and when fully established was transplanted into the field itself by hand. Harvesting was by hand using a grass knife and the co-operative assistance of kin and neighbours. The bundles of cut paddy were dragged to the flat piece of land at the edge of the field and 'mashed' or threshed by bulls trampling on them. The grains were then bagged and transported to one of the small mills in the area where they were turned into 'brown' or parboiled rice.

Up till this time the industry had grown to what it was very much by its own efforts, and had at its pre-war peak contributed 11 per cent of gross exports with comparatively little assistance and regulation on the part of government, although the Board of Agriculture had tried to improve the quality of rice planted. With the advent of the Second World War the industry entered a crucial phase which affected its whole future, as for the first time it was used by the colonial administration as a major feature in its plans to obtain as much contribution to the war effort as possible. Here two developments are of paramount importance: the establishment of the Rice Marketing Board as the sole purchasing agent for all rice produced in the country, and the introduction of large-scale mechanized rice farming on an experimental basis in an area called, appropriately, Burma.

The RMB was set up to avoid the wild speculation which had occurred in the last war, and it has continued in its role of sole buyer and seller of rice until today. The Board buys rice and pays according to the grade. The documentation is handled by the miller and where necessary any fees and loans due to him are removed before payment is forwarded to the farmer. The rice is then blended into export grades and grades for local sale and shipped accordingly. Compared with other government agencies in the industry it has been noticeably successful.

The Mahaicony–Abary Rice Development Scheme covered some 11,000 acres and was established on the basis of mechanized and extensive cultivation. It produced quite substantial amounts of rice for the war effort, though as a scheme it had a lot of organizational problems. In 1952 it was incorporated into the Rice Development Company (RDC) and included the large central mill which was rebuilt at Abary. As R. T. Smith says, 'It has done good work of an experimental nature, and has provided some services such as machinery hire and milling facilities to farmers in the area. As a commercial venture it has been a total failure.'[15] The RDC has now become the Guyana Rice Corporation, but continues to be a financial embarrassment to the government. The one indisputable achievement of the RDC was to demonstrate that mechanized rice cultivation was possible in Guyana, and this has had far-reaching consequences for the industry. However, this policy was implemented by the colonial administration in the light of the urgent needs of the war situation without any proper evaluation of the wider implications and long-term effects it might have. It showed a rather naïve faith in the effectiveness of machines in agriculture, and although the mechanized cultivation aspect showed some return, the complete failure of the same approach applied to the large-scale mill illustrates how wildly speculative the policy really was.

During the war the acreage under cultivation increased by 50 per cent and the amount of rice exported doubled. However, apart from the Mahaicony–Abary Rice Development Scheme this was all achieved through traditional practices of hand cultivation. After the war, the Development Plan for the Colony contained several schemes for large-scale empoldering of land which would be suitable for the expansion of rice cultivation, and some of these have come to fruition, though there are several which still await implementation.

Another planned development of great consequence to the industry in the post-war situation was the negotiation in 1946 of a five-year agreement by the RMB to supply most of the British West Indian islands with rice at fixed prices. Fixed prices proved to be a mistake, and with the rising costs of the post-war situation the Guyanese farmers did not do well, and acreage and exports fell, despite frantic efforts to get the other territories to agree to at least a temporary increase in price, which only Trinidad and Barbados accepted reluctantly. However, the principle had been accepted that where possible Guyana should be the sole supplier of rice to the British West Indies.[16] There seems little doubt that this provision of a protected market on its doorstep was a major factor in the subsequent development of the industry. This concession appears to have been made because of the apparent inability of the region's traditional Far Eastern suppliers to meet their pre-war commitments, and is in sharp contrast to the way in which the industry was treated after the First World War. It was now presumably more convenient for the colonial power to allow the growth of the local industry.

By 1950 the acreage under cultivation had returned to its war-time level, and during the 1950s it more than doubled. At the same time the export price doubled, the price paid to farmers doubled and the total output of rice almost doubled[17] as Guyana tried to ride the post-war boom in food prices with its new-found guaranteed market and lack of competition.

The developments during this decade transformed the industry into what it is today and will have to be examined in more detail. One of the most striking factors is the very rapid expansion of the acreage under cultivation and here the activities of the government are very relevant. Under the Ten Year Plan for Development and Welfare 1947–56 work was started on the Courantyne Drainage and Irrigation Project, which included the Black Bush Polder Scheme which came to feature so much in the agricultural and political life of the country during the coming decade. Black Bush contained over 30,000 acres, of which 27,000 were to be devoted to rice, and came into full operation only in the early 1960s. Another scheme started in the Ten Year Plan was the Boeraserie Conservancy Scheme which provided water supply for sugar estates as well as land settlement schemes and added over 26,000 acres of rice land. Later schemes which came to fruition in the 1950s and early 1960s were Tapacuma (30,000 rice acres), Vergenoegen (2,000 rice acres), Mara (1,400 rice acres) and Garden of Eden (1,200 rice acres). Some of these schemes were drainage and irrigation projects, whilst others were specific land settlements, the most important of which was Black Bush. There are clear indications that a good deal of previously unused land was converted to rice throughout the 1950s and early 1960s without any assistance from government. Much of this land was either not well suited or well prepared for rice cultivation, as is borne out by the fact that despite this increase in acreage and a massive move to mechanized cultivation throughout the industry, the yield per acre has not risen at all, and in many areas it has in fact fallen.

During this period of growth the government did give a great deal of assistance to the rice industry in a variety of ways, and this was especially true during the two People's Progressive Party (PPP) governments, under the leadership of Dr Cheddi Jagan, between 1957 and 1964. More will be said about the reasons for this later, but in general terms, when the PPP returned to office in 1957 they not only increased the size of the development budget which they had inherited from G$91 million to G$102·5 million, but also increased the proportion allocated to agriculture from 27·5 to 33 per cent. Furthermore, when the plan was prematurely superseded in 1959, of the money actually spent to that date, some 42·8 per cent had gone to agriculture.[18] From early in the 1950s the RMB had provided a scheme whereby they guaranteed the loans made to farmers by importers for the sale of tractors and other equipment. This proved very popular, not least of all with the importers, who had a seller's market with all their risks covered. This is reflected in the figures for the importation of tractors, which averaged over 350 per year, whilst in 1960 the numbers were 777 and 783 respectively. Combine harvesters were also imported at the rate of 30 or so per year, though in 1960 alone the number was 128.[19] In 1965 Caffey and Efferson estimated that there were approximately 3,000 tractors farming some 240,000 acres, thus giving the not unreasonable figure of one tractor to eighty acres.[20] However, as I will show later, this allocation was not spread evenly throughout the country. From 1954 until 1960 the government also provided duty-free gasolene to agriculture, and the rice industry received the lion's share throughout, rising from 70 per cent in 1954 to 87 per cent in 1960.[21]

The British Guiana Development Programme 1960–4, drawn up by Mr Kenneth Berrill, laid quite explicit emphasis on the expansion of the rice industry as a major component of the Programme: 'the feature that needs comment here is that the expansion of farming in British Guiana in the next five years is heavily reliant on the expansion of rice acreage'.[22] Although, as has been mentioned above, a good deal of this expansion was by private initiative, the government's Land Settlement Schemes did play a significant part in the process, especially Black Bush Polder. This large scheme of some 30,000 acres or more was planned to contain three communities of homesteads for 1,586 families. Each of these would have leased to them 15 acres of rice land and 2 acres for a house lot and ground provisions. The total cost was estimated originally at some G$18·67 million, or approximately G$11,800 per family[23] although the final cost is reputed inevitably to have been higher than this. The scheme was intended to provide land for experienced farmers who needed to expand their activities but who could not do so in the area where they were living. Despres describes how whilst he was there the operation was turned into a political exercise, with the PPP taking five of the seven seats on the selection committee and using the scheme as a system of political patronage to loyal party members, who were overwhelmingly East Indian. Of the 3,300 applications received at the time he was in the area, less than 200 were from Afro-Guyanese, and only 3 of the 150 families settled so far were from this section of the society.[24] The pattern continued in later years, and the subject became a matter of major political controversy and has eventually passed into the country's political folklore.

The PPP now freely admits that the selection of settlers for the scheme was faulty, though not that this was due to political or racial bias, which leaves the fascinating problem of to what extent the central government's policy was administered in a partial manner locally. The lands were given overwhelmingly to landless Indians, many of whom had little or no interest in rice farming and the abuse of the overall system was extensive, with farmers subletting their land and living away from the scheme in many cases. The organization was very poor, and continues to be so, largely because of jobs being distributed by political patronage. The land preparation and harvesting is done through centralized machinery pools and there are many complaints of crop losses through machines failing to turn up at the right time and of machines standing idle for long periods awaiting repair.

The government also helped the rice farmer working privately owned land in a number of ways. Most important was the Rice Farmers Security of Tenure Ordinance of 1956 which established a scale of rents for different qualities of private estates, set a fixed profit margin, and an Assessment Committee system to regulate the rates. This prevented landowners from turning their tenants off the land at will. There were also expanded agricultural extension services, improved credit through credit co-operatives and machinery and equipment pools organized by the RMB and the Rice Producers' Association (RPA), which also received a subsidy from the RMB. The RPA had been recognized since 1946 and provided eight of the sixteen members of the RMB board, with the other eight being nominated by the Governor. In 1960 the PPP Government changed the structure of the Board so that the RPA provided eleven of the sixteen members, the remaining five being nominated by the Minister of Trade and Industry. The Board also now elected its own Chairman instead of having him nominated by the Governor. Thus for the first time the rice producers of Guyana had control of the most important body in the industry through the RPA. However, the RPA is controlled by the PPP, for since 1957 they have contested the RPA elections as a party and have continually won.

In 1965, after the PPP had lost power, the structure of the RMB was altered yet again, with the total membership being reduced to eleven, of which eight were nominated by the Ministry of Trade, and three by the RPA. This effectively removed control from the PPP/RPA and it is a frequent boast of PPP supporters that the best profits were made whilst the RPA had control of the Board and that with the advent of the PNC appointees there was a period of annual losses. The reasons for these losses will be discussed later, but one reason which has been advanced is that the PPP had encouraged the RMB to pay excessively high purchase prices to farmers. Certainly, as has been mentioned, the prices paid to farmers throughout the 1950s and early 1960s rose dramatically and it does seem that the RMB paid out as much as possible in purchase prices or assistance. In an extensive submission to the Rennison Committee on the rice industry in 1957, A. F. MacKenzie, the Director of Agriculture, stressed that he felt that the RMB was not sufficiently protected by reserves, pointing out that the G$1 million in these reserves was the same amount as when the RMB had been set up in 1946, despite the great increase in business since then. He indicated further that because of the low reserves the RMB frequently found itself at times of peak purchasing activity over-drawn to the extent of G$2 million.[25] His warning was apposite, for in 1964/5 as the result of a politically induced glut rather than a shortage, the RMB sustained losses of over G$4 million.

Problems of development

I have thus suggested that the period of the 1950s and early 1960s was an era of great expansion and development for the Guyana rice industry and the East Indian population who formed the bulk of those involved. This is closely related to the rising sense of East Indian political confidence as the country moved ahead under the firm control of 'their' party. But not everything in the industry's garden was lovely, and there were some very major problems loom-ing on the horizon.

As has been mentioned, the expansion of rice output was largely achieved by the expansion of the margin of cultivation and not by any improvement in productivity. As the Annual Report of the Department of Agriculture stated in 1960: 'The efficiency of paddy production leaves much room for improvement. Farmers have been paying more attention to increasing production by cultivating new lands than to securing higher yields per acre and a better quality of the crop.'[26]

This emphasis on extensive rather than intensive cultivation pro-duced a number of serious technical problems which still remain. First, because of the poor drainage and irrigation facilities on much of the new land it was not possible to practise the traditional form of Guyanese rice planting. Instead of transplanting young seedlings from a nursery plot or broadcasting germinated seed ('jarai') into a flooded field, which became a popular substitute for transplanting, the farmers on the new land had to go over to dry cultivation. This entails the broadcasting of the seed onto the dry land after plough-ing, where it awaits the arrival of sufficient rain to flood the field until it ultimately germinates. Obviously this is much more of a hit or miss process than the 'jarai' or transplanting methods and indeed the growth of the plants is very uneven. Since the land has no proper water control in the first place it is dependent on the rain as to whether the field is parched or flooded, though even in the latter case the farmer is often loth to remove excessive water in case he should be short later. In such situations it is not possible to practise very scientific farming, which is becoming more and more necessary with the introduction of more sophisticated breeds of plant.

In addition to the general problems of farming in such conditions, the expansion onto marginal land brought with it a number of other serious problems such as that of 'red rice'. This is a variety of wild rice which if not strictly controlled will quickly infest a field and seriously affect the quality of the crop. It is a sturdy plant which grows alongside the normal ones and is harvested with them, but it has a short grain and a great tendency to shatter in milling so that it produces a large number of broken grains. This not only lowers the grade of the rice but the broken grains soon discolour too, which lowers the grade even more. 'Red rice' is very much a product of extensive mechanical cultivation, for this form of cultivation is not able to use the traditional practices for its eradication, and there are as yet no chemical means of combating it. As early as 1957 the Rennison Committee stated:[27]

> The Committee were informed that the high incidence of 'red rice' in crops grown under mechanised conditions had focussed attention on the urgent need for research to devise a means for its eradication. . . . Indeed 'red rice' has now become a most serious and intractable problem.

By 1960 the situation in some places was very bad:[28]

> A survey was carried out by the Extension Staff of this Department in the main rice producing areas in order to assess the incidence of 'red rice'. The figures disclosed that in areas where dry cultivation has been practiced the incidence of 'red rice' had reached the enormous figure of up to 90% recorded in the Mahaica–Mahaicony area. In areas where wet cultivation was practiced and particularly with transplanted rice, 'red rice' was below 2% on the West Coast of Demerara and the Essequibo islands.

In some areas the problem became so acute that farmers suffered severe financial loss and stopped rice growing entirely. This represents one of the main reasons for the decline in acreage which has occurred in recent years.

Extensive rice cultivation was only possible through mechanization, and although this has brought great benefits to the industry and the farmers, it has also brought great problems. There was of course the inevitable one of the introduction of complex machinery into a developing country, with inexperienced operators breaking machines and inexperienced mechanics being unable to repair them, but this stage is effectively passed and these machines have come to be a fully accepted part of the normal farming process. A more serious and long-term problem has been that of farmers buying inappropriate equipment. In some ways this should have been short lived whilst farmers were unfamiliar with the new equipment and bought the wrong machine for their needs. Although this did inevitably happen, more seriously, farmers bought machines where it was doubtful if they needed them at all. There was a definite failure to recognize that there is a minimum level below which mechanized farming is not economic. As MacKenzie stated in his submission to the Rennison Committee in 1953:[29]

> A very arbitrary division can be drawn between mechanisation
> problems for the small farmer, that is a farmer with a farm
> of less than say twenty acres at the most. Under present
> conditions it is clear that to purchase mechanical equipment
> would not be in the best interests of the farmer. The capital cost
> of the normal sized tractors is far too high for the amount of
> work that the machines would be put to on that particular
> farm.

TABLE 7.1   *Increase in rice acreage and tractor ownership in a West Demerara community, 1956 and 1972*

	Overall rice acreage planted by villagers	No. of tractors owned by villagers
1956[30]	1470	7
1972	1588	73
Increase %	8	943

Yet this is precisely what happened. A tractor became not only a wonderful new tool for progressive farmers, but also a status symbol to have parked under their houses. And it was under the house that many of the tractors stayed for much of the time, as areas became so over-mechanized that there was not enough work for them to be used economically. As was mentioned before, the report of Caffey and Efferson presents a picture of an overall allocation of approximately one tractor for 80 acres, which they seem to find satisfactory. However, this global statistic covers a situation of a very unbalanced distribution. The figures in Table 7.1 relate to a community on the west coast of Demerara which is considered to be a highly efficient rice producer. Unfortunately this situation is not accounted for by an alteration in the land holding pattern, for the average acreage per family remains approximately what it was in 1956 (6·5 acres) and the number of families planting rice in the community has gone up by almost the same amount as the total acreage (7·5 and 8 per cent respectively).

In his submission to the Rennison Committee in 1957 the Director of Agriculture felt that tractors could not be economical if used for less than 800 hours per year. This he felt represented about 100 acres to be worked by each machine. David suggests that an economic level is 1,000 hours of work per machine per year and concludes that even on a very optimistic estimation it is not possible for tractors in the Guyanese situation to work for more than 700–750 hours per year.[31] In the West Demerara community referred to above, the average machine has 21·75 acres to plough per crop or 43·5 per year. Although the actual distribution varies, it is in the vast majority of

TABLE 7.2 *Increase in purchase price of rice and cost of tractors, 1956 and 1972*

	Purchase price of 180 lb. bag of extra no. 1 rice*	Massey-Ferguson small tractor
1956	G$ 16·90	G$ 3,500
1972	G$ 18·75	G$ 8,500
Increase %	11	143

*This is a high grade which farmers in West Demerara commonly achieve; 17·7 per cent of the RMB's total purchases were of this grade in 1969/70.

cases still well below the level of 100 acres per machine referred to in the Rennison Committee report.

Farmers throughout the Guyanese rice industry are therefore heavily committed to a highly mechanized form of farming based on very dubious economic justification, and recent trends in the rice industry at both the national and international level have exposed this weakness. The income of farmers in the early 1950s was based on production using family labour, and in a country with both a rapidly growing population and high unemployment the opportunity cost of this labour was low. Now with the move over to mechanized cultivation farmers are committed to using a much more expensive labour substitute, over the price of which they have no control. With rising costs and latterly the high rate of inflation in Western industrial countries, the effect on primary producing industries, like the rice industry, which are dependent on imported machinery, has been severe, as can be seen in Table 7.2.

Whilst prices paid to farmers continued to rise and there were fairly good yields coming from the new lands being taken up, this dependency situation was hidden or ignored. However, with the growth of the red rice problem, and as the other problems associated with poor land preparation and water control, such as weed and bug infestation, became more apparent the full extent of the industry's difficulties were revealed. This is well illustrated by the declining yield per acre, which fell as a national average from 15·3 bags (140 lb.) per acre in 1959/60 to an all-time low of 9·6 bags per acre in 1968/9.[32] There has been a slight recovery from then as a result of extensive government campaigns, though the situation is far from good. As with the case of the tractor population the local distribution can be quite different to the national picture, and in intensive farming areas such as West Demerara and Essequibo the yields are frequently more than twice the national average, with 20–5 bags (140 lb.) per acre common. This points out how at the lowest level the yields per acre are abysmally low.

'Red rice' and the other infestations not only lower the yield per acre but they also lower the quality of rice produced, and in this area too the Guyanese rice industry has faced some major problems in recent years. As described previously, most commonly rice is milled near to where it is grown and in a single-stage huller. These machines are not capable of separating out the various constituents of the paddy and are not capable of milling white rice. This requires the much more complex and expensive multi-stage mill, and there are increasing numbers of these. In addition the traditional drying facilities of a concrete floor and sunshine are very rudimentary and very erratic, so that a farmer often watches his crop decline in quality as it is locked in the store, or worse still on the concrete, by wet weather. The practices involved in the soaking of the paddy prior to steaming also apparently leave much to be desired as they are usually held responsible for the offensive odour which Guyanese rice is widely considered to have. Within the traditional market of the West Indies this has not mattered too much in the past, but for the future this could make a considerable difference and many commentators have pointed to the importance of improving quality throughout the industry. As Caffey and Efferson said in 1965:[33]

All of this rice was medium-grain, off-white parboiled rice
which due to the large East Indian population of both British
Guiana and the islands of the West Indies and to long-term
consumption habits was preferred, or at least accepted
without objections by the mass of the consumers in the region.

When production expanded beyond this level, however, other
world export markets were not interested in medium-grain,

146

medium-quality, off-white, red-rice contaminated parboiled rice. Outside of Asia, mostly India, there is little demand for medium-grain, medium-quality parboiled rice. The countries importing rice and paying hard currency for their imports are demanding mostly long-grain, high-quality raw white rice, and, long-grain, high-quality parboiled rice. There is also some export demand for medium-grain, high-quality raw white rice. The rice now stored in the warehouses throughout British Guiana does not fit these specifications.

The milling section of the industry has frequently been singled out as an area where immediate improvements could be made to the overall benefit of the industry. The Rennison Committee made its views on the current state of mills in the country known quite clearly, and in doing so echoed the views of almost all the experts who had examined the problem till then, and some who were to follow:[34]

> The committee found the present organisation of the milling processes of the Industry unsatisfactory and set themselves the vital task of trying to find a practicable solution for the rationalisation of milling. . . . At the outset all members unanimously agreed that while single-stage huller-type mills had played their part in the development of the Industry, they were now out of date and unsuited to any area which was producing rice as a market crop. The immediate objective of the Industry must be to replace single-stage milling throughout the country.

In 1957, when this was written, there were 206 private mills in the country, with very few multi-stage mills apart from the RDC ones. The figures for 1970 are 123 single-stage mills (62 per cent) and 76 multi-stage mills (38 per cent).[35] Thus the single-stage huller, 'unsuited to any area which was producing rice as a market crop', is still the predominant method of processing: the modernization and rationalization of this section of the industry still has a long way to go. This uneven development in which the expansion of production, with its simple emphasis on mechanization and acreage extension, at the expense of the more capital-intensive milling improvements needed, is another example of the ways in which easy strategies were followed rather than balanced development.

The picture which I have been trying to present so far is of an industry which grew initially out of a set of historical circumstances centring round indentured labour from India and the opportunities which these labourers found as they moved out of the plantation environment, which only received extensive government recognition with the demands of a war-time situation. It then became involved in the development process which followed the ending of hostilities and tried as best it could to reap the benefits of the post-war shortages and the new market opportunities which lay on its doorstep. In doing so it took a number of easy options which paid off at the time but which turned out to have unfortunate long-term consequences. In the process it attracted a good deal of government assistance of both a direct and indirect nature and featured prominently in the plans of both development economists and local politicians.

Mention has already been made of how the PPP Government between 1957 and 1964 gave a good deal of assistance to the rice industry and in particular to the East Indian participants in it. These political factors reached their high point in the years from 1961 to 1963 when large amounts of rice were sold to Cuba at an artificially high price. In 1964 the PPP Government was brought down after a long and bitter campaign by the opposition parties and their allies, and which brought the country to the verge of civil war.

The Cuban trade was immediately stopped by the new People's National Congress/United Force Government, with the result that there were some 60,000 tons of rice which could not be disposed of. This had eventually to be sold at disastrously low prices and largely accounts for the massive loss of more than G\$4 million which the RMB sustained in 1964/5 and of G\$2·8 million in 1965/6.[36] Largely as a result of this situation the RMB cut its purchase prices in 1966 by between 20 and 27 per cent. This reversed the whole trend of the previous decade and a half and was not only highly unpopular with the farmers but was also inevitably seen by them and others in a political light as a way of getting back at the supporters of the PPP. However, there appears to have been a good deal of justification for the reduction on the general grounds of international prices, for as Caffey and Efferson pointed out in 1965:[37]

> For the average grade, No. 1, the support price was BWI\$ 9.00 per 180-pound bag in 1950, was increased to BWI\$ 16.00 in 1955, further increased to BWI\$ 17.60 in 1960, and has been maintained at BWI\$ 18.95 in 1964 and 1965. . . . At this support level, British Guiana rice is being supported at the same level as United States rice of much higher quality and from 20 to 25 per cent above the world price level for rice of equivalent quality.

At the same time the government altered the composition of the RMB to take control from the RPA and put it more firmly in its own hands. For the rice farmers of Guyana the honeymoon was over, as consequences of decisions, both public and private, taken for their short-term benefit, both political and economic, came home to roost.

The years since then have been difficult ones for both the government in dealing with the rice industry, and for the farmers themselves as they are increasingly squeezed between rising production costs and falling income. The farmers generally see the situation in political and racial terms with a strong feeling that they are being cheated and exploited and express a constant longing for a return to the halcyon days of yesteryear, of which the Cuban market is the perennial symbol.

For its part the government is now coming round to a concerted programme to get the industry on a reasonable footing, though this has yet to bear full fruit; it is based on an attempt to improve the quality of the rice produced by planting improved varieties which can be made into profitable white rice of good quality whilst also improving the processing operations in both the mills and the RMB, The variety chosen, Starbonnet, is an American breed which requires expensive fertilization and careful husbandry, so that it cannot be grown in all areas. With increasing supplies of the new variety coming in, combined with greatly improved equipment at the RMB, there is a prospect of increasing penetration into lucrative packaged rice markets in the Caribbean and elsewhere. There is also a policy for providing loans and subsidies to farmers with a need to improve their equipment or facilities to enable them to grow the new variety, rather than have large overall price increases, although this programme has largely become bogged down in local political disputes amongst a welter of accusations of favouritism and exploitation. But on the whole the total policy might just succeed in putting the industry on a viable economic base at last.

Conclusions

The question which we must now face is how the Frank model can help us to understand these events. As I mentioned earlier there are a number of ways in which this model does not fit the situation in the rice industry, and several of the model's shortcomings in dealing with such situations were mentioned. However, there are two factors in the Guyanese situation which make it highly relevant, and these are the degree of expatriate business control of the economy, especially in the sugar and bauxite industries, and the nature of local political autonomy under colonialism during the 1950s and 1960s.

Although the large expatriate firms do not participate directly in the rice industry, apart from their significance as suppliers of farm equipment, spares and chemicals, they nevertheless have a heavily dominant role in all sectors of the economy and are largely responsible for export earnings. This situation had long been noted and was strongly resented by many radical thinkers. As a party with socialist aims and led by an avowed Marxist, the PPP had long had the nationalization of the sugar and bauxite industries as one of its major policies. In 1953 the PPP under Jagan formed the first popularly elected government of the colony under a new constitution: after four months of office they were removed by the British Government and the constitution suspended amongst charges of a Communist takeover plot. From 1953 until 1957 there was an appointed interim government.

This experience had a traumatic effect on the PPP, and when they were again elected to office in 1957 in the first elections since the suspension of the constitution, they had learned the lesson of the dangers of trying to hasten too quickly under a colonial administration.[38] Jagan realized that, in view of the British reaction to the relatively mild steps he had taken in 1953, any attempt to tackle the expatriate firms in the sugar and bauxite industries would inevitably lead to a head-on clash and another constitutional crisis. He and his party were unlikely to survive such an experience a second time, and so were faced with the dilemma of how to achieve any real benefit and progress for the country under their administration. The rice industry was an obvious choice which offered a number of distinct advantages:

(1) It was likely that any stimulation or assistance to the industry would bring a return, since the industry was riding a world boom and had a guaranteed market on its doorstep.

(2) The industry could be helped by a number of drainage schemes which were already in the planning pipeline. As an additional benefit the PPP reaped the credit for bringing several of them to fruition, although planning had started some time before.

(3) Here was a way of channelling more development into the rural areas and away from the urban areas and the sugar estates.

(4) The rice industry was mainly worked by East Indians, who were overwhelmingly PPP supporters, and this would be a way of rewarding them for their support. In view of the racial cleavages of Guyana's social and political system, it is easy to see Jagan as a simple machine politician in this respect cynically rewarding his followers. However, a number of commentators feel this is misleading.[39] Undoubtedly reward to supporters was a major factor, but not the overwhelming one that it might appear to be.

(5) Perhaps most important of all, it was a sector of the economy in which there were no expatriate domination nor direct involvement of the colonial government. Furthermore it was an area controlled and regulated by the Guyana Government through

the RMB and whose markets were obtained preferentially through government negotiation.

In short it was the only major area of the economy where the government could have a large measure of unhampered control and with a real prospect that in the short term there would be benefits and improvements which could be held to be the outcome of government policy. It was the only way in which anything significant could be done to the economy without offending the entrenched interests of the expatriate firms in the other major industries and their colonial protectors. It must have been a politically attractive opportunity.

Economically something needed to be done, since the economy's rate of growth, especially during the period of the interim government, had been depressingly slow and it is doubtful if it kept pace with the rapidly expanding population.[40] In such a situation the economic justification for placing emphasis on the expansion of the rice industry did make some sense, for as Brewster has pointed out, the periods of growth for rice were the converse of those of the rest of the economy during this time.[41] Politically too the Jagan government's rice policy had received recognition for what it attempted to do. The New World Associates have described the development of the rice industry as the first breakthrough for Guyana from the 'tyranny' of the sugar plantations.[42]

This, therefore, is how I see the unsettled and in some ways unhappy recent history of the development of the Guyanese rice industry and the application of the Frank model; an application at one remove. It is the situation of a radical nationalist political party attempting to make innovations and changes in a situation of entrenched expatriate corporate domination of the economy and trying to keep within the rules of the colonial system. The outcome was a series of changes which brought short-term benefits, but in the long term had unfortunate consequences. It is a pattern which could well be repeated throughout the Third World.

Notes

1 This paper is largely based on material collected during a period of field research conducted between August 1971 and November 1972. It was financed by the Social Science Research Council and the University of Edinburgh, and I should like to express my appreciation to both these bodies for their assistance.

2 Dwarka Nath, *A History of Indians in Guyana*, London, 1970, p. 263.

3 See Jay Mandle, 'The plantation economy: an essay in definition', *Science & Society*, vol. XXXVI, 1972; George Beckford, *Persistent Poverty*, New York, 1972, pp. 49–62.

4 Colin Henfrey, 'Foreign influence in Guyana', in Emanual de Kadt, ed., *Patterns of Foreign Influence in the Caribbean*, London, 1972, p. 54.
5 Cedric Grant, 'Company towns in the Caribbean', *Caribbean Studies*, April 1971.
6 Nath, *op. cit.*, p. 263.
7 *The Rice Industry: a Case for Increased Prices for Rice and Paddy*, Guyana Rice Producers' Association, Georgetown, 1970.
8 Wilfred David, *The Economic Development of Guyana 1953–1964*, London, 1969, p. 90.
9 Andre Gunder Frank, *Latin America: Underdevelopment or Revolution*, New York, 1969.
10 Ernesto Laclau, 'Feudalism and capitalism in Latin America', *New Left Review*, no. 67, 1971, pp. 19–38.
11 *Ibid.*, p. 25.
12 Nath, *op. cit.*, p. 220.
13 Beckford, *op. cit.*, pp. 3–29; Mandle, *op. cit.*, pp. 58–62.
14 David, *op. cit.*, p. 103; Carleen O'Loughlin, 'The rice sector in the economy of British Guiana', *Social and Economic Studies*, vol. 7, no. 2, 1958, p. 142.
15 Raymond T. Smith, *British Guiana*, London, 1962, p. 64.
16 A. Kundu, 'Rice in the British Caribbean Islands and British Guiana 1950–75', *Social and Economic Studies*, vol. 13, no. 2, 1964, p. 258.
17 Nath, *op. cit.*, p. 257.
18 Leo Despres, *Cultural Pluralism and National Politics in British Guiana*, Chicago, 1967, p. 245.
19 Kundu, *op. cit.*, table 13, p. 267, and *Annual Reports of the Department of Agriculture*, Georgetown, 1950–60.
20 H. R. Caffey and J. N. Efferson, *An Appraisal of Rice Production and Marketing Problems in British Guiana*, Government Printer, Georgetown, 1965, p. 5.
21 Kundu, *op. cit.*, table 13, p. 267, and *Annual Reports of the Department of Agriculture*, Georgetown, 1954–60.
22 *Report on the British Guiana Development Programme 1960–1964*, Sessional Paper, no. 2, 1960.
23 Depres, *op. cit.*, p. 247.
24 *Ibid.*, p. 248.
25 *Report of the Rice Committee Appointed by H.E. The Governor on 2nd November 1957* (Rennison Committee), Government Printer, Georgetown, 1958. G$1 is equivalent to 50c. US.
26 *Annual Report of the Department of Agriculture for 1960*, Georgetown, 1961, p. 4.
27 Rennison Committee, *op. cit.*, pp. 5 and 6.
28 *Annual Report of Department of Agriculture, 1960*.
29 Rennison Committee, *op. cit.*
30 Raymond T. Smith, 'Economic aspects of rice production in an East Indian community in British Guiana', *Social and Economic Studies*, vol. 6, 1957.
31 David, *op. cit.*, p. 102.

32 Guyana Rice Marketing Board, *Annual Report 1969–70*, Georgetown, 1971, p. 25.
33 Caffey and Efferson, *op. cit.*, pp. 8, 9.
34 Rennison Committee, *op. cit.*, p. 10.
35 *Annual Report of the Ministry of Agriculture for the Year 1970*, Georgetown, 1971, p. 113.
36 Nath, *op. cit.*, p. 116.
37 Caffey and Efferson, *op. cit.*, p. 7.
38 Roy Glasgow, *Guyana: Race and Politics among Africans and East Indians*, The Hague, 1970, p. 114.
39 Henfrey, *op. cit.*
40 *Ibid.*, p. 54.
41 Havelock Brewster, 'Planning and economic development in Guyana', *New World Fortnightly*, no. 41, Georgetown, 1966; reprinted in N. Girvan and O. Jefferson, eds, *Readings in the Political Economy of the Caribbean*, Kingston, Jamaica, 1971.
42 New World Associates, 'Working notes towards the unification of Guyana', part VI, *New World Quarterly*, vol. 1, no. 1, Georgetown, 1963; reprinted in N. Girvan and O. Jefferson, eds, *Readings in the Political Economy of the Caribbean*, Kingston, Jamaica, 1971.

8 Rural social differentiation and political goals in Tanzania

Rayah Feldman

Tanzania has become noted throughout the world for her serious attempts to achieve socialism by peaceful means. She has thus enjoyed the support of both liberals and revolutionaries—each believing that the direction of her development was towards goals that they could approve. But liberals and revolutionaries make uneasy bedfellows and some scepticism is generated by seeing them together. There are certain ambiguities in the Tanzanian road to socialism which can perhaps explain their partnership but which at the same time need examination. These ambiguities may conceal the contradictions which prevent the road from ever reaching its destination.

The Tanganyika African National Union (TANU) has for some years declared itself as revolutionary. At present Nyerere has argued that the achievement of socialism in Tanzania does not necessitate the kind of class struggle which has characterized European history. It is by these assertions and by their expression in practice that TANU has seemed to stay in the clear with both liberals and Marxists. In recent years, however, a discussion from the left has grown both as to whether revolutionary policies are possible without a class struggle, and more importantly, whether such policies can be revolutionary if *inequalities* rather than *conflict* are the basis of their practice. If TANU is trying to reduce or merely eliminate inequalities, say the left, then she is ignoring the contradictions arising from Tanzania's involvement in the world imperialist system. If she ignores them she cannot create socialism.

Out of this perception of the problems of achieving socialism in Tanzania, a discussion has been generated as to the nature of these contradictions and their manifestation within Tanzanian society. There have been two themes in the argument which has developed. The first stresses the relationship of dependency between the neo-

154

colonial states and the imperialist countries, and the second, relatively less stressed, concerns the emergence of a capitalist class within the agricultural sector in Tanzania.

Arrighi and Saul have argued that there have been three major types of surplus absorption in modern African economies—the export of profits and investment income in general, discretionary consumption by a small labour aristocracy, and productive investment mainly outside the capital goods sector, and they suggest that this form of development tends to inhibit the creation of stimuli to encourage investment in the traditional agricultural sector.[1] But even where some such stimuli exist, they note briefly the problems of the structure of rural society as it tries to absorb its own surplus productively. Evidence from throughout sub-Saharan Africa has shown that in response to the creation of markets, particularly for export crops, an entrepreneurial incipient capitalist class of farmers has developed, increasingly differentiated from other farmers. Where governments have tried to control them through, for example, co-operatives and marketing boards, they have been found to manipulate these institutions to their own ends.[2]

Nevertheless discussion of rural social differentiation in Tanzania has never led to its being seen as a major contradiction in the achievement of socialism, except by implication in a paper by D. Feldman in which it was argued that economic, technical, and organizational problems confronting production co-operation in agriculture had to be faced, but that in the absence of a solution to them, individual entrepreneurship and concomitant economic differentiation were likely to follow.[3] It is possible to criticize this position on the grounds that economic dependency itself creates the criteria for development and that an independent basis for the economy could also produce new criteria which would cause one to re-evaluate obstacles in the way of a particular development path.

In the meantime this line of critique has scarcely been taken up. What has happened in the 1970s is that the contradictions stressed in the dependency notion have been given an enormous boost in the debate in Tanzania by a paper by a recent graduate of the University of Dar-es-Salaam, Issa Shivji. In 'The silent class struggle' Shivji relegates the issue of rural stratification to a minor position in the question of the contradictions of Tanzanian society.[4] He argues that Tanzania is a peculiar form of neo-colony, but that in spite of strenuous attempts to nationalize the key sectors of industry she remains a neo-colony, and that as such the development of the productive sectors of her economy is hindered. His essay is an attempt to show that the major antagonistic relationship within Tanzanian society is between the workers and peasants—the masses—and the forces of imperialism. However, the increasingly state-controlled structure of the economy has inseparably linked this with 'a secondary contradiction between the economic bureaucracy and the revolutionary leadership'.[5] Shivji does not examine the class base of 'the economic bureaucracy' or petty bourgeoisie in detail. It is enough for him to document a link between the industries they 'control' as government appointees, and international capitalism, to show that they are likely to be counter-revolutionary.

He notes, almost as a digression, that the 'economic bureaucracy' may be allied with the large-scale farmers, thus conferring the only political importance they have on the latter group. This lacuna in his paper is taken up in a critique of it by J. Saul which says:[6]

> He [Shivji] may underestimate the extent to which capitalist relationships have emerged in the rural areas and the possibility that the socio-economic forces which result are potentially complementary to and supportive of petit-bourgeois elements in the state bureaucracy. They may, therefore, as a matter of urgency require confrontation in their own right.

In this paper I take up these questions in the debate. What is the relationship at the local level between different groups of peasants? Can we call them classes; if so what means are available to them to perpetuate their position; and what are the links between them and the bureaucracy? The other question which I raise is the way in which the new relationships which have been created between peasants affects the interpretation of TANU's political message and hence the responsiveness of farmers to the government call for rural socialism.

The material on which this chapter is based is taken from fieldwork in a commercial maize-growing area—Ismani—particularly in Kihengeni village.

Background to Ismani

Ismani is an area of approximately 200 square miles lying at the northern end of the Iringa district in the south of Tanzania. Until the late 1940s it was sparsely populated by a part of the Hehe tribe who live throughout Iringa. They were subsistence farmers, and lived in an inhospitable environment since, although the land was fertile, there was a shortage of water for domestic consumption, and what there was tasted unpleasant and brackish.

After the war the demand for maize within Tanzania rose steadily, and a market was created in Iringa with the establishment in Iringa town of a major mill. An expansion of maize production occurred in all parts of the district which had access to markets, resulting in land shortage in some parts, and a decline in soil fertility. It was at this time that Ismani was 'discovered' by African entrepreneurs seeking to create new farms and expand existing maize production. Many of the early farmers had been involved in commercial agriculture for some time, while others had been employed or had run small-scale businesses. As they were given land by the 'native' population such farmers were in a position to hire labour to clear the bush, and within a few years, when the traditional cultivation method of slash and burn was no longer feasible, they were also among the first to use tractors and ox-ploughs to cultivate their land. For these farmers, the area cultivated, sometimes over one or two hundred acres, marked a radical departure from the few subsistence acres of former times.

By contrast most farmers came with little or no capital. In 1957 over 60 per cent had less than 10 acres and this was still the case in 1969.[7] These farmers continued to cultivate predominantly by hoe, though they also hired tractors and ox-ploughs.

The immigration to Ismani was very intensive, and while in the first years of settlement, farmers gained free access to land merely by applying to the village headman (*Jumbe*), after some years there was no longer any empty bush available for allocation in this way, and land changed hands by private arrangement either through sale or through a rental agreement. This naturally meant that some farmers were now in a position to accumulate increasingly large acreages—by 1969 a few farmers owned over 500 acres, while many others were landless, holding land only through annual tenancy agreements.[8]

Ismani has, over time, come to be regarded as the maize granary of Tanzania, producing in 1969 approximately one-fifth of that country's maize supply. Despite claims by the local officials of the Agricultural Department that Ismani farmers were 'mining the soil', and that fertility would disappear leaving the area a dustbowl, farmers were, until 1970, continuing to derive most or all of their livelihood from the sale of maize, and the yields, using no improved techniques, were higher than those of surrounding places. Nevertheless in comparison with its boom period of the 1950s and early 1960s, Ismani has experienced a decline, and for the majority of the farmers, there has been little hope of actually advancing their living standard from the cultivation of maize.

The way in which development has taken place in Ismani— involving the commercialization of relations of production and of land tenure—has meant that not only have inequalities developed between farmers, but also that qualitatively the relationships between them have changed, and can increasingly be characterized in terms of class.[9]

In this chapter the implications of the new kinds of economic

157

relations which have been created in Ismani are examined. I shall look first at the way in which these relationships are expressed and perceived by the people themselves, and at the difficulties of viewing them solely in terms of class. This is so both because of the multiplexity of relationships in which people are involved, and also because the short time-span in which successful entrepreneurs and concomitant quasi-capitalist relations of production have arisen, as well as the risk attached to entrepreneurship, have militated against the development of class consciousness. They have also left some traditional conceptions of status relatively intact, as can be seen from the composition of the ten house cell leaders.

I shall argue though that the system of production in Ismani with the possibility of individual accumulation does provide a means whereby successful entrepreneurs can perpetuate their position even beyond their own lifetime. This possibility is enhanced given the existing structure of the education system in Tanzania. Moreover, the bigger farmers dominate the most crucial rural institution linking the rural area to the central government—the co-operative society. Co-operative policies have been pursued which are favourable to them, but more importantly, the co-operative societies give them a voice through which they can interpret government policies to the rest of the people.

Ismani has also provided the test-case for the peaceful establishment of rural socialism. The response of local political leaders, in keeping with their class interests, to the prospect, and ultimately the implementation of collectivization, indicates some of the contradictions within pre-*Ujamaa* Tanzanian society between its democratic institutions and the realities of its social structure. In the event, the attempt to collectivize the entire population of Ismani, landlords and peasants, large- and small-scale farmers, was unsupported by the existing local leadership, and though finally carried through, culminated in the assassination of the Iringa Regional Commissioner on Christmas Day, 1970.

Class and class consciousness

This chapter is too brief to document the differences in wealth between Ismani farmers. Nor, for a discussion of rural stratification, is it worth while to stress merely the inequalities between farmers. H. Alavi has pointed out that the distinctions between different categories of peasants, for example, middle and poor peasants, 'appear to focus attention on *relative differences* in wealth (or poverty) . . . rather than on *class relations*'[10] (my emphasis). Alavi notes too that these categories refer to peasants belonging to different 'sectors' of the rural economy. It is difficult to establish within Tanzania to which particular sector different categories of peasants belong. The subject is particularly complex because of the inter-connectedness of these sectors as other chapters within this collection show. The point about class relations is, however, crucial, and this section while only loosely categorizing different groups of farmers, concentrates on the kinds of relations which exist between them.

These relationships are analytically of importance for two reasons. First, because some people stand in a superordinate economic position to others as a result of their control of resources such as land, labour, farm machinery, etc., and it is these resources which allow them potentially to become a class. Secondly, because social and economic differences are not just quantitative, but express certain kinds of relationships and the possibility that people will become aware of them cannot be dismissed.[11] This is particularly important given the implication, and frequently the overt content, of Tanzanian Government ideology.

Objective class relations, however, without any consideration of consciousness, can give only a very partial picture of social stratifi-cation. For this reason I examine here the limits on class conscious-ness in Ismani, and how this effectively enables the dominant class to maintain its position. It may be objected that given the absence of class consciousness in Ismani one is not justified in speaking of classes there at all. Yet to argue this would be to overlook the fact that one can begin to observe in Ismani the dominance in important areas of social life of people whose position is based on economic primacy, and more importantly, their ability to perpetuate their dominance across generations.

The basis of the system of dominance in any society is extremely important. Lloyd Fallers has suggested that in the pre-colonial period, African societies in general, especially centralized ones, did exhibit some kind of stratification, although evaluations of prestige were made in terms of political rather than economic criteria. He argues that in traditional African societies 'the most important facilities (that are the expressions of authority and the means of strengthening and extending it) are people'.[12] The size of tribute is then a function of the scale of the subordinate labour force. While this is undoubtedly true, it skirts over the essential feature of this kind of social structure which was its very low level of technology and productive capacity. This allowed little more than personal service to be 'conspicuously consumed'. It is this fact that contributed both to the importance of the size of the dependent population and to the strongly egalitarian character of African tribal life despite the widespread existence of a small political elite. Fallers concedes the economic and political impact of colonialism, particularly in the increasing differentiation of roles, but ends on a vague note arguing the possible growth in Africa of stratification on the basis of income and occupational prestige. It is, however, precisely the kind of structural differentiation which has occurred in Africa, and the economy on which it is based, that determines the nature of the type of stratification which is emerging out of the colonial experience. Structural differentiation implies not just the creation of new roles, but also of new relationships. Capitalist economic relationships are both highly differentiated in terms of roles, and also inherently involve relations of inequality which have had little counterpart in pre-colonial African society.

Part of the difficulty of assigning class positions to people in capitalist societies, is that economic and non-economic institutions are ostensibly separate—hence the possibility of maintaining Weber's distinction between class and status. Congruence between economic position and political and social positions is neither so clearly visible as in other types of system such as feudalism, nor so easily ignored as in traditional tribal systems. The most visible congruence exists between occupation and other positions, which is why analyses of stratification have usually used occupation as a starting point, both in industrial studies, and also in studies of urban Africa. However, differentiation through changing economic relationships and opportunities leading to the individual ownership of property has also occurred in African rural areas where it cannot be readily described or interpreted in terms of occupation. It is therefore necessary to examine in what way political dominance and social prestige in Ismani stems from, and is related to, the accumulation of property and new uses of wealth. It is only in this sense that any group which exerts dominance in Ismani society could properly be called a class, in contrast to holders of political authority in tribes, who derived their authority from the number of people who owed some kind of allegiance to them, generally expressed in terms of wide kinship ties.

Even where economic supremacy is not converted into either social or political control, the institutionalized system of private property and the market enable the capitalist entrepreneur to assert an autonomy in the economic sphere inconceivable within another mode of production. Thus through access to factor markets, the entrepreneur can continue to maintain and increase the scale of his operations with very little involvement in local community affairs. Indeed, probably because of their political vulnerability, and also because of their activities outside Ismani, the two richest men of Kihengeni played very small parts in local affairs, while continuing to control the largest individual acreages of land and other commercial enterprises.

It might be expected that class groups would have formed on the basis of joint economic interests between individuals and that such groupings would operate to defend the interests of one group against another. Specifically in the case of Tanzania where the government is launching its strength against the capitalist, one might expect these to close ranks and attempt some kind of joint action in recognition of their threatened mutual interests. Conversely the poorer elements of the community, who do not own land, cattle, or other capital, might be expected to work together to attempt to implement the government's ideology which they would perceive as promoting their best interests.

Such a view assumes that in the first place there are both capitalist and non-capitalist farmers who recognize their joint interest. In the case of the former group, however, there is a distinction between a threat by the government and a threat from poor farmers or labourers. The threat from the government is real, but it is largely mitigated by the fact that many of the large farmers are themselves much more representative of the government than are the small ones, controlling the institutions through which the political message is diffused. To the extent that the threat is posed in individual terms, i.e. expropriation of land, a recognition of mutual interest would be for the whole group of somehow objectively defined 'larger' farmers to join together regardless of whether they themselves were likely to lose from expropriation. Some farmers did appear aware that they were threatened in this way, and they associated by name with others in the same position. Before 1970, however, the threat was more apparent than real, and so farmers did not mobilize at all on this basis. In one Ismani village, Mbwawani, however, where, through the actions of one farmer, the threat was made explicit, and expropriation of existing farmers became part of the *Ujamaa* policy, factions were beginning to form, based on this issue, as the policy proceeded during 1970. After the *Ujamaa* policy was implemented in Ismani towards the end of 1970, the mobilization of larger farmers hostile to the programme grew rapidly, culminating in the arrest of over twenty large Ismani farmers following the murder of the Iringa Regional Commissioner, Wilbert Klerruu. These farmers had clubbed together to raise about 25,000 shillings for the defence fund of the assassin.

The threat posed by the *Ujamaa* policy brings the question of the nature of classes in Ismani into a very acute form. By its nature it was likely to accelerate any incipient growth of antagonistic class relationships. Without *Ujamaa* the capitalist farmers had no real reason to feel threatened by the government. Indeed, a good deal of morality could be attributed to them given their commitment to ideals of hard work and increasing production. However, discussions did occur between large farmers about the possible consequences of the implementation of *Ujamaa* well before 1970, and individual farmers were making their own private contingency plans.

The other question still remains of whether the capitalist farmers felt threatened by the economic groups subordinate to them—a question that is perhaps better restated in terms of whether they had anything to be threatened by. It is too facile to speak of any opposition arising through the exploitation of labour, or even through relations of tenancy and landlordism. This is because the economic changes that are still occurring in the countryside in Tanzania are so regionally varied that the degree of exploitation of labour is as much a function of the relative backwardness of other areas as of a localized expression of economic differences. Because of this many farmers are able to employ seasonal and migrant labourers, many of whom themselves see labouring for others as a stage in their own life cycle before they gain the independence of running a viable domestic farm unit at home. This is not to say that they are not exploited, but that unless the cause of their exploitation could be laid at the door of Ismani farmers there would seem to be no common link which could even cause them to define their situation as one of conflict.[13] In any case the supply of labour at the price offered during the fieldwork period was beginning to dwindle, partly because of the abolition of the local rate,[14] and partly because of developments in the areas from which the labour force was drawn, mainly Njombe and Mbeya districts.

Another important point to note about the use of the employer–employee relationship as an index of class formation is that almost everyone in Ismani employs labour at least seasonally, and at the same time is himself an employee for some of the time if work is available. There is of course a difference of status attached to various jobs, and the least prestigious is casual labour which is the usual nature of agricultural work. Few permanent residents of Ismani work for others at all systematically as agricultural workers, so the village as a community is not internally divided on this basis. To be an employer of certain kinds of labour, i.e. casual agricultural or domestic labour, no more singles anyone out from the community, than it would to be able to build one's own mud-walled, thatched cottage.[15] The point here is that despite the widespread existence of wage employment there are not many situations in which antagonistic relations can develop between the residents of the community on the basis of their position in the labour market.

The other important area characterized by relationships of inequality and exploitation is that of land holding. In this sphere Ismani villagers are involved with each other as landlords and tenants. Approximately a quarter of the population of Kihengeni cultivated rented land, though since this figure refers almost entirely to the permanent residents, it probably underestimates the true proportion, since a large, though undocumented number of seasonal migrants rent land. However, the data also show that landlordism is not highly correlated with other indices of economic position. Instead landlords are middle to poor farmers who acquired land in the early days of settlement and who now lack the means to cultivate it, at least on the scale they would like to.[16] Alternatively they are farmers who have moved away from Kihengeni to get more fertile land elsewhere, or who have returned to their home areas. There is no evidence that independent small holders have been forced out by large farmers. Rather larger land holders have avoided reducing the size of their holdings when facing financial difficulties by becoming landlords.

Just as everyone is or has been at some point an employer of labour, so the peculiar seasonally orientated character of Ismani has enabled many farmers at some time to be landlords. It is difficult to give accurate data about this because people tended to deny renting out land. However, the demand for rented land, particularly from town dwellers, was high, and it had become a norm to expect payment. How payment of rent for land was viewed can be seen clearly from a series of questions and answers in a Rural Development Seminar held in Kihengeni in March 1970.

Question: 'What happens if I have ten acres of land and I can only cultivate five acres? My friend who is doing *kibarua* (casual work, labouring) in town wants five acres. Why should I give it to him free, when he is doing *kibarua* (i.e. he is getting paid) and otherwise would have to go to the *Jumbe* and clear bush?' The implication of this question is that the landowner was only loaning the land for one season to someone who had work and who thus also had money to pay for it. The cost of rental is much less than to clear new bush,[17] and anyway the *kibarua* (worker), because he is working, doesn't have time to clear. In other words, the landlord is doing the town worker a favour by giving him five acres, and he is therefore entitled to some reward, even though he has already indicated that 'he cannot cultivate' those five acres and so there is no opportunity cost to him in letting the *kibarua* use it. Nevertheless this view exonerates the landlord from accusations of exploitation. The point is brought home by the reply to the question by the District Rural Development Officer, who referred to *Ubepari* (capitalism), the issue which had prompted the question in the first place.

Answer: 'That case is quite different from *Ubepari*. I'm talking about people who deliberately rent out land for profit.' Landlords viewed in this way are not seen as exploiters. Indeed the payment of rent is then only conceived as a monetization of the traditional payment in kind which was made to anyone from whom one borrowed land.[18]

Another element which colours the relationship of landlord to tenant in Ismani is patronage. Not every landlord by any means can be held to be a patron to his tenant. Indeed the patron–client relationship, to the extent that it can be observed in Ismani, is not institutionalized. It can be defined as a relationship of dependence with diffuse rather than specific elements linking the two parties to it. Many landlords are, as noted, absent, as are many tenants, for most of the time, and their link with their tenant is entirely impersonal and transitory. There are, however, a number of more complex relationships between individuals which include a relationship with land as one component. For instance it is customary for the tractor driver of a tractor owner to be allowed to cultivate two or three acres of his employer's land without charge either for the land or for the use of the tractor. Other relationships in which people were given land stemmed from kinship or tribal links. In such cases, although payment was usually exacted for the land, there was an onus on the landlord to provide land for the tenant. This was his obligation as kinsman or tribesman. In such a relationship if the client/tenant fell ill the patron/landlord would be obligated to feed him though at a later date might claim some compensation. Again where the landlord–tenant ties, as in such cases, are multiplex it is not difficult to see why the landlord does not see himself as exploiting the tenant. Even in the question at the Rural Development Seminar quoted earlier, some element of multiplexity is implied: 'If I have a *friend* who is doing *kibarua* . . .'

The preceding passages have indicated not only that landlords and employers of labour do not feel threatened and are not seen as posing a threat to those whom they employ or lease land to, but also that no conflict of interests is directly apparent between the groups standing in these kinds of relationships to one another. In this way the development of explicitly antagonistic relationships is prevented, and with it, the formation of class consciousness.

The establishment and perpetuation of class differences

(1) *Entrepreneurship*

The possibility of the emerging economic system in Ismani creating a class structure which can be perpetuated, requires that mechanisms exist whereby this can be achieved. If these are weak, economic differences have not yet succeeded in creating a social order based on class. To the extent that they already exist one can say that there is an incipient class system. Its particular form is determined both by the relation of the local economic system to the wider economy, and immediately by the significant relationships characterizing the local economic system, for example whether landlords, large farmers, or entrepreneurs outside agriculture are the most important holders of economic power.

The most important potential means of consolidating and perpetuating economic inequality in Ismani has been through the accumulation of capital, though a number of factors have militated against the growth of strongly coherent and defined social classes based on the ownership of property. Most importantly the whole process has only occurred over a relatively brief period, most farmers starting with either very few or no resources, and very few farmers have yet been able to raise their stock of wealth very substantially over the rest of the population. The short time-span has not yet allowed distinctive cultural characteristics to evolve between economic groupings which would also enable them to be defined as distinctive status groups, with a style of life which itself gains independent importance for the persistence of class differences. Another important limitation on the accumulation of capital has been the high risk associated with commercial entrepreneurship, so that property acquired may be rapidly lost, even within the lifetime of a single entrepreneur, and especially over more than one generation.

Despite these limitations the possibility for individual entrepreneurs to develop and expand both agricultural and non-agricultural enterprises is still the most important single factor enabling the growth and persistence of economic differences. Property alone has the capacity to grow, to be transmitted between generations, and to transmute itself into other means of protecting the privileges it confers, notably through education, and as we shall see later, more indirectly, through politics.

The chief means open to farmers to perpetuate their position at any one moment in time was to invest in capital goods. These ranged from cattle to transport, and included houses, shops, and farm machinery. The majority of wealthy farmers were unwilling to invest in agriculture because of its low returns and the institutional factors which militated against remedying this situation.[19] However, investment became the mark of a 'progressive' farmer, whether large or small.

Many farmers indicated a positive valuation on the reinvestment of profit or earned income emphasizing not only the importance of hard work, a message echoed in the ideology of self-reliance, but also the judicious use of one's resources for investment. Hard work had for most been a necessary preliminary to the acquisition of wealth, either through agriculture, or in some kind of paid employment, but further investment was essential if one wanted to consolidate one's position. To educate one's children could give one's family standing

165

and might have a long-term payoff, but it provided no short-term security. For this, investments must be made, and productive assets acquired. The most important of these has been land, but can now include a variety of other things, notably transport or farm machinery.

For early farmers there was no difficulty in acquiring land, and they therefore used it as extensively as possible, ploughing profits back into farming and other investments. For farmers who today do not own their own land the situation is reversed. Because of the low returns from agriculture, they are often forced to make their money in other ways in order to acquire the minimal resource of land.

While obviously access to labour is a crucial resource of any farming household, with the diversification of economic activities and the partial mechanization of agricultural production itself, the owner-ship of a whole range of assets comes to define the economic poten-tial of a household—but still only its potential. At first sight it would appear that the man with a tractor, a lorry, or a house used for rent is one whose position is assured, but the rate of failure of investment is very high. Lorries and other vehicles including tractors are often bought in poor condition leaving the owner with insufficient money to maintain them properly. Houses can remain partially built, when the money to pay the builder and to buy the materials has run out, and then the rains will destroy much of the existing building, so in-creasing the final cost to prohibitive levels. Tractor owners can fail to cultivate their own fields because they are so busy looking for the funds to repair their machines or for fuel. Traders who have paid for licences leave themselves with insufficient capital to stock their shops and bars.

Although these kinds of failures are repeated year after year, and many middle and even poorer farmers have seen far better days, nevertheless, farmers continue to attempt to accumulate more property. Besides the possibility of successful enterprise there are locally no institutionalized means of guaranteeing a good position, for those who do not have special qualifications. The only existing avenues are agriculture and commerce. Even landlordism does not provide an alternative means of wealth from the land. It is therefore a situation in which only the successful entrepreneur can guarantee himself the privileges of a good standard of living, of the ability to educate all his children, and to maintain an adequate output of maize. This accounts for the widespread attempts at further investment among farmers, attempts which in many cases are doomed to failure.

(2) *Education*

The fact that it has been entrepreneurship rather than inheritance which confers prestige, and that entrepreneurship is very uncertain and competitive, means that neither the successful nor the unsuccessful can form clearly defined strata even though at a particular point in time people hold similar class positions. Financial success does confer prestige but only as long as it lasts—more permanent criteria of prestige derive from other less fickle sources. But what we call commercial entrepreneurship is also the basis of capital accumulation, and so success in that field does mean that the differentiation between entrepreneurs and others can be the basis of more permanent class formation. The history of Ismani as a history of entrepreneurship is too brief to test this hypothesis, but evidence from other parts of Africa would appear to confirm it.

There is, however, an alternative, or at any rate, a supplement, to capital accumulation which potentially can ensure the persistence through generations of economic, and ultimately cultural, differences which accumulation alone cannot. This is the education of children, by means of which parents hope to gain for their children secure employment, generally outside the agricultural sector, with concomitant income and security for themselves. Until recently graduates of primary schools in Tanzania could expect to find some kind of clerical employment but increasing unemployment among primary school leavers has made it clear that to secure employment one must have passed through at least some years of secondary school. I therefore tried to discover if there was any pattern among the Kihengeni villagers in the level of education reached by children of families at different economic levels.

Whatever results emerge from my data are, given the smallness of the sample, extremely tentative. But, as will be seen, they do suggest that in absolute terms few children are ever able to leave the village except as migrants to work in towns or to become farmers or petty traders in other rural areas. The number who, from my sample, which covered nearly all the permanent residents of the village and many seasonal farmers, reached secondary education, and hence the possibility of incorporation into the State infrastructure, or what Shivji calls the 'national bourgeoisie', was only ten out of a total of 399 children born to this sample. It is, however, important to know who those few are. In the first place one simply wants to know whether in a poor peasant society there can be equality of educational opportunity given the great scarcity of educational resources. The term peasant is stressed here because of the connotation it has of a gap between rural peoples and a non-rural class.[20] This is particularly important in connection with education because education is geared to the needs and assumptions of the non-rural strata, and the point at which an individual can be said to have 'succeeded' in education is the point where he can become incorporated into the non-rural part of the society on the basis of the skills he has acquired.

Secondly, if we know who is becoming educated to the level of the national bourgeoisie, networks can be drawn from the village to people of influence outside it. Shivji for instance asserts:[21]

> The fundamental contradictions in Tanzanian society are not to be found in the rural peasantry (including the big farmers) but in the content and nature of the relationship of Tanzania's economy with international capital. . . . This is not to say that rural stratification should not be analyzed. It must be done . . . but within the context of Tanzania's economy as a whole. The important question within *this* context is: 'Who controls Tanzania's economy?' . . . The farmers of Iringa and Kilimanjaro *do not* control Tanzania's economy as a whole. If they are important at all it is because they may be allied with the economic bureaucracy which in turn is allied with the international bourgeoisie.

Shivji's underrating of the importance of the farmers in Tanzanian society leads him to ignore the contradiction between the big farmers and Tanzanian policies, which exist not because the latter are tools of the 'international bourgeoisie', but because of their own vested interests as a group. Furthermore, what my data suggest, however tentatively, is that the 'economic' and 'political' bureaucracies may actually have roots in an indigenous economic base, and that that, as much as any alliance with the 'international bourgeoisie', influences the kinds of domestic policies they espouse.

While the Arusha Declaration recognized that private property was incompatible with disinterested implementation of socialist policies by political leaders and civil servants, it could not destroy the link. Richer peasants have more chance of themselves becoming part of the bureaucracy than the poorer ones. However effectively the Arusha Declaration is implemented, the bureaucracy's class base through filiation, kinship, and marriage still remains. It is necessary therefore to see whether in fact the data support the contention that it is the economically more privileged who are able to educate their children to secondary level. Table 8.1 indicates that children of families in the higher income category have approximately twice the chance of reaching secondary education of the children of poorer families.

Even these figures are misleading since at least two of the families placed in the lower income category, on account of the Kihengeni household head's financial position in 1969, were in fact better off from the viewpoint of their children's education. One household head, a divorcée, had her son maintained by her former husband, a policeman. The other was a retired carpenter who, while his children were at school, had a relatively high income.

These details indicate the difficulty of assigning people to an economic position at one point (the present) and inferring their class position. Changes within a lifetime, either due to changes in marital status, or in age, or for other reasons, need to be considered in explaining either present or past behaviour. If we take these changes into account, then at least two of the four lower income category households, who educated their children to secondary level, cannot really be considered part of that category for this purpose.

Of the six families in the higher income categories who educated

TABLE 8.1 *Number of families in Kihengeni with at least one child attending, or having attended, school at different levels, according to head of household's income category**

	Income category	
	1	2
	(*n* = 54)	(*n* = 34)†
Standard 1–4 ⎱ Primary	32 (59·3%)	23 (67·6%)
Standard 5–8 ⎰	16 (29·6%)	14 (40·6%)
Standard 9–12 Secondary	4 (7·4%)	6 (17·1%)

* The income categories were constructed as follows:
  Category 1—Farmers cultivating less than 5 acres with or
  without other income sources, and those cultivating
  between 6 and 20 acres without any alternative stable
  income source.
  Category 2—Farmers cultivating over 20 acres with or without
  other income sources and those cultivating between
  6 and 20 acres who had a stable alternative income
  source.
† The totals exceed the total number of households in each
  category since a household was counted each time at least
  one child was attending or had left school at the level
  shown.

their children to secondary level, four had houses in Iringa town and two permanently maintained a household there. Until 1969 it was not possible to complete primary education in Ismani, and so any child who went on to secondary school must have had at least some of their primary education either in Iringa town or elsewhere: either at boarding school or where they could stay with a relative. (Unfortunately I collected only information about the present level of education reached, and so do not know the educational history of each child.) From those farmers in this group for whom I have sufficient information it would seem that either they are older men who have maintained their economic position or they are economically still very active and continuing to enlarge their scale of operation.

They can look forward to financial assistance and security from their children as they advance in education and finally achieve well-paid employment.

It would be misleading to attribute only economic motives to parents who wish to educate their children, but given the economic effects of education, it has been important to show that pre-existing differentiation in the countryside tends to be reinforced through unequal access to educational opportunity, partly through the direct and indirect cost of education, partly through locational advantages like the possibility of access to urban primary schools, and partly through the 'modernity' of outlook of the entrepreneur—the effect frequently of his own earlier educational advantages.

Two main conclusions emerge from this brief discussion of educational opportunity in Ismani. First, it provides some documentation, albeit flimsy, of the link between the national bureaucracy and the wealthier stratum of farmers, and in particular suggests that there is a structural aspect to the way this bureaucracy is generated. It is not simply a question, as the Arusha Declaration implied, of the political leaders and senior civil servants themselves acquiring property because of their salary advantages. I am tentatively proposing on the basis of evidence from Ismani that they are already—and some quite significantly—rooted in property. This should not be overstated. It has been pointed out by Fanon and others that the middle classes of underdeveloped countries lacking independent economic power, attempt to transform the State, which they do control, into the source of economic power.[22] However, because as we have seen, rural society is stratified, the movement of its children out of the rich peasantry into the middle classes helps to confirm the control of the rich peasantry in the countryside and reinforces it through support from its bourgeois offshoots.

The second conclusion is really a modification of the first. The very limited extent to which we can see this process occur in Ismani, and the large number of wealthier families whose children do not become educated and are thus obliged to stay in the rural areas, subject to the vagaries of fortune associated with capital accumulation, in practice means that classes are not so easily perpetuated in this way as might at first sight appear to be the case. It is nevertheless significant that of those few children who do go on to higher levels of education such a high proportion have been in, or are part of, wealthier families.

Politics and political leadership

Despite the very real economic inequalities that exist in Ismani, the level of competition and exploitation, and the unequal access to education between economic groupings, I have not been able to document the existence of class consciousness at any of the levels described. Class, however, assumes a particular significance in local politics since it is here that the economic differentiation of Ismani farmers finds its clearest expression because local political institutions are dominated by the wealthier farmers. Given the political orientation of the Tanzanian Government, this fact becomes very important as local institutions both give expression to, and execute much of, government policy and ideology. Local leaders, however, by virtue of the positions they hold, vary in the extent to which they actually shape local policy, or give expression to national ideology. In this section, therefore, I distinguish between different leadership positions, and the kinds of people who fill them, and show the implications this has for the expression of government policy at the village level.

Ten house cells and their leaders

Tanzanian national politics and administration have penetrated the rural areas as far, in principle, as the individual household. Since 1964, the ten house cell system has provided the basis for TANU organization on an extremely small scale.[23] The ten house cell leaders hold the lowest level of office within the national hierarchy. An examination of who they are, what they are supposed to do, and how they actually carry out their tasks, illuminates the position of other local leaders, and also introduces some of the contradictions within the operation of the TANU party and governmental system at the local level.

The ten house cell system was established initially in Dar-es-Salaam for two major purposes: first, to strengthen the organization of TANU at the local level, and secondly, to improve the level of control in order to maintain security and order. The first purpose involves an immediately identifiable ambiguity between the concrete organization of TANU in terms of paying dues, holding meetings, conveying information between different levels of the democratic centralist hierarchy, and the fulfilment of TANU objectives in the fields of development and ideology—in other words in terms of political mobilization. Thus one important question which needs examination is the nature of the cell leader's political role.

Social control was conceived essentially in terms of security both of the State, e.g. against spies, and of persons, e.g. against thieves.[24] In Ismani, as in other rural areas with rudimentary policing and judicial facilities, the cell system fills a clear gap in the maintenance of social order.

There is a third area of activity involving cell leaders which touches

171

on both the preceding ones but which seems to have been outside the initial scope of the system. This is the area of local administration where cell leaders, either acting on behalf of their individual offices, or as members of the Village Development Committee (VDC), are allotted discretionary powers to allocate plots for buildings or cultivating, or to grant various kinds of licences, etc., to members of their cells.

The explicit political function of cell leaders in Ismani is fairly well defined. They form the large body of the VDC which is composed of all the cell leaders of its area plus the chairman of TANU and the TANU secretary and any other elected or appointed officials, e.g. members of village or ward level TANU committees (elected) and local level appointed officials such as Agricultural Field Officers and Rural Development Officers. Although the chairman of the VDC is not necessarily himself a cell leader, he can only be elected by them and a few other selected individuals. VDCs in Tanzania are coterminous with TANU branches. TANU elections are held annually for branch officials who then represent their branch both on branch working committees and also at regional and district levels.[25] However, at the elections for TANU representatives in Ismani only cell leaders and a few others involved in TANU are allowed to vote. This is in spite of the fact that many other people hold TANU cards, but it is because each level of TANU elects the higher level (according to the principle of democratic centralism) and the ten house cell is regarded as the lowest level of the party hierarchy. This gives the cell leaders an involvement with TANU which is not shared by the members of their cells, because, despite the initial formulation of ten house cells as being composed of party members, the cells in Ismani are composed of all people living within a given area whether they are party members or not. But it is a curious involvement with TANU since, unlike party representatives in most party systems, even one-party ones, they are not elected on the basis of their activism in the party or on its behalf, nor particularly for their commitment to its ideology.

Ten house cell leaders were hardly purveyors of the TANU political message in Ismani. Neither they nor the members of their cells, nor other influential people, saw them as creatures of TANU. The chairman of TANU of Iringa region during a long speech to a Rural Development Seminar in Kihengeni did not mention the political aspect of the cell leader's work, stressing only the security aspect of their role.

The cell leaders could only be seen engaged in essentially non-political activities, and these were the ones stressed in any description or comment on their function. The Divisional Executive Officer of Ismani referred to the following functions of the cell leaders: They must, he said, send agendas to the VDC based on cell requests, e.g. to dig wells, build schools, or ask for water, and they are also responsible for dispute settlement. He did not mention any functions either of mobilization or of party organization within the cells. However, or perhaps because of this, TANU as an organization only functioned sporadically even outside the cells, and TANU general meetings were hardly ever held.

But if TANU as an organization did not figure prominently in the activities of the cell leaders, this does not mean that they were totally uninvolved in political issues, and did not exercise a limited amount of political control outside the immediate framework of TANU, by means of VDC meetings and *Maendeleo* (development) projects. One of the major tasks of cell leaders is to sit on committees, and represent their cell members to higher level officials. Many recommendations are eventually accepted and so the cell leader's voice, through the VDC, can be important. Indeed, it is ultimately the cell leader alone who makes the decisions on behalf of his cell—he does not represent their democratically-reached decisions. One prominent Kihengeni cell leader said he never had meetings with the householder in his cell. 'They would never come to a meeting. In the rainy season they would say they were busy, and in the dry season they would be busy drinking. If you offered them beer to come it would be a different matter.' Of course cell members can make their opinions felt in other ways than through meetings.[26] However, because it is a representative committee the VDC, by not being open to everyone, confers a status on its members elevating the ten house cell leader above the other villagers, and so gives him some legitimacy for those few executive powers which he holds.

A great deal of the cell leader's work is concentrated on administration, particularly the administration of local self-help projects. Self-help has an important place in TANU ideology. As understood by TANU, however, self-help calls for a strong government impetus and the use of local leaders to organize projects and even, if necessary, to coerce unwilling participants. Many of its characteristics follow directly from the colonial period. The organization of self-help is seen as a major political task of the cell leaders. This has the effect of making politics and administration largely indistinguishable, and also of removing any distinctive ideological content from local political *practice*, besides the almost universal 'ideological' emphasis on *development*.

Politics, in the sense of questions of the distribution of power, enters into the work of the cell leader in an oddly non-ideological way when, as the representative of the people, he is called upon to defend the interests of his members. Levine has some very interesting material from Dar-es-Salaam which shows the limitations of the cell leader's power even in a situation where he is ostensibly representing the interests of workers against the wealthier sections of the population.[27] In Ismani I recorded a case where the cell leader supported his member who was flagrantly violating principles of *Ujamaa* ideology. In 1970, in one village, 100 people registered to form an *Ujamaa* village. They asked a certain large farmer, William, the son of a wealthy and influential Ismani farmer, for land to cultivate collectively, because he had land nearby which he had not cultivated for two years. He refused to give it to them, saying that he had already given it to sixteen other people outside the group of a hundred, so that they could cultivate it collectively. Both sides to the dispute were represented by cell leaders at a VDC meeting. One cell leader, who was one of the sixteen, claimed that they were William's neighbours, although in fact this turned out not to be true. The consensus at the meeting was that William was using the story of the sixteen to avoid losing his land, and it was decided that the land should go to the group of a hundred, permitting the sixteen to join them if they wished.

This example shows how William's 'neighbours" cell leader was giving support to his members regardless of the position of TANU, while the 'village' cell leader supported the members of the registered village. There was no mechanism for, or indeed any mention of the possibility of, a TANU opponent who was a cell leader being removed from his office. The absence of an explicit commitment on the part of the cell leaders to be ideological leaders of TANU means, therefore, that TANU at the grass-roots can be undermined in certain situations using the structure ostensibly set up to protect it. When a single farmer in another village cultivated a farm which had been set aside for joint cultivation by members of the TANU Youth League, a delegation of ten house cell leaders was sent from the VDC to investigate and ask the man to stop cultivating. The delegation never went.

Thus the cell system as it operates in Ismani has two weaknesses built into it from the viewpoint of political mobilization. By lacking a common commitment to TANU in terms of ideology, cell leaders are not likely to unite as a joint force of leaders to promote TANU ideals. It is even possible for them to oppose each other, not just for factional issues, but on the basis of the implementation of policies to which TANU as a party is committed. Secondly, because just anyone can be a cell member, the ten house system can actually detract from mobilization towards the party, by separating the people from the party's representatives at higher levels of the hierarchy.

All this implies that the political role of the cell leaders both as party organizers and militants is very restricted. However, they remain important in the community as a result mainly of the part they play in dispute settlement and the maintenance of order. They also have clearly perceived welfare functions; they would, for example, intervene if they saw husbands beating their wives excessively. In these kinds of situations, appeals are made to norms of tradition and respectability to justify the actions of the cell leader. It is then quite natural for the cell leaders to associate with elders who themselves do not hold elected office. This is also done when disputes are heard. The cell leaders have in fact taken over many of the functions of village elders who formerly, or in other places, held their position by virtue of their age and seniority.

The cell leaders in Kihengeni, to some extent, constitute an economic elite in the community, though to a much lesser extent than those who have held office in the co-operative society, or at higher levels of TANU. They are older and wealthier though than the majority of villagers, and have spent longer in the village. It is, therefore, at first sight surprising that only two of eleven cell leaders in Kihengeni had held any other local public office. But this observation corroborates the view that the cell leaders are not important as ideological mobilizers, or even as party organizers. While that is partially the result of the way the cell system is organized, it also reflects the lack of any deep involvement by the cell leaders in party affairs. K. S. Kawago has written of Iringa urban cell leaders:[28]

> There have been instances when someone was elected . . . without investigating whether he was a member of TANU. . . . Some of those chosen were not party members. Fortunately those leaders agreed to join the party after getting into office. But often such people are not versed in party policies so they fail to perform all the functions expected of a cell leader. They seem to concentrate their effort on settling family disputes brought before them, and make little effort to educate themselves in party policies.

This description holds good in Ismani too. The cell leaders are much more fundamentally 'elders' of the village concerned largely with welfare and dispute settlement. At the elections for TANU branch officials for the branch including Kihengeni, only one cell leader of that village was even nominated, though several other officials of the co-operative society and other *ad hoc* committees were nominated and elected. Their lack of participation in wider political institutions reinforces the cell leaders' social control function, just as Kawago indicated for Iringa town, leaving the field for active political involvement open to others who comprise a much more exclusively wealthy stratum. The effect of this on the nature of political messages reaching the peasants will now be examined.

Co-operative societies, and TANU political goals

The lack of political involvement by cell leaders and the concomitant importance of the co-operatives and higher level committees of

175

TANU which are closely connected in personnel, makes the class basis of the local leaders particularly important in view of the ideological character of the political messages in Tanzania. The co-operative movement in Tanzania has historically had connections with national politics, providing a training ground for post-independence national leaders. At the present time, while the ruling TANU party and the co-operatives function quite separately nationally, they both reach into the rural areas and provide not just a forum for the achievement of local power, but also for their leaders, a straddling of the distance between the villages and the centres of decision-making. The TANU branches in Ismani have been seen to have little autonomous influence, linked as they are to the VDCs, ten house cell leaders, and general administration and social control functions. Besides sporadically held public meetings they have an existence in that the local TANU leaders sit on higher level committees and at meetings convey messages from the central government to the people.

Co-operative societies in Ismani as elsewhere in Tanzania were established to supersede the role of Asian traders who acted as middle men. The first co-operative in Iringa District was set up in Ismani in 1954 by a number of leading farmers to organize their own transport and marketing of maize. Initially they demanded a share membership of 100 shillings, a sum that was vetoed by the colonial administration as effectively excluding the majority of their fellow farmers. The size of the sum proposed indicates the exclusiveness of the stratum of farmers who set it up. The first co-operative had grown by the early 1960s into three societies responsible for the whole of Ismani, which organized the marketing of all the crops grown in the area. Only a few rich farmers with their own means of transport could by-pass the co-operatives and sell their crops directly to the marketing boards, but non-membership cost them nothing since they did not need credit from the co-operatives as they were able to raise loans directly from the bank or private sources.

The other main function of the co-operative societies was to organize the allocation of credit to farmers. However, by 1967 no more loans were being issued through the Ismani co-operative societies because of farmers' failure to repay earlier debts. But even when credit was given, the co-operative could do nothing to affect the distribution of incomes between farmers. It is clear from one society's records that credit was either allocated according to the scale of farming, or even in suspiciously large amounts to members of the committees and their relatives.[29] Thus, despite the egalitarian ideals of the co-operatives, in practice they simply reinforced the divisions which already existed between the farmers. They were assisted in doing so by the commercial criteria they were supposed to apply to the allocation of credit, which tended to exclude those farmers who most needed assistance.[30] While such help would not necessarily be most effective in the form of credit, a discriminatory policy could only aggravate the problem of income distribution.

It is in this perspective that one must see the leadership of the co-operative societies. The activities of co-operatives are almost exclusively concerned with problems of marketing and credit for farm inputs, and not at all with older concerns of reciprocal exchange which characterized subsistence production systems. Whether the co-operative societies represented the choice of entrepreneurial farmers to reduce the exploitation directed against them, or whether the societies were established as a result of government policy, it was still the same kinds of people—those who were active and successful as commercial farmers—who put themselves forward as leaders. There was no incompatibility between the class base of the co-operatives' leadership, and the policies which they were encouraged to pursue as part of a commercial institution.

At the level of ideology, however, the discrepancy was great, since the ideals of both the Rochdale model on which co-operatives in British Africa were ostensibly based, and the Tanzanian conception of socialism, involve equality and participation by all members. Part of the co-operatives' objectives was to serve as tools to broaden the opportunities for development. In this they have been seen by both government and people to have failed. But the fact that some literacy, understanding of the operation of the market, and even the mystique of book-keeping has confined the demand for access to the leadership to those few who anyway stand to gain most from co-operatives, has helped to minimize the expression of the co-operatives' failings amongst their membership. Losses to farmers resulting from societies' inefficiency and corruption can even confirm the leading members in their positions by reducing the active participation of ordinary members.[31]

The propertied class base of the leadership of the co-operative societies has another dimension which is the subject of the discussion here. The involvement of the wealthier farmers in the co-operative societies tends to be only one manifestation of an active concern with political issues. It is here that the contrast with ten house cell leaders is sharpest. The latter are the source of quasi-traditional dispute settlers. The former are the source of elected TANU representatives to divisional, district, and regional committees. The ten house cell system is able, as noted earlier, to encourage this difference since the cell leaders alone can elect TANU representatives who themselves are not cell leaders. Indeed the involvement with the co-operative societies can become a credential for further TANU work. The chairman of TANU in Kihengeni area, a man who cultivated 100 acres, said that he was elected because of his experience in committee work. He had been for many years variously chairman and vice-chairman of the co-operative society.

The fact that TANU committees and the co-operatives are so closely bound together locally means that the effort of 'political mobilization' for the policy of *Ujamaa* is in the hands of people who in general could not but be harmed by its implementation in Ismani. Yet it is they whose task it is to receive and pass on the political messages from the government to the rest of the people. The co-operative societies, even more than TANU through the VDCS, serve as a convenient mouthpiece for government policy and ideology at public meetings. The main speakers at these meetings are the District or Regional level civil servants and the co-operative society and TANU leaders, often the same people. Even when *ad hoc* committees are formed for very specific purposes, as for example in Kihengeni, a committee to administer new house-building, or in Mbwawani, a women's co-operative beer-selling club, their members are elected from the same 'activists'. The Mbwawani women's co-operative was interesting in this respect since it consisted of the wives of wealthy farmers and also demanded a share membership of 100 shillings which excluded most women. Yet this women's co-operative was held up as an example of *Ujamaa* in action. Such people naturally gave support to *Ujamaa* policies in their public utterances, but while stressing their benefits, consistently played down the concrete effects they were likely to have on large farmers, landlords, and employers whom they most closely represented.

The message of *Ujamaa* put forward by this economically dominant class of local political leaders was a Utopian vision of government-aided local improvements of benefit to all, such as schools, hospitals, roads, electricity, better water supplies, and extensive government assistance in agriculture, if only the people would live together in villages (which they already did), and cultivate together—a vague proposal which could and did mean a few hours' collective work per week on meagre plots of hitherto uncultivated land, additional to their privately owned land. Capitalism was condemned, often most forcibly by TANU leaders who were the largest landowners, but capitalism did not in practical terms extend to landlords or employers. It was an attractive message which could unify everyone and affirm the leaders' solidarity with the national ideology. The majority of farmers were not involved with the idea and understood it little.[32] It did not encourage participation because no social change was offered, only desultory communal cultivation little different from the communal work of self-help projects.

The effect was a dilatory and ineffective progression towards *Ujamaa* in Ismani, with villages forming committees and organizing collective work on relatively small empty plots of land. The *Ujamaa* committee in Kihengeni was chaired by the wealthy chairman of the co-operative society. This kind of response has been observed in other rural areas in Tanzania where commercialization of agriculture has been in progress for some time. It probably would have continued like this in Ismani had not one local activist precipitated a crisis that involved the intervention of the President himself, by demanding the expropriation of large landowners.

The campaign was directed specifically against one farmer, the richest in the whole of Ismani, a man who owned buses, lorries, houses, and much farm machinery, besides over 500 acres of land. He had not been involved with either TANU or the co-operative society. He refused to contribute part of his land to the *Ujamaa* farm which was proposed on land which was currently under cultivation in Mbwawani village. Leaders consistently played down this matter for it raised the very issue that could threaten them. Instead they argued that it was better to have a communal farm without expropriation than to have no communal farm at all, thus evading the whole argument underlying the affair. However, the dispute became increasingly public, and finally resulted in direct government involvement in the establishment of *Ujamaa* in Ismani.

In 1970 *all* land in Ismani was taken over by the government and redistributed only to registered members of *Ujamaa* villages to cultivate collectively, as well as three acres to be cultivated individually by each member. Other productive assets such as tractors, lorries, and businesses were individually retained. There were very deep divisions between the people. Many of the larger farmers including some of those who had held positions of leadership left. Nearly all seasonal farming stopped since the seasonal cultivators were not members of the *Ujamaa* villages. Finally, in December 1970 on Christmas Day, the Regional Commissioner of Iringa who had directed the programme of land reform was assassinated by a large farmer in a village in Ismani. Wealthy farmers throughout the district contributed 25,000 shs. for a defence fund and twenty-three were arrested and detained in preventive detention.

Many of the farmers affected were pleased by the reform since they actually gained land. However, in the first year, 1970/1, nearly all cultivation costs for both private and communal plots were borne by the government, and thus not felt by the farmers during this initial reform period. There was some concern expressed though that the leadership of the *Ujamaa* villages still included wealthy people owning tractors, businesses, and private farms outside Ismani.

One can speculate as to why the reform in Ismani was so partial, whether it was constrained by administrative or political difficulties. It is, however, clear that as far as it went, it could not occur without

179

imposition from above and outside, despite the presence of local institutions ostensibly committed to government goals, because the class interests of the leaders in those institutions conflicted with the prevailing ideology. The violent aftermath to the collectivization confirms the existence of class divisions whether they were formerly perceived or not.

Conclusion

This chapter has explored the way class relationships have developed in a particular rural area of Tanzania. While Ismani is in many ways unusual, it is least unusual with respect to the economically differentiating effects of commercial development in agriculture. Such effects have been observed in many of the more developed parts of Tanzania, as elsewhere in Africa.[33]

While it is important to explain how colonial and neo-colonial relationships have shaped the social structure of modern African states at the national level, the concomitant changes in rural societies must be examined if the further course of development is to be understood. The class structure within the rural areas themselves shapes the conditions for future rural development whatever political strategy is adopted. In the case of Tanzania the implication of rural class divisions is particularly significant since government policy is directed explicitly against the interests of those responsible for expressing it to the people. The chapter has shown that ideological exhortation cannot by itself arouse the consciousness of the people if such consciousness is to threaten the interest of the leaders who express it. This is as true at the rural level as it is nationally.

Much of this chapter has been devoted to an examination of the lack of class consciousness amongst the peasants and the clear monopolization of political leadership by the economically dominant class. There does exist considerable economic differentiation. At the same time, however, antagonistic relationships have yet to be fully developed, and therefore there has been little or no class consciousness. A government wishing to create a social revolution, therefore, has the choice of creating consciousness by allowing these antagonisms to grow through further differentiation ('letting the kulaks run') or suppressing this process and imposing social change from above, as was done in Ismani. Whether the latter can really result in a true social revolution has still to be demonstrated.

Notes

1 G. Arrighi and J. Saul, 'Socialism and economic development in tropical Africa', *Journal of Modern African Studies*, vol. 6, no. 2, 1968, pp. 141–69.

2 See for example J. S. Saul, 'Marketing co-operatives in Africa', in P. Worsley, ed., *Two Blades of Grass*, Manchester University Press, 1971.

3 D. Feldman, 'The economics of ideology', in C. Leys, ed., *Politics and Change in Developing Countries*, Cambridge University Press, 1969.

4 I. Shivji, 'The silent class struggle', *Zenit*, Reprint 6, Lund, 1971.

5 *Ibid.*, p. 45.

6 J. S. Saul, 'Who is the Immediate Enemy?', in *ibid.*

7 For a more detailed discussion of the background to Ismani see R. Feldman, 'Ismani', in F. G. Bailey, ed., *Debate and Compromise*, Basil Blackwell, Oxford, 1973.

8 See R. Feldman, 'Custom and capitalism—changes in the basis of land tenure in Ismani, Tanzania', *Journal of Development Studies*, forthcoming.

9 Cf. the effect of commercial development among the Agni of the Ivory Coast in R. Stavenhagen, *Les Classes Sociales dans les Sociétés Agraires*, Anthropos, Paris, 1969.

10 H. Alavi, 'Peasants and revolution', in J. Saville and R. Miliband, eds, *The Socialist Register*, Merlin Press, London, 1965.

11 Cf. P. Hill, *Rural Hausa*, Cambridge University Press, 1972—in which she totally neglects the relational aspect of economic differentiation. See for example pp. 57–84.

12 L. A. Fallers, 'Social stratification and economic processes in Africa', in M. J. Herskovits and M. Horwitz, eds, *Economic Transition in Africa*, North-western University Press, Evanston, 1964.

13 See G. Simmel, *Conflict and the Web of Group Affiliations*, Free Press, Chicago, 1955.

14 A local rate of 45 shillings per household head was abolished at the end of 1969. Many farmers claimed they had more difficulties recruiting casual labour subsequently.

15 Cf. the use of domestic servants among the poorest families in Mexico City, of which Oscar Lewis comments that it was not a particular mark of prestige or wealth. See O. Lewis, *The Children of Sanchez*, Secker & Warburg, London, 1961, p. xviii.

16 Cf. M. Stahl, *Contradictions in Agricultural Development*, Institute of African Studies, Uppsala, 1973.

17 R. Feldman (forthcoming), *op. cit.*

18 For a long time I thought that the very frequent use of 'borrow' (*kuazima*) in connection with land renting was a euphemism because farmers were unwilling to disclose that they rented out land. However, it is characteristic both of the way renting is rationalized by landlords, and of the system of rental. This is on an annual basis, and the casual expectation of the tenant with regard to his security, or even the availability of land from a particular landlord, fits in with a 'conditional' conception of renting—'If I have some land to spare you can "borrow" it.' Both the reasons for renting and for leasing out land are quite different from the 'borrowing' of land by strangers in former times.

19 See R. Feldman, 1973, *op. cit.*

20 Cf. E. Wolf, *Peasants*, Prentice-Hall, Englewood Cliffs, 1966.

21 Shivji, *op. cit.*, p. 6.
22 E.g. F. Fanon, *The Wretched of the Earth*, Penguin, Harmondsworth, 1967, p. 122.
23 The system was based on the Chinese ten house cell system.
24 Ten house cells were introduced in Japan against Christian spies in the 1640s. See S. Fukawa, 'Neighbourhood associations in Japanese cities and their political implication', unpublished MA thesis, London University, 1964.
25 See G. Hyden, *Political Development in Rural Tanzania*, E. African Publishing House, Nairobi, 1969, for a closer examination of the organization of local political institutions, especially p. 138.
26 See for example N. Van Hekken, *The Ten House Groups in Ngamanga*, Afrika Studiecentrum, Leiden, mimeo, 1969.
27 K. Levine, 'Cell leaders in Dar-es-Salaam', in J. F. O'Barr and Joel Samos, eds, *Cell Leaders in Tanzania*, East African Publishing House, Nairobi, 1974.
28 K. S. Kawago, 'The operation of TANU cells in Iringa', in J. H. Proctor, ed., *The Cell System of the Tanganyika African National Union*, Tanzania Publishing House, Dar-es-Salaam, 1971.
29 See R. Feldman, 1973, *op. cit.*
30 See M. J. Collinson, 'Agricultural planning in Tanzania', in G. Helleiner, ed., *Agricultural Planning in East Africa*, East African Publishing House, Nairobi, 1968, for a statement of the principles of agricultural credit in Tanzania.
31 Cf. J. S. Saul, 'Marketing cooperatives in Tanzania', in P. Worsley, ed., *Two Blades of Grass*, Manchester University Press, 1971.
32 A survey conducted in Mbwawani indicated very limited conceptions of its specifically socialist objectives.
33 Cf. especially R. Stavenhagen, *op. cit.*, for an account of remarkably similar developments to those in Ismani, amongst the Agni of the Ivory Coast.

9 The Gezira Scheme: production of cotton and the reproduction of underdevelopment
Tony Barnett

Frank's work on the nature of underdevelopment has now become a part of the conventional wisdom in academic reflection.[1] The model which he employs is attractive and apparently very simple. It is that of the parasitic metropolis and the parasitized satellite. However, this apparent simplicity, together with the writer's polemic, does obscure some important theoretical considerations. These considerations are not important solely in relation to their theoretical implications, but also in relation to the strengthening and sharpening of the substantive analysis which derives from the theory.

On the whole, Frank's model is rather too static and schematic. We are presented with what might be described as a vertical model. This model operates in terms of a number of concepts, such as 'expropriation', 'surplus', but somehow or other, the entire structure fails to move. At least, it does move, but only like a conveyor belt, transporting surplus from point A to point B. The social, economic, and political reality is far more complex, requiring a less mechanistic model. What is required is some kind of account which includes the more organic features of the historical economic and social processes which have been, and continue to be, at work in the relationship of underdevelopment.

The main inadequacies in Frank's formulation revolve around two points. The first is that we are told that the world capitalist system actively underdevelops other parts of the world. However, within Frank's work this system is shown as either about to engulf an *undeveloped* area, or as having already engulfed it. We are not acquainted with the types of process which have been central in the historical experience of this articulation. This gap in Frank's model may be a result of his concentration on Latin American material. But, if the formulation is to be generalizable to other parts of the world, then certain refinements should be introduced.

On the whole Frank concentrates his analysis on Chile and Brazil. In both these areas we are faced with a very specific form of colonization. It is a form of settler colonization akin perhaps to the cases of Australia and New Zealand. In such cases, the indigenous population is reduced to insignificance, and the society is in essence a settler colony. In such examples, it is not difficult to see how the historical process of underdevelopment could occur, and more importantly, continue. It is a case of the exertion of total coercion, resulting, in many cases, in the virtual extermination of any indigenous population. This initial exercise of naked force is then followed by the construction of a new social and economic structure, which entirely serves as a satellite of the colonizing society.

Contrasted with this type of colonialism are two other types. On the one hand there is what might be called the 'South African' type, where the native population remains in existence, but is totally suppressed by explicitly repressive means. On the other, there is the case where in the imperial era, the colony is an administered society. The majority of the population are indigenous, the minority are mainly administrators (not settlers) who come for short periods from the colonizing society. This type of society attains its political independence, but effective economic control is maintained very largely by external forces. In so far as the majority of the world's underdeveloped societies fall in to the last category, it is necessary to demonstrate how Frank's model can be made relevant to these societies, both in their colonial and post-colonial experience.

There are two problems in applying the model to this third type of society. The first is that of demonstrating the manner in which the social and economic system of the underdeveloped society became articulated with the expanding capitalist system. For, although there was clearly an element of naked force in the events through which the articulation occurred, it would be naïve and analytically unsubtle to leave the explanation at that point. The process of articulation whereby societies became consociates as well as contemporaries took place through the medium of human actors operating within the context of specific sets of social structural constraints and opportunities. The work of some of the French anthropologists, such as Meillassoux[2] and Dupré and Rey,[3] gives us some indication of the complexity of such processes. For example, the slave trade from the coast of West Africa was not solely a series of raids which permitted the extraction of the human cargo by sheer brute force. In fact, the entire structure of the society and economy of the coastal and inland regions underwent a process of adaptation and change, all ultimately directed toward filling the waiting cargo holds at the coastal factories. But at lower levels of the vertical structure, horizontal substructures developed which satisfied local interests, and therefore contributed to the maintenance of the vertical relationships.

In a similar manner it is necessary to be able to demonstrate how the changes in economic, social, and political organization occurred in less spectacular cases. For example, in cases such as those of plantation agriculture, small-holder cashcrop agriculture, and mining. These are clearly historical questions: but they have considerable importance for understanding the contemporary social structure of those societies which have been encapsulated by a global system of production and exchange.

The second problem arises partly from the essentially vertical nature of the Frank model, but also, I think, from his concentration on the South American material. This is the problem of the persistence of the metropolis–satellite linkages in a situation of neo-colonialism. Frank concentrates on showing us how the vertical links from the furthest satellite to the ultimate metropolis are brought into existence historically. He uses the concepts of surplus and expropriation in order to describe the relationship between the poles at the various levels of the system. However, this seems to avoid a central issue which can be summed up in the following question: 'What kinds of horizontal social, economic and political formations develop within the context of the general relationship which allow it to continue in existence?' Or, to put it another way, how does the social structure of underdevelopment reproduce itself, and renew itself? To return to my earlier analogy, we are not concerned with a conveyor belt of any ordinary kind; this is a very remarkable conveyor belt which not only transports goods, men, and services from one place to another, but also renews itself at the same time. Indeed, one might say that at each stage of the relationship between a metropolis and a satellite, a little of the surplus expropriated comes to settle, enabling that element in the total chain to continue in existence and therefore maintain the drain. A related point which I want to take up in this chapter is concerned with the work of Arghiri Emmanuel. Emmanuel, in his book *Unequal Exchange*,[4] argues that the exchange of goods and services between rich and poor countries is essentially unequal because of the manner in which prices ruling between nations are determined. Thus, he argues that in contrast to the conventional view that producers' incomes are determined by the market price, in fact a much more complex causal relationship is the case. The actual sequence is that the wage paid to labour in fact determines the price at which a commodity can be sold on the world market. I would want to argue that Emmanuel's point, in as much as it holds, only does so in the early days of economic articulation between two systems of production. After the initial interpenetration has occurred, a conventional price, socially and more importantly, politically determined and defined, becomes the 'normal' price. Thus, the relation between price and wage (or producer income more generally, perhaps as a form of labour-rental) is essentially a *reflexive* one. It is determined in the final analysis by a whole series of conventional definitions of what constitutes a 'normal' price, and by the political trials of strength which accompany this process of assigning a market value to land and labour. In this process, these elements become 'factors of production'. This is not to suggest that the present-day market price for Gezira cotton is determined by the level of income accruing to labour. On this point I disagree with Emmanuel. However, I would suggest that the range of price elasticity of demand for cotton on the world market has been influenced by the traditional prices which have been paid, and that these are directly related to the original value which was assigned to labour. It is only in situations of extreme shortage, such as the early 1950s and 1970s, that these traditional prices seem to lose their influence on the actual market prices. However, the notion of a return to 'normality' outside such periods implies that cotton, and therefore the labour which produces it, has a 'normal' price which ought not to be exceeded.

Having outlined these broad theoretical points, I now want to show how they are relevant to the analysis of an empirical case, that of the Gezira Scheme in the Sudan.

The Gezira Scheme—an outline

The Gezira Scheme is situated in the triangle of land south of Khartoum. Two sides of the triangle are formed by two rivers, to the east the Blue Nile, and to the west the White Nile. The southern boundary of the Gezira area can be taken as the railway line which runs from Sennar in the east to Kosti in the west. The total area of the Gezira region is about five million acres, but the Scheme itself occupies slightly under two million acres. The government corporation which today runs the Scheme is called the Sudan Gezira Board. It employs directly about 10,000 staff of all grades. The agricultural operations are performed by the 70,000 tenants, their families, and various types of hired labourers. The whole Scheme therefore gives employment and some kind of livelihood to a very large number of people—probably something in the region of a quarter of a million.

Although other crops are cultivated, the dominant one is long staple cotton. The production of the Gezira Scheme constitutes a major part of the total Sudanese exports of cotton, which in turn forms a considerable part of all Sudanese exports. For example, in 1969 cotton exports were worth £s51·8 million out of a total of £s86·3 million exported from the Sudan.[5]

The cultivation of cotton on this scale in the Gezira is facilitated by a complex irrigation system. This is based upon two dams on the Blue Nile, one (the older) at Sennar, and the other at Al Roseires. Further details concerning the operation of the Scheme are to be found elsewhere,[6] and I shall restrict my general description to what has already been presented.

The bulk of what follows will concentrate upon certain aspects of how the Gezira Scheme came into being, and is maintained in its present form—a form which has altered only slightly from the original ground plan. This continuity of social relationships and of organizational structure is in itself an important feature of the entire position of dependence in which the Sudan stands to other dominant socio-economic systems. The Gezira Scheme is but one focus of the more general articulation between the whole Sudan and the global system of production and distribution.

I shall consider four empirical areas which will illustrate the theoretical concerns which have already been introduced. These are:

(1) the reasons why the Gezira Scheme was established;

(2) the way in which the role of labour was defined in the context of the Scheme;

(3) the effects of concentration on cotton mono-culture on the micro-social structure, and particularly on the formation of classes; and

(4) the definition of the value of labour, and the organizational complex which enables that definition to be maintained.

Clearly, a purely sociological consideration of these problems is bound to result in considerable distortion. What I shall attempt in looking at these problems will be an integrated analysis, showing how economic relations are created and maintained by political factors and social factors, and how in fact all three types of analysis necessarily form an integrated whole.

There were two reasons for the creation of the Gezira Scheme. Both of these grew directly out of the industrial history of the United Kingdom. The key factors were:

(1) the traditional role which had been occupied by the cotton textile industry in Britain throughout the nineteenth century; and

(2) the dependence of the United Kingdom upon its colonies for supplies of raw materials and markets.

(1) *The British cotton industry*

By the end of the nineteenth century and the beginning of the twentieth, the Lancashire cotton industry, which had until that time occupied a paramount position in the world, was facing increasing competition from Germany, the United States, and even China. These areas were competing with Lancashire both for markets and for the raw materials. This had two connected effects. On the one hand the Lancashire industry was increasingly unable to compete in the production of coarse cotton textiles. It therefore began to concentrate increasingly on the fine end of the trade. It was only this change in production which enabled Lancashire to maintain its position as a leading textile area.

However, this move towards the production of the finer textiles was not unaccompanied by risks. The finer product required a finer raw material: it required long staple cotton rather than short or medium staple varieties. The areas of the world in which this type of cotton was to be found were quite restricted, limited in the main to Egypt, and to a lesser extent the United States and Peru.

With the development of the domestic textile industry in the USA, the American crop was less available to Lancashire. At the same time, the quantity of the Egyptian crop was falling year by year. This was a result of the increasingly oppressive taxation of the *fellahin*, who by the end of the nineteenth century were leaving the land in considerable numbers. As a result the price of raw cotton rose astronomically. In 1904 it rose from $5\frac{3}{4}d$. per pound to $9d$. a pound.[7] The overall scarcity of long staple cottons, arising from increased competition and decreasing supplies, was in turn exacerbated by cotton hoarding on the part of the Manchester and Liverpool cotton purchasing houses.

The whole affair came to a head in 1913, when in a number of parliamentary debates, MPs from Lancashire constituencies—acting as mouthpiece for the British Cotton Growers' Association[8]—suggested in very strong terms that the only way to solve the problems of Lancashire was by creating a safe and dependable supply of long staple cotton. It was necessary to derive the cotton from an area in which Britain would have a virtual monopoly of purchase. As one Member of Parliament put it:[9]

> The greatest cotton industry in this country can never be in
> the position in which we should like to see it so long as it
> is dependent entirely, or almost entirely, for its supplies of
> raw materials on foreign countries.

In so far as a colony could not be considered a 'foreign country', bound as it was politically and economically to the British metropolis, it was clear that the dependable source of supply would have to be created in some suitable part of the Empire.

Thus, the initial loan by the British Government for building the dam and irrigation system in the Sudan was pushed through Parliament largely through the efforts of the cotton interests, particularly the British Cotton Growers' Association. By creating a monopoly area for the supply of the raw material, the survival of the Lancashire industry was ensured for a few more decades.

(2) *The dependence of the United Kingdom on its Empire*

This in itself was, however, only one aspect of the more general imperial concern which influenced the creation of the Gezira Scheme. On the one hand the Gezira Scheme was brought about to ensure the existence of protected sources of raw materials. On the other, the Sudan itself was a necessary element in the wider imperial strategy. Its occupation by Britain was essential for the protection of the route to India through the Suez Canal, and thus for the protection of some of the important Far Eastern markets in which cotton textiles (as well as other manufactures) were to be sold. However, in the occupation of colonies, it was always necessary to maintain the costs of administration at the lowest possible level. Indeed, as far as possible, colonial possessions were expected to finance their own administration. In the case of the Sudan, this was very difficult. Prior to the development of cotton, the main export was gum arabic. And at the time of the Anglo-Egyptian invasion, the economy was in a somewhat parlous state as a result of the combination of bad harvests and bad administration during the period of Mahdist rule. So, in effect, the requirements of colonial policy—that a colony should be self-supporting as far as possible—the requirements of imperial strategy—protection of the Suez Canal route to the east—and the requirements of the Lancashire textile industry—a safe supply of raw long staple cotton—all came together in the creation of the Gezira Scheme.

The general processes underlying this historical development are, of course, by no means peculiar to the case of the Sudan. They are familiar in any area where underdevelopment through colonization has taken place. Indeed, it is because of the general features of the Gezira case that it is relevant to present it in the present theoretical context. In all cases of colonization, similar combinations of political, economic and sociological factors will be at work. It is to one of the central interactions of these elements that I now turn.

The definition of labour and its role in the production process

Arghiri Emmanuel suggests that a central feature of the relationship between rich and poor countries is that they stand in a relationship of unequal exchange. This notion of unequal exchange involves a process of social and political definition of what constitutes a 'fair

189

price' for a product. In short, as has been suggested in a number of places[10] there is nothing technological or necessary about relative pricing of either commodities, or, in the final analysis, of labour. Pricing is a process of definition which derives directly from the social relationships ruling between human actors in a given historical situation. Social evaluation, price evaluation, and power must be treated as inseparable elements in any piece of empirical analysis. The crux of Emmanuel's argument is that the exchange value of a commodity which is produced in a poor country is largely determined by the value which is placed upon labour used in the process of production. Thus, the low incomes which are received by labour in underdeveloped countries are not the result of low prices which are being paid for their products. Rather, the converse is the case. The low prices which a commodity brings on the market are the result of the low incomes which are paid to the labour.

Our concern, then, is with the processes whereby the value of agricultural labour was determined in the Gezira Scheme, and the processes by means of which it is maintained at a low level relative to the value of labour in the industrialized nations.

However, to express the problem in these terms is a serious oversimplification. It is an oversimplification because, traditionally, labour in the Gezira did not have any 'value' in the economic sense. 'Value' as a term applied to labour implies that it is a saleable commodity which can be the subject of calculative determination. Prior to the Gezira Scheme, the majority of the inhabitants of the area away from the rivers (where the situation was rather different) led a semi-nomadic, transhumant life. In the dry season they wandered from place to place in search of water and sparse grazing for their cattle. In the rains they lived in their villages and cultivated *dura* (*Sorghum vulgare*) on the land around them. Economic production was organized in terms of the lineage and the tribe. The head of a lineage or the sheikh of a tribe would make decisions as to the precise mode of exploiting the environment in any particular season. On the basis of his decisions, agricultural operations would be performed. In fact, the lineage or the tribe can be considered as in some ways resembling the 'family labour farm' described by Chayanov.[11] Within this system of economic organization, land was not a commodity in the sense of being commonly bought and sold. It was, though, frequently vested in one man[12] or in one family. But this was a situation of individual right in land, the use of which was held in trust for the entire group.

Not all people held these individual rights. There were in fact three reasonably distinct strata in the society. These were the landed, the landless, and the slaves (*abiid*). The land was exploited in a number of ways. A landed man would work his land with the labour of his extended family and of his slaves. A landless man, or a man with only a small area of land, would sharecrop the land of a landed individual. The relationship between these two men is, however, distorted by the use of the term 'sharecrop' because this concept emphasizes the purely economic aspect of their links. In fact their relationship will have been very multiplex, for the entire system of relationships between man, land, and man, functioned so as to bind men together into political units. The implications of this kind of social structure in the post-irrigation period will become clear later in the chapter. For the moment, though, two points should be borne in mind. First, land was not a commodity, with a cash value. It was not in fact (in the central areas of the Gezira) entirely central to the economy, for it shared that position with cattle. It was worked as a family labour farm, sufficient labour being expended upon it to produce a subsistence minimum where and when this was possible. Thus, the land had use value, but did not have exchange value. Secondly, the economy was not such that it could produce any considerable surplus, which could then be marketed. Although taxes were paid in grain and cattle under the Turkish and the Mahdist regimes, they often had to be extracted under considerable duress. On the whole the products of the land had only use value and were rarely used to raise cash. This is not to say that the economy was entirely unconnected with other economies. Such a statement would be grossly misleading. Coffee was imported from Ethiopia, and also some gold was purchased from Omdurman.[13] However, these were special purchases, they do not indicate any great degree of dependence on the wider economy, nor any great degree of articulation with it. In the circumstances, these trade goods were not so central to the way of life as to necessitate the constant transformation of labour and land into exchangeable commodities with a view to being able thereby to purchase more coffee or more gold.

In the same way that the land and its products were not commodities, in the specific sense of having exchange value, so labour itself had only use value; it did not have a cash value attached to it. It was not a marketable commodity. An important feature of Chayanov's notion of a family labour farm is that in the peasant economy, production is for subsistence plus taxes, and labour is used to exploit the land to a level where some culturally acceptable level of subsistence is achieved. It is not used in such a way as to aim at a maximization outcome, because the possibility of maximization only arises with the possibility of exchange. Thus in a system where economic decisions are made in terms of subsistence, it becomes virtually impossible to attach cash value to land or to labour.

During the period following the reconquest of the Sudan in 1898 and the downfall of the Mahdist state, the central Sudan underwent considerable changes. For our purposes it will be sufficient to note four of these:

(1) Land tenure and land rights had become extremely confused during the period of the Mahdiyya and immediately afterwards. This resulted from considerable population movement together with other forms of disruption associated with the political situation both during the Mahdiyya and during the period of the Anglo-Egyptian invasion.

(2) In 1904 experiments began with irrigated cotton cultivation along the Nile.

(3) Many foreign speculators—mainly Greek and Egyptian—came to the Sudan with the invading Anglo-Egyptian force. These people began to buy land from the local people who claimed to have rights to it, but who often did not have such a right.

(4) The government passed a Land Ordinance and executed a cadastral survey with a view to establishing land rights in the Gezira area. They feared the effects of land speculation, perceiving the possibility that this could create large numbers of landless people who might ultimately form the basis of a political threat. The effects of land legislation were to restrict sale of land to people of Sudanese nationality, or to the government itself.

Thus land was legally defined in such a way that it could now be treated as a commodity, exchangeable against cash. This legislation and the new definition which was implicit in it could be seen as a direct result of the influx of speculators, coming as the first wave in the historical process of articulation between the Gezira economy and the wider global economy of the British Empire. Land was now divided into discrete parcels, each parcel having an individual's name attached to it. Indeed, Bohannan's comment fits the case precisely when he says:[14]

> Man–man relationships in space, with concomitant rights
> to exploit the environment [were] replaced by legally enforceable
> man–thing units of the property type, the man becoming a
> legal entity the thing a surveyed parcel of land!

Land, in other words, was not converted into a totally free commodity exchangeable against cash, but, significantly, into one exchangeable only within certain limits—either with the government or those who were considered to be of Sudanese nationality.

This change, particularly the fact that it was carried out under the aegis of an invading military administration, has considerable relevance for my later discussion. In the situation of confusion which followed the invasion, rights in land often accrued to particular sections of the population. On the whole those who had been enthusiastic supporters of the Mahdi were unable to exercise their rights of ownership. For these reasons of political disqualification, rights in land tended to accrue to those who had either not supported the Mahdi, or at least had not been among his more enthusiastic supporters.

The point to note here is that the right to land which accrued to the new landholders under the colonial regime was much more a right to individual ownership than it had ever been prior to the reconquest. The nature of land was defined in terms of categories which formed part of the total system of economic, political, and legal philosophy of the new administration. These new categories also, of course, formed an integral part of the total system which was now engulfing the Gezira and the Sudan. That this type of redefinition of the relevant economic and legal categories could occur was a result of the monopoly of power held by the invading Anglo-Egyptian administration. But it is important to note that it was not solely a result of the monopoly of power. New political configurations provide new structural opportunities, and those people who had not been prominent Mahdists were in a position to grasp these opportunities. The outcome was not only a redefinition of legal categories, therefore, it was also, of course, a fundamental change in the structure of social relations between men through the medium of land.

The nature and the depth of the change is in many ways epitomized in the very organization of the Gezira Scheme. The Scheme was set up as a combination of government, commercial, and local involvement. Thus, the colonial government had the responsibility for construction and maintenance of all the irrigation works; the management of the Scheme was in the hands of a British company, the Sudan Plantations Syndicate; labour was to be supplied by the native inhabitants of the Gezira.

This formal division of responsibility is in itself a structuring of the organization in terms of the categories of neo-classical economic thought. The government leased the land on a very long-term basis from those who had rights in it. In so far as they could only sell to the government or to other Sudanese, and the government was offering a good rent for the unirrigated land, there was no difficulty in the way of gaining control of the land. Thus the government in effect became the landowner—there was never any real possibility of the land being returned to the original owners.

The Sudan Plantations Syndicate supplied the managerial ability, and the people of the area supplied the labour power upon which the entire enterprise was based. What had happened was that the three factors of production of neo-classical economics—land, labour, capital—were now represented by the government, the tenants, and the Sudan Plantations Syndicate. The whole undertaking was represented as a commercial partnership. Indeed the proceeds of cotton sales were divided up in proportion between the three factors. The government was to receive 40 per cent, the Sudan Plantations Syndicate 20 per cent, and the tenants collectively 40 per cent. However, although the enterprise was represented as a partnership, it was in reality only a partnership between the government and the Sudan Plantations Syndicate. The tenants had no direct say in the running of the Scheme. Indeed, it was not until the late 1940s, with the beginnings of the trade union movement in the Gezira, that they were to any great degree taken into consideration.

The tenants were not intended to be labourers in the sense of being paid a wage. Part of the ideology of 'partnership' was that the tenants in the Scheme were to form the basis of a class of 'yeoman farmers' such as were at that time said to form the backbone of the current British greatness. It was intended that this goal should be achieved through allocating each tenant an area of land within the rotation. On this land he, together with his family, was supposed to grow cotton, *dura*, and perhaps a fodder crop, usually *lubia* (*Dolichos lablab*). The cotton was to be collected by the Sudan Plantations Syndicate and marketed by them, the proceeds of the sale to be divided as described above.

The tenant's position was very clearly defined by means of a contract which specified his obligations to the Sudan Plantations Syndicate. This contract is worth quoting as it demonstrates very clearly the real nature of the 'partnership'. The tenant had to accept the following conditions in order to be able to cultivate the land:[15]

> If the tenant neglects or is careless in the cultivation of
> his crops the Syndicate shall have the right without the
> consent of the tenant to take such steps as the Syndicate may
> consider proper for the safeguarding of the crops, and any
> expenses incurred thereby shall be a debt from the tenant to
> the Syndicate and may without his consent be deducted by the
> Syndicate from his share of the crop proceeds.

In contrast, the Syndicate was allowed considerably more independence of action. Thus its obligations were as follows:[16]

> The Syndicate shall supply water necessary for the irrigation
> of the said Scheme of crop rotation but if at any time by
> reason of the breakdown of machinery, canals or other irrigation
> work or any other compulsory circumstances the supply of water
> to the said land is interrupted the tenant shall have no claim
> against the Syndicate for any compensation on account of the
> water not reaching the land under cultivation.

Indeed the underlying unequal nature of this contract of supposed 'partnership' is epitomized in the final paragraph, which clearly stated: 'The English copy of the Tenancy Agreement shall . . . form the official contact. The Arabic translation thereof is merely for the information of the tenants.'[17] The tenant's role in the Gezira Scheme was defined in terms of English legal categories and in the English language. He had many obligations, but few rights. But above all he now became a legal person defined in terms of a legal system originating in a capitalist, European society.

Whereas production in the pre-Scheme Gezira had been organized in terms of a variety of multiplex social relations, in which the economic, the political, and the kinship strands had all been internally related, the tenant in the new situation was related to the newly created means of production solely as an economic actor—in other words as 'labour'. More than this, though, he was no longer producing only for subsistence purposes. Previously his product had had little or no exchange value, and neither had his labour. Now he was almost totally concerned with producing a commodity— cotton, which for him had only exchange value, and his labour was now a commodity. And the value of his labour as a commodity was determined by the traditionally low standard of living characteristic of the Gezira. Its value was set at the level at which an individual could maintain himself and his family within the existing circumstances, and under the existing set of expectations. It is the mechanisms which operate to maintain the value of labour at this level or at least to prevent it from rising very fast, which ensure the operation of the Scheme on the present basis. One such mechanism is that of credit. The way in which informal credit at the village level operates in the Gezira Scheme is absolutely central to the maintenance of low prices for cotton and low incomes for the producers. The system of credit has to be understood in terms of the developing class structure in the villages of the Scheme.

The formation of social classes in the Gezira villages

The change in social organization within the irrigated area over the past thirty years has seen the clear formation of economic classes. These classes did not, of course, develop spontaneously. They developed from the combination of pre-existing social forces and social configurations with the particular structural opportunities provided by the Scheme itself.

Although it was assumed by the British that a tenancy could be worked by a man and his family, this has never been entirely the case. At peak periods, such as weeding and picking, it has always been necessary for the tenants to employ labour. This labour consists of non-tenants from the Gezira as well as non-Sudanese and Sudanese labour migrants. The payments made to the tenants for their cotton have (with the exception of the early 1950s) never been sufficient to enable them to meet the costs of this hired labour. They have always had to resort to borrowing in excess of the cash advances made to them by the Sudan Gezira Board, in order to pay for these labourers.

However, not all tenants are in fact entirely dependent upon their tenancies for their income. There is a stratum of rich tenants who have sources of income in addition to their tenancies. They own shops, lorries and may have sons who are in salaried employment. These people, and others in similar positions who are not tenants (for not every inhabitant of a Gezira village is a tenant), have been able to provide the credit requirements of those wholly dependent on their tenancy. Credit tends to flow along kinship channels. This is certainly the case where the larger loans of cash are concerned. Therefore that section of the population who originally had titles to the land, or who became involved in trade because they had land which could be used for growing *dura*, and could thus form the base of trading activities, have developed into a class of money-lenders. However, credit is not extended in the same measure to all who request it. Large loans on easy terms will be made to relatives or to those who are definable as relatives. Non-relatives can only obtain credit at very high rates of interest, in restricted amounts, and in particular ways. These differences in the credit arrangements, depending on one's position in the kinship, and class structures, ensure the continued separation between those who have wealth and those who do not. The wealthy and their relatives maintain a relatively high standard of living, depending upon their lending and other entrepreneurial activities rather than upon their tenancies. The poor tenants are entirely dependent upon their tenancies, and the returns from a tenancy are rarely sufficient to support a family. Indeed, in some cases, tenants have negative incomes.[18] They are only maintained through the small amounts of credit which they can obtain from the rich. The whole dependence and debt relationship, it must be emphasized, is in no way vicious, disguised as it is by the dominant Islamic ideology concerning charity.

It is, though, at this point of the analysis that one of the processes by which the entire Gezira Scheme is maintained in being as a link in underdevelopment becomes clear. The credit arrangements at the village level are vital to the reproduction of the overall structure. The tenant dependent upon his tenancy is able to live on his low income only because he can get credit. Therefore the cotton which he produces can be sold for a low price. In order to remain viable, in order to subsist, he has to depend upon credit. This credit is given in two ways: either at a shop from which he purchases food, a system akin to 'putting it on the slate' in Britain, or he sells the grain which he grows on his tenancy to the shopkeeper or other money-lender.

In the final analysis, both these sources add up to much the same thing. If he has an outstanding debt to a shopkeeper at the harvest, he will normally be expected to pay off the whole sum, or a large proportion of it, in grain. Whether he sells his grain directly for cash (a system called *shail*) or settles his outstanding account, he receives the low price ruling at the time of the harvest. The lender then stores the grain, and later sells it in the towns at a profit of 100 per cent or more. The profit which the shopkeeper makes on the transaction will in general be used to purchase a variety of imported foodstuffs and consumer goods, which are then sold to the tenant. The tenant is highly dependent on purchasing food and consumer goods from the shops because the Scheme within which he works has removed from him, to a very considerable degree, the possibility of complete production for his own subsistence and that of his family. Thus, in effect, the continued operation of the Gezira Scheme depends upon the willingness of the lenders to lend, and their ability to spend their profits from these transactions on the purchase of imported goods.

This mechanism, which serves to finance an important part of the operation of the Scheme, has both social and economic effects. It enables the labour upon which the Scheme is predicated to continue to exist; it also reinforces, and indeed deepens the class divisions which have developed in the social structure. Frank concentrates much of his analysis of underdevelopment around the model of the metropolis and the satellite. The interesting feature of this model is the way in which the conflicting interests of the social metropolis and satellite, at each level, operate in fact to maintain the vertical linkage of underdevelopment. The contradiction in the total economic relationship between, for example, the Sudan and its markets, which is one of unequal exchange, is just one case of this general type of relationship. The relationship between poor and rich tenants is another example of how this overall relationship is maintained at the micro level. Low income permits low prices; low incomes also generate a need for credit. This reinforces the class divisions in the society, and at the same time allows the whole structure to continue in being. And within the overall structure, each of the two classes has interests in the maintenance of their existing immediate relationship.

The role of the administrators and the structure of the organization

However, important as this micro-level aspect of the Gezira Scheme is in maintaining the overall system of production, it has to be considered within the overall context of the Scheme. The class relations

197

at the village level, which have been sketched here in terms of credit relations, do not function in isolation. They are part of a much more complex system of social relationships, which contribute to the overall reproduction of the total socio-economic structure of the Scheme within the context of the Sudanese political economy. One way of approaching this wider aspect of the problem is to consider the role of the administrators of the Scheme, and, in particular, to examine their class origins, their aspirations, and the manner in which these operate together to influence their behaviour as administrators. One crucial area which is to be considered at this point is the way that the administrators define the quality of the tenants' labour. Earlier, it was suggested that in the initial period of the Scheme's development, the price for which the cotton could be sold on the world market was directly related to the value given to the tenants' labour by the colonial administration. The maintenance of the relationship between administrative-governmental evaluation of the tenants and the formation of a market price can still be detected in the present-day operation of the Scheme. We can begin by looking at the relationship between market price of the labour factor and the social evaluation of labour in some more detail.

What is being suggested is that there is some relationship between the social definition of a particular group in a society, and the price which their labour can command on the market. Now, quite clearly, this relationship, if it exists, is in no sense a simple one. It is a relationship which is mediated through a whole complex of socio-historical interpretations and definitions; it is a reflexive, processual relationship.

A productive role in a society is allocated a value, this value manifests itself as a wage payment (or some other form of payment) in return for the effort expended. However, such a price does not reflect any measure of actual labour input, but only a measure of the socially dominant *estimation* of the value of labour input. In other words, it represents the socially defined exchange value of the commodity labour. Neither does this payment reflect any necessary technical or technological constraints on payment. Constraints do not exist of themselves, but through processes of social definition. The mechanism which fixes the price of labour, reflects the social relationships ruling between groups in a society. In other words, there is a bargaining and power element involved, and this bargaining element is indicative in its outcome of the power relationships between groups.

The neo-classical model of price as a response to supply and demand is acknowledged within the tradition as an approximation to reality. In reality we are most often concerned with situations of what that tradition calls 'imperfect competition'. This notion of 'imperfect competition' applies only to the point in socio-economic life where goods and services are being exchanged, not to that point where they are being produced. 'Exchange' is a concept which describes the social relationship between those who produce a product, or supply a factor of production, and those who purchase that product or that factor. The value allocated to a product or factor in this case cannot be considered in isolation from the more general political (in the broadest sense of the word) relationships between social groups.

The processes whereby price, power relationships, and definition of the value of labour are related, can be illustrated by examining the Gezira Scheme in terms of the following problem areas:

(1) the way in which the present-day relationships between the tenants and the administrators are structured in such a way as to maintain the traditional price for tenant's labour, and for his services as an organizer of the labour he hires;

(2) the way in which the present-day definitions of value are maintained through social structures which have their origins in the past;

(3) the way that a specific organizational structure functions so as to enable the reproduction of the social relations of production; the organization acts as an arena in which a defined value is acted out and confirmed in the eyes of the administrators, and thus perpetuated.

The formal organization in the Gezira Scheme (or in any large-scale concern) is based upon various assumptions as to how groups within that organization can be expected, or ought, to act. These are in turn based on the assumptions which the originators of the organization make about the 'correct' relationships between these groups in society generally. In so far as an organization does in fact conform to these expectations in its functioning, the appropriate definitions of the value of the participants are confirmed in practice. In other words, the existing relations of production are supplied with the preconditions of their reproduction and in the process a contribution is made to the overall reproduction of the social structure.

In the Gezira Scheme, the tenants, on becoming involved in a contractual relationship, became defined as a factor of production—'labour'. However, the process by which this occurred has to be explored in more detail. In order to do this, the origins of the organization of the Gezira Scheme must be examined. In particular this organization must be analysed in terms of the assumptions which its founders made about the ideal relationsips which ought to be the case between the management and workers.

The organizational form adopted in the Gezira Scheme was from its earliest days highly authoritarian in tone and hierarchical in structure. This was to be expected. The Sudan Plantations Syndicate was a commercial enterprise, having its origins in the latter part of the nineteenth century. The type of organizational thinking which informed the planning of the operational organization has its roots in two traditions of administrative thought. One root was that of the accepted methods of industrial organization. The prime movers in the implementation of the Scheme were the members of the British Cotton Growers' Association. These men were predominantly industrialists from Lancashire, connected in various ways with the cotton industry. Their interest was to obtain a constant supply of cotton for their industries. Their experience of large-scale organization was gained mainly in the industrial environment of nineteenth-century Lancashire. The rules of thumb by which such men would expect an organization such as that planned in the Gezira to function would have been drawn from their own industrial and commercial milieu. The emphasis was inevitably on control rather than on communication. In so far as 'labour' was to be controlled and manipulated, it is indeed questionable whether the lower levels of the organization, where it had immediate contact with labour, did receive any conscious degree of consideration.

We can then assume a situation where the assumptions which informed the organization were similar to those informing industrial organizations in the metropolis. Strict control of the labour force through the medium of a hierarchically structured organization was a basic assumption. The kind of explicit theory about the nature of organizations which might have been influential in that industrial milieu was that of J. Slater Lewis, the Manchester mechanic and industrialist, whose book *The Commercial Organization of Management*[19] was one of the earliest discussions in Britain of the theory of commercial management. His basic assumptions about industrial organizations rested upon the need for efficiency and control, and are illustrated in this very characteristic extract:[20]

> A manufacturing organization is, in a sense, an engine of warfare—industrial warfare—hence it is obvious that readiness, efficiency and perfection of organization must receive very careful, if not paramount consideration as against the claim of profit and dividend.

This type of theory was, though, only one strand in the organizational ground plan of the Gezira Scheme. There was another strand, which was perhaps more important. This was what might be called the 'theory of the organization of native labour'. This body of theory which existed and was influential within the entire imperial tradition made a number of assumptions which resulted in an even greater emphasis on the control function of an organization. There are three assumptions in this strand of thought: first, native labour is by its nature recalcitrant, and therefore requires authoritarian treatment; second, native labour lacks initiative, and therefore requires very detailed directives and instructions; and third, native labour can, within certain limits, be improved, and the 'civilizing' function of authoritarian methods in some way legitimizes those methods.

The evidence for this kind of definition of the nature of native labour is scattered throughout the documentation of the imperial period. However, the following extract from a (hurried) letter written by a senior British inspector in the Scheme in 1928 will illustrate the point:[21]

> The custom of the native of the Gezira was to use slaves for
> all possible manual labour and the poorer Arabs went out after
> rain and worked hard for 10 days or so getting their
> Dhurra sown and cleaned when they left it for 2 months to
> ripen and then spent a hard week collecting it, and paying
> their Taxes and few debts, and they then lived for the rest of
> the year in a very cheap and lazy fashion attending weddings
> and funerals and doing odd jobs of trading in oil and
> tobacco or something similar.

Within the limits set by these two strands of thought about the nature of labour, it becomes clear how the definition of the value of Gezira tenants was inevitable. 'Labour', defined as being in need of control by the assumptions drawn from the metropolitan industrial milieu, became further specified in the context of the assumptions about the nature of *native* labour. The outcome of this was that when the tenants' labour became a commodity it was a commodity which could exist at a particular standard of life, and required particular techniques of management.

The second element in our discussion of how power relationships are represented by the price paid to the labour factor involves an examination of the wider social structure within which an organization such as the Gezira Scheme operates. The argument is that the administrative state of the colonial period, together with the administrative class of that time, has been replaced in the present by an administrative class operating within a successor administrative state. As the Gezira Scheme has now been nationalized, so its Sudanese administrators have taken on the role of the British administrators. This class relates to 'labour' through the organization. In so far as the organization remains virtually unchanged, so the perceptions which it allows the administrators of the nature and role of labour are in many ways analogous to those which were allowed to the British administration of an earlier era. What are the origins of those Sudanese administrators?

When the Sudan was reconquered by the British in 1898, a military administration was established. However, such a state was unable to function without the aid of an indigenous staff at its lower levels. In 1902 Gordon Memorial College was opened, with the aim of providing for the state's needs of clerks, book-keepers, and secretaries. In line with this requirement for skilled lower level office staff, the administration also needed officials in the rural areas. These two requirements meant the involvement in the running of the colonial state of two sets of Sudanese participants. On the one hand a group of urban-based *sous-officiers*, on the other a group of rural, tribal headmen.

This was the period (up to about 1925) when the Sudanese political economy was undergoing a process of progressive articulation with the metropolitan economy of Britain. The foundation of Gordon Memorial College in 1902 and its upgrading to secondary school status in 1913, together with the Power of Nomad Sheikhs Ordinance in 1922 and the Power of Sheikhs Ordinance in 1927, are the indicators of this process of increasing articulation at the political and administrative level. The founding of Gordon Memorial College opened the way for power to pass into the hands of the traditional urban administrative and merchant class of the Central Sudan, the *gellaba*. The Power of Nomad Sheikhs Ordinance crystallized the previously fluid power structure within the nomadic tribes. Under this and other such legislation, the rural social structure underwent considerable changes. From a situation of fluidity where power and social organization had been basic responses to population pressure and environment, a move to relative stasis occurred. Instead of the social structure receiving its main impetus from ecological relationships, it now received directives from a centrally organized government and administration. This had occurred to some extent in the past, particularly during the Mahdiyya. However, the technology of control had been far less efficient in the past, as is witnessed by the inability of the Mahdist state to control the centrifugal tendencies in Sudanese society.[22]

The *gellaba* had occupied an important position within the Sudanese state during the Turkish period (1822–81) and during the Mahdiyya (1881–98). However, this had always been an uneasy role, particularly during the latter period, when there had been a constant balancing act between the dependence of the Khallifa's administration upon their clerical and other skills, and his suspicion and dislike of them as an urban group.[23] With the reconquest, the rural headmen and the *gellaba* came to occupy relatively secure positions within the colonial state. Most of the entrants to Gordon Memorial College were from *gellaba* backgrounds,[24] and the centralized administration could not function efficiently without them and the rural headmen. However, it is with the role of the *gellaba* class that we shall be concerned in what follows.

The *gellaba* were not solely an administrative class, although they have so far been treated as though this were the case. In fact, they were a mixture of minor officials, merchants and artisans. In the roles of merchant and official they were vital to the process of vertical articulation between the Sudanese satellite and the British metropolis. They were equally vital in the process of deepening articulation within the Sudan. The administrators, who came to be known as the *effendiyya*, were a vital part of the administration. The merchants were equally vital in the process of economic articulation. They consisted, and still consist, of people involved in a whole range of scales of enterprise. The largest operators were based in the capital, Khartoum, or in Omdurman, the smallest in some of the villages and small towns throughout the Sudan.[25] In short, this group played an important role in the process of encapsulation of the Sudan into the economic and political structure of the British Empire. In the course of this process, they became beneficiaries of the new political economy, and began to accept parts of the ruling definition of how the system of government and administration worked. Most important, while resenting their own exclusion from power, they very often accepted some of the assumptions of the British colonial government as to the nature of the rest of the Sudanese population. Because they accepted these kinds of assumptions, and at the same time identified with the British administration, they were inevitably centrally involved in the struggle for political independence. This involvement began in an organized form with the formation of the Graduates Congress in 1922, composed of graduates of Gordon Memorial College.

With the transition to political independence in 1956, the *effendiyya* gained control of the State administration. With the Sudanization of the Gezira Scheme from 1950 onwards they began to take control of the field administration of the Scheme. The first recruits were considered to be an elite. This was because the Gezira Scheme, widely seen both within and outside the Sudan as a tremendous success, was in many ways an elite organization, the backbone of the entire Sudanese economy. These early recruits were trained by the British inspectors, and learned to do their job along the same lines as it had been done by these men.

As has already been noted, the overall ethos of the administration was one of authority and hierarchy. It was this ethos which informed the training of these new administrators drawn from the *effendiyya*. In particular, it should be noted, they learned an established attitude towards the tenants. The tenants were supposed to be the labour factor in the overall process of production, and were on the whole characterized by laziness, lack of initiative, and a marked preference for leisure over work. In effect, then, the new inspectors came to

203

occupy not only the formal work roles of the British inspectors of the commercial company, but also many of their attitudes to and assumptions about the tenants. This organizational role was reinforced by the origins of this group within the overall social structure of the colonial Sudan. In so far as the economy of the Sudan was (and still is) so heavily dependent on the Gezira Scheme, those who succeeded to the administration were almost bound to accept the existing theories as to how the Scheme ought to operate. The constraints upon the Sudanese economy as a primary producer remained the same as they had been throughout the colonial period, and any attempt to question or change the structure of administration in the Gezira was fraught with considerable danger; it might threaten the stability of the entire economy. The outcome of this process has been a situation whereby the historical definition of the value of labour, and its position in the operation of the Scheme, was taken over by the new administrators. This process occurred in the context of the same organization which continues to occupy a crucial position in the articulation of the Sudanese economy with dominant economies.

This brings us to the third element in the discussion. The social relations of production cannot just be said to have been taken over. The process by which this happened has to be demonstrated. In this demonstration lies part of the explanation of the central problem of this chapter—the process of reproduction of the relations of production by which the vertical relations of underdevelopment are maintained and renewed in the process of cotton production. Reproduction of the relations of production—in this case the organization and the resulting relations between the inspectors and the tenants—hinges upon the reproduction of the inspectors' definition of the nature of the tenants and their part in the enterprise.

The organization of the Gezira Scheme is based upon the assumptions which have been described. These concern the nature of labour and the organizational technology required to handle it. The emphasis is on control rather than on participation. This emphasis is of course in the interest of the inspectors. The greater the perceived need for control, the greater is the need for inspectors to run the Scheme. The way in which the definition of the tenants as lazy and unwilling labour has been maintained, and the continuing need for inspectors therefore reinforced, can be illustrated through an examination of the history of devolution policy in the Scheme.

During the period when the Sudan Plantations Syndicate ran the Scheme, the colonial government began to be concerned at the degree of power that the companies were wielding within the Sudan. Concern was felt in particular at the authoritarian manner in which the Scheme was administered. Pressure was therefore brought on the companies to involve the tenants in the running of the Scheme. This is the origin, in the 1930s, of the policy of devolution. This policy was intended to cut down the number of inspectors required, make the organization less authoritarian, and involve the tenants in the day-to-day running of operations. The policy never really succeeded, due largely to a number of factors extraneous to the Scheme itself. The policy was, however, given new life after nationalization and independence, but has failed again. This time the failure is due as much to the unwillingness of the inspectors to operate it as to any external factors.

In a survey of all the inspectors in the Gezira Scheme carried out in 1971,[26] it was found that a very large proportion of them were strongly opposed to the policy of devolution. This proportion was in excess of 50 per cent. They considered that any attempt to implement devolution detracted from the need for control and efficiency. Inasmuch as the general impression among these men is that tenants are on the whole lazy and inefficient, then the majority opinion was that authority and supervision were the only qualities which would enable the Scheme to continue to function. It is particularly worth noting that this feeling was most strongly expressed by the older inspectors, who also tend to be from *gellaba* origins.

In fact the characteristics of the tenants which the inspectors interpret as laziness and inefficiency are largely the result of the design of the Scheme itself, and the way that it functions. Briefly, it is true to say that the Gezira Scheme was designed to be operated by families, each working its own holding, and employing very little labour. This holding (the tenancy) was supposed to produce sufficient income to support the family unit. However, the nuclear family unit (which has developed partly as a response to the Scheme) cannot in general supply enough labour to run a tenancy. Therefore, labour is employed in large amounts. This confirms the inspectors' presupposition that the tenants are lazy. Furthermore, tenants' incomes from cotton can be very low indeed, discouraging them from working on that crop, and encouraging them to give their attention to their staple food crop, *dura*.

However, as we have seen, one major element in the present-day price for which cotton can be sold is the historical definition of the value of labour. This has had an important reflexive effect in determining the selling price of cotton and the level of income which the tenants receive. This in turn discourages them from giving very much attention to their cotton, thus confirming the preconceptions of the field staff about them as inferior labour. It also produces a need for the tenants to depend upon informal credit. The first of these is a major element in the reproduction of the organizational form and the field staff as a class. The second of these is a major element in

205

the class relationships which have developed at the micro level. Both phenomena play a central role in the overall reproduction of the relations of production, and in this case, also of the vertical structure of underdevelopment.

In conclusion, it will be useful to summarize the argument. There are five main points:

(1) The Scheme came into being as a result of an internally related set of economic and political factors. These developed from certain features of British industrial structure and imperial history in the latter part of the nineteenth century.

(2) In the process of colonization, the socio-economic structure of the Gezira underwent a fundamental change. The point upon which I have concentrated is the way that land was converted into a commodity and labour into a factor of production.

(3) This process enabled certain strata in the Gezira social structure to achieve a position of economic dominance. Their position as money-lenders maintains a structure of production which permits cotton to be produced at a low price relative to the price of imported manufactured goods. This position in the production process on the part of the creditors maintains and deepens the class divisions which have developed within the Scheme.

(4) The definition of the tenants as 'labour' within which the Sudanese administrators operate allows the reproduction of their own class relationship with the tenants, and thus of the authoritarian organization of the Scheme.

(5) These two elements, the relations between village debtors and village creditors, and the inspectors' definition of the nature of tenant labour, are essential to the reproduction of the whole relationship of underdevelopment between the Sudanese satellite and the metropolitan economies.

Notes

1 A. G. Frank, *Capitalism and Underdevelopment in Latin America*, Penguin, Harmondsworth, 1971.
2 C. Meillassoux, 'Essai d'interprétation du phénomène économique dans les sociétés traditionnelles d'auto-subsistance', *Cahiers d'Études Africaines*, vol. 4, 1960; see also 'From reproduction to production', *Economy and Society*, vol. 1, no. 1, 1972.
3 G. Dupré and P. P. Rey, 'Reflections on the pertinence of a theory of the history of exchange', *Economy and Society*, vol. 2, no. 2, 1973.
4 A. Emmanuel, *Unequal Exchange*, New Left Books, London, 1972.
5 Economic Commission for Africa, *Summary of Economic Data, Sudan 1970*, no. 39, October, 1971, p. 3.

6 Notably in A. Gaitskell, *Gezira: a Story of Development in the Sudan*, Faber & Faber, London, 1959; and in A. S. Barnett, 'A sociological study on the Gezira Scheme, Sudan', unpublished Ph.D. thesis, University of Manchester, 1973. The research for this thesis was financed by a grant from the Social Science Research Council.

7 A. W. Abdel Rahim, 'An economic history of the Gezira Scheme 1900–1956', unpublished Ph.D. thesis, University of Manchester, 1968.

8 An organization of individuals associated with cotton manufacture who had an obvious interest in the growth of that commodity. For further information see Gaitskell, *op. cit.*

9 *Hansard Parliamentary Debates*, fifth series, vol. 50, col. 17, 1913.

10 For example, by E. Nell in his essay 'Economics: the revival of political economy' in R. Blackburn, ed., *Ideology in Social Science*, Fontana, London, 1972, pp. 79 ff.

11 A. V. Chayanov, *The Theory of Peasant Economy*, Irwin, Homewood, Illinois, 1966.

12 A. R. C. Bolton, 'Land tenure in the Sudan', in J. D. Tothill, ed., *Agriculture in the Sudan*, Oxford University Press, London, 1948, p. 191.

13 J. R. Randell, 'El Gedid: a Blue Nile Gezira village', *Sudan Notes and Records*, vol. 39, 1958.

14 P. Bohannan, 'Land, "tenure", and land-tenure', in D. Biebuyck, ed., *African Agrarian Systems*, published for the International African Institute by Oxford University Press, London, 1963.

15 Reproduced in Gaitskell, *op. cit.*, p. 342.

16 *Ibid.*, p. 341.

17 *Ibid.*, p. 342.

18 A. S. Barnett, *op. cit.*, p. 121.

19 J. Slater Lewis, *The Commercial Organization of Management*, London, 1896, quoted in L. Urwick and E. Brech, *The Making of Scientific Management*, Management Publications Trust, London, 1946, vol. 2.

20 *Ibid.*, p. 83.

21 Letter to the Managing Director of the Sudan Plantations Syndicate, 22 March 1928, in Durham University Sudan Archives, Box 218.

22 This point is well demonstrated in P. M. Holt, *The Mahdist State in the Sudan 1881–1898*, Clarendon Press, Oxford, 1958.

23 *Ibid.*, p. 235.

24 Sudan Government, *Report of the Commission of Inspectors on the Gordon Memorial College*, Khartoum, 1929, p. 28, para. 21.

25 They in turn articulated with smaller merchants who had their origins in the more remote areas of the country.

26 A. S. Barnett, *op. cit.*, chapter 10.

10 Economic anthropology and the sociology of development: 'liberal' anthropology and its French critics

John Clammer

There is a complementarity between the work of Andre Gunder Frank[1] and that of recent French economic anthropology. Frank presents an analysis which explores the relations of dependence and exploitation between metropolitan centres and their satellites. The French anthropologists examine similar problems in terms of relations between modes of production, looking at the links between pre- and non-capitalist modes, and between those and capitalism itself. In turn, the whole discussion revolves around the question of the applicability of economic concepts deriving from capitalism to economic systems whose characteristics are different from or in opposition to the capitalist mode.

My project in this chapter will be to attempt to throw some light on this second area by way of a critical examination of the largely unknown (certainly to sociologists) and unappreciated literature deriving from the French economic anthropologists who are concerned with this issue and, in passing beyond the level of a critique, to relate the theoretical importance of this group to the twin issues of the nature of the fundamental conceptual basis of economic anthropology (and therefore of economics) on the one hand, and to the bearing of this on the more classical concerns of the sociology of development on the other. In so doing it is to be hoped that we might be both able to supply some theoretical discussion of the 'missing term' which lies between the analysis of the workings of international capitalism at a general level and the implementation of detailed studies of the operation of these forces at a truly local level in indigenous contexts, and to thereby make some move towards the integration of economic anthropology and the sociology of development, disciplines which are not conceptually, and should not be institutionally, distinct. The wider purpose must therefore be seen not so much as the transcending of Frank's seminal work, but as an attempt to give some substantial theoretical flesh to his often imprecise formulations.

But an understanding of the nature and purposes of the radical rethinking of the French neo-Marxists must be seen against the background of the whole Anglo-American tradition in economic anthropology, for it is from the criticism of this tradition, and in particular some of its key figures—Firth, Dalton, Bohannan, and Polanyi—together with a return less to Marx himself than to certain ideas inspired by him, that the positive programmes of the French radicals emerge. It is to the nature of this Anglo-American tradition that we must therefore turn.

The 'liberal' tradition

Contemporary economic anthropology has been largely dominated in recent years by the controversy surrounding the validity of applying concepts derived from 'classical' or conventional economics to the anthropological sphere. I do not intend to survey the details of this controversy: this has already been done perfectly adequately.[2] Instead I propose to examine the principal ideas of perhaps the single most creative economic anthropologist in recent history: Raymond Firth. This approach has the additional advantage of highlighting the main theoretical concerns of modern economic anthropology, for it is these that Firth has largely created or addressed himself to.

I will begin my exposition of Firth with the statement of four propositions which are axiomatic to his whole approach to economic anthropology.[3] First there is the distinction between what is commonly called 'primitive technology' and economic anthropology proper, defined as an essentially institutional study. Secondly there is the suggestion that the conceptual clarifications achieved by economists of the essential nature of *economic* problems, particularly where they relate to the behaviour of people in choice-making situations in the context of the disposal of available resources, can be imported into the study of economic anthropology. Thirdly there is the methodological proposition that the understanding of the nature of particular social systems can only be achieved when the nature of the particular economic system embodied in the social system is itself understood. And finally there is the claim that the divorce from 'primitive technology' and the borrowing of economic concepts has increased the interest in analytical problems to the extent that theory, including the subject's reflection on its own nature, has become a paramount concern of economic anthropologists.

The role of material 'things' is basic to any economy yet it has become increasingly apparent that economics, particularly when applied to small-scale communities, is essentially the study of *re-lationships*. And the economic anthropologist, because of the nature of his material, is obliged to recognize the reciprocity between forms of social relationship and the movement of material goods. The corollary of this is of course the proposition that there is an indissoluble relationship between any social system and its related economic system, such that one cannot be adequately explained or understood without reference to the other. Indeed this polarity of 'economic' and 'social' becomes more unreal the more one examines it. This may seem self-evident to the economic anthropologist who may be working at a fairly low level of abstraction, but it carries with it the interesting point that, if it is true, the possibility of divorcing social from economic factors becomes less viable at every level, which admits the possibility of systematic error into areas of economics which are tempted to regard the economic system as a self-regulating and abstract scheme of essentially mathematical relationships between abstract entities. Notions such as 'value' and 'demand' are empty unless they are seen in an essentially social context, and the economist must logically admit that if he is willing to import his own high-level abstract concepts into economic anthropology, then the contrary must be true. Thus Firth is correct in asserting that while certain economic concepts may or may not seem applicable to economic anthropology, there is no *a priori* way of deciding this: it must be tested empirically in the individual case by the anthropologist who has the data. Firth's debt to Malinowski in arriving at this position of the economic transactions being regarded as acts with a social meaning rather than as transmissions of objects is clear even though he diverges on almost all points of detail.[4] There arises from this the second and normative point, i.e. the assertion that economic anthropology *should* and indeed *must* be a theoretical and analytic discipline and not simply a descriptive one. Firth's recognition that anthropology is essentially a comparative study makes this problem acute by calling into question the theoretical basis of the subject at the two levels of (*a*) the general applicability of economic concepts in economic anthropology, and (*b*) the *universal* applicability of any given concept once it has been tested and found sound in a particular case.

Firth's general position on this is clear when speaking of a particular economic concept he says:[5]

> Evidence of gross difference between primitive, peasant and industrial economic systems is obvious. But absence of general markets for goods and services of all kinds and the lack of impersonal market relationships *does not mean the lack of any concept of economic advantage* ... the differences *lie*

primarily in the structural and institutional fields. On the basic principles of choice in the use of resources and perception of relative worth in an exchange, there is a continuum of behaviour over the whole range of human economic systems. From this point of view it may be argued that the relation sometimes postulated as a disjunction between economics and anthropology is of the same order as the relation between economics and economic history. When the anthropologist or historian applies an empirical institutional test to theoretical economic propositions, the propositions themselves may be found to need amplification or modification by specifying more precisely the conditions in which they operate. But anthropologist no more than historian needs to reject the whole apparatus of economic analysis.

Firth's position explicitly, then, is that it is possible, on the basis of the general uniformity of human economic reactions, to employ the basic approach of economic analysis in primitive contexts, given that the relationship between primitive system and modern analysis is a dialogue in which both sides may come to be seen in a different light. This, I take it, is the reason behind Frankenberg characterizing Firth's position as 'neo-classical'.[6] Let us expand this a little as it is the key to Firth's whole approach.

Firth starts from the assumption that all men in all societies are faced with the same economic problem: how to allocate scarce resources between alternative uses, given that some uses are more highly valued than others. He sees the main task of economic anthropology to be the study of how men organize their activities in solving the problem of allocation within the limits set by their physical environment, as transformed by culture, their technology and state of knowledge, their social structure and values. He denies that men in primitive and peasant societies are mere automata driven by the demands of their environment and social structure, and sees them as exercising choice in having to economize as men do in more complex societies. In analysing this aspect of conduct, anthropologists can use economic categories and economic analysis. Thus while primitive economies lack most of the specialized economic institutions that we associate with industrial societies, these alone need not be the object of economic analysis, and other forms of relationships may equally well be abstracted and examined, such as the processes of how people allocate their time between production of different categories of goods, of how goods and services are distributed and exchanged, how labour is mobilized and utilized, and the factors influencing decisions on these matters. These economic relationships function as part of a wider system of social involvements and moral imperatives, which are to be found also in industrial

211

societies: the difference between types of economic systems is one of degree, not kind. This view has been challenged on the basis that certain *essential* features of economies as we (i.e. Western economists) know them are missing from primitive systems. I think that Firth has partly forestalled this criticism by allowing that while, as he explicitly admits in many places, there are vast differences between primitive and modern economies, nevertheless, given that they can withstand the empirical tests for validity, individual economic concepts can be utilized universally, which is *not* what the anti-Firthian economists are arguing about.[7] The failure to resolve this problem seems to stem from an essential lack of communication: the economists who deny the validity of their concepts when applied to primitive cases are denying this possibility on the basis of the greater or lesser *lack* of certain of these *same* key concepts in the primitive economy in question. What we *should* be arguing about is how far *any* alien concepts can be used to explain a system which does not share the same presuppositions as the culture from which those concepts arise. In the context of this chapter I do not wish to enter this question. My point in making it is to demonstrate that the controversy as to whether or not we can employ classical economic concepts is empty until we specify the terms on which to argue. A resolution of the problem cannot even be attempted on the basis laid down by Frankenberg, Dalton,[8] and others. In this context involving Firth as the 'neo-classical' protagonist is pointless in that while he recognizes Malinowski's maxim that 'Nothing is so misleading in ethnographic accounts as the description of facts of native civilizations in terms of our own' (*Argonauts*), he is not blindly applying a set of economic points of reference to all economies and hoping for universally valid results. His claim that[9]

> what is required of Economic Anthropology is the analysis of material in such a way that it will be directly comparable with the material of modern economics, matching assumption with assumption and so allowing generalizations to be ultimately framed which will subsume the phenomena of both price and non-price commodities into a body of principles about human behaviour which will be truly universal

is not contrary to the more modest claim that we have characterized Firth as holding earlier when it is remembered that Firth is not claiming that he *has* found such a body of universal principles, but that this is the ideal, the paradigm of what any science should achieve. To argue that he is here misconceiving the nature of the human sciences is one thing and is a quite different issue altogether from arguing that he has contradicted his more moderate position.

This is not, however, to deny that there are problems. It is indeed true for instance that Firth's work contains no reference to the problems of dependence and exploitation, nor in any serious way (until very recently) to traditions of economic thought which lie outside of classical capitalism. To simply plead empiricism is clearly not enough—this is largely what the epistemologies of Structuralism and Marxism have struggled against. Similarly the misleading and theoretically inadequate 'underlabourer' conception of economic anthropology—the 'filling the gaps in the economist's data'—exists in Firth's view of the subject in large measure. Equally the view that the problem that 'where the economic anthropologist is still uncertain of his role is in the degree to which he should or can raise to a more abstract level the propositions he derives from the data he empirically gathers' is just a function of the present state of knowledge is naïve in the extreme.

In the light of this we must begin anew. Many of the arguments of Dalton, Polanyi, Sahlins, Burling, and Herskovits[10] may simply be misconceiving the nature of the problem. Few would wish to argue that the precise conceptual vocabulary of theoretical economics can be introduced *in toto* and without modification into economic anthropology. In practice the process is much more *ad hoc* than this, as Barth, Paine,[11] and others have shown. To begin afresh we must recognize (a) what is to be meant by 'economic analysis', (b) the characteristics of the societies being studied by the economic anthropologist, and (c) the limitations of concepts from any other discipline when applied to anthropology. Anthropologists, while correctly recognizing that much can be learnt from other disciplines, have undoubtedly leaned far too heavily on the concepts that those subjects have developed for themselves. Economic anthropology, perhaps more than most other specialized sub-branches of the activity, must develop its own concepts appropriate to its own peculiar needs.

The French critique

It is in response to these problems that a wide ranging critique of 'liberal' economic anthropology has arisen in France, drawing its inspiration from Marx largely by way of Althusser. While not recognizing themselves as composing a 'school' in the narrow sense, the common presuppositions, interests and purposes of the anthropologists I shall examine are so closely related that they may nevertheless be called by this term. The use of Althusserian language, aspects of his methodology, the common interest in Marx's mature works (and in particular *Capital*) as opposed to his early ones and the extension of certain Althusserian preoccupations (and in particular that of modes of production) equally allows us to identify something stronger than a mere tendency. In this sense also, the movement is a neo-Marxist one, rather than a 'classical' one, as I will attempt to make clearer. I will thus proceed by examining in some detail the contributions of Dupré and Rey[12] and Claude Meillassoux[13] to this debate, for it is in the works of these that the clearest exposition is to be found. Other and less central contributors (for example E. Terray,[14] M. Godelier,[15] and Coquery-Vidrovich[16]) I will make reference to only where a clear link with my central exposition (and subsequent critique) can be seen to exist.

Dupré and Rey's discussion (like that of Meillassoux's of 1972) begins with the rejection of the classification and interpretation of economic systems based exclusively on *forms of exchange*, and in particular of the models presented by Bohannan and Dalton[17] and Polanyi,[18] and in the bringing into opposition with this a Marxian analysis of the relationships between capitalist and 'traditional' modes of production and of the 'theory of the reproduction' of such formations. The details of the internal critique of Bohannan and Dalton, and Polanyi, I will leave to one side, and attempt to draw out only those aspects of the discussion concerned directly with Dupré and Rey's opposition to liberal economics as obscuring the true nature of dependence and exploitation.

What has to be explained is the historical problem that in many instances economic 'change' (or 'development') exerts its influence over 'traditional' economies by impelling them from being 'market-less economies', through the stage of being 'economies with peripheral markets' to their economic climax, 'economies in which the market principle is dominant'. But the real question is whether such a progression is to be explained by a liberal ('idealist') model which sees the seeds of the 'market principle' which comes to penetrate the entire society in pre-market institutions (whether in African societies, or in the Classical World, as with Polanyi) and which 'develops by means of its own forces, independently of any other structure than that of exchange', or by an historical one which 'does not conceal the fact that the famous "market principle" only developed through the coloniser's violent intervention against the previous mode of production'. What is needed, therefore, is a method which can take account of this in a concrete way—a method possessing 'theoretical unity', rather than one which operates through the fake oppositions of liberal economics, and particularly one which repudiates the view that market and non-market economies stand in a relationship of 'reciprocal exclusion', i.e. that 'the market system and other systems are absolutely incompatible'. Equally such a method must combat the insidious belief that 'from the moment the market is introduced the hitherto anthropological analysis gives way to the principles of liberal economics'.

The demonstration of this thesis involves Dupré and Rey in two linked expositions, one of the 'role of exchange in the reproduction of the conditions of production' in lineage societies, the other of the argument that[19]

almost in the centre of each particular system the place of exchange in the articulation of these systems will be justified by its role in the process of one system's domination of another, and this role will be determined in the last instance by the dominant mode of production.

The former exposition, of which I will try and point out the essence (and some of its equally essential difficulties), is based upon an analysis by Meillassoux[20] of the significance of exchange between the elders of lineage groups. Meillassoux quite rightly identifies the fact that the control that the elders possess over the goods produced in a lineage cannot be explained by reference to their powers of physical coercion, which they do not have, nor by reference to their control of technical knowledge, over which they have no monopoly, nor by reference to their kinship relations, which are only the expression of and not the basis for social cohesion. On the contrary their power is based on the twin abilities to 'reserve for themselves control of social knowledge' (genealogies, marriage regulations, etc.) and the corollary of this 'the spheres of artifice' (magic, divination, etc.) on the one hand, and on the other[21]

above all, they reserve for themselves control of the cadets' and their own access to women, and they guarantee this control by holding the 'elite goods' which are indispensable for marriage. This last weapon of the elders has an original character compared with the weapons considered above: it is that whereas all the others were *individual weapons* of each particular elder within his particular group, this is a *collective weapon* belonging to all *the elders of the* different lineage groups.

In detail, then, the elders maintain control of the material aspects of matrimonial exchanges, they thereby 'guarantee the control of the demographic reproduction of the lineages' and they in addition retain control over the exchange of slaves, thereby controlling also the 'redistribution of men from demographically strong lineages towards demographically weak ones'.

It is, according to the argument, this demographic reproduction which is the leading condition for, in lineage societies, the reproduction of the conditions of production. This contrasts with Marx's 'ancient societies' where this reproduction must be sought in the 'defence or acquisition of land, preservation of the global liberty of the community or enslavement of the defeated community'. Social structure can also be accounted for in that 'control of the reproduction of the technical conditions of production (unit of labour demographically adapted) guarantees the reproduction of the social relations (dependence of the cadets with respect to the elders)'.

It might well be asked what has happened to the notions of dependence and exploitation in the course of all this? The very existence of a relation of dependence suggests to Dupré and Rey that exploitation, something not normally associated with 'lineage' societies, may in fact exist in such typically 'anthropological' societies, provided that an adequate definition of exploitation is employed. To show that this is the case involves a rejection of Godelier's definition that 'Exploitation begins when appropriation of the surplus is effected without counterpart',[22] on the grounds that this suggests that exploitation would not really occur in any kind of society, and that it also implies that[23]

capitalists exploit less in so far as they provide a more significant counterpart, that is, in so far as they consign a greater part of the surplus product to the development of the forces of production and a lesser part to their personal consumption,

a position antithetical to that of Marx. The true answer indeed should be sought in Marx's early view that exploitation occurs when the product turns against the producer and increases his subjection:[24]

We propose the following definition of the concept: exploitation exists when the use of the surplus product by a group (or an aggregate) which has not contributed the corresponding surplus of labour reproduces the conditions of a new extortion or surplus labour from the producers.

Exploitation, then, is a notion with a potential range of application extending far beyond the conventional boundaries of capitalism.

From the recognition of this to an application of the definition to the relationship between 'traditional' modes of production and the capitalist one is an obvious step (at least in so far as the historical contact between colonial capitalism and lineage social formations is concerned). This contact is seen by Dupré and Rey as falling into three phases: (1) the period of slave trade when 'the European market economy got its supplies essentially by playing on the internal contradictions of the lineage social formations'; (2) a transitional phase, that of 'colonialism proper' which is 'characterized by ambiguity: it is a matter of using the economic basis characteristic of lineage society to establish the conditions of transition to capitalism'; and (3) 'At the end of this process a new type of social formation is to be constituted where the capitalist mode of production is dominant; and with capitalism once established, it is to be dominated by the capitalism of the metropolitan country, that is, to depend on it for its reproduction: this is neo-colonialism.'[25] It must be noted however that Dupré and Rey's claim that 'in each of the systems [capitalist and lineage] *exchange* plays a dominant role in the reproduction of one of these systems over another system with which it is articulated'[26] is based on some measure of semantic confusion, involving as it does the belief that the term has the same application in all its uses and in relation to all kinds of economic systems, even to the extent of assimilating the notion of a *medium of exchange* to their unitary model, a move which brings them perilously close to the logic of the vilified Dalton–Bohannan–Polanyi position, despite disclaimers to the contrary.[27] The relationship between systems of exchange and the transition from one mode of production to another stand in need of considerable clarification (of which more below) even assuming that (*contra* Meillassoux) the transition is ever a complete one, an assumption not supported by history, as the authors agree.[28] In the conclusion to their paper Dupré and Rey summarize and expand their 'phase' characterization of the encroachment of capitalist domination over traditional modes of production, and draw attention to the fact that several modes of production can simultaneously co-exist in a colonial or neo-colonial context. In so doing they place themselves in a close relationship with Meillassoux who is in large measure concerned with the expansion of this latter point. (The internal connections between Meillassoux's and Dupré and Rey's theoretical positions are numerous and I will point them out where they are relevant.)

Meillassoux's contribution to the present debate is to be found mainly in three papers which draw heavily upon the material presented in his notable book in the field of African economic anthropology. The essence of his theoretical position may be found in the two later papers (1972, 1974) and it is upon these that I will concentrate.

The importance of Meillassoux should not, however, be traced to his generalized, patriarchal and neo-evolutionist and, curiously enough, in terms of its ethnographic basis, highly particular and localized, general theory,[29] but to the insights contained at the end of his 1972 paper and developed in his 1974 one. In essence these relate to the claim that 'agricultural self-sustaining formations' ('*sociétés traditionnelles d'auto-subsistance*') contain within themselves all the necessary means of coping with the basic social, economic and other needs of their members. The grafting onto them of production for external markets can only bring about their transformation into class societies, or it will fail, or such communities are (or should be) dissolved and replaced by a new type of unit. However,[30]

> paradoxically, the capitalist exploiters, who are often better Marxists than Marxist theoreticians, are aware of the potentiality of this contradictory situation. The agricultural self-sustaining communities, because of their comprehensiveness and their *raison d'être* are able to fulfil functions that capitalism prefers not to assume in the under-developed countries: the functions of social security. The cheap cost of labour in these countries comes from the super-exploitation, not only of the labour from the wage-earner himself but also of the labour of his kin group.

In other words movement between the urban capitalist sector and the rural 'traditional' one in, for instance, South Africa, is to be explained not by psychology or demography, but by reference to the economic fact that people who are obliged to become wage-labourers in a neo- or quasi-colonial situation are forced back on the 'traditional' sector to obtain precisely those services which the capitalist does not provide—sickness, unemployment, and old age benefits. Much of the so-called 'dual economy' theory is thus to be seen as an attempt[31]

> to conceal the exploitation of the rural community, integrated, . . . as an organic component of capitalist production to feed the temporarily unproductive workers of the capitalist sector and supply them with the resources necessary to their survival. Because of this process of absorption within the capitalist economy, the agricultural communities, maintained as reserves of cheap labour, are being undermined and perpetuated at the same time, undergoing a prolonged crisis and not a smooth transition to capitalism.

Equally the pool of labour power itself is reproduced in the 'traditional' context and then drawn off into the capitalist sector. The two 'spheres' of the economy thus stand in and perpetuate with respect to each other a relation of exploitation, inequality and dependence.[32]

The situation in practice is not a static one, however. For on the one hand the capitalist system must avoid a *direct* intrusion of capital into the traditional sector, if that sector is to continue unchanged, a restraint that capitalism rarely finds it possible to sustain. (In this later paper (1974) Meillassoux continues to use the term 'self-sustaining' sector, a term not really applicable after the advent of capitalism–colonialism.) Equally, on the other hand, attempts to 'fix' the traditional system, to confine it to some unchanging pattern, are similarly doomed to failure, for without the equally traditional means of outlet–territorial expansion, means of demographic control and avenues of creativity, the 'native' sector is set on the road to sterility and impoverishment. Contradictions *within* and *between* the spheres of a 'dual' economy are thus closely and internally linked.

Critique

There are some severe difficulties, both logical and empirical with these theses, which I will briefly indicate. In the first place Dupré and Rey's argument is a systematic perpetration of the sin of Africocentrism: the belief widespread in England, and apparently also in France, that African societies and their institutions exhaust all that is of theoretical or empirical interest in anthropology. Many of the failings of the argument stem from adopting this position, but then in not pursuing it with complete singlemindedness and thereby failing to take note of counter-evidence from other parts of the same continent. The logical and empirical difficulties are equally so closely related that I will not attempt to examine them separately.

The first point to establish is a general conceptual one—that Dupré and Rey nowhere define the key notion of 'mode of production' and consequently succeed in making it a very flexible stick with which to beat the 'liberals'. More particularly the inner connections between a mode of production and its corresponding system of distribution (the latter the classical concern of the liberals, according also to Meillassoux) are left to one side, and more significantly, so is any discussion of the very tenable argument that a 'mode of production' (logically) contains the means of its own reproduction: this is *part of its definition*. Instead, distribution and exchange are confused, the latter is reduced to *explaining* the 'reproduction of the conditions of production' and the whole is assimilated to a highly dubious (and highly generalized) theory of elder dominance within and between 'lineage societies'.

The dubiousness of this theory derives from its premises, which can be summarized as follows (and seen to be dubious as soon as they are clearly stated):

(1) that goods produced by the 'cadets' are entirely controlled by the elders;

(2) that 'social knowledge' is exclusively in the hands of the elders, while 'technical knowledge' is not (even if such a distinction is valid);

(3) that the elders conspire amongst themselves and between lineages to retain this exclusive knowledge;

(4) that thereby they control demographic reproduction (there is confusion between various uses of the term 'reproduction' and

about the relationships between demography and kinship: the elders control *matrimonial exchanges*);

(5) that they thereby control the reproduction of the lineages;

(6) that (contrary to Meillassoux's original formulation) the elders do possess powers of physical coercion whereby they can reduce a cadet to slavery;

(7) that, unlike 'ancient societies', relationships between lineages are *not* based on warfare or conceptions of property or territoriality, but on the 'exchange' and 'conspiracy' functions between elders ('conflict takes place in a field determined externally by exchange between the elders')[33];

(8) that the relationship between 'economy' and 'social structure' is a relatively simple one, mediated by the concept of 'control of reproduction of the technical conditions of production' (which in turn involves a 'power' or hierarchy model of social relations where the Dupré–Rey–Meillassoux argument is to hold); and finally

(9) that the claim that 'demographic reproduction appears to be the essential condition for the reproduction of the conditions of production in lineage society'[34] is something more than the tautology and truism that it appears to be.

The theory is additionally not an historical one: it has to do only with the *maintenance* of 'dependence' and not with its *establishment*, a claim which embodies a view of the relationship between 'structure' and 'history' of dubious utility to a Marxian.

Our criticisms of Meillassoux's position specifically fall into an additional set of categories. In the course of his 1972 paper his argument leads him into a critique of liberal economics directed against the belief that, stemming from the alleged universality of the 'laws' of capitalism, non-capitalist economies are simply underdeveloped forms of capitalism, and that therefore the methods of liberal economics apply equally to all kinds of economic formations. This in turn involves an attack on certain key 'liberals', and in particular Sahlins and Raymond Firth, which does little justice to the range and complexity of the thought of either of those writers or the real nature of their positive contributions to economic anthropology, and commits such elementary errors as castigating Firth for not distinguishing use-value from exchange-value or for only dimly perceiving the 'possible influence of social situation on behaviour instead of the reverse'.[35] Such claims cannot be justified, and can only be partly excused if seen as overstatements for the purpose of highlighting an allegedly contrary view held by Meillassoux. This is supported by the claim that 'all liberal economic anthropology is centred on problems of distribution and never on those of production'.[36] While this is undoubtedly true, the existence of a logical connection between production and distribution is never seen by Meillassoux as a factor determining the whole way in which the 'problematic' of economic anthropology must be phrased. Related to this is the belief that the approach to pre-capitalist (Meillassoux uses the word *pre* without qualms) formation pioneered by Marx in the 'pre-capitalist economic formations' should be abandoned in favour of the method of *Capital*.[37] The full implications of this are not elaborated upon. Meillassoux's claim, therefore, is that we should concentrate on 'the social organization of production: who is working with whom and for whom? Where does the product of the labourer go? Who controls the product? How does the economic system reproduce itself?'[38]

Meillassoux's discussion of Marx's distinction between land as a 'subject of labour' and as an 'instrument of labour' then leads him into a two-part theory: (*a*) the distinction between hunting/gathering and agricultural societies, based on certain false and Africocentric assumptions such as that[39]

the hunters, once they share the common product, are free from any reciprocal obligations or allegiance. The process gives no ground for the emergence of a social hierarchy or of a centralized power, or even the extended family organization. The basic social unit is an equalitarian but unstable band with little concern for biological or social reproduction,

which can only be seen as a wilfully negligent misinterpretation of known ethnographic facts; (*b*) an argument (and it is not clear if the argument is offered as a model or an empirical generalization) of 'elder domination' closely related to that of Dupré and Rey, but largely confined to relations of production *within* the 'agricultural community' and which somewhat modifies their conception of the role of exchange:

These relations of production are materialized through a redistributive system of circulation. . . . This is not a system of exchange, properly speaking, since the products are never offered for each other and therefore not subjected to the appraisal of their respective value. It is rather a continuously renewed cycle of *advance* and *restitution* of subsistence.

The other major divergence lies in Meillassoux's seeing the elders as *directly* determining this cycle of subsistence by receiving and managing the produce of the 'cadets' and in turn advancing them food and seed. So in turn 'Control over subsistence is not control of the means of production but of the means of physiological *reproduction*, used to reproduce the life of the human producer'.[40]

221

In other words the leaders of such societies 'rely less on the control of the *means of material production* than on the *means of human reproduction*: subsistence and women'.[41] The assimilation of 'subsistence' to the category of 'reproduction' is significant, but leaves very unclear the exact rationale for creating an (artificial?) distinction in 'agricultural societies' between subsistence and 'means of material production'. Additionally, as Gledhill puts it:[42]

> One of the most striking features of 'primitive economic organisation' is the way in which competition for status is often kept sharply separate from the question of the organisation of society at the 'subsistence' level. Restrictions on the convertibility of goods between spheres, restrictions on the alienation of property, most notably land and one's own person, the principle of redistribution and the specification of rights of access to the means of production, all these conditions control distribution within the 'substantive' economic infrastructure, whilst scarcity and competition—one might borrow Lévi-Strauss' use of the term 'entropy' here—are restricted to a secondary level of activity and circulation.

The control of women and matrimonial policy is again the key to this. The same criticisms brought against Dupré and Rey apply equally (and perhaps more so—his model is cruder) to Meillassoux's theory of patriarchy.

Towards a broader theory

The whole of the foregoing analysis has directed attention to some (and only some) aspects of the relationship between colonial or neo-colonial capitalism and local economies and social structures and in particular as this relates to the concepts of 'structural dependency' and 'exploitation'. There are certain obvious gaps, especially in Meillassoux's argument, amongst which might be included any analysis of *commodity extracting* exploitation as opposed to *labour power extracting* exploitation, and the question of how far certain kinds of relations of *dependency* necessarily imply relations of *exploitation* and the development of links between all these things and indigenous social structures. Similarly one finds parallel inadequacies in Frank's analysis when it comes to the question of the *exact* nature of the articulation (or rather disarticulation) between the urban–industrial and rural–peasant sectors in underdeveloped countries. The famous Frankian metaphor of a 'chain' of metropolitan–satellite relationships stretching from the world centres of capitalism to the most isolated peasant[43] needs a corresponding clarification. Many of the ways in which this clarification might be achieved are suggested by the 'French School's' approach. For instance the *co-existence* of several modes of production, including traditional with capitalist modes, and the implications of this in terms of their articulation must be incorporated into a 'metropolis–satellite' model. The significance of the seemingly purely internal anthropological debate on the subject of markets thus reappears in a new light when seen in this context. In other words the question of the nature of exchanges between sectors reasserts itself, and in so doing points again to the logically necessary internal connection between production and distribution, and once again underlines the analytical vacuousness of concentrating upon 'modes of production' to, at the worst exclusion of, and at the best trivialization of, systems of distribution. Indeed we must turn to the fundamental question of the definition of 'mode of production', and of its utility as an analytical tool once defined.

Terray, in opening his analysis of Meillassoux's *Anthropologie économique des Gouro de Côte d'Ivoire*, starts from a criticism of the narrow definition of 'mode of production' employed in that work. This criticism has two aspects—that to reduce the concept of a mode of production to 'the enunciation of a few general characteristics of "self-subsistence economies" is . . . a waste of its operational fruitfulness' and that the implication that all such societies have the *same* mode of production excludes the attempt 'to explain the great variety of social and ideological relations observed in such societies'.[44] The point behind this is that, according to Marx, a simple description of an economy does not exhaust the concept of 'mode of production'. (A point also obscured by Meillassoux in his 1972 paper when he simply remarks, 'Recognition of various economic formations comes generally from the observation of different "ways of living", such as hunting, cultivating, cattle herding, etc. which must not be confused with modes of production, *though they may coincide with the latter.*')[45] Meillassoux's confusion is essentially that he restricts 'mode of production' to the *productive activities* themselves (the process of appropriation), thus excluding not only the juridico–political and ideological superstructures, but even the *relations of production*, all of which he then has to reintegrate into his analysis. (His production/distribution dichotomy can also be seen as stemming from this.) In fact, as Terray following Étienne Balibar points out, 'productive forces and relations of production do not relate to two separate categories of "things" but are two aspects of one single "reality"'[46] (i.e. the economic base of a mode of production). And, as he goes on,[47]

these same factors are involved in definite social relations
which constitute the structure of the process of production,
seen as the social appropriation of the product. Here we find

223

relations of production which allocate the agents and means of production, and the division of the product which follows that allocation.

And again, 'Thus a study of relations of production is only possible through the enumeration and examination of relations of distribution.'

A mode of production in its most limited sense, therefore, is something more than a description of the process of appropriation, for it must encompass both the forces of production and the social relations of production. Two principal issues arise from this. First there is the claim that we can undoubtedly establish that, while it is legitimate to function with more than one operational definition of 'mode of production', the usage in question *must be defined* in each case, and precisely what the implications of the usage chosen are must be indicated. Many of Meillassoux's difficulties stem from a lack of awareness of the range of his concepts. The Althusserian use of the term 'mode of production' is an instance of this, where not only is the concept extended beyond its limited usage, but exists specifically within the context of a particular kind of structural analysis.[48] Secondly there is the question of what happens when we go looking for modes of production, and the suggested answer, that we always find more than one in a 'combination of one dominant and the other(s) subordinate, the articulation of the relationship between them resulting in the concrete social formation under examination.

By a circuitous route we have thus arrived back at our central theme as originally posed (in practice of course all these 'subsidiary' issues are tied to it). The expansion of his argument indeed leads Terray into a vigorous defence of Meillassoux against Dupré and Rey and their 'discovery' of exploitation and class antagonisms in lineage societies and their belief that evidence for this can be found in Meillassoux's own writings. This defence is partly based on an empirical argument, that their conception of chiefly office is incorrect in that they do not see that 'The elder plays the same part in matrimonial exchanges as he does in material production: in both cases his power is simply a function of his office.' In other words:[49]

> To put it more generally, Rey and Dupré see the moment of tribute as determinant in the cycle of tributes and redistributions: the elder monopolizes the product of the labour of the juniors and hence presides over the redistribution. On the contrary, to me the moment of redistribution comes first and the moment of tribute is only its necessary consequence.

But the defence is also based on the belief that committing this error of partiality leads him to assimilate their position to bourgeois economics:[50]

Pierre-Philippe Rey and Georges Dupré did not consider the process of reproduction as a whole, but only at the *single moment of circulation*: it may be this that led them to see the relations between elder and junior as between exploiter and exploited. The errors into which this attitude has led bourgeois political economy are common knowledge. . . . The ethnologist ratifies this 'representation' when he isolates the moment of circulation in the process of reproduction: like the bourgeois economist he then asks himself whether the relations of circulation are the site of an equilibrium or an antagonism and his answer will depend on whether he favors a static or a dynamic ethnology.

While warmly agreeing with Terray's criticism of Dupré and Rey, it must not be forgotten that very similar points can in fact be made against Meillassoux himself (although not necessarily against the *Anthropologie économique des Gouro*). We should also retain some awareness of the general anthropological principles lying behind the notions of 'surplus' and 'distribution':[51]

The idea of surplus is still obscured by the notion that many people still hold that there is a necessary causality between the existence of a surplus and that of the exploitation of man by man. This raises the general problem not of the mechanisms, but of the 'principles' of distribution, since the latter can be either equal or unequal among the members of a society. One and the same society may, moreover, follow different principles; depending on the objects which are to be distributed. The Siane ensure equal access for everyone to the use of land and to subsistence foodstuffs. Luxury goods, however, such as tobacco and salt, depend on the initiative of each individual. As for actual wealth-feathers, shells, pigs—the material basis for ceremonial acts and for access to women, these are controlled by the elders of the families and the important men (*bosboi*), whose prestige and power they symbolize. But this inequality does not signify at all that there is exploitation of some by others.

The broader theory towards which we are working will thus involve the making clear of a number of distinctions. Some of these are obviously conceptual ones—the problem of the definition of 'mode of production', the identification of such modes, their articulation, and their relationship to other aspects of the social formations in question. Related to this will be the notion of 'exploitation' in non-capitalist contexts and the links between 'exploitation' and 'dependence' when non-capitalist societies come into contact with capitalist ones. Also closely associated with this is the question of where social classes enter the arena, and at what point a class analysis becomes possible. The importance of conceptual clarity is thus of primary importance both within economic anthropology, and as economic anthropology bears upon the expansion of the Frankian model. The broadening of the vocabulary of anthropology also results from this. Anthropology as a whole has very successfully (to date) insulated itself from the conceptual repertoire not only of sociology, but of Marxism as well.

A second group of distinctions emerges from this. The distinction between *types* of relationships between capitalism and its subject peoples are rarely made clear from within the 'macro-perspective' of the sociology of development. In the light of the foregoing discussion we can see that significant differences exist between (*a*) settler colonization and the *destruction* of indigenous societies, (*b*) surplus expropriation colonization where material wealth is removed, and (*c*) labour expropriation, where the native population is essential and has to be preserved. The relationships between colonial or neo-colonial capitalism and indigenous social structures will vary correspondingly. Thus not only Frank, but also Baran with his theory of the *decomposition* of pre-capitalist structures, need modification.[52]

A third group of issues involve anthropology itself in a clarification of some of its most basic and classical preoccupations in the light of the present debate. At the level of practice the uncovering of the *horizontal* as well as the *vertical* linkages that exist in all social situations is clearly an aspect of this. At the level of theory we must reject the 'underlabourer' conception of anthropology, providing the cultural flesh for the planning or 'development' economists' bones,[53] and argue instead that it has a key role in not only illuminating some of the darker areas of the theories of the sociology of development, but in establishing the very basis upon which such theories are constructed. In this respect the classical problems of the 'location' of the economy in the wider social system, the arresting issue (for an economist!) of the 'surplusless economy',[54] the relevance of economic theory nurtured in a capitalist system for societies of an entirely different form of organization (and of course the relevance of that theory for explaining behaviour *within* a putatively capitalist system) all assert their importance. If the wall between economics and epistemology starts to get dangerously thin at this point, this is only to be expected. The general point that should at all costs be established is that the link between the hitherto isolated theoretical concerns of economic anthropology not only should not be, but cannot be, divorced from the concerns of a critical sociology of development. Indeed, an anthropologist's discussion of the concept of 'development', which should perhaps have stood at the head of this essay, rather than be implied throughout, is a case in point.

Notes

(Note: all textual citations are to the English-language editions of the works in question where they exist.)

1 A. G. Frank, *Capitalism and Underdevelopment in Latin America*, New York, 1969.
2 R. Frankenberg, 'Economic anthropology', and P. S. Cohen, 'Economic analysis and economic man', in R. Firth, ed., *Themes in Economic Anthropology*, Association of Social Anthropologists Monograph 6, London, 1970.
3 For references see R. Firth, *Economics of the New Zealand Maori*, Wellington, 1959, pp. 25–6 and R. Firth, *op. cit.*, 1970, pp. 1–28.
4 Firth, *op. cit.*, 1970, p. 11; and R. Firth, 'The place of Malinowski in the history of economic anthropology', in R. Firth, ed., *Man and Culture: An Evaluation of the Work of Bronislaw Malinowski*, London, 1957.
5 Firth, *op. cit.*, 1970, p. 6.
6 Frankenberg, *op. cit.*, p. 57.
7 R. Firth, *Primitive Polynesian Economy*, London, 1939, pp. 347 ff.
8 G. Dalton, 'Theoretical issues in economic anthropology', *Current Anthropology*, February 1969; also G. Dalton, 'Economic theory and primitive society', *American Anthropologist*, vol. 63, 1961.
9 Dalton quoting R. Firth, *Primitive Polynesian Economy*.
10 K. Polanyi, *Origin of our Time: The Great Transformation*, London, 1946, and K. Polanyi, C. W. Arensberg and H. W. Pearson, *Trade and Market in the Early Empires*, Chicago, 1957; M. D. Sahlins, 'Political power and the economy in primitive society', in G. E. Dole and R. L. Carneiro, *Essays in the Science of Culture*, New York, 1960; R. Burling, 'Maximization theories and the study of economic anthropology', *American Anthropologist*, vol. 64, 1962; M. J. Herskovits, *Economic Anthropology*, New York, 1952.
11 F. Barth, *The Role of the Entrepreneur in Social Change in Northern Norway*, Oslo, 1963; R. Paine, 'Entrepreneurial activity without its profits', in *ibid.*
12 Georges Dupré and Pierre-Philippe Rey, 'Reflections on the pertinence of a theory of the history of exchange', *Economy and Society*, vol. 2, no. 2, 1973. In French in *Cahiers Internationaux de Sociologie*, vol. 46, 1968.
13 C. Meillassoux, *L'Anthropologie Économique des Gouro de Côte d'Ivoire*, Paris, 1970; 'From reproduction to production', *Economy and Society*, vol. 1, no. 1, 1972; 'Imperialism as a mode of reproduction of labour power', unpublished seminar paper, mimeo, 1974; 'Essai d'interprétation du phénomène économique dans les sociétés traditionnelles d'auto-subsistance', *Cahiers Études Africaines*, vol. 4, 1960.
14 E. Terray, *Marxism and 'Primitive' Societies*, London and New York, 1972. In French, *Le Marxisme devant les Sociétés Primitives: Deux Études*, Paris, 1969.

15 M. Godelier, *Rationality and Irrationality in Economics*, London, 1972. In French, *Rationalité et Irrationalité en Économie*, Paris, 1966.
16 C. Coquery-Vidrovich whose paper in *Cahiers d'Études Africaines*, no. 29, 1968, provides a good deal of Dupré and Rey's background material.
17 P. Bohannan and G. Dalton, eds, *Markets in Africa*, Evanston, 1962.
18 K. Polanyi, C. M. Arensberg and H. W. Pearson, eds, *Trade and Market in the Early Empire*, Chicago, 1957.
19 Dupré and Rey, *op. cit.*, p. 144.
20 Meillassoux, *op. cit.*, 1960 and 1972.
21 Dupré and Rey, *op. cit.*, p. 145.
22 M. Godelier in *Les Temps Modernes*, vol. 20, 1965.
23 Dupré and Rey, *op. cit.*, p. 151.
24 *Ibid.*, p. 152.
25 *Ibid.*, pp. 156–7.
26 *Ibid.*, p. 158, my italics.
27 *Ibid.*, pp. 159–60.
28 *Ibid.*, p. 162.
29 E.g., Meillassoux, *op. cit.*, 1972, especially pp. 98–101.
30 *Ibid.*, p. 102.
31 *Ibid.*, p. 105.
32 Meillassoux, *op. cit.*, 1974.
33 Dupré and Rey, *op. cit.*, p. 148.
34 *Ibid.*, p. 147.
35 Meillassoux, *op. cit.*, 1972, p. 95.
36 *Ibid.*, p. 95.
37 *Ibid.*, p. 98.
38 *Ibid.*, p. 98.
39 *Ibid.*, p. 99.
40 *Ibid.*, p. 100.
41 *Ibid.*, p. 101.
42 J. Gledhill, 'Economics and the theory of games in social anthropology', *Journal of the Anthropological Society of Oxford*, vol. 2, no. 2, 1971, p. 67.
43 A. G. Frank, *op. cit.*, p. 17.
44 Terray, *op. cit.*, p. 97.
45 Meillassoux, *op. cit.*, 1972, p. 98, my italics.
46 Terray, *op. cit.*, p. 98.
47 *Ibid.*, p. 98.
48 L. Althusser and E. Balibar, *Reading Capital*, London, 1970.
49 Terray, *op. cit.*, pp. 175–6.
50 *Ibid.*, pp. 173–4, my italics.
51 Godelier, *op. cit.*, p. 275.
52 P. Baran, *The Political Economy of Growth*, London, 1957.
53 M. Edel, 'Economic analysis in an anthropological setting', *American Anthropologist*, vol. 71, no. 3, 1969.
54 H. W. Pearson, 'The economy has no surplus: a critique of a theory of development', in K. Polanyi, *et al.*, *op. cit.*

11 The theory of internal colonialism: the South African case

Harold Wolpe

The view that there are close parallels between the *external* relationships established by colonial powers over colonized peoples and the relationship of ethnic, cultural, national, or racial groups *within* some Latin American societies, the United States, and South Africa, has led to the use of the notion of 'internal colonialism' in the analysis of these societies.[1]

The specific feature which is said to distinguish 'internal' from 'normal' colonialism is the fact that in the former the colonizing 'nation' or 'race' or other group occupies the same territory as the colonized people. As Simons and Simons put it:[2]

> The imperial colonial qualities of the society . . . become visible by comparison with the typical colony. In its normal form, the colony is a distinct territorial entity, spatially detached from its imperial metropolis.

In all other important respects, the implication is, the components of the 'normal' imperial–colonial relation are to be found within the borders of a single state to an extent which justifies the view that it constitutes an internal colonialism. In particular, it is argued in this approach, that the 'underdeveloped' (and 'underdeveloping') condition, of subordinate ethnic and racial groups and the geographical areas they occupy within the boundaries of the state, is produced and maintained by the same mechanisms of cultural domination, political oppression, and economic exploitation which, at the international level, produce the development of the advanced capitalist states through the imperialist underdevelopment of the colonial satellites.

Notwithstanding the apparently unproblematical use of the terms 'imperialism' and 'colonialism' in the passage cited above (and in the writing on 'internal colonialism' generally), it is obvious from the literature that there are differing conceptions of imperialism and colonialism, and that these are not all equally suitable for conversion into a notion of 'internal colonialism'. Lenin's insistence in his *Imperialism: the Highest Stage of Capitalism*, that the *export* of capital is a crucial distinguishing feature of imperialism and, therefore, of colonialism in the monopoly stage of capitalism, is only one relevant example. It is, therefore, of considerable importance to analyse the conceptions of colonialism and imperialism which serve as the model from which the notion of 'internal colonialism' is derived by analogy.

In making such an analysis it will be argued first that, while the internal colonial thesis purports to rest on class relations of capitalist exploitation, in fact it treats such relations as residual. That is to say, the conceptualization of class relations, which is present in the theory, is accorded little or no role in the analysis of relations of domination and exploitation which are, instead, conceived of as occurring between 'racial', 'ethnic', and 'national' categories. To this extent, the 'internal colonial' thesis converges with conventional race relations theory (in particular, the theory of plural society), and, as I shall show, suffers from the same analytical limitations as the latter.

It will be argued, secondly, that in so far as the theory of internal colonialism does accord relevance to relations of capitalist exploitation it does so in a manner which denudes the analysis of all historical specificity and thereby deprives the concept of analytical utility.

The question remains as to whether or not it is possible to develop a satisfactory and rigorous concept of 'internal colonialism' which will provide the foundation for an adequate analysis of the internal structure and development of certain social formations. This problem will constitute the subject-matter of the third section in which an attempt will be made to provide an historically specific account of South Africa which is both based on concepts which define capitalism generally and, at the same time, uncovers in a rigorous way its internal colonial character.

Internal colonialism

In the theory of internal colonialism, the colonial relation appears to be characterized by two main elements. First, the colonial relationship is conceived of as occurring between different countries, total populations, nations, geographical areas or between peoples of different races, colours, and cultures. As Blauner, for example, expresses it:[3]

The colonial order in the modern world has been based on the dominance of White Westerners over non-Westerners of colour: racial oppression and the racial conflict to which it gives rise are endemic to it, much as class exploitation and conflict are fundamental to capitalist societies.

Secondly, the colonial relationship is characterized, in a general way, as involving domination, oppression, and exploitation. Again Blauner provides a convenient statement:[4]

Colonialism traditionally refers to the establishment of domination over a geographically external political unit, most often inhabited by people of a different race and culture, where this domination is political and economic, and the colony exists subordinated to and dependent upon the mother country. Typically the colonisers exploit the land, the raw materials, the labour, and other resources of the colonised nation; in addition a formal recognition is given to the differences in power, autonomy and political status, and various agencies are set up to maintain this subordination.

It is these two features which constitute the core of internal colonialism, that is, of colonialism internal to a particular society. Casanova, for example, states: 'Internal colonialism corresponds to a structure of social relations based on domination and exploitation among culturally heterogeneous, distinct groups.'[5] And Tabb puts it thus: 'The economic relations of the ghetto to White America closely parallel those between third world nations and the industrially advanced countries.'[6]

With regard to South Africa, the argument has been formulated as follows by the South African Communist Party:[7]

South Africa is not a colony but an independent state. Yet masses of our people enjoy neither independence nor freedom. The conceding of independence to South Africa by Britain in 1910 . . . was designed in the interests of imperialism. Power was transferred not into the hands of the masses of the people of South Africa, but into the hands of the *White minority* alone. The evils of colonialism, insofar as the *non-White majorit,'* was concerned, was perpetuated and reinforced. A new type of colonialism was developed, in which the oppressing *white nation* occupied the same territory as the oppressed people themselves and lived side by side with them.

On one level, that of *White South Africa*, there are all the features of an advanced capitalist state in its final stage of imperialism. There are highly developed industrial monopolies, and the merging of industrial and finance capital. The land is farmed along capitalist lines, employing wage labour, and producing cash crops for the local and export markets. The

231

South African monopoly capitalists . . . export capital abroad. But on another level, that of *'non-White South Africa'*, there are all the features of a colony. The indigenous population is subjected to national oppression, poverty and exploitation, lack of all democratic rights and political domination by a group which does everything it can to emphasize and perpetuate its alien 'European' character. The African Reserves show the complete lack of industry, communications, transport and power resources which are characteristic of . . . territories under colonial rule. . . . Typical, too, of imperialist rule, is the reliance by the state upon brute force and terror, and upon the most backward tribal elements and institutions which are deliberately and artificially preserved. *Non-White South Africa* is the colony of *White South Africa* itself. [My emphasis throughout.]

The characterization of colonial relations as occurring between nations, countries, races and so on finds its most rigorous formulation in the work of Blauner. He states:[8]

Unfortunately, social science lacks a model of American society and its social structure in which racial division and conflict are basic elements rather than phenomena to be explained (or explained away) in terms of other forces or determinants. To close this theoretical gap, in part, I rely on the framework of colonialism in the present study.

And again: 'racism and racial oppression are . . . independent dynamic forces (not ultimately reducible to other causal determinants)'.[9]

Since, in this argument, Blauner asserts the *independence* and *irreducibility* of 'race' (although curiously he also argues that 'racism developed out of the same historical situation [as colonialism] and reflected a world economic and power stratification')[10] he cannot conceptualize the relationship of 'race' to the social structure and we are, therefore, left only with racial and ethnic groups abstracted out of the social formation. Indeed, Blauner appears to be aware of this problem, but to have no answer to it:[11]

Yet the colonial perspective cannot by itself provide the theoretical framework necessary to grasp the complexities of race relations and social change in America. When the colonial model is transferred from the overseas situation to the United States without substantial alteration, it tends to miss the total social structure, the context of advanced industrial capitalism in which our racial relations are embedded. . . . This

suggests a major defect of my study. It lacks a conception
of American society as a total structure beyond the central
significance that I attribute to racism.

In two other versions of the theory of internal colonialism no
assumption of the independence of race, ethnicity, or culture is made,
but the analysis nevertheless does not go beyond Blauner. In the
first of these versions, the contrast is implicitly drawn between
capitalist societies which are culturally, ethnically, and racially
homogeneous, and in which relations of class exploitation are
dominant, and those societies in which both capitalist exploitation
and internal colonial relations exist side by side (with the latter
frequently dominant). Two questions arise here. First, what is the
relationship between the system of class exploitation and domination
and the relations of racial, ethnic, cultural or national exploitation
and domination characteristic of internal colonialism? Second, in
what way does internal colonial exploitation differ from class
exploitation? On these questions the theory is silent. Thus Casanova,
for example, asserts:[12]

> The colonial structure and internal colonialism are
> distinguished from the class structure since colonialism is
> not only a relation of exploitation of the workers by the
> owners of raw materials or of production and their
> collaborators, but also a relation of domination and exploitation
> of a total population (with its distinct classes, proprietors,
> workers) by another population which also has distinct classes
> (proprietors and workers).

While this passage is useful for the way in which it points to the,
or rather to one of the, modes of class exploitation (that is, the
appropriation of surplus value) entailed in imperialism, it nevertheless fails to link 'the exploitation of the workers' to the exploitation
of one 'total population' by another and nor does it explain the
meaning of exploitation in the latter case.

Similarly, Johnson states: 'The population of internal colonies is
subject to discriminatory practices over and above those characteristic of relations between dominant classes and underclasses.'[13] But,
despite a lengthy discussion of 'Class relations and colonial relations',
he is unable to clarify the relationship between 'discriminatory
practices' and class relations or the differences between the two. He
can only *assert* the differences:[14]

> The major differences in the relations between the dominant
> classes and institutions of society and marginal under-classes
> on the one hand, and internal colonies [An internal colony
> constitutes a society within a society based upon racial,

linguistic and/or marked cultural differences as well as differences of social class. H.W.] on the other hand, revolve around different means of social control. It is important to emphasize that *all* the classes of the dominant society rest upon the colonial population.

What appears from the above passages is that no attempt is made to identify the specific mode of exploitation and domination characteristic of internal colonialism which purports to differentiate it from class exploitation and domination. Instead, there is a general reference to exploitation, used in a descriptive sense, and to undefined states of racial or ethnic oppression and these are in no way linked to the system of class exploitation. The consequence of this is that, as in Blauner's analysis, internal colonial relations are not only left obscure but are said to hold between racial, ethnic, and cultural groups which are analysed as if they are autonomous of the total social structure.

In the second version of the theory in which no claim is made that race and ethnicity are independent of the social structure, a similar result is arrived at by a different path. The analysis of the South African Communist Party is the case in point here. In this case, as is clear from the passage from the Party's Programme quoted above, class relations are simply *assimilated* to race relations. Thus 'White South Africa' is identified with the 'capitalist state' and the capitalist system, while 'non-White South Africa' is identified with 'the colony'. From this point on the analysis of class relations gives way to the description of White domination and exploitation of Blacks in terms of the internal colonial analogy.

It is possible to argue that where there is a complete coincidence between race and class the concepts defining the relationship between classes may be utilized in defining the relationship between races or ethnic groups.[15] Where this is not the case (and it is not the case in South Africa), the substitution of racial groups for classes in the analysis requires a specification of the nature of the relationship between the former groups. Such a specification is not forthcoming in the Programme and, consequently, we are once more left with racial groups which stand in a vaguely defined relationship of domination and subordination and whose relations to the class structure are left completely unanalysed.

This conclusion is underlined by the fact that the characterization of internal colonialism as a relation between racial or ethnic entities necessarily involves, despite the recognition that these entities themselves have complex class structures, an analysis which treats these categories as homogeneous. If this were not the case, if the analysis were to be made in terms of class relations, then the internal colonial relation could no longer be conceptualized as a relation between racial, ethnic, etc., groups. But the consequence of the failure to relate classes *within* racial or ethnic groups to the class structure of the society as a whole, is that racial or ethnic entities are treated abstractly and as if their internal class structures are irrelevant to their existence as groups and to their political and ideological practices. Indeed the simultaneous recognition of the diversity of classes within racial groups and their conceptualization as homogeneous categories of internal colonialism forces the Programme of the Communist Party into a contradictory position: 'Power [in 1910] was transferred not into the hands of the masses of people of South Africa, but into the hands of the White minority alone.'[16] This is followed with:[17]

> All Whites enjoy privileges in South Africa. They alone can
> vote and be elected to parliament and local government bodies.
> They have used this privilege to monopolise nearly all
> economic, educational, cultural and social opportunities.
> This gives the impression that the ruling class is composed
> of the entire White population. In fact, however, real power
> is in the hands of the monopolists who own and control the
> mines, the banks and finance houses, and most of the farms and
> major industries.

The theory of plural society

The unexplained autonomy of racial, ethnic, and cultural groups and the obscurity of the relationships between them which we have shown to be the outcome of the theory of internal colonialism, brings this theory within a conceptual framework which is similar to that of the theory of plural society. Despite the very different origins of these theories they suffer from identical analytical limitations. The nature of these limitations, which have been briefly adverted to above, may be elaborated and made clearer by a discussion of the main propositions of plural theory.

It is well known by now that Furnivall[18] was the first to characterize a colonial society as 'plural' and since then, in one sense or another, the notion has been widely used in the analysis of certain societies outside West Europe and the United States, particularly by M. G. Smith with reference to the West Indies.[19] What was the intellectual context in which this concept emerged and became increasingly utilized by Western social scientists in their accounts of non-Western societies? The answer to this question sheds some light on one of the central theoretical difficulties inherent in the attempt to develop a concept of plural society.

Throughout the 1950s and 1960s structural-functionalism, as developed by Talcott Parsons, was the most widely accepted (among social scientists that is) sociological theory, at least in the United States and possibly Britain. The basic propositions of this theory, in so far as they are relevant for present purposes, may be summarized as follows: all social systems are made up of the interaction of individuals. Such interaction is not random, on the contrary, it is highly structured. That structure is produced consensually through the values and norms of the common cultural system, which determine the actions of individuals. The differentiation of individuals into groups, and, most importantly, their allocation to institutionalized roles (including authority or power positions) is carried out in accordance with the common, accepted norms. Because cohesion is produced through voluntary adherence to the rules, conflict is at a minimum; in any event conflict is not systematically generated, it is managed in accordance with the norms and may even function to enhance cohesion.

Despite the fact that it was claimed that these propositions constituted the core of a *general sociological theory*, it soon became apparent that the theory was actually regarded as appropriate only to certain societies which, in fact, were believed to be highly stable, relatively free of conflict, and consensual. That is to say, the general theory turned out to be a *specific model* for the analysis of social systems which were thought to be integrated around a common value system. It need hardly be added that the social systems to which the model was held to be appropriate were the 'advanced industrial societies' of Western Europe and the United States.

By contrast, colonial and former colonial societies were seen by Furnivall and later by Smith to be characterized by conflict, cultural heterogeneity and an absence of common values. Not consensus, but domination, is asserted to be the basis of social order and cohesion in such societies. If consent is the basis of social solidarity in Western societies then clearly a different 'model' had to be devised for societies held together largely by coercion. At this point the 'conflict theorists' enter the stage with the various 'theories' of plural society.

While the construction of two quite different models in this way seems to imply the assumption that some societies are totally free of conflict and bound together solely by consensus, while others are racked with conflict and bound together only by coercion, in fact it is clear that no such assumption is made. Thus as Lockwood has pointed out in relation to Parsons:[20]

The presence of a normative order, or common value system does not mean that conflict has disappeared, or been resolved in some way. Instead, the very existence of a normative order mirrors the potentiality of conflict.

236

Both Rex and Van Den Berghe seem to adopt a similar position, as the following passages show:[21]

> Could not a similar plan of study [i.e. the plural model. H.W.] be employed in the analysis of British society? For myself I am prepared to accept that the scheme is less applicable in a society like our own than in the colonial situation. Class divisions in Britain are certainly not as far-reaching as are the differences between race groups in the colonies.
>
> Nonetheless I think that our analysis of our own society would be enriched by studies which started by assuming conflicting valuations rather than some sort of social consensus.

> I prefer to regard pluralism as a variable, and to include cases of stratification based on 'race', caste, estate, or class . . . as instances of pluralism, even though the constituent groups share the same general culture.[22]

Since both consensus and conflict and 'plural' groups are common to all societies, what determines the decision to apply a plural conflict model rather than a consensus model? It would seem that the decision is not based on any conceptual distinction but on *ad hoc* empiricist judgments. Thus in the passages cited we have nothing more than the *preference* of the authors (Van Den Berghe: 'I prefer to regard pluralism as a variable'; Rex: 'For myself I am prepared to accept that the scheme is less applicable in a society like our own') based simply on an assessment of the *degree* of conflict which manifests itself in any period. This is hardly a satisfactory basis for deciding what 'model' ought to be applied to the analysis of a particular society.

It is possible to argue, however, that the pluralism of a society does not rest merely on the degree of conflict but also on the nature of the groups and the content of the conflict between them. While it is not always clear what the different plural theorists are arguing, it would seem that plural societies are sometimes differentiated from others on the grounds that the *salient* groups in the former societies are racial, cultural, religious, national but *not* classes or strata. This seems to have been Rex's argument at one stage and Van Den Berghe's in his *South Africa, A Study in Conflict*.[23]

Two problems arise here. First, since such ethnic, cultural, etc., divisions are obviously found in societies not normally regarded as plural or internal colonial (e.g. Flemish people and Walloons in Belgium; French and English in Canada; Catholic and non-Catholic in France and Holland; Irish and Welsh in Britain) it is difficult to see how plural societies or internal colonial societies can be distinguished on this basis. But second, and more importantly, to treat such groups as autonomous and as *the* salient groups in the society has the consequence of excluding from the analysis precisely those other structures and relations (in particular the mode of production, the class structure, and class relations) which are necessary to an explanation of the nature and relationships of those groups. The point is that to base an analysis on the criteria (race, religion, etc.) by which groups define themselves and the conflict between them is to take as given precisely what requires explanation. For what needs to be accounted for is why these particular groups come into existence and into conflict with one another. This requires an analysis of the conditions which generate particular conflicts and which affect their nature and intensity.

Therefore, what is needed is, on the one hand, a description of the ideology and political practices of the ethnic, racial, and national groups and, on the other, an analysis of how they relate to the mode of production and social formation in which they are located. It is thus insufficient to stop at the first stage because this is too abstract from the social totality in which the groups are embedded and which explains them.

Some writers, particularly M. G. Smith and Van Den Berghe, have attempted to define the nature of plural groups more rigorously. Although their conceptions differ in a number of respects (which need not be discussed here) they are in fundamental agreement that there are two basic features which differentiate plural groups and, therefore, plural societies from others. In Van Den Berghe's formulation these features are:[24]

(1) segmentation into corporate groups that frequently, though not necessarily, have different cultures or subcultures; and
(2) a social structure compartmentalized into analogous, parallel, non-complementary but distinguishable sets of institutions.

In this view, the corporate groups are incorporated around 'complementary but distinguishable institutions'. These institutions, and therefore the groups, operate independently of the other groups and institutions in the society. If this were not the case, that is, if they—the institutions and groups—were integrated with one another, the society could not be regarded as plural.

Given the plurality and autonomy of these institutions and groups, on what basis can they be regarded as constituting a society? Van Den Berghe and Smith give rather different answers to this question but both answers are open to the same objections. According to Van Den Berghe:[25]

At one extreme, societies characterized by a high degree of social pluralism are integrated only through a set of central political institutions controlled by the dominant group, and of economic institutions in which members of different groups interact asymmetrically.

And Smith argues that[26]

> Pluralism is a condition in which members of a common society are internally distinguished by fundamental differences in their institutional practice. Where present, such differences are not distributed at random; they normally cluster, and by their clusters they simultaneously identify institutionally distinct aggregates or groups, and establish deep social divisions between them. The prevalence of such systematic dissociation between the members of institutionally distinct collectivities within a single society constitutes pluralism. . . . In a plural society where the rulers form a culturally distinct numerical minority, the aggregate depends for its formation, unity, order, and form primarily on the concentration . . . of regulative powers by the ruling section through the political framework.

It is to be noted that for Smith the pluralism relates only to the basic institutional system which 'embraces kinship, religion, property and economy, recreation, and certain sodalities. . . . It does not normally include government.'[27]

The criticisms already made of plural 'theory' apply equally to these conceptions and need not be repeated here. There is, however, an additional point to be made. It is one thing to argue that groups within a society may, in certain respects, follow different institutional practices; it is quite another thing to suggest that these institutional practices are independent of one another and of the structure of the social formation. On what basis, for example, can it be maintained that only the political system links the plural institutional orders so as to enable a plural society to be referred to as a society whereas the economy does not? Again, once it is argued that the political and the economic institution do hold the society together despite the plurality of the institutions, how can it be maintained that the other institutional orders remain autonomous? The assertion of institutional 'segregation' and autonomy presses plural theory to its logical conclusion and emphasizes the abstractness of its formulation. This is so since we are asked to understand institutions independently of any relationship outside of their own 'boundaries'.

One result of this is that there is no way in which it can be meaningfully asked (let alone be answered) within this 'theory': how can the development and maintenance of distinguishable institutional practices be explained?

The above discussion of internal colonialism suggests that this theory presents society as a composite of class relations and ethnic, race, cultural, or national relations. To this extent the theory may be distinguished from conventional analyses of race, ethnic and similar relations, since in the latter approach these relations are accorded sole salience. On the other hand, the theory of internal colonialism is unable to explain the relationship between class relations and race or ethnic, etc., relations. As a consequence, the latter relations come once more to be treated as autonomous and in isolation from the class relations. To this extent there is a close convergence between internal colonialism and conventional race relations theory, more particularly, as our analysis has shown, when the latter is based on a plural model of society.

For this reason, internal colonialism remains vulnerable to the analytical limitations which we have shown to apply to plural theory.

Imperialism and modes of production

The obfuscating consequences of an analysis in terms of racial, ethnic, cultural, or national entities is nowhere clearer than in the use of the notion of exploitation to describe relations between such entities. The reason for this is that while the concept of exploitation can have a rigorous and explicit meaning in defining class relations, it becomes a vague, descriptive term in the characterization of relations between such entities as racial, national, or cultural groups. Bettelheim, in commenting on the notion of the exploitation of the 'poor countries' by the 'rich ones', has made the same point, in relation to 'normal' colonialism. He states:[28]

> Because the concept of *exploitation* expresses a *production relation*—production of surplus labour and expropriation of this by a social class—it necessarily relates to *class relations* (and a relation between 'countries' is not and cannot be a relation between classes).

He argues that 'it is not possible to give a strict meaning to the notion of exploitation of one *country* by another *country*', and he concludes:[29]

> Henceforth it is necessary to think of each 'country' as constituting a social formation with a specific structure, in particular because of the existence of *classes* with contradictory interests. It is this structure that determines the way in which each social formation fits into international production relations.

With only slight amendments this passage applies equally to the case of internal colonialism. Thus, we may say, that in order to avoid the abstraction involved in treating racial or ethnic groups as undifferentiated and homogeneous, we must think of each such group as having a 'specific structure, in particular because of the existence of classes with contradictory interests'. It follows that the concrete social totality is constituted by the complex articulation of class relations within racial or ethnic groups, as well as the relation of classes across these groups together, we may add, with the ideological and political practices which 'fit' these relationships.

This consideration leads directly to the crucial further question of historical specificity. It should be clear from what has so far been argued that the concept of colonialism upon which the internal colonial thesis is based is extremely vague and unspecific. In part, this is due to the failure to distinguish between forms of colonial, political, ideological, and cultural domination and modes of imperialist economic exploitation. In turn this conflation stems from the failure to distinguish differing modes of imperialist economic exploitation with the result that different forms of colonial domination cannot be explicitly related to different modes of exploitation.

More specifically, much of the analysis of imperialism and underdevelopment (and of internal colonialism) has been based on the assumption that in the era of capitalist imperialism, exploitation everywhere takes place according to a single, invariant mode. There are two variants of this argument, but both contend that capitalist relations have, as Laclau puts it, 'effectively and completely penetrated even the most apparently isolated sectors of the underdeveloped world'.[30]

In one variant capitalism is equated with commodity exchange—with the market economy—and consequently the participation of the underdeveloped world in the market is construed as evidence of the total transformation of the indigenous economies into capitalist economies, albeit subordinate ones. This is the position advanced by Frank in his analysis of Latin America. But, Laclau argues,[31]

Frank's theoretical schema involves three types of assertion:
1. Latin America has had a market economy from the beginning; 2. Latin America has been capitalist from the beginning; 3. the dependent nature of its insertion into the capitalist world market is the cause of its underdevelopment. The three assertions claim to refer to a single process *identical in its essential aspects* from the 16th to the 20th century.

The consequence of this, as Laclau has shown, is that it becomes impossible to define 'the specificity of the exploitative relationship' in operation at a specific moment and this flows directly from

Frank's failure to base his analysis on the concept of relations of production. Thus, an analysis based on the concept of relations of production would have shown, in the particular case of Latin America, not the complete penetration of capitalism but rather that the[32]

> pre-capitalist character of the dominant relations of
> production in Latin America was not only *not* incompatible
> with production for the world market, but was actually
> intensified by the expansion of the latter. The feudal regime of
> the haciendas tended to increase its servile exactions on the
> peasantry as the growing demands of the world market
> stimulated maximization of their surplus. Thus, far from
> expansion of the external market acting as a disintegrating
> force on feudalism, its effect was rather to accentuate and
> consolidate it.

It is thus clear from Laclau's argument that it cannot be assumed from the emergence of a dominant capitalist market, that non-capitalist economies which participate in that market are, thereby, automatically transformed into capitalist modes of production.

In the second variant of this argument, the analysis is, indeed, based on the concept of the mode of production. In this case it is assumed that the effect of the emergence of capitalism as a dominant mode of production is the necessary and rapid disintegration of non-capitalist productive relations. This view seems to be based on Lenin's discussion of imperialism and Marx's analysis of primitive accumulation.

In *Imperialism: The Highest Stage of Capitalism* Lenin stated:[33]

> The export of capital influences and greatly accelerates the
> development of capitalism in those countries to which it is
> exported. While, therefore, the export of capital may tend
> to a certain extent to arrest development in the capital
> exporting countries, it can only do so by expanding and
> deepening the further development of capitalism throughout
> the world.

In *Capital* Marx formulated the notion of primitive accumulation in the following terms:[34]

> The capitalist system presupposes the complete separation of
> the labourers from all property in the means by which they can
> realize their labour. . . . The process, therefore, that clears
> the way for the capitalist system, can be none other than the
> process which takes away from the labourer the possession of
> his means of production; a process that transforms on the one

hand, the social means of subsistence and of production into capital, on the other, the immediate producers into wage-labourers. The so-called primitive accumulation, therefore, is nothing else than the historical process of divorcing the producer from the means of production.

However, neither Lenin's general characterization of the development of capitalism through imperialism in the era of monopoly capitalism, nor Marx's theoretical analysis of the constitution of capitalism through primitive accumulation, can be construed as concrete historical accounts of the actual progression of imperialism and capitalism either within particular social formations or on a world scale. To interpret Marx and Lenin in this way, as, for example, the Programme of the South African Communist Party clearly does, is precisely to obliterate the analysis of the relationship of capitalism with non-capitalist modes of production and thereby to exclude the possibility of analysing the specificity of the exploitative relations which concretely characterize social formations.

In fact, the relationship of capitalist to non- or pre-capitalist modes of production may vary in a number of ways and for different reasons. Thus, in one place the relationship of capital to a non-capitalist mode of production may revolve around the extraction in different ways—by plunder, or the exchange of non-equivalents or by means of the process of price formation—of the commodities produced by the latter. Geertz's study of Inner Java is an example of this. At another place, the main focus of the relationship may be on the extraction, not of the product, but of labour-power. South Africa, as I will show below, is an example of this type of relationship. While in both of these cases the associated political policy turns on the domination and preservation of the non-capitalist societies, in other instances the particular mode of economic exploitation may be accompanied by a policy aimed at or having the effect of destroying the non-capitalist societies.

The relevance of this for the present discussion may be clarified by the following elaboration. In the course of its development, the capitalist mode of production enters into relationships with other, non-capitalist, systems of production—the very origins of capitalism in the interstices of feudalism testifies to this. Relations with other modes of production first occur within the boundaries of the nation state. First with trade and later with the development of monopoly capitalism and the export of capital, capital increasingly enters into new relationships with other, non-capitalist, modes of production, beyond the borders of the nation-state. These relations, which are exploitative in the strict sense of the term—they involve directly or indirectly the extraction of the surplus from the direct producers—

characterize, in general, the period of capitalist imperialism. These relations of imperialism are constituted within a particular context of political domination and are sustained and supported by a mode of ideological and political practice which varies with the mode of exploitation. But, as Lenin pointed out, both imperialism and colonialism undergo historical changes:[35]

> Colonial policy and imperialism existed before the latest
> stage of capitalism, even before capitalism. Rome, founded
> on slavery, pursued a colonial policy and practised imperialism.
> But 'general' disquisitions on imperialism which ignore, or put
> into the background, the fundamental differences between
> socio-economic formations, inevitably turn into the most vapid
> banality. . . . Even the capitalist colonial policy of previous
> stages of capitalism is essentially different from the colonial
> policy of finance capital.

In certain conditions of imperialist development, ideological and political domination tend to be expressed not in terms of the relations of class exploitation which they must sustain but in racial, ethnic, national, etc., terms and, in all cases, this is related to the fact that the specific mode of exploitation involves the conservation, in some form, of the non-capitalist modes of production and social organization, the existence of which provides the foundation of that exploitation. Indeed, it is in part the very attempt to conserved an *control* the non-capitalist societies in the face of the tendency of capitalist development to disintegrate them and thereby to undermine the basis of exploitation, that accounts for political policies and ideologies which centre on cultural, ethnic, national, and racial characteristics.

In certain circumstances capitalism may, within the boundaries of a single state, develop predominantly by means of its relationship to non-capitalist modes of production. When that occurs, the mode of political domination and the content of legitimating ideologies assume racial, ethnic, and cultural forms and for the same reason as in the case of imperialism. In this case, political domination takes on a colonial form, the precise or specific nature of which has to be related to the specific mode of exploitation of the non-capitalist society.

These points can be illustrated and perhaps made clearer by an analysis of internal colonialism in South Africa.

Internal colonialism in South Africa

It was suggested in the previous section that one important economic basis of colonial domination is the economic relationship which imperialism establishes between capitalist and non-capitalist modes of production. I also argued that that relationship may take different forms.

In volume II of *Capital*, in dealing with the circuit of capital and in particular the commodities which comprise the means of production Marx stated:[36]

> Within its process of circulation, in which industrial capital functions either as money or as commodities, the circuit of industrial capital whether as money-capital or as commodity capital, crosses the commodity circulation of the most diverse modes of social production, so far as they produce commodities. No matter whether commodities are the output of production based on slavery, of peasants . . . of state enterprise . . . or of half-savage hunting tribes, etc.—as commodities and money they come face to face with the money and commodities in which the industrial capital presents itself and enter . . . into its circuit. . . . The character of the process of production from which they originate is immaterial. They function as commodities in the market, and as commodities they enter into the circuit of industrial capital as well as into the circulation of the surplus value incorporated into it. . . . To replace them [i.e. the commodities entering the capitalist circuit in the above manner] they must be reproduced and to this extent the capitalist mode of production is conditional on modes of production lying outside of its own stage of development.

While in the above passage Marx's remarks are restricted to commodities which are also means of production, it seems clear that they apply equally to labour-power which is physically produced in a non-capitalist mode of production but which is converted into a commodity by its appearance on the capitalist labour market.

It is this feature, the introduction into the capitalist circuit of production of labour-power physically produced in a non-capitalist economy, that denotes one important feature of imperialism. This 'crossing' of different modes of production modifies the relationship between wages and the cost of reproducing labour-power in favour of capital. It is precisely this relationship which is the foundation of 'internal colonialism' in South Africa.

In fact, the South African social formation is made up of several modes of production but it is not possible in this paper to discuss all of these or to explore the complex relations between them. For present purposes the analysis may be restricted to the relationship between the dominant capitalist economy and the mode of production in the African areas (Reserves).

The capitalist mode of production in South Africa (as elsewhere) is one in which

(1) the direct labourers, who do not own the means of capitalist production, sell their labour-power to the owners of the means of production who are non-labourers; and

(2) the wage the labourer receives for the sale of his labour-power for a certain period is only a portion of the value created by him during that period, the balance being appropriated as unpaid labour (surplus value) by the owners of the productive means.

This second condition is, of course, related to Marx's conception of labour-power as a commodity and expresses the specific form in which the surplus is extracted from the direct producers in the capitalist mode of production.

The ratio between the surplus product and the necessary product which accrues to the labourer in the form of wages is, in Marx's terms, the rate of surplus value. This rate will obviously vary in accordance with changes in the distribution of the product between necessary and surplus labour. The greater the proportion of the working day devoted to necessary labour, the lower the rate of surplus value and consequently the rate of profit, all other things remaining equal. It follows that the conditions which determine the amount of time spent on the necessary product are of crucial importance in capitalist production.

In general commodities exchange at their value. The value of labour-power is determined in the same way as that of other commodities—by the amount of socially necessary labour time which has been expended in its production. As Marx put it:[37]

> The value of labour power is determined, as in the case of every other commodity, by the labour time necessary for the production and consequently also the reproduction of this special article. . . . Given the individual, the production of labour power consists in his reproduction of himself or his maintenance. Therefore the labour-time requisite for the production of labour-power reduces itself to that necessary for the production of . . . the means of subsistence; in other words, the value of labour-power is the value of the means of subsistence necessary for the maintenance of the labourer.

The subsistence necessary for the reproduction of labour-power is extended in at least two ways by Marx: 'the sum of the means of subsistence necessary for the production of labour-power must include the means necessary for the labourers' substitutes, that is, his children';[38] in addition: 'The expenses of . . . education . . . enter *pro tanto* into the total value spent in its production.'[39]

There are a number of ways in which the proportion of the working day which is allocated to necessary labour may be decreased. Thus, for example, the value of labour-power may be decreased or, again, the length of the working day may be increased and most importantly for the present argument, labour-power may be acquired at a cost below its value.

As Meillassoux has pointed out, the means of subsistence acquired by the labourer can be divided into two parts—the direct wages paid to the worker in and during employment, and indirect wages which he receives in the form of social security benefits, for example, unemployment payments, family allowances, health services, education and so on.[40] In its most advanced form indirect wages are institutionalized in the social welfare arrangements of the welfare state, but obviously, these arrangements are the outcome of a lengthy historical process.

Under certain conditions the capitalist mode of production is able to avoid, to a greater or lesser extent, the payment of indirect wages; that is, it is obliged to pay only the immediate sustenance of the labourer but it can avoid paying for his subsistence during unemployment, or for the subsistence of children or costs of education, etc.

The most important condition enabling capitalism to pay for labour-power below its cost of reproduction in this way is the availability of a supply of labour-power which is produced and reproduced outside the capitalist mode of production.

In South Africa this condition was (and still is, although to a decreasing extent) met by the presence of a non-capitalist mode of agricultural production in the areas of African concentration (particularly, but not exclusively, in the Reserves). In this mode of production land is held communally by the community and worked by social units based on kinship, and the product of labour is 'pooled' and then redistributed directly by means of an allocation through the kinship units in accordance with certain rules of distribution. Alternatively, where the land is held in individual tenure, it is worked by a kin group between the members of which, certain reciprocal obligations of support are in force. Whatever the mode of production, however, the crucial element is the existence of reciprocal obligation of support.

Given the nature of the relations of production and distribution in such an economy, the potentiality exists of utilizing labour-power drawn from it into the capitalist sector without fundamentally altering those relations. Thus, as Meillassoux argues, if the necessary subsistence for the entire year can be produced by labour which is limited to a part of the year, then labour-power will be potentially available to the capitalist sector for the remainder of the year. This potential labour-power can be brought into the circuit of capitalist

247

production provided that the capitalist sector 'finds the means to extract it practically, without the direct intrusion of capital into the self-sustaining sector', an intrusion which would destroy the relations of production and, therefore, the basis of the production of labour-power in the sector external to capitalism.[41] It is presumably in this kind of situation that various 'political' measures may be taken to force labour-power onto the market. On the other hand, if the subsistence produced during the productive season is insufficient to meet all necessary needs then, provided there are no actual productive possibilities beyond the period of agricultural production, the propulsion of labour-power onto the market may occur through the operation of economic forces.

In either case, the significant aspect is that the capitalist sector benefits from the means of subsistence produced in the non-capitalist mode of production to the extent that it is relieved of paying a portion of the necessary means of subsistence by way of indirect wages. This, as I have shown in a previous paper, has the important effect of raising the rate of surplus value.[42] The uniqueness or specificity of South Africa, in the period of capitalism, lies precisely in this: that it embodies within a single nation–state a relationship characteristic of the external relationship between imperialist states and their colonies (or neo-colonies).

Bettelheim has pointed out that[43]

> Inside social formations in which the capitalist mode of production is dominant, this domination mainly tends to expanded reproduction of the capitalist mode of production, that is, to the dissolution of the other modes of production and subsumption of their agents to capitalist production relations. The qualification 'mainly' indicates that this is the *predominant tendency* of the capitalist mode of production within the social formations under consideration. However, this predominant tendency is combined with another *secondary* tendency, that of 'conservation–dissolution'. This means that within a capitalist social formation the non-capitalist forms of production, before they disappear are 'restructured' (partly dissolved) and thus subordinated to the predominant capitalist relations (and so conserved).

Within the advanced capitalist states themselves the dominant tendency more or less rapidly brought about the complete or almost complete dissolution of the non-capitalist relations of production. The explanation for this, in each society, and the specification of the processes involved require, of course, their own historical analysis.

In South Africa, on the contrary, the dominant tendency has been inhibited by the secondary tendency of 'conservation–dissolution'.

That is to say, the tendency of capital accumulation to dissolve the very relationship (with the non-capitalist economies) which makes that accumulation possible (at a particular rate) is blocked by the contradictory tendency of capital to conserve the relationship and with it the non-capitalist economies, albeit in a restricted form for the reasons already outlined.

The political expression of this imperialist-type relationship takes on a colonial form. This is so because, at one level, the conservation of the non-capitalist modes of production necessarily requires the development of ideologies and political policies which revolve around the segregation, and preservation and control of African 'tribal' societies. The ideological focus, it must be stressed, is always necessarily on the 'racial' or 'tribal' or 'national' elements, precisely because of the 'tribal' nature of what is being preserved and controlled.[44]

So, too, the policies pursued and the laws passed must have the same focus. Therefore, the attempt to conserve these societies in the face of disruptive tendencies centres on guaranteeing the availability of some land (1913 Land Act) to the 'tribe', the preservation of the social and political organization of the 'tribe', and thus the retention of much 'Native' law and so on. At the same time the disruptive tendencies create problems of control for the capitalist state and these are met by a vast superstructure of administrative control both through the state and through 'tribal' authorities. The counterpart of all this is the structure of domination exercised over the African labour force through the pass laws, urban areas acts, police, Bantu administration department, and so on.

In the paper referred to above I showed concretely and in some detail how the specific changes in ideology and political policy— the transition from 'Segregation' to 'Apartheid'—reflected changing relationships between the African redistributive economics and the capitalist sector with particular reference to the supply of cheap labour-power. In brief the preservation of the conditions (migrant-labour, fixed land area, low capital investment in African agriculture) which enable labour-power to be extracted from the African societies serve to destroy the productive capacity of these societies (given the increase in population, and consequent over-population on the fixed land means, backward farming methods, etc.). The diminution of the product from these Reserve economies generates rural impoverishment and, also, in the absence of the assumption by the capitalist sector of responsibility for indirect wages, extreme urban impoverishment. The consequence is increasing African pressure on wages and on rural conditions, pressure which becomes elaborated into an assault on the whole political and economic structure in the 1940s and 1950s. Apartheid may be seen as the attempt of the capitalist state to maintain the system of cheap migrant-labour, in the face of this opposition, by means of the erection of a 'perfected' and 'modernized' apparatus of political domination.

Although, in this section, the focus has been on the extraction of labour-power by a capitalist mode of production from non-capitalist productive systems, it must be stressed that it is not intended to suggest that this is the only form such a relation may take. I indicated above that imperialism may also operate by appropriating the product of non-capitalist societies or, indeed, by destroying those societies such that the producers are 'freed' of the means of production. These types of relations give rise to varying forms of political domination.[45]

Conclusion

As I indicated earlier, the analysis presented here is partial in that it does not deal with the full complexity of the relationships between all the different modes of production in South Africa. Nevertheless, sufficient has been said to show the fundamental difference between this approach and those criticized in the chapter. Although only briefly, specific racial ideologies and political policies, despite their pervading racial content, have been shown to reflect and to relate to a specific reality 'external' to themselves—the modes of production and their interrelationships. In particular, the point has been stressed that specific modes of political domination which assume a racial or ethnic and, therefore, a colonial rather than a class form have to be analysed in terms of the specific relations of economic exploitation.

Notes

1 See, for example: R. Blauner, 'Internal colonialism and ghetto revolt', *Social Problems*, vol. 16, no. 4, 1969, pp. 393–408, and *Racial Oppression in America*, Harper & Row, New York, 1972; G. M. Carter, T. Karis and N. M. Stultz, *South Africa's Transkei, the Politics of Domestic Colonialism*, Heinemann, London, 1967; P. Gonzalez Casanova, 'Internal colonialism and national development', *Studies in Comparative International Development*, vol. 1, no. 4, 1965; A. G. Frank, *Capitalism and Underdevelopment in Latin America*, Monthly Review Press, New York, 1967; A. Lerumo, *Fifty Fighting Years*, Inkululeko Publications, Johannesburg, 1971; L. Marquand, *South Africa's Colonial Policy*, South African Institute of Race Relations, Johannesburg, 1957; H. J. Simons and R. E. Simons, *Class and Colour in South Africa, 1850–1950*, Penguin, Harmondsworth, 1969; South African Communist Party, *The Road to South African Freedom*, Ellis Bowles, London, n.d.; R. Stavenhagen, 'Classes, colonialism, and acculturation: a system of inter-ethnic relations in Mesoamerica', *Studies in Comparative International Development*, vol. 1, no. 6, 1965.
2 Simons and Simons, *op. cit.*, p. 610.

3 Blauner, 1972, *op. cit.*, pp. 12–13.
4 Blauner, 1969, *op. cit.*, p. 395.
5 Gonzalez Casanova, *op. cit.*, p. 33.
6 W. K. Tabb, *The Political Economy of the Black Ghetto*, W. W. Norton, New York, 1970, p. 15.
7 South African Communist Party, *op. cit.*, pp. 25–6.
8 Blauner, 1972, *op. cit.*, pp. 11–12.
9 *Ibid.*, p. 2.
10 Blauner, 1969, *op. cit.*, p. 395.
11 Blauner, 1972, *op. cit.*, p. 13.
12 Gonzalez Casanova, *op. cit.*, p. 33.
13 D. L. Johnson, 'On oppressed classes', in J. D. Cockroft, A. G. Frank and D. L. Johnson, *Dependence and Underdevelopment*, Doubleday, New York, 1972, p. 282.
14 *Ibid.*, p. 281.
15 Cf. Stavenhagen, *op. cit.*
16 South African Communist Party, *op. cit.*, p. 25.
17 *Ibid.*, p. 27.
18 J. S. Furnivall, *Colonial Policy and Practice*, Cambridge University Press, 1948.
19 M. G. Smith, *The Plural Society in the British West Indies*, University of California Press, Berkeley, 1965.
20 D. Lockwood, 'Some remarks on "The Social System"', *British Journal of Sociology*, vol. 7, 1956, p. 137.
21 J. Rex, *Race, Colonialism and the City*, Routledge & Kegan Paul, London, 1973, p. 256.
22 P. L. Van Den Berghe, 'Pluralism and the polity: a theoretical exploration', in L. Kuper and M. G. Smith, eds, *Pluralism in Africa*, University of California Press, Berkeley, 1969, p. 68.
23 J. Rex, 'The plural society in sociological theory', *BJS*, vol. 10, 1959, and 'The plural society: the South African case', *Race*, vol. 12, no. 4, 1971; University of California Press, Berkeley, 1967.
24 Van Den Berghe, 1969, *op. cit.*, p. 67.
25 *Ibid.*, p. 71.
26 M. G. Smith, 'Institutional and political conditions of pluralism', in Kuper and Smith, *op. cit.*, pp. 27, 32.
27 Smith, 1965, *op. cit.*, p. 82.
28 C. Bettelheim, 'Theoretical comments', in A. Emmanuel, *Unequal Exchange: A Study of the Imperialism of Trade*, New Left Books, London, 1972, p. 301. Ernesto Laclau in a personal communication has pointed out that the unequal exchange of non-cquivalents also constitutes an exploitative relation. This, however, in no way affects the general point being made by Bettelheim since an analysis of the class structure of 'countries' in a relationship of unequal exchange is no less important than in the case of production relations.
29 *Ibid.*, p. 300.
30 E. Laclau, 'Feudalism and capitalism in Latin America', *New Left Review*, no. 67, May–June 1971, p. 21.
31 Frank, *op. cit.*; Laclau, *op. cit.*, p. 22.

32 *Ibid.*, p. 30.
33 V. I. Lenin, *Selected Works*, Lawrence & Wishart, London, 1969, p. 214.
34 K. Marx, *Capital*, Foreign Languages Publishing House, Moscow, 1962, vol. I, p. 714.
35 Lenin, *op. cit.*, p. 228.
36 Marx, *op. cit.*, vol. II, pp. 109, 110.
37 *Ibid.*, vol. I, p. 171.
38 *Ibid.*, p. 172.
39 *Ibid.*
40 C. Meillassoux, 'Imperialism as a mode of reproduction of labour power', unpublished seminar paper, 1974.
41 *Ibid.*
42 H. Wolpe, 'Capitalism and cheap labour-power in South Africa: from segregation to apartheid', *Economy and Society*, vol. 1, no. 4, 1972.
43 Bettelheim, *op. cit.*, p. 297.
44 Stavenhagen, *op. cit.*, makes a similar analysis in relation to the 'corporate' nature of the Indian Community but he does not articulate the relationship between this and the precise mode of economic exploitation.
45 I leave open whether the notion of 'internal colonialism' has any proper application in conditions of racial discrimination where, however, the internal relations within the society are overwhelmingly capitalist in nature, that is, where non-capitalist modes of production, if they exist at all, are marginal.

12 Structural dependency, modes of production and economic brokerage in rural Peru

Norman Long

This paper discusses three types of analysis which focus upon the system of linkages between local rural economies and the wider socio-economic framework of Third World countries. The argument is illustrated with examples drawn from studies of rural Peru.

The Peruvian case is particularly interesting in that recently several Peruvian anthropologists and sociologists have attempted to interpret the problems of underdevelopment in Peru by analysing the mechanisms by which the expropriation and utilization of economic surplus takes place at local and regional levels; and have characterized the types of dependency relations and inequalities that exist between different sectors of the national economy and in the social structure generally. Hence they have drawn attention to structural imbalances that exist between the major urban centres and the rural hinterland, between the highland region and the coast, and have shown how, at the local level, there also exist internal patterns of domination. A subsidiary aim of this paper, then, is to review some of this work, since it remains less well known in English-speaking circles. The examination of socio-economic and political relations at the international level lies outside the scope of the discussion.

Structural dependency and metropolitan–satellite relations

The structure of underdevelopment has been conceptualized by Frank[1] in terms of metropolitan–satellite relationships which, at the regional level, are characterized by a series of unequal economic and social exchanges between urban and rurally located groups exercising different degrees of power. A similar type of analysis has been developed by Stavenhagen[2] in his study of the differential access to economic and political resources exercised by 'Indians' and *ladinos* in Mexico and Guatemala, by Cotler[3] who examines the

253

regional inequalities that exist between highland and coastal areas of Peru and who argues that this is reinforced by the existence of certain social and cultural stereotypes contrasting 'Indian' with *mestizo* culture; and by Burgos,[4] Castillo,[5] and Preston[6] each of whom present data on the pattern of domination found in the Andes between urban-based *mestizo* groups and the peasant Indian population.

Frank starts with the view that underdevelopment is a logical outcome of the expansion of the capitalist system to colonial areas; but rejects the dualistic interpretation which argues that the pattern of external domination produces a structure of dualism in underdeveloped countries such that there exists, on the one hand, a modern partly industrialized urban sector and, on the other, a traditionalized and economically backward peasant sector. These two opposing sectors are said to be poorly articulated and it is this lack of integration which constitutes a major obstacle to socio-economic development. In opposition to this view, Frank maintains that the sectors of an underdeveloped economy are in fact well integrated in terms of a structure of metropolitan–satellite relationships which results from the penetration of capitalism into even the remotest corner of the Third World.

As an alternative model he suggests that we visualize 'a whole chain of metropolises and satellites, which runs from the world metropolis down to the hacienda or rural merchant who are satellites of the local commercial metropolitan centre but who in their turn have peasants as their satellites'.[7] Hence we find that close economic, political, and social ties bind the satellites to each metropolis, which expropriates their economic surplus (or a large part of it) to use for its own economic development. Ties of economic dependence are matched by a concentration of political power and social resources in metropolitan centres. This manifests itself most dramatically in the way that the members of a relatively small, urban-based national elite control the economic and political life of the masses. According to Frank, this tendency towards centralization is an essential element of the capitalist system.

He also suggests that the economic and socio-political connections between satellite and metropolis generate increasing interdependence of their bourgeoisie, who develop a mutual interest in maintaining the system. This growing interconnection also produces increasing polarization between dominate and subordinate groups: 'A symptom of this polarization is the growing international inequality of incomes and the absolute decline of the real income of the low income recipients.' And it is also shown by the 'acute polarization at the lower end of the chain, between the national and/or local metropolises and their poorest rural and urban satellites whose absolute real income is steadily declining'. Eventually this 'polarization sharpens political tension . . . until the initiative and generation of the transformation of the system passes from the metropolitan pole, where it has been for centuries, to the satellite pole'.[8]

It is at this point in the historical process that revolutionary action is called for: it is Frank's conviction that radical structural change and self-perpetuating economic growth will only come to Latin America and other similar underdeveloped areas once the national and regional bourgeoisie are overthrown and the links in the chain of dependency relationships broken.

Frank's thesis then is both an attempt to offer a new analytical perspective for the study of economic development and social change in the Third World, and also a piece of political writing. I am concerned here only with the analytical usefulness of his scheme, not with its implications for political action.

One recent attempt to apply the concepts of structural dependency and internal domination to problems of rural development and change is that by Matos Mar, et al.[9] This study opens with an account by José Matos Mar of the general socio-historical circumstances of Peruvian development in which he argues that the pattern of external domination established by Spanish colonial rule and continued by the advanced industrial countries is repeated in a multiplicity of ways within the nation and its differentiated social sectors. Like Frank, 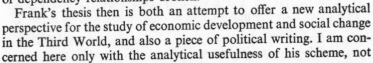 Matos rejects the commonplace dualistic interpretation of the problem of underdevelopment. He argues that the rural–agricultural and urban–industrial sectors cannot be regarded as separate, opposed structures or social systems for they are mutually related to one another in a complex web of relationships. He proposes instead to use the concept of 'plural' society.[10] This concept he believes emphazises both the 'singularity' of Peruvian society, its unique history and persisting cultures, while also giving attention to the patterns of inequality and dependence which have emerged as a result of its incorporation into a wider system of international relations of an economic and political nature.

A similar position is maintained by Fuenzalida and Alberti in a later chapter, when they state:[11]

> In contrast to the concept of a dualistic society which is
> defined by reference to its internal disarticulation, a plural
> society is defined in terms of a specific mode of articulation
> whose fundamental character is imprinted by the persistence of
> pre-industrial types of domination.

This formulation differs somewhat from the Frankian thesis in that it emphasizes the continuation of forms of domination other than that specifically created by the capitalist system. However, the phenomenon of domination remains central to their analysis and provides the unifying element of what they call a pluralist system of the 'arborescent' type. Similar to Frank's notion of metropolitan–satellite relations, this metaphor is employed to describe a structure where[12]

the units of each subordinate level are connected to one another only by means of a superior instance. It depicts a mode of articulation which is highly centralized and in which the different instances of power assume gradually more capacity for decision, control a larger amount of wealth and have access to a wider range of information as one approaches the summit.

At the base of such a structure there is a variety of different types of rural social systems, represented in Peru by so-called 'traditional' haciendas of the southern highlands, modernized haciendas of the coastal region, indigenous peasant communities and smallholder settlements. These systems, however, are interrelated within a specific micro-regional context and tied into the overall pattern of domination at national level. Hence the concepts of 'domination', 'pluralism', and 'micro-region' are closely interdependent analytically.

As a general statement of the kind of orientation required to analyse problems of rural development in Peru such a formulation represents a considerable advance on previous conceptual frameworks. However, certain difficulties arise when the various authors try to elaborate their interpretation in the context of field data on the Chancay Valley of coastal Peru. For example, although there is a discussion of the micro-region and pluralism, much of the analysis is taken up with a specification of the different modes of social organization represented by the haciendas of the lowland zone of the valley, by the communities of the higher altitudes and by the settlements of smallholders, and far too little attention is given to how these systems are interrelated economically and/or politically and of the ways in which the region is tied into the wider national structure. Thus more emphasis in fact is given to pluralism than to regional structure.

Nevertheless in this study Cotler develops two models which he claims enable one to gain a better understanding of the patterns of domination in rural Peru and of the changes that result from socio-economic change. He calls these models the 'triangle *without* a base' and the 'triangle *with* a base'.[13] His discussion centres around the comparison of two contrasting situations: one characterized by being 'typically traditional' such as can be observed in the Peruvian highlands,[14] and the other an area undergoing more economic change as we find in the Chancay Valley.[15]

Cotler first identifies the general social conditions associated with the 'traditional' hacienda system. These are: (*a*) low level of urbanization; (*b*) low socio-economic differentiation; (*c*) primitive technology and low level of productivity; (*d*) absence of effective communications; and (*e*) high incidence of illiteracy. Although not necessary, these conditions are sufficient for the emergence and persistence of 'traditional' relations of dominance.

Within this context, Indian peasants of the highlands have few alternatives open to them and are forced to submit to whoever has control over the key resources of the area (e.g. land and education). These dominant figures (normally non-Indians or *mestizos*) link the local structure with the outside and have access to important institutions of national significance. For example they control the regional markets and local politico-administrative institutions. The peasants may be permanent or temporary workers or sharecroppers who provide labour and other service to the *hacendado* (i.e. the landowner and patron). The stability of the system is maintained by a normative structure which functions as a rationalization of the

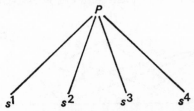

FIGURE 12.1   *Traditional patronage pattern of domination*

status quo: the *mestizo* is perceived by the peasants as the most powerful source of potential benefits and the only person who can improve their condition. Because of this the peasants lack group solidarity and compete with one another for the favours and protection of the *hacendado*.

The combination of structural conditions and the form of existing social relations and values severely limits the possibility of changes being generated internally. The peasantry is atomized and subordinate. Diagrammatically the structure of social relations can be depicted as in Figure 12.1, where P is the patron, and s^1, etc., are subordinates. The model isolates two basic elements: the complete atomization of the subordinates, and the funnelling of relations through the patron who controls access to external persons and institutions.

Using this model as a baseline, Cotler then goes on to outline the means by which this structure can be transformed. He deals only with externally generated changes. Change is produced by the following processes:

(1) The creation of new alternatives. For example, the intervention of the State in the construction of roads and other types of

257

infrastructure that open up new sources for work for peasants in the area. Another example is the appearance of traders or intermediaries who compete with *hacendados* for the marketing of agricultural produce. In certain circumstances this can substantially undermine the authority and social position of *hacendados*, stimulate the production of cash crops among peasants, and lead to the invasion of hacienda land.[16]

(2) The development of mass communications which can broaden cultural horizons, bringing about a reorientation in the normative structure and resulting in certain changes in the relations between *hacendados* and peasants.

(3) The falling away of institutional support at State level given to *mestizos* and *hacendados*; and the appearance of political parties, trade unions and student organizations which mobilize the peasantry. Also powerful national bodies like the church and military may sever their close ties with local elites.

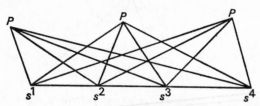

FIGURE 12.2 *Complex pattern of domination*

The final outcome of such processes can be depicted as the closing of the base of the triangle as peasants develop more solidarity among themselves and as new kinds of apex emerge (see Figure 12.2). In this way the monopoly of material and social resources is broken and the taking of decisions becomes based on the mutual adaptation of groups and social categories that have the power to negotiate concerning the content and form of exchange. These changes are characteristic of the transformation of the traditional pattern of domination into one based more on consent and bargaining, though patron–client relations may not be totally eliminated and power imbalances may still be present. The main feature of the new structure is the existence of several apexes representing dominant groups operating in varying fields of action: in the market, in local government, or in relation to national government agencies. Thus a simple metropolitan–satellite structure is replaced by a more complex one.

Cotler's two models have been used by Fuenzalida and Alberti to analyse the differences between haciendas, Indian communities, and smallholder settlements in the Chancay Valley. The authors suggest that one can treat these two models as representing opposite ends

SEE
MITCHIE
1977

of a morphological continuum and that the settlements in the valley can be placed on this continuum according to how far they approximate to either of these ideal–typical situations. Several different dimensions are considered: the question of administrative functions and structures, the control of economic resources, the availability and use of information, and the types and intensity of external contacts.

From this they conclude that the commercial haciendas of the region approximate most closely to the pattern of traditional domination described by Cotler, whilst the Indian communities, where land and resources are still largely held under a system of communal ownership, fall towards the other end of the continuum, with the smallholder settlements coming at some midway point between these two extremes.

The haciendas exhibit a pattern of centralization whereby the hacienda administration controls most of the organizational, economic and natural resources of the settlement. This severely limits the possibility of workers forming effective bodies like trade unions and associations to protect their own interests. In contrast, the Indian communities show a greater propensity to engage in co-operative modes of organization. The bulk of their pastoral land remains firmly in the control of the community and the District Council composed of local residents collaborates with community leaders in the running of local government and services. Clubs and political party organizations abound and are active in representing the interests of their members in local and national affairs. Although there is evidence of growing economic differentiation between larger and smaller landowners and a small commercial sector consisting of shopkeepers and traders, there is no clearly defined politico-economic elite.

The smallholder settlements are characterized chiefly by the existence of major social divisions which inhibit the development of strong horizontal linkages at the base of the triangle. This seriously affects the functioning of local government: in one of these settlements there are two District Councils in competition for control. Also political parties and clubs are poorly organized and internally divided. The most important criterion of social status is one's economic standing and it is this which tends to correlate with the degree to which farmers are in regular contact with urban areas. Land is gradually becoming more unequally distributed as a relatively small group of better-off farmers acquire access to larger extensions and control the water supplies necessary for irrigation.

Each of these types of local organization is embedded in a regional and national structure which places restrictions on the kinds of structural changes that can occur. For example, Fuenzalida and Alberti point out that marked changes occurred in the haciendas with increased external contacts and the growth of the regional capital of Huaral. This led to the establishment of trade union organizations which resulted in a decline in the power of the hacienda administration *vis-à-vis* peasant workers. But it also coincided with a series of economic crises brought about by fluctuating prices for export crops on the world market. Thus the net result was only a marginal improvement in the position of workers. Indeed changes in ownership and control had to await the intervention of the State which, under its new land reform policy, has expropriated them and transformed them into production co-operatives.[17] The socio-economic life of Indian and smallholder settlements is likewise affected by the fact that they must export their crops and labour through urban markets controlled by more powerful commercial and industrial groups. And, in addition, they are dependent on government and other agencies for the provision of the capital and technical expertise necessary for the development of their agriculture.

The main finding of this study, however, is that there exists in regions like the Chancay Valley of Peru a whole complex of dependency relations, some of the traditional patronage type described by Cotler for highland haciendas and others based on the differential control of the means of capitalist production, of the markets and of politico-administrative bodies. Hence the hacendado is frequently replaced by the rural merchant and agricultural entrepreneur, and in other contexts by the political broker tied to a national political party.

I now examine, in the light of the above empirical data, the analytical utility of the structural dependency approach. The main burden of my discussion will be to show that Frank's model is too simplistic to provide a satisfactory framework for understanding the complexities and variations in metropolitan–satellite relations and that it contains a number of assumptions which seem unwarranted. I shall also offer some criticism of Cotler's formulation.

In the first place Frank's analysis assumes that the intrusion of capitalism leads to the elimination of pre-capitalist forms of organization. This is evident from his assertion that Latin America has been capitalist from the time that it was incorporated into the world market during the colonial period. He rejects social and economic dualism and at the same time refuses to allow for the persistence of certain feudal-type relations or other non-capitalist modes. Yet, as Laclau has argued, this is to confound two quite separate issues. To claim that feudal-type relations survive into the modern capitalist era, albeit somewhat modified in form, is not the same as adhering to a dualistic interpretation. Indeed, while rejecting dualism one might still argue 'that the modernity of one sector is a function of the backwardness of the other', showing, for example, how 'the maintenance of feudal backwardness at one extreme and the apparent progress of a bourgeois dynamism' at the other are actually functional for the persistence of underdeveloped forms of capitalism.[18] Moreover, as the Peruvian studies show, both capitalist and non-capitalist modes of production frequently co-exist within the same empirical situation, involving the same or neighbouring peasants in qualitatively different types of production relations.

According to Laclau, this weakness in Frank's argument arises fundamentally from his failure to define at all precisely what he means by capitalism. In common with certain other writers, he tends to deal with the problem from the point of view of commodity exchange rather than production relations. It is because of this that he can argue that the enlargement of the world market during the sixteenth century which led to the colonization of the Third World was thoroughly capitalist in nature, and that it brought about the destruction of feudalism. Drawing upon Marx, Laclau stresses the necessity of distinguishing between *capital* and *capitalism*. He writes:[19]

> Did the structural conditions of capitalism exist in 16th century Europe when, according to Frank, the process of capital domination started in Latin America? Could we consider free labour to be the rule then? By no means. Feudal dependence and urban handicrafts remained the basic forms of productive activity. The existence of a powerful commercial class which greatly enlarged its stock of capital through overseas trade did not in the least modify the decisive fact that this capital was accumulated by the absorption of an economic surplus produced through labour relationships very different from those of free labour.

A similar point could be made for contemporary rural Peru where labour may be recruited through a patron–client system like that of the traditional haciendas, or from the extended family on a non-wage basis, although the product itself may be sold in external markets which form part of the wider capitalist economy.

Frank's analysis, then, is primarily concerned with demonstrating how the establishment of a market economy, now based on the demands of capitalist production in advanced industrial countries and in national metropolitan centres, leads to the setting up of metropolitan–satellite relations which operate to maintain a structure of unequal exchange between the groups involved. This functions not only in economic terms but also has it social, political, and cultural components. The studies by Cotler, Fuenzalida and Alberti indicate the variations in this pattern as it pertains to rural Peru.

Further difficulties arise over the use of the concept of 'dependence'. According to Dos Santos,[20]

> dependence is a *conditioning situation* in which the economies
> of one group of countries are conditioned by the development
> and expansion of others. A relationship of interdependence
> between two or more economies or between such economies
> and the world trading system becomes a dependent
> relationship when some countries expand through self-impulsion
> while others, being in a dependent position, can only expand as
> a reflection of the expansion of the dominant countries, which
> may have positive or negative effects on their immediate
> development. In either case, the basic situation of dependence
> causes these countries to be both backward and exploited.
> Dominant countries are endowed with technological, commercial,
> capital and socio-political predominance over dependent
> countries . . . and can therefore exploit them, and extract part of
> the locally produced surplus. Dependence, then, is based upon an
> international division of labour which allows industrial
> development to take place in some countries while restricting
> it in others, whose growth is conditioned by and subjected to
> the power centres of the world.

Whilst this may characterize in general terms the types of relationships that exist between advanced industrial and underdeveloped economies, and may be extended to cover similar patterns at national and regional levels, it necessarily avoids specifying the other elements in the relations between the nations or groups concerned which may not so easily be categorized in terms of dependence. I do not deny the importance of satellite status but a fuller analysis of the complexities involved would, I believe, be better achieved if the study of exploitative relationships was matched by some account of the patterns of co-operation and collaboration that also exist. Indeed the existence of dependency relations normally entails the maintenance of co-operative elements based on some degree of mutual interest in order that the former might be perpetuated; and there are also important types of horizontal exchanges that occur between the satellites themselves, as is shown, for example, in the Chancay Valley where peasants from smallholder settlements work as temporary labourers on the haciendas.

This predilection for depicting relationships exclusively in terms of dependency or verticality also distorts Cotler's view of traditional haciendas. His model assumes that horizontal relationships among peasant workers are relatively unimportant and that the relationship between patron and workers is one of extreme domination. Yet other hacienda studies show that there is considerable exchange of services and produce among peasant workers. This functions to counteract temporary food and labour shortages which individual households sometimes suffer and it helps to build up some degree of trust between particular households that may later become important for the contracting of marriages or for organizing religious fiestas.[21] Indirectly of course these relationships contribute towards the maintenance of the *status quo*. Recent evidence also questions the assumption that haciendas severely exploited their workers and suggests that frequently smallholder peasants were much worse off economically than those tied to 'feudal lords'.[22]

It would seem, therefore, that in order to develop the Frankian type of analysis we need to be much more precise in defining what is implied by the concept of dependence as it relates to different structural contexts. Dos Santos and others have clarified the matter in relation to economic and political dependence at the macro-international level, and some attempts too have been made to define it in terms of sectoral or inter-regional inequalities that exist within nations. However, major difficulties arise when this concept is extended in micro-studies to deal with specific types of interpersonal relationships. A basic conceptual problem here is that participation in any kind of interpersonal relationship involves some degree of dependence on the part of the parties concerned since having a relationship with someone implies the exclusion of other possible alternatives. Hence it is important to try to specify the conditions under which different types and degrees of structural dependency or domination exist. Cotler's attempt to set out the structural conditions associated with the pattern of domination found on haciendas fundamentally fails because it does not distinguish the hacienda situation from that of other types: all of the conditions he lists could apply equally well to other situations of a peasant or tribal nature.

Another weakness in Frank's formulation is that he assumes that metropolitan–satellite relations are arranged in a simple hierarchical ordering. He writes of the chain of metropolises and satellites stretching from the world metropolitan centres to national, regional and local satellites, down to the lowest level in the structure involving the most isolated peasant farmer or agricultural worker.[23] Although it may be possible to show that this pattern pertains for certain cases, it is clearly inadequate for understanding other situations where more direct links with national centres exist. Recent research in the central region of highland Peru has shown, for instance, that many villages of the zone operate a whole series of economic and social transactions directly with Lima the capital (some 250 miles away) and have only minimal contact with the local regional city of Huancayo. In

263

order to explain this one would need to take account of various factors: the development of communications between the capital city and its hinterland, the spatial location of certain produce markets, the rate and types of labour migration from the villages to the mines and cities of the coast, and the development of certain patterns of social organization (e.g. migrant clubs, and fiesta and political associations) which provide the means by which close relations with the capital city are maintained.[24]

The notion of metropolitan–satellite relations also assumes that changes in the development and organization of satellites are largely dependent on forces emanating from the metropolitan centres. While this may be substantially true if we are identifying the initial sources of major structural change, later in the process satellites themselves may come to play a determining role in the allocation of national and regional resources. This is documented for both Latin America and Africa where certain provincially-based political parties and interest groups may succeed in obtaining more favourable terms for their areas of origin. Frank's argument directs attention away from the analysis of such matters and suggests that instead we view the actions of such groups from the point of view of how their protagonists come to be absorbed into the national bourgeoisie and thus no longer represent the 'real' interests of their provincial compatriots. Hence the elite members of a satellite acquire metropolitan status *vis-à-vis* their followers, and the system remains unimpaired. Such an interpretation espouses an essentially static view of development and underestimates the part played by internal factors in promoting economic and social change or in contributing towards the maintenance of inequalities between sectors of the economy or society.

This tendency to see structural change from the point of view of the impact of exogenous factors is characteristic of Cotler's analysis as well. He interprets changes in hacienda organization as a response to changes in the external environment. Hence he stresses the importance of the emergence of new employment opportunities, the development of national political parties and changes in the relations between national and regional elites. Clearly one would not wish to reject such an interpretation but the mere listing of types of environmental changes cannot explain the differential impact which these forces have had on different haciendas. To explain this one needs to examine much more closely the types of internal differences that exist between haciendas (e.g. in the types of relationships that exist among tenants and between them and their *hacendado*). It might also be important to examine the cumulative effect of demographic change leading to changes in the distribution of resources as holdings become more fragmented or when peasants slowly encroach upon the land of the *hacendado*.[25]

Given these qualifications, however, the study of structural dependency and internal domination is obviously important if we wish to understand more fully the impediments to economic growth and social change among rural peoples of the Third World. Such an approach does not necessarily make assumptions about the nature of traditional or 'pre-modern' societies, nor does it assume that traditional patterns are eliminated by more modern forms. It sees the outcome in terms of the evolution of a more capitalistically-orientated society but it does not assume that this will closely parallel that of Western Europe. Indeed it emphasizes that because the socio-historical conditions are so different for these countries, their paths of change will be markedly different. Hence studies of rural situations should examine both the modes of incorporation consequent upon greater involvement in the capitalist system and also the variations that are found in different ecological, economic, and socio-cultural zones. As yet analysis of these problems is in its infancy: the research by Frank has pointed the way but it is weak in that it tends to over-stress the uniformities in the pattern and does not address itself adequately to the variations that arise, except in so far as it treats these as the result of the concatenation of highly specific historical circumstances.

The articulation of modes of production

The next type of approach offers some way out of the conceptual and analytical difficulties posed by the metropolitan–satellite model. It attempts to do this by focusing more explicitly on the problem of the interconnections between different modes of production.

The discussion of modes of production in the Third World has recently concerned itself with the ways in which the capitalist mode articulates with, and eventually comes to have a controlling influence over, traditional or non-capitalist modes. The criticism of Frank's thesis by Laclau,[26] the work by the French Marxist anthropologists like Terray,[27] and Dupré and Rey,[28] and the critique of Myrdal's writings by Ulyanovsky and Pavlov,[29] each represents an attempt to come to grips with the multi-structural character of economic systems in the Third World through an analysis of production systems. Through this it is hoped to gain insight into the mechanisms by which particular types of production relations are maintained and how they are connected with other modes existing within the same macro socio-economic framework. When applied to the analysis of underdevelopment this approach aims to explain how and why certain non-capitalist forms of production persist despite their involvement in modern marketing systems based on commodity exchange.

While Frank is right in emphasizing the importance of exchange processes it is equally important to attempt to relate patterns of circulation and distribution to production. Hence Meillassoux[30] argues that exchange elements (whether they be located within a predominantly capitalist or non-capitalist system) must be examined in relation to the part they play in reproducing the material conditions of existence. For example, in the lineage-based subsistence societies in West Africa studied by him the circulation of women through marriage, which is controlled by the lineage elders, is critical for the reproduction of the productive unit itself thereby allowing the producers to benefit in the future from their past labour. He also shows that the movement of children between classificatory fathers and the adoption of strangers into the system enables adjustments to take place in order that certain lineages, which (because of differential fecundity and accidents of birth and death) are low on labour, may be replenished. Indeed he extends his argument to suggest that many of the customs concerning gift-giving, reciprocity, and dowry arrangements can be interpreted in terms of this notion of reproducing or maintaining the basic conditions of subsistence production. Similar functions are performed by various institutions and processes which encourage capital accumulation for investment in production in capitalist societies.

Dupré and Rey have developed this type of analysis to provide some account of the ways in which the capitalist mode impinges upon non-capitalist modes at different stages in the development of Third World economies. Their argument shows that in certain contexts a capitalist mode of production can indirectly contribute to the persistence of non-capitalist forms. During the early trading period the capitalist mode supplied important goods and even injected money into the subsistence system but these items were absorbed into the system and did not undermine the traditional production process. Hence we find in West Africa a flow of trade goods into the interior in return for slaves and other products. In some cases (e.g. the Bemba of Zambia) the supply of important items like guns and gunpowder led to significant changes in political organization, but it did not affect agricultural production much.[31] Later with colonial rule the capitalist mode came to have a dominant influence over non-capitalist modes as commercial and industrial capital was invested in production itself. This resulted in the development of small-scale commercial agriculture, plantation systems, mining, and limited industrialization. Yet despite these changes some rural areas continue to be primarily concerned with satisfying subsistence needs and keep almost intact their traditional modes of production. This is well illustrated by Watson's study of the Mambwe of Zambia. Watson argues that although the Mambwe are well integrated into the urban–industrial economy through the export of labour to the mines, their

266

system of subsistence production is unchanged and will remain so providing the ratio of women to men left in the rural area is kept at approximately 2 : 1, and there is no pressure on existing land resources.[32]

I want now to show how one might begin to develop an analysis of different modes of production and their interconnections in rural Peru. However, before doing so some clarification of concepts is necessary.

By 'mode of production' we mean that complex made up of the forces of production (i.e. technical rules, resources, instruments of labour, and labour-power) and the social relations of production. Production is the process by which men with their labour-power and instruments of labour transform the object of labour (in this case, land) in order to reap some material or economic return. The object of labour and the instruments used constitute what we call the means of production, but the process itself requires the participation of men who are brought together in terms of a specific set of social relations. These social relations are principally defined in terms of the ownership and control of the means of production and of the social product.[33] Thus in theoretical terms a mode of production equals the combination of social relations of production and the level of development of the productive forces: comparing, for example, the capitalist with the feudal mode we find that both systems exhibit qualitatively different relations and forces of production.

Certain difficulties arise, however, when we attempt to apply this formal definition to particular empirical material. Montoya argues, for example, that although it is possible to show that various types of production systems found in highland Peru have roughly similar levels of productive forces they in fact represent a wide variety of systems based on different types of social relations.[34] It would seem better, therefore, to differentiate between them by describing the different patterns of ownership and control that exist.

Taking social relations of production as the main criterion, Montoya identifies four main non-capitalist modes in rural Peru: the traditional hacienda, the smallholder–private property type, the sharecropping type (of which there are several variants), and the indigenous or peasant community type. Since most regions of Peru are fairly heterogeneous in terms of production systems, an analysis of the economic structure of any one area would normally involve consideration of each of these modes and of how they interconnect. Here it is important to recognize that although there is a tendency for a particular mode of production to be associated with a certain type of settlement and land tenure system, several modes (both capitalist and non-capitalist) will normally be found to co-exist within the same context.

This point is well illustrated by studies of highland haciendas.[35] The hacienda mode of production can be characterized in the following way:

(1) It consists basically of two classes of persons: the landowners (or persons who rent the land from the State) called *terratenientes*; and the tenant-workers called *colonos*. In between these two classes is a small group of administrators or foremen, sometimes recruited from the *colonos*, employed by the hacienda.

(2) The *hacendado* has legal control of the land, but *colonos* have effective possession of their plots for usufructuary purposes. In addition there is land which is set aside for the *hacendado* himself.

(3) The contract between the *hacendado* and *colono* is general and often of a verbal kind. It gives land to the *colono* for his personal use and in return secures his services for various duties. Hence the 'rent' is paid for in labour.

(4) Labour service generally takes three forms:

(a) Agricultural work by the *colono* on the lands of the *hacendado*. This is normally fixed in terms of a set number of days per week, month or year. The normal requirement is about two or three days per week or 100 to 150 production days in the year. The rest of the *colono*'s time, when he is not involved in helping the *hacendado* in other ways, can be spent cultivating his own plot. This arrangement enables him to satisfy his basic subsistence requirements, though how successful he is will of course be affected by his household demands and the size of the plot.

(b) Domestic work for the *hacendado*. Depending on the number of *colonos* available each one must complete a work quota as servant in the house of the *hacendado* either on the hacienda or in the town house where he lives. The wife too must periodically assist in domestic chores and the children are normally expected to look after his chickens and small animals.

(c) Periodic work on the clearing of roads and water channels and repairing the *hacendado*'s house and outbuildings. Frequently the *colono* must also assist in carrying the *hacendado*'s produce to the town markets for sale.

At some haciendas additional forms of service include the lending of oxen (if the *colono* possesses them) to the *hacendado* when the latter needs them for ploughing or the drying of potatoes which are stored for sale later in the season.

(5) In addition to providing a small plot of land to the *colono*, the *hacendado*'s obligations consist of:

(a) the giving of small gifts of money for work done on the hacienda (this is only a token amount and is not a salary);

(b) the provision of alcohol and cigarettes for workers when engaged in collective work parties (*faenas*);

(c) the offer of pasturage for the tenant's animals and of firewood for cooking purposes;

(d) the provision of food for servant workers and persons involved in *faenas*.

This dominant pattern of production relations is frequently combined with other types. In addition to the *colonos* there are also often 'sub-*colonos*'. These are usually younger men who have not yet been allocated their own plots for cultivation. In return for food produce they will substitute for a *colono* when he is called for work parties. Also in some cases there is sub-letting of plots. Under this system the sub-tenant is obliged to work for the original tenant for a specified number of days in the week just as the *colono* does for the *hacendado*. Hence within the hacienda we may find similar patterns of patronage operating at lower levels in the structure.

Another variation is that sometimes there is differentiation among the *colonos* themselves whereby some are granted more land than others, and may be required to do more labour service. There are also *colonos-comuneros*. These are peasants living outside the hacienda who have insufficient land of their own to satisfy their subsistence needs and who seek work on the hacienda. Whilst some of them may be recruited temporarily for a fixed payment in money or kind, others are able to acquire plots and provide labour for the *hacendado* in the same way as do resident *colonos*. But unlike the resident *colonos* these *colonos-comuneros* continue to live in their peasant communities and retain an interest in cultivating their own small holdings there too.

A similar type of contract exists between the *hacendado* and *colono* on livestock haciendas. Here the *colono* is required to herd the flocks of sheep and graze the llamas of the *hacendado* and in return is allowed to retain a proportion of the new-born each year, normally in the order of one in ten new animals. In addition he must send all the animals down to the *hacendado*'s land to provide manure when requested, must sell his own animals through the *hacendado*, and undertake whatever other duties that the *hacendado* demands.

The hacienda mode of production then binds the tenant–worker closely to the *hacendado* who owns and, in the last analysis, also controls the means of production. The *colono* however is generally tied to the *hacendado* not only by economic ties but by other types of relationships based on *compadrazgo* (co-parenthood) and on membership of a common religious congregation.[36] Nevertheless, an understanding of the system requires a detailed analysis of how these other types of relationships reinforce and maintain the social relations of production.

It is also important to emphasize that the hacienda mode of production is not geared to subsistence production, for the *hacendado* is primarily interested in exporting produce to local or external markets. Hence the city and the market feature as central points of orientation and the *hacendado* frequently has a part to play in the commerce and administration of the region.[37]

This mode of production is linked to other modes: there is a peasant family, sharecropping system within the hacienda which operates through the exchange of labour between kinsmen and neighbours, and the hacienda draws in other types of labour (of a wage and non-wage form) from nearby communities and settlements and employs its own cadre of administrators. In some areas of Peru haciendas are linked to nearby mining centres through the provision of food and labour for the mines and occasionally the *hacendado* is himself a mine owner. Also on the coast we find a tenant system combined with a capitalist mode of production: some of the cotton and sugar haciendas, for example, have both tenant–workers and an agricultural proletariat. The latter group work regularly for the hacienda on certain parts of the production process and run the factories where the product is processed. Each hacienda then represents a combination of social relations based on different modes of production.

If we were to extend this analysis to cover the other non-capitalist modes we would find a similarly complex pattern of relations with other modes and with various capitalist forms. For example, in peasant communities we normally encounter not only a mode of production based on the exploitation of communally owned land, but also a smallholder-private property system combined with different sharecropping arrangements, and a small but significant capitalist sector based on private ownership of the means of production, wage labour and commercial agriculture. Moreover, a careful study of production units would reveal that various types of exchanges occur between these systems (e.g. labour, capital, and technology transfers), and that, like the hacienda system, these relationships are further consolidated by various types of non-economic exchanges (e.g. participation in religious fiestas, political activities, and family and kinship relations).

The complexities involved in developing such an analysis can best be illustrated by considering the participation of particular household units in different modes of production. Thus a peasant family owning a small plot of land might from time to time also supply labour to nearby haciendas or commercial farms, or, if it has the resources to do so, it might rent or sharecrop land owned by a neighbouring family. In addition, this same family might be linked to the mining sector through the labour of one of its members, or it might engage in some handicraft production of pottery or ponchos which it will sell or exchange in the local market. Hence the existence of other modes of production (both capitalist and non-capitalist) affords the peasant family operating predominantly under a smallholder system the means by which it can acquire supplementary income or additional resources to cover various production and non-production expenditure. On the other hand, the *hacendado*, or capitalist farmer, also benefits from this arrangement for the continuance of a small-holder mode ensures that he can obtain a supply of temporary peasant labour when he needs it.

This suggests that the reproduction of the social relations of production for one mode is dependent on the continuity of other social relations of production found in other modes. As I indicated above, the smallholder family production system found among tenants on the traditional hacienda caters for the material means of subsistence for peasants whilst at the same time enabling the *hacendado* to extract surplus labour from them. Similarly, the co-existence of large commercial farms, based on a capitalist or semi-capitalist mode of production, and smallholder agriculture tends to generate a series of exchanges between them: peasants become temporary wage labourers for landowners of the district and may sometimes become bound to them through debt relations (i.e. they borrow money or acquire seeds, fertilizers, or equipment on credit). In addition to receiving money for their work, peasants frequently look towards these land-owners for other favours (e.g. they may act as brokers for them in their negotiations with government or help in the financing and organization of local fiestas). Socio-economic exchanges of this kind, which involve individuals who depend primarily on different modes of production, seem especially likely to persist in zones where agricultural production is characterized by relatively low levels of capitalization and high production risks, as is the case with much of highland Peru.

A consideration of modes of production also leads to an analysis of the ways in which different production systems are articulated with different types of local and regional markets. Here we need to distinguish between markets of the more traditional type (*ferias*), which predominantly cater for exchanges among peasant producers who bring their products to the market to sell or barter for other goods, and the distribution markets which buy up local produce for sale in the major urban centres. In other situations certain types of produce are exported directly from the farms to the cities by middle-men and wholesale merchants, like those described by Forman and

271

Riegelhaupt for north-east Brazil.[38] As yet no detailed work has been done on regional marketing systems in Peru: the Chancay Valley study makes little mention of this and Castillo's study of Pisac in the southern highlands concentrates almost exclusively on the peasant marketing sector and says little about the activities of the large-scale merchants in the area.[39] However, the work by Burgos on Ecuador, which includes a detailed discussion of marketing in one provincial area, is suggestive of the way in which market studies could be married to an analysis of differing modes of production. He shows that there are imbalances in the control over market resources held by different participants and suggests that pricing mechanisms operate to perpetuate a pattern of structural dependency between peasant producers and market middlemen.[40]

While the Frankian type of analysis emphasizes the ways in which different rural systems are integrated into regional and national marketing structures, showing how the capitalist market economy comes to dominate other forms, it fails to comprehend the sets of relationships which exist between different modes of production at either the regional or national level. Furthermore although Cotler *et al.* recognize the co-existence of different settlement types and therefore implicitly point to the need to examine the ways in which various non-capitalist and capitalist modes of production are interlinked, they too concentrate upon vertical relationships and do not explore the types of horizontal relationships that exist both within and between different modes. This is most strikingly demonstrated by Cotler's failure to take account of the ways in which tenant-workers on traditional haciendas develop relationships among themselves and with other non-resident peasant families for economic, social and religious purposes. He also of course takes no note of the fact that haciendas normally draw upon other forms of labour from outside as well. The attempt to apply Cotler's two models to other settlement types in the Chancay Valley falls down because it tends to treat these as separate organizational entities, when from the point of view of a mode of production analysis they are clearly interconnected. Each type contains a smallholder mode of production and this is variously linked to other modes through transfers of labour, capital, and technology. It is this set of relationships which characterizes the main features of the regional socio-economic structure.

Economic brokerage

A third type of analysis, which to my mind has not yet addressed itself explicitly enough to the question of underdevelopment, is that represented by anthropological studies of rural entrepreneurs and economic brokers. The main focus of this research is the study of those individuals and social categories who play a major part in connecting local production systems with the wider socio-economic framework and who control the crucial sets of relationships involved. Depending on the researcher's theoretical interests, this work either tends to stress the entrepreneurial function (i.e. the management of capital and other resources invested in an enterprise) or it discusses the question of economic brokerage (i.e. the control of the important sets of relationships that provide the main links with the regional or national economy) or occasionally it deals with both.[41]

Such studies are of central importance for the analysis of under-development since they identify the groups and individuals holding strategic positions in the system of linkages between local rural economies and the wider regional and national structure. Through this we may gain further insight into the mechanisms by which economic surplus is extracted and can establish to what extent it is invested in local production. It also enables us to describe the social characteristics of economic brokers (e.g. whether they are 'locals' or 'cosmopolitans', whether they run multiple enterprises and invest in agricultural production, the extent of their urban experience and contacts, whether they hold local or extra-local political office, etc.) and to examine the networks of social relationships used by them to consolidate their positions. Studies by Strickon,[42] Geertz,[43] Long,[44] Cohen,[45] Parkin,[46] and others have shown, for example, how in differing contexts relationships based on kinship, tribal affiliation, common religious bonds, *compadrazgo*, or patron–client relations are utilized to secure entrepreneurial advantage. While most of this research is concerned with processes at the local community level, some anthropologists have begun studying brokers at the national and international levels. For example, Gonzalez has produced a fascinating account of the transactions which occurred between members of an industrial elite in the Dominican Republic and USAID officials over the provision of development aid.[47]

Clearly Frank's suggestion that in Latin America it is the *hacendado* or rural merchant who functions as the local metropolis to whom various peasants are tied in satellite status is a gross simplification of the complexities involved. But it does point to the importance of studying such roles. The same is true of Cotler's attempt to characterize the position of the *hacendado* in southern Peru. It is my contention that whilst the analysis of modes of production enables us to identify the types of horizontal relations that occur at local level and helps to describe the ways in which these function to maintain certain types of vertical (or metropolitan–satellite) relations, we are left with a gap in our analysis if we do not also attempt to understand in detail the activities and strategies of such brokers. We have to analyse, that is, how they organize their resources and how they

273

interact with other social groups. This I believe cannot be done merely by describing institutional roles as Cotler has done for the traditional *hacendado*, nor by giving a structural account of modes of production. The analysis has to be moved on to a somewhat different plane so that we can take more of an actor-orientated perspective and make use of case-study methods.

I cannot here spell out the theoretical assumptions of such an approach, nor can I summarize the substantive findings of my recent studies of economic brokers in the central region of highland Peru.[48] Instead I intend to indicate briefly the kind of contribution that such an approach can make to the study of the articulation of local with regional and national systems.

A defining characteristic of a broker is that he operates in both local and extra-local arenas. For economic brokers this means that they must have links with local production and distribution systems and with external markets. Hence a major task for analysis is to establish how and on what criteria these relationships are built up and maintained. This entails an understanding of the social and economic characteristics of the local and external contexts within which brokers operate and of the range and types of resources available to them. The study of such aspects is complex because it requires an appreciation of how particular individuals manage their affairs in several, often geographically distant, localities.

Existing literature suggests that in the remoter regions of Peru, where the hacienda mode of production predominates, we find a pattern of centralization whereby the major landowners also control marketing and transportation, play an important part in the commerce of the region, and hold major administrative and political offices.[49] These individuals form part of a regional *mestizo* elite that is interconnected through a web of ties based on kinship, affinity, and common economic and political interests. There will of course be variations in the degree of success achieved by particular *hacendados*, but their direct involvement in production ensures a ready supply of labour when they need it and a clientele for the marketing of produce. In addition, they have contacts in town which provide up-to-date information on price fluctuations for particular crops and they are able to build up close ties with larger-scale merchants. This contrasts with the position of the poor peasant producer who may sell his produce through local markets but is handicapped by his poor control over Spanish and by his general lack of information on market conditions.

In other areas where there is a more developed economy and few haciendas the pattern appears to be much more complex. Here we find a multiplicity of economic brokers specializing in the marketing and transportation of different products and operating at different economic scales. Detailed analysis would need to distinguish carefully between different brokerage roles: between, for example, the agricultural middleman, the livestock trader, the timber merchant, the middleman dealing in craft goods, and the transporter. Each of these occupational categories requires slightly different types of local and external networks for the operation of their businesses; and there are marked differences in the extent to which they are involved in local production systems.

In some situations, like the Chancay Valley, the marketing of crops is handled by agricultural entrepreneurs who control reasonably large tracts of land and who themselves produce for export. These individuals are frequently connected to the local peasant population through kinship, affinity, and friendship ties and make use of these relationships in the running of their enterprises. The main problem they face is that of weighing up the various costs and benefits associated with the utilization of these relationships in order to achieve some satisfactory economic return: kinship relationships in particular tend to generate a whole series of uncertainties and difficulties concerning the nature of the obligations and rewards that can be expected.[50] Like the *hacendado*, the hallmark of the successful agricultural entrepreneur is his ability to combine different types of social relations deriving from different modes of production and from different institutional contexts. This enables him to build up a relatively stable set of ties which become functional for mobilizing labour and other resources for production and marketing. It is this bringing together of diverse elements which, I believe, sets him apart from the stereotype of the capitalist entrepreneur.[51]

Some of these brokers devote a considerable amount of time to building up contacts in external markets and this can cut into their time available for other commitments. This may account for the fact that there is a tendency in these situations for traders to specialize in the marketing of particular products (e.g. agricultural or livestock produce, or timber) and in the use of certain markets (e.g. the mining towns, Lima or regional centres). According to the literature, a common mechanism used for consolidating ties with merchants and business associates is by inviting them to become godparents to one's children: this establishes a *compadrazgo* (co-parenthood) bond which it is said generates a high degree of trust (*confianza*) between the persons concerned.[52] Another pattern emerges among groups that have evolved a network of rural–urban ties based on *paisano* relationships: these are relationships involving persons of common village origin. The availability of such ties enables rurally-based traders to avoid some of the difficulties of operating through 'strangers' in urban markets and of being thrown into open competition with traders from other regions. The establishment of regular trading

275

arrangements with compatriots is clearly of advantage to urban-based merchants as well, for they may wish to maintain links with their home communities for family and investment reasons.[53]

The types of economic brokers so far mentioned are all closely connected with agricultural production and normally own land themselves. However, there is another type that specializes in the transportation rather than the buying and selling of produce. Transporters (*transportistas* or *fleteros*) are a common phenomenon throughout Peru. They are primarily concerned with the movement of produce from the rural areas to the urban wholesale and consumer markets, though they also bring consumer goods from the major cities to the regional centres. These individuals own lorries and are contracted by middlemen and distribution agents for the transportation of goods and produce. Because of this they tend to evolve close links with marketing entrepreneurs in both the village and town contexts, and are continually seeking to extend and consolidate these commercial networks. In contrast to agricultural middlemen, they apparently do not place premiums on developing close ties with the peasant farming population and seldom invest in land (possibly because of the tremendous geographical mobility necessitated by their occupation which makes it difficult to manage a farm at the same time).

In addition, transporters frequently form themselves into associations which have the implicit, if not explicit, aim of protecting their economic interests. These associations serve to develop a system of mutual assistance among members for obtaining help on the road when one of their vehicles breaks down or when they need information for securing new contracts, and provide some protection against competition from rival transporters. Of particular interest from this point of view is one group from the central highlands of Peru who are members of a fiesta club which was formed to organize the annual fiesta of San Sebastian, a local patron saint. These transporters are interrelated through a network of kinship, affinal and *compadrazgo* ties and co-operate each year in the financing and running of the fiesta. They maintain close bonds of friendship during the rest of the year and are often seen together at weekends drinking in the local bars, exchanging gossip and information about the people they have worked for and about the places they have visited. At the time of the fiesta, which lasts for nearly a week and during which various religious and secular activities take place, the club invites prominent businessmen from the towns and other notables of the region to take a major part in the proceedings, and they are suitably dined and wined. This serves to reinforce existing relationships and to develop new contacts that may prove useful in the coming year's business activities.[54]

276

These brief comments must suffice to indicate the importance of examining the ways in which particular occupational requirements tend towards the development of somewhat different types of local and extra-local networks, and of relating this to the types of material and social resources available to particular brokers. It is of course also necessary to describe the socio-economic opportunity structure that operates at local level for this will determine the types of brokerage roles that can emerge and whether or not it is possible for individuals of peasant origin to move into these positions. Obviously in a situation where land is concentrated in a few hands there will be less opportunities for economic mobility and the crucial brokerage positions will tend either to be held by large landowners of the district or by town-based merchants. The opportunities for work and for acquiring education will also be important factors to take into account.

This suggests that variations in the socio-economic structure of a region will have a significant effect on the pattern of linkages that develop between rural areas and the towns and cities. The hacienda centralized structure described by Cotler and Frank's model of metropolitan–satellite relations depict, at best, only one variant. There are, as I have argued, other more complex arrangements. The discussion of brokers has stressed the importance of examining the networks of inter-personal ties that develop between rural and urban areas, not merely the general institutional dimensions. It has also pursued the idea that it is essential to examine the types of exchanges that occur within the brokerage group itself. This emphasizes the study of horizontal relationships within local metropolises as well as the consideration of vertical links between brokers and their clients. While it might be possible to cast the argument in terms of an analysis of social classes, I think the study of brokers from the point of view of their social networks, which may cross-cut class formations, is equally important.

Such an approach complements a mode of production analysis for it distinguishes between different brokerage roles in terms of the extent to which particular categories or individuals are involved in production or utilize sets of social relations that derive from various modes of production. The analysis also links up with studies of the organization of markets and of buyer–seller relations which have been a major concern in economic anthropology for many years.

Conclusion

This paper has dealt with three analytical approaches to the study of linkages between local rural structures and the wider socio-economic framework of Third World countries, focusing on the Peruvian case in detail. A substantial part of the argument was

277

devoted to a critical appraisal of the structural dependency models formulated by Frank and Cotler.

Frank's approach was criticized for a number of reasons. It concentrates upon the penetration of the capitalist market economy and gives little attention to the ways in which different types of production systems, capitalist and non-capitalist, co-exist at local, regional, and national levels. It describes underdevelopment in terms of a pattern of metropolitan–satellite or vertical relations and neglects the importance of horizontal ties for sustaining dependency structures. The stress on colonialist or imperialist forces as the main sources for change tends to overlook the significance of internal social and cultural factors that interact with these to produce historically specific outcomes.

Although Cotler takes cognizance of forms of domination other than that associated with capitalism, he too emphasizes vertical relations and fails to comprehend the interconnections between different production systems. He also stresses exogenous factors in his interpretation of structural change.

A somewhat different perspective is provided by the group of French Marxists who have re-kindled interest in the analysis of the articulation of different modes of production and of the processes by which specific types of production relations are reproduced. This approach is particularly valuable for comprehending the multi-structural nature of Third World economies for non-capitalist modes often persist in the face of economic change and can be expected to do so in the foreseeable future. The usefulness of this type of analysis was briefly explored through an examination of the 'traditional' hacienda mode of production and its connections with other modes in highland Peru. I also indicated how one might apply a similar analysis to non-hacienda zones where there exist a multiplicity of modes based on capitalist, semi-capitalist, and non-capitalist production relations.

In the last part of the chapter I discussed the relevance of anthropological studies of entrepreneurs and economic brokers. These studies enable us to identify the social characteristics of, and strategies adopted by, individuals and social categories who play a major part in connecting local production systems with the wider socio-economic structure, and who control the crucial sets of relationships involved. Whilst a mode of production analysis explains how certain social relations of production function for the extraction of economic surplus, the study of brokers analyses how particular individuals acquire positions of economic power and attempt to maintain their pre-eminence. It also shows how sets of relations deriving from different modes of production and from different institutional contexts can be combined for entrepreneurial profit.

It is my view, then, that the bringing together of these two types of analysis is likely to afford a more penetrating study of socio-economic structures and underdevelopment than the highly simplistic and over-generalized model of structural dependency propounded by Frank and his followers. Moreover, it has the added advantage of being compatible with the study of class formations in the Third World, a field of research that has received considerable attention in the literature in recent years.

Notes

1 Andre Gunder Frank, *Capitalism and Underdevelopment in Latin America*, Monthly Review Press, New York and London, 1967.
2 Rodolfo Stavenhagen, 'Classes, colonialism, and acculturation', *Studies in Comparative International Development,* vol. I, no. 6, 1965.
3 Julio Cotler, 'The mechanics of internal domination and social change in Peru', *Studies in Comparative International Development*, vol. III, no. 12, 1967–8.
4 Hugo Burgos, *Relaciones Interétnicas en Riobamba*, Instituto Indigenista Interamericano, Ediciones Especiales, 55, Mexico, 1970.
5 Herman Castillo Ardiles, *Pisac*, Instituto Indigenista Interamericano, Ediciones Especiales, 56, Mexico, 1970.
6 David Preston, 'Internal domination: small towns, the countryside and development', Working Paper no. 11, Department of Geography, University of Leeds, 1972.
7 Frank, *op. cit.*, pp. 146–7.
8 *Ibid.*, p. 150.
9 José Matos Mar, *et al.*, *Dominación y Cambios en el Perú Rural*, Instituto de Estudios Peruanos, Lima, 1969.
10 Throughout this work the notion of 'plural' society is used rather loosely and there is no discussion of the sociological literature on this topic.
11 Matos Mar, 1969, *op. cit.*, p. 289.
12 *Ibid.*, pp. 289–90.
13 These models have also been used by F. Lamond Tullis in a study of the factors affecting the rise and success of peasant movements in central Peru; see *Lord and Peasant in Peru*, Harvard University Press, Cambridge, Massachusetts, 1970.
14 By 'highland Peru' Cotler means the southern regions of Puno, Cuzco, Apurimac and Huancavelica, and the central area of Ancash. This excludes economically more dynamic regions like Junin and Cajamarca.
15 Cotler's analysis assumes the existence of marked socio-economic and cultural differences between the highland and coastal areas of Peru, and of imbalances in trade and capital flows. For details on inter-regional trade see, Keith Griffin, *Underdevelopment in Spanish America*, George Allen & Unwin, London, 1968, pp. 63–5.
16 See, for example, the case of the Convención Valley where the development of coffee as an export crop led to a major peasant movement,

in Wesley Craig Jr, *El Movimiento Campesino en La Convención, Perú*, Instituto de Estudios Peruanos, Serie: Documentos Teóricos no. 1, Lima, 1968.

17 It is debatable of course whether workers have much effective control under the present system, since decision-making tends to rest in the hands of a group of technocrats appointed to supervise their running.

18 E. Laclau, 'Feudalism and capitalism in Latin America', *New Left Review*, no. 67, 1971, p. 31.

19 *Ibid.*, p. 27.

20 T. Dos Santos, 'The crisis of development theory and the problem of dependence in Latin America', *Siglo*, vol. 21, 1969. Reprinted in Henry Bernstein, *Underdevelopment and Development*, Penguin, Harmondsworth, 1973, pp. 76-7.

21 For more details see, Solomon Miller, 'Hacienda to plantation in northern Peru: the processes of proletarianization of a tenant farmer society', in Julian H. Steward, ed., *Contemporary Change in Traditional Societies, vol. III: Mexican and Peruvian Communities*, University of Illinois Press, Chicago and London, 1967. There is an excellent analysis of the functions of horizontal as against vertical relations in a Brazilian *fazenda* (which organizationally resembles the hacienda) by Allen W. Johnson, *Sharecroppers of the Sertão*, Stanford University Press, California, 1971.

22 See Juan Martinez Alier, 'Los huachilleros en las haciendas de la sierra central del Perú desde 1930: algunos hipótesis preliminares', *II Simposio sobre Historia Económica de América Latina*, Rome, 1972.

23 In some respects Frank's model resembles 'central-place theory' developed by geographers for characterizing the socio-spatial arrangement of villages, towns, and cities, and which differentiates them in terms of increasing size and specialization of socio-economic functions (see Brian J. L. Berry, *Geography of Market Centres and Retail Distribution*, Prentice-Hall, Englewood Cliffs, 1967, especially chapter 5). But whereas geographers are mainly interested in ecological formations, Frank focuses on the problem of superordinate–subordinate relationships.

24 See Norman Long 'Kinship and associational networks among transporters in rural Peru: the problem of the "local" and the "cosmopolitan" entrepreneur', *Kinship and Social Networks*, Institute of Latin American Studies, University of London, mimeo, 1972; Long, 'The role of regional associations in Peru', in M. Drake *et al.*, eds, *The Process of Urbanisation*, The Open University, Bletchley, 1973; also Bryan Roberts, 'The interrelationships of city and provinces in Peru and Guatemala', in W. A. Cornelius and F. M. Trueblood, eds, *Latin American Urban Research, 1974*, forthcoming.

25 See, for example, Teofilo Altamirano Rua, 'El cambio del sistema de hacienda al sistema comunal en un area de la sierra sur del Perú: el caso de Ongoy', thesis, University of San Marcos, Lima, 1971.

26 Laclau, *op. cit.*

27 Emmanuel Terray, *Le Marxisme devant les Sociétés Primitives: Deux Études*, Maspero, Paris, 1969.

28 Georges Dupré and Pierre-Philippe Rey, 'Reflections on the pertinence of a theory of the history of exchange', *Economy and Society*, vol. 2, no. 2, May 1973.

29 R. Ulyanovsky and V. Pavlov, *Asian Dilemma: A Soviet View and Myrdal's Concept*, Progress Publishers, Moscow, 1973.

30 Claude Meillassoux, 'From reproduction to production', *Economy and Society*, vol. 1, no. 1, February 1972. See also his *Anthropologie Économique des Gouro de Côte D'Ivoire*, Mouton & Cie, Paris, 1964.

31 See Andrew Roberts, 'Migrations from the Congo (AD. 1500 to 1850)', in Brian M. Fagan, ed., *A Short History of Zambia*, Oxford University Press, Nairobi, 1966, pp. 109–14.

32 William Watson, *Tribal Cohesion in a Money Economy*, Manchester University Press, 1958.

33 An excellent theoretical discussion of the concept of mode of production is contained in Étienne Balibar's 'The basic concepts of historical materialism', in Louis Althusser and Étienne Balibar, *Reading Capital*, Pantheon Books, New York, 1970. There remain, however, certain analytical difficulties in applying a mode of production analysis, as Marx developed it in his studies of capitalism, to non-capitalist systems. Not least of these is the problem of avoiding a Western ethnocentric bias when we attempt to specify the structures pertaining to 'the ownership' of the means of production, or what Balibar has called 'the property connexion', when dealing with non-Western societies, especially those of a tribal organization. Louis Dumont makes a similar point when he questions the application of Marxist ideas and Western sociological concepts to the study of Indian society and history. See his 'The individual as an impediment to sociological comparison and Indian history', in *Religion, Politics and History in India*, Mouton, Paris/The Hague, 1970.

34 Rodrigo Montoya, *A Propósito del Carácter Predominantemente Capitalista de la Economía Peruana Actual*, Ediciones Teoría y Realidad, Serie: Formación Social y Estructura Económica, no. 1, Lima, 1970.

35 See, for example, Gustavo Palacio, 'Relaciones de trabajo entre el patrón y los colonos en los fundos de la provincia de Paucartambo', *Revista Universitaria del Cuzco*, año XLVI, no. 112, 1957; and José Matos Mar, *Las Haciendas en el Perú*, Instituto de Estudios Peruanos, Lima, 1967.

36 Miller, *op. cit.*

37 Montoya, *op. cit.*, p. 19.

38 Shepard Forman and Joyce F. Riegelhaupt, 'Market place and marketing system: towards a theory of peasant economic integration', *Comparative Studies in Society and History*, vol. 12, 1970.

39 Castillo, *op. cit.*

40 Burgos, *op. cit.*, pp. 279–86.

41 For theoretical statements on entrepreneurship, see Fredrik Barth, *The Role of the Entrepreneur in Social Change in Northern Norway*, Universitetsforlaget, Bergen, Oslo, 1963, introduction; and Peter Kilby, ed., *Entrepreneurship and Economic Development*, Free Press, New York, 1971. On brokerage roles, see Eric R. Wolf, 'Aspects of group

relations in a complex society: Mexico', *American Anthropologist*, vol. 58, no. 6, 1956; Clifford Geertz, 'The changing role of the cultural broker: the Javanese Kijaji', *Comparative Studies in Society and History*, vol. 2, 1960; and Sydel F. Silverman, 'Patronage and community-nation relationships in central Italy', *Ethnology*, vol. 4, no. 2, April 1965.

42 Arnold Strickon, 'Carlos Felipe: kinsman, patron and friend', in A. Strickon and S. M. Greenfield, eds, *Structure and Process in Latin America*, University of New Mexico Press, Alberquerque, 1972.

43 Clifford Geertz, *Peddlers and Princes*, University of Chicago Press, Chicago and London, 1963.

44 Norman Long, *Social Change and the Individual*, Manchester University Press, 1968.

45 Abner Cohen, *Custom and Politics in Urban Africa*, Routledge & Kegan Paul, London, 1969.

46 David J. Parkin, *Palm, Wine, and Witnesses*, Intertext Books, London, 1972.

47 Nancie L. Gonzalez, 'Patron–client relationships at the international level', in A. Strickon and S. M. Greenfield, eds, *op. cit.*

48 Norman Long, see above papers on Peru. The research was financed by the Social Science Research Council, with additional assistance from the Foreign Area Fellowship Program, and was co-directed by Dr Bryan Roberts.

49 See Cotler, *op. cit.*; Matos Mar, *op. cit.*, 1967.

50 See Norman Long, 'Commerce and kinship in the Peruvian highlands', paper presented to annual meeting of the American Anthropological Association, Toronto, November 1972.

51 Compare this with Barth's views on entrepreneurship.

52 See Eric Wolf and Edward Hansen, *The Human Condition in Latin America*, Oxford University Press, New York, London and Toronto, 1972, pp. 131–5.

53 See Norman Long, 'The role of regional associations in Peru', *op. cit.*

54 See Norman Long, 'Kinship and associational networks among transporters of highland Peru', *op. cit.*

Index

283

Routledge Social Science Series

Routledge & Kegan Paul   London, Henley and Boston

39 Store Street,
London WC1E 7DD
Broadway House,
Newtown Road,
Henley-on-Thames,
Oxon RG9 1EN
9 Park Street,
Boston, Mass. 02108

Contents

*Authors wishing to submit manuscripts for any series
in this catalogue should send them to the Social Science Editor,
Routledge & Kegan Paul Ltd, 39 Store Street,
London WC1E 7DD.*
● *Books so marked are available in paperback.*
○ *Books so marked are available in paperback only.*
*All books are in metric Demy 8vo format (216 × 138mm approx.)
unless otherwise stated.*

International Library of Sociology
General Editor John Rex

GENERAL SOCIOLOGY

Barnsley, J. H. The Social Reality of Ethics. *464 pp.*
Brown, Robert. Explanation in Social Science. *208 pp.*
● Rules and Laws in Sociology. *192 pp.*
Bruford, W. H. Chekhov and His Russia. *A Sociological Study. 244 pp.*
Burton, F. and **Carlen, P.** Official Discourse. *On Discourse Analysis, Government Publications, Ideology. About 140 pp.*
Cain, Maureen E. Society and the Policeman's Role. *326 pp.*
● **Fletcher, Colin.** Beneath the Surface. *An Account of Three Styles of Sociological Research. 221 pp.*
Gibson, Quentin. The Logic of Social Enquiry. *240 pp.*
Glassner, B. Essential Interactionism. *208 pp.*
Glucksmann, M. Structuralist Analysis in Contemporary Social Thought. *212 pp.*
Gurvitch, Georges. Sociology of Law. *Foreword by Roscoe Pound. 264 pp.*
Hinkle, R. Founding Theory of American Sociology 1881–1913. *About 350 pp.*
Homans, George C. Sentiments and Activities. *336 pp.*
Johnson, Harry M. Sociology: *A Systematic Introduction. Foreword by Robert K. Merton. 710 pp.*
● **Keat, Russell** and **Urry, John.** Social Theory as Science. *278 pp.*
Mannheim, Karl. Essays on Sociology and Social Psychology. *Edited by Paul Keckskemeti. With Editorial Note by Adolph Lowe. 344 pp.*
Martindale, Don. The Nature and Types of Sociological Theory. *292 pp.*
● **Maus, Heinz.** A Short History of Sociology. *234 pp.*
Myrdal, Gunnar. Value in Social Theory: *A Collection of Essays on Methodology. Edited by Paul Streeten. 332 pp.*
Ogburn, William F. and **Nimkoff, Meyer F.** A Handbook of Sociology. *Preface by Karl Mannheim. 656 pp. 46 figures. 35 tables.*
Parsons, Talcott and **Smelser, Neil J.** Economy and Society: *A Study in the Integration of Economic and Social Theory. 362 pp.*
Payne, G., Dingwall, R., Payne, J. and **Carter, M.** Sociology and Social Research. *About 250 pp.*
Podgórecki, A. Practical Social Sciences. *About 200 pp.*
Podgórecki, A. and **Łos, M.** Multidimensional Sociology. *268 pp.*
Raffel, S. Matters of Fact. *A Sociological Inquiry. 152 pp.*
● **Rex, John.** Key Problems of Sociological Theory. *220 pp.*
Sociology and the Demystification of the Modern World. *282 pp.*
● **Rex, John.** (Ed.) Approaches to Sociology. *Contributions by Peter Abell, Frank Bechhofer, Basil Bernstein, Ronald Fletcher, David Frisby, Miriam Glucksmann, Peter Lassman, Herminio Martins, John Rex, Roland Robertson, John Westergaard and Jock Young. 302 pp.*
Rigby, A. Alternative Realities. *352 pp.*
Roche, M. Phenomenology, Language and the Social Sciences. *374 pp.*
Sahay, A. Sociological Analysis. *220 pp.*
Strasser, Hermann. The Normative Structure of Sociology. *Conservative and Emancipatory Themes in Social Thought. About 340 pp.*
Strong, P. Ceremonial Order of the Clinic. *267 pp.*
Urry, John. Reference Groups and the Theory of Revolution. *244 pp.*
Weinberg, E. Development of Sociology in the Soviet Union. *173 pp.*

FOREIGN CLASSICS OF SOCIOLOGY

● **Gerth, H. H.** and **Mills, C. Wright.** From Max Weber: *Essays in Sociology. 502 pp.*

● **Tönnies, Ferdinand.** Community and Association *(Gemeinschaft und Gesell-schaft).|Translated and Supplemented by Charles P. Loomis. Foreword by Pitirim A. Sorokin. 334 pp.*

SOCIAL STRUCTURE

Andreski, Stanislav. Military Organization and Society. *Foreword by Professor A. R. Radcliffe-Brown. 226 pp. 1 folder.*

Broom, L., Lancaster Jones, F., McDonnell, P. and Williams, T. The Inheritance of Inequality. *About 180 pp.*

Carlton, Eric. Ideology and Social Order. *Foreword by Professor Philip Abrahams. About 320 pp.*

Clegg, S. and Dunkerley, D. Organization, Class and Control. *614 pp.*

Coontz, Sydney H. Population Theories and the Economic Interpretation. *202 pp.*

Coser, Lewis. The Functions of Social Conflict. *204 pp.*

Crook, I. and D. The First Years of the Yangyi Commune. *304 pp., illustrated.*

Dickie-Clark, H. F. Marginal Situation: *A Sociological Study of a Coloured Group. 240 pp. 11 tables.*

Giner, S. and Archer, M. S. (Eds) Contemporary Europe: *Social Structures and Cultural Patterns, 336 pp.*

● **Glaser, Barney and Strauss, Anselm L.** Status Passage: *A Formal Theory. 212 pp.*

Glass, D. V. (Ed.) Social Mobility in Britain. *Contributions by J. Berent, T. Bottomore, R. C. Chambers, J. Floud, D. V. Glass, J. R. Hall, H. T. Himmelweit, R. K. Kelsall, F. M. Martin, C. A. Moser, R. Mukherjee and W. Ziegel. 420 pp.*

Kelsall, R. K. Higher Civil Servants in Britain: *From 1870 to the Present Day. 268 pp. 31 tables.*

● **Lawton, Denis.** Social Class, Language and Education. *192 pp.*

McLeish, John. The Theory of Social Change: *Four Views Considered. 128 pp.*

● **Marsh, David C.** The Changing Social Structure of England and Wales, 1871–1961. *Revised edition. 288 pp.*

Menzies, Ken. Talcott Parsons and the Social Image of Man. *About 208 pp.*

● **Mouzelis, Nicos.** Organization and Bureaucracy. *An Analysis of Modern Theories. 240 pp.*

● **Ossowski, Stanislaw.** Class Structure in the Social Consciousness. *210 pp.*

● **Podgórecki, Adam.** Law and Society. *302 pp.*

Renner, Karl. Institutions of Private Law and Their Social Functions. *Edited, with an Introduction and Notes, by O. Kahn-Freud. Translated by Agnes Schwarzschild. 316 pp.*

Rex, J. and Tomlinson, S. Colonial Immigrants in a British City. *A Class Analysis. 368 pp.*

Smooha, S. Israel: Pluralism and Conflict. *472 pp.*

Wesolowski, W. Class, Strata and Power. *Trans. and with Introduction by G. Kolankiewicz. 160 pp.*

Zureik, E. Palestinians in Israel. *A Study in Internal Colonialism. 264 pp.*

SOCIOLOGY AND POLITICS

Acton, T. A. Gypsy Politics and Social Change. *316 pp.*

Burton, F. Politics of Legitimacy. *Struggles in a Belfast Community. 250 pp.*

Crook, I. and D. Revolution in a Chinese Village. *Ten Mile Inn. 216 pp., illustrated.*

Etzioni-Halevy, E. Political Manipulation and Administrative Power. *A Comparative Study. About 200 pp.*

Fielding, N. The National Front. *About 250 pp.*

● **Hechter, Michael.** Internal Colonialism. *The Celtic Fringe in British National Development, 1536–1966. 380 pp.*

Kornhauser, William. The Politics of Mass Society. *272 pp. 20 tables.*

Korpi, W. The Working Class in Welfare Capitalism. *Work, Unions and Politics in Sweden. 472 pp.*

Kroes, R. Soldiers and Students. *A Study of Right- and Left-wing Students. 174 pp.*

Martin, Roderick. Sociology of Power. *About 272 pp.*

Merquior, J. G. Rousseau and Weber. *A Study in the Theory of Legitimacy. About 288 pp.*

Myrdal, Gunnar. The Political Element in the Development of Economic Theory. *Translated from the German by Paul Streeten. 282 pp.*

Varma, B. N. The Sociology and Politics of Development. *A Theoretical Study. 236 pp.*

Wong, S.-L. Sociology and Socialism in Contemporary China. *160 pp.*

Wootton, Graham. Workers, Unions and the State. *188 pp.*

CRIMINOLOGY

Ancel, Marc. Social Defence: *A Modern Approach to Criminal Problems. Foreword by Leon Radzinowicz. 240 pp.*

Athens, L. Violent Criminal Acts and Actors. *104 pp.*

Cain, Maureen E. Society and the Policeman's Role. *326 pp.*

Cloward, Richard A. and **Ohlin, Lloyd E.** Delinquency and Opportunity: *A Theory of Delinquent Gangs. 248 pp.*

Downes, David M. The Delinquent Solution. *A Study in Subcultural Theory. 296 pp.*

Friedlander, Kate. The Psycho-Analytical Approach to Juvenile Delinquency: *Theory, Case Studies, Treatment. 320 pp.*

Gleuck, Sheldon and **Eleanor.** Family Environment and Delinquency. *With the statistical assistance of Rose W. Kneznek. 340 pp.*

Lopez-Rey, Manuel. Crime. *An Analytical Appraisal. 288 pp.*

Mannheim, Hermann. Comparative Criminology: *A Text Book. Two volumes. 442 pp. and 380 pp.*

Morris, Terence. The Criminal Area: *A Study in Social Ecology. Foreword by Hermann Mannheim. 232 pp. 25 tables. 4 maps.*

Rock, Paul. Making People Pay. *338 pp.*

● **Taylor, Ian, Walton, Paul** and **Young, Jock.** The New Criminology. *For a Social Theory of Deviance. 325 pp.*

● **Taylor, Ian, Walton, Paul** and **Young, Jock.** (Eds) Critical Criminology. *268 pp.*

SOCIAL PSYCHOLOGY

Bagley, Christopher. The Social Psychology of the Epileptic Child. *320 pp.*

Brittan, Arthur. Meanings and Situations. *224 pp.*

Carroll, J. Break-Out from the Crystal Palace. *200 pp.*

● **Fleming, C. M.** Adolescence: Its Social Psychology. *With an Introduction to recent findings from the fields of Anthropology, Physiology, Medicine, Psychometrics and Sociometry. 288 pp.*

● The Social Psychology of Education: *An Introduction and Guide to Its Study. 136 pp.*

Linton, Ralph. The Cultural Background of Personality. *132 pp.*

● **Mayo, Elton.** The Social Problems of an Industrial Civilization. *With an Appendix on the Political Problem. 180 pp.*

Ottaway, A. K. C. Learning Through Group Experience. *176 pp.*

Plummer, Ken. Sexual Stigma. *An Interactionist Account. 254 pp.*

● **Rose, Arnold M.** (Ed.) Human Behaviour and Social Processes: *an Interactionist Approach. Contributions by Arnold M. Rose, Ralph H. Turner, Anselm Strauss, Everett C. Hughes, E. Franklin Frazier, Howard S. Becker et al. 696 pp.*

Smelser, Neil J. Theory of Collective Behaviour. *448 pp.*

Stephenson, Geoffrey M. The Development of Conscience. *128 pp.*

Young, Kimball. Handbook of Social Psychology. *658 pp. 16 figures. 10 tables.*

SOCIOLOGY OF THE FAMILY

Bell, Colin R. Middle Class Families: *Social and Geographical Mobility. 224 pp.*
Burton, Lindy. Vulnerable Children. *272 pp.*
Gavron, Hannah. The Captive Wife: *Conflicts of Household Mothers. 190 pp.*
George, Victor and **Wilding, Paul.** Motherless Families. *248 pp.*
Klein, Josephine. Samples from English Cultures.
    1. Three Preliminary Studies and Aspects of Adult Life in England. *447 pp.*
    2. Child-Rearing Practices and Index. *247 pp.*
Klein, Viola. The Feminine Character. *History of an Ideology. 244 pp.*
McWhinnie, Alexina M. Adopted Children. *How They Grow Up. 304 pp.*
● **Morgan, D. H. J.** Social Theory and the Family. *About 320 pp.*
● **Myrdal, Alva** and **Klein, Viola.** Women's Two Roles: *Home and Work. 238 pp.*
    27 tables.
Parsons, Talcott and **Bales, Robert F.** Family: Socialization and Interaction Process. *In collaboration with James Olds, Morris Zelditch and Philip E. Slater. 456 pp. 50 figures and tables.*

SOCIAL SERVICES

Bastide, Roger. The Sociology of Mental Disorder. *Translated from the French by Jean McNeil. 260 pp.*
Carlebach, Julius. Caring For Children in Trouble. *266 pp.*
George, Victor. Foster Care. *Theory and Practice. 234 pp.*
    Social Security: *Beveridge and After. 258 pp.*
George, V. and **Wilding, P.** Motherless Families. *248 pp.*
● **Goetschius, George W.** Working with Community Groups. *256 pp.*
Goetschius, George W. and **Tash, Joan.** Working with Unattached Youth. *416 pp.*
Heywood, Jean S. Children in Care. *The Development of the Service for the Deprived Child. Third revised edition. 284 pp.*
King, Roy D., Ranes, Norma V. and **Tizard, Jack.** Patterns of Residential Care. *356 pp.*
Leigh, John. Young People and Leisure. *256 pp.*
● **Mays, John.** (Ed.) Penelope Hall's Social Services of England and Wales. *368 pp.*
Morris, Mary. Voluntary Work and the Welfare State. *300 pp.*
Nokes, P. L. The Professional Task in Welfare Practice. *152 pp.*
Timms, Noel. Psychiatric Social Work in Great Britain (1939–1962). *280 pp.*
●   Social Casework: *Principles and Practice. 256 pp.*

SOCIOLOGY OF EDUCATION

Banks, Olive. Parity and Prestige in English Secondary Education: a Study in Educational Sociology. *272 pp.*
● **Blyth, W. A. L.** English Primary Education. *A Sociological Description.*
    2. Background. *168 pp.*
Collier, K. G. The Social Purposes of Education: *Personal and Social Values in Education. 268 pp.*
Evans, K. M. Sociometry and Education. *158 pp.*
● **Ford, Julienne.** Social Class and the Comprehensive School. *192 pp.*
Foster, P. J. Education and Social Change in Ghana. *336 pp. 3 maps.*
Fraser, W. R. Education and Society in Modern France. *150 pp.*
Grace, Gerald R. Role Conflict and the Teacher. *150 pp.*
Hans, Nicholas. New Trends in Education in the Eighteenth Century. *278 pp. 19 tables.*
●   Comparative Education: *A Study of Educational Factors and Traditions. 360 pp.*
● **Hargreaves, David.** Interpersonal Relations and Education. *432 pp.*
●   Social Relations in a Secondary School. *240 pp.*
    School Organization and Pupil Involvement. *A Study of Secondary Schools.*

6

● **Mannheim, Karl** and **Stewart, W. A. C.** An Introduction to the Sociology of Education. *206 pp.*
● **Musgrove, F.** Youth and the Social Order. *176 pp.*
● **Ottaway, A. K. C.** Education and Society: An Introduction to the Sociology of Education. *With an Introduction by W. O. Lester Smith. 212 pp.*
Peers, Robert. Adult Education: *A Comparative Study. Revised edition. 398 pp.*
Stratta, Erica. The Education of Borstal Boys. *A Study of their Educational Experiences prior to, and during, Borstal Training. 256 pp.*
● **Taylor, P. H., Reid, W. A.** and **Holley, B. J.** The English Sixth Form. *A Case Study in Curriculum Research. 198 pp.*

SOCIOLOGY OF CULTURE

Eppel, E. M. and **M.** Adolescents and Morality: *A Study of some Moral Values and Dilemmas of Working Adolescents in the Context of a changing Climate of Opinion. Foreword by W. J. H. Sprott. 268 pp. 39 tables.*
● **Fromm, Erich.** The Fear of Freedom. *286 pp.*
● The Sane Society. *400 pp.*
Johnson, L. The Cultural Critics. *From Matthew Arnold to Raymond Williams. 233 pp.*
Mannheim, Karl. Essays on the Sociology of Culture. *Edited by Ernst Mannheim in co-operation with Paul Kecskemeti. Editorial Note by Adolph Lowe. 280 pp.*
Merquior, J. G. The Veil and the Mask. *Essays on Culture and Ideology. Foreword by Ernest Gellner. 140 pp.*
Zijderfeld, A. C. On Clichés. *The Supersedure of Meaning by Function in Modernity. 150 pp.*

SOCIOLOGY OF RELIGION

Argyle, Michael and **Beit-Hallahmi, Benjamin.** The Social Psychology of Religion. *256 pp.*
Glasner, Peter E. The Sociology of Secularisation. *A Critique of a Concept. 146 pp.*
Hall, J. R. The Ways Out. *Utopian Communal Groups in an Age of Babylon. 280 pp.*
Ranson, S., Hinings, B. and **Bryman, A.** Clergy, Ministers and Priests. *216 pp.*
Stark, Werner. The Sociology of Religion. *A Study of Christendom.*
  Volume II. *Sectarian Religion. 368 pp.*
  Volume III. *The Universal Church. 464 pp.*
  Volume IV. *Types of Religious Man. 352 pp.*
  Volume V. *Types of Religious Culture. 464 pp.*
Turner, B. S. Weber and Islam. *216 pp.*
Watt, W. Montgomery. Islam and the Integration of Society. *320 pp.*

SOCIOLOGY OF ART AND LITERATURE

Jarvie, Ian C. Towards a Sociology of the Cinema. *A Comparative Essay on the Structure and Functioning of a Major Entertainment Industry. 405 pp.*
Rust, Frances S. Dance in Society. *An Analysis of the Relationships between the Social Dance and Society in England from the Middle Ages to the Present Day. 256 pp. 8 pp. of plates.*
Schücking, L. L. The Sociology of Literary Taste. *112 pp.*
Wolff, Janet. Hermeneutic Philosophy and the Sociology of Art. *150 pp.*

SOCIOLOGY OF KNOWLEDGE

Diesing, P. Patterns of Discovery in the Social Sciences. *262 pp.*

● **Douglas, J. D.** (Ed.) Understanding Everyday Life. *370 pp.*
● **Hamilton, P.** Knowledge and Social Structure. *174 pp.*
Jarvie, I. C. Concepts and Society. *232 pp.*
Mannheim, Karl. Essays on the Sociology of Knowledge. *Edited by Paul Kecskemeti. Editorial Note by Adolph Lowe. 353 pp.*
Remmling, Gunter W. The Sociology of Karl Mannheim. *With a Bibliographical Guide to the Sociology of Knowledge, Ideological Analysis, and Social Planning. 255 pp.*
Remmling, Gunter W. (Ed.) Towards the Sociology of Knowledge. *Origin and Development of a Sociological Thought Style. 463 pp.*
Scheler, M. Problems of a Sociology of Knowledge. *Trans. by M. S. Frings. Edited and with an Introduction by K. Stikkers. 232 pp.*

URBAN SOCIOLOGY

Aldridge, M. The British New Towns. *A Programme Without a Policy. 232 pp.*
Ashworth, William. The Genesis of Modern British Town Planning: *A Study in Economic and Social History of the Nineteenth and Twentieth Centuries. 288 pp.*
Brittan, A. The Privatised World. *196 pp.*
Cullingworth, J. B. Housing Needs and Planning Policy: *A Restatement of the Problems of Housing Need and 'Overspill' in England and Wales. 232 pp. 44 tables. 8 maps.*
Dickinson, Robert E. City and Region: *A Geographical Interpretation. 608 pp. 125 figures.*
The West European City: *A Geographical Interpretation. 600 pp. 129 maps. 29 plates.*
Humphreys, Alexander J. New Dubliners: *Urbanization and the Irish Family. Foreword by George C. Homans. 304 pp.*
Jackson, Brian. Working Class Community: *Some General Notions raised by a Series of Studies in Northern England. 192 pp.*
● **Mann, P. H.** An Approach to Urban Sociology. *240 pp.*
Mellor, J. R. Urban Sociology in an Urbanized Society. *326 pp.*
Morris, R. N. and **Mogey, J.** The Sociology of Housing. *Studies at Berinsfield. 232 pp. 4 pp. plates.*
Mullan, R. Stevenage Ltd. *About 250 pp.*
Rex, J. and **Tomlinson, S.** Colonial Immigrants in a British City. *A Class Analysis. 368 pp.*
Rosser, C. and **Harris, C.** The Family and Social Change. *A Study of Family and Kinship in a South Wales Town. 352 pp. 8 maps.*
● **Stacey, Margaret, Batsone, Eric, Bell, Colin** and **Thurcott, Anne.** Power, Persistence and Change. *A Second Study of Banbury. 196 pp.*

RURAL SOCIOLOGY

Mayer, Adrian C. Peasants in the Pacific. *A Study of Fiji Indian Rural Society. 248 pp. 20 plates.*
Williams, W. M. The Sociology of an English Village: *Gosforth. 272 pp. 12 figures. 13 tables.*

SOCIOLOGY OF INDUSTRY AND DISTRIBUTION

Dunkerley, David. The Foreman. *Aspects of Task and Structure. 192 pp.*
Eldridge, J. E. T. Industrial Disputes. *Essays in the Sociology of Industrial Relations. 288 pp.*
Hollowell, Peter G. The Lorry Driver. *272 pp.*
● **Oxaal, I., Barnett, T.** and **Booth, D.** (Eds) Beyond the Sociology of Development.

Economy and Society in Latin America and Africa. 295 pp.

Smelser, Neil J. Social Change in the Industrial Revolution: *An Application of Theory to the Lancashire Cotton Industry, 1770–1840. 468 pp. 12 figures. 14 tables.*

Watson, T. J. The Personnel Managers. *A Study in the Sociology of Work and Employment, 262 pp.*

ANTHROPOLOGY

Brandel-Syrier, Mia. Reeftown Elite. *A Study of Social Mobility in a Modern African Community on the Reef. 376 pp.*

Dickie-Clark, H. F. The Marginal Situation. *A Sociological Study of a Coloured Group. 236 pp.*

Dube, S. C. Indian Village. *Foreword by Morris Edward Opler. 276 pp. 4 plates.*
India's Changing Villages: *Human Factors in Community Development. 260 pp. 8 plates. 1 map.*

Fei, H.-T. Peasant Life in China. *A Field Study of Country Life in the Yangtze Valley. With a foreword by Bronislaw Malinowski. 328 pp. 16 pp. plates.*

Firth, Raymond. Malay Fishermen. *Their Peasant Economy. 420 pp. 17 pp. plates.*

Gulliver, P. H. Social Control in an African Society: a Study of the Arusha, Agricultural Masai of Northern Tanganyika. *320 pp. 8 plates. 10 figures.*
Family Herds. *288 pp.*

Jarvie, Ian C. The Revolution in Anthropology. *268 pp.*

Little, Kenneth L. Mende of Sierra Leone. *308 pp. and folder.*
Negroes in Britain. *With a New Introduction and Contemporary Study by Leonard Bloom. 320 pp.*

Tambs-Lyche, H. London Patidars. *About 180 pp.*

Madan, G. R. Western Sociologists on Indian Society. *Marx, Spencer, Weber, Durkheim, Pareto. 384 pp.*

Mayer, A. C. Peasants in the Pacific. *A Study of Fiji Indian Rural Society. 248 pp.*

Meer, Fatima. Race and Suicide in South Africa. *325 pp.*

Smith, Raymond T. The Negro Family in British Guiana: *Family Structure and Social Status in the Villages. With a Foreword by Meyer Fortes. 314 pp. 8 plates. 1 figure. 4 maps.*

SOCIOLOGY AND PHILOSOPHY

Adriaansens, H. Talcott Parsons and the Conceptual Dilemma. *About 224 pp.*

Barnsley, John H. The Social Reality of Ethics. *A Comparative Analysis of Moral Codes. 448 pp.*

Diesing, Paul. Patterns of Discovery in the Social Sciences. *362 pp.*

● **Douglas, Jack D.** (Ed.) Understanding Everyday Life. *Toward the Reconstruction of Sociological Knowledge. Contributions by Alan F. Blum, Aaron W. Cicourel, Norman K. Denzin, Jack D. Douglas, John Heeren, Peter McHugh, Peter K. Manning, Melvin Power, Matthew Speier, Roy Turner, D. Lawrence Wieder, Thomas P. Wilson and Don H. Zimmerman. 370 pp.*

Gorman, Robert A. The Dual Vision. *Alfred Schutz and the Myth of Phenomenological Social Science. 240 pp.*

Jarvie, Ian C. Concepts and Society. *216 pp.*

Kilminster, R. Praxis and Method. *A Sociological Dialogue with Lukács, Gramsci and the Early Frankfurt School. 334 pp.*

● **Pelz, Werner.** The Scope of Understanding in Sociology. *Towards a More Radical Reorientation in the Social Humanistic Sciences. 283 pp.*

Roche, Maurice. Phenomenology, Language and the Social Sciences. *371 pp.*

Sahay, Arun. Sociological Analysis. *212 pp.*

● **Slater, P.** Origin and Significance of the Frankfurt School. *A Marxist Perspective. 185 pp.*

Spurling, L. Phenomenology and the Social World. *The Philosophy of Merleau-Ponty and its Relation to the Social Sciences. 222 pp.*

Wilson, H. T. The American Ideology. *Science, Technology and Organization as Modes of Rationality. 368 pp.*

International Library of Anthropology
General Editor Adam Kuper

● **Ahmed, A. S.** Millennium and Charisma Among Pathans. *A Critical Essay in Social Anthropology. 192 pp.*
Pukhtun Economy and Society. *Traditional Structure and Economic Development. About 360 pp.*

Barth, F. Selected Essays. *Volume I. About 250 pp.* Selected Essays. *Volume II. About 250 pp.*

Brown, Paula. The Chimbu. *A Study of Change in the New Guinea Highlands. 151 pp.*

Foner, N. Jamaica Farewell. *200 pp.*

Gudeman, Stephen. Relationships, Residence and the Individual. *A Rural Panamanian Community. 288 pp. 11 plates, 5 figures, 2 maps, 10 tables.*
The Demise of a Rural Economy. *From Subsistence to Capitalism in a Latin American Village. 160 pp.*

Hamnett, Ian. Chieftainship and Legitimacy. *An Anthropological Study of Executive Law in Lesotho. 163 pp.*

Hanson, F. Allan. Meaning in Culture. *127 pp.*

Hazan, H. The Limbo People. *A Study of the Constitution of the Time Universe Among the Aged. About 192 pp.*

Humphreys, S. C. Anthropology and the Greeks. *288 pp.*

Karp, I. Fields of Change Among the Iteso of Kenya. *140 pp.*

Lloyd, P. C. Power and Independence. *Urban Africans' Perception of Social Inequality. 264 pp.*

Parry, J. P. Caste and Kinship in Kangra. *352 pp. Illustrated.*

Pettigrew, Joyce. Robber Noblemen. *A Study of the Political System of the Sikh Jats. 284 pp.*

Street, Brian V. The Savage in Literature. *Representations of 'Primitive' Society in English Fiction, 1858–1920. 207 pp.*

Van Den Berghe, Pierre L. Power and Privilege at an African University. *278 pp.*

International Library of Phenomenology and Moral Sciences
General Editor John O'Neill

Apel, K.-O. Towards a Transformation of Philosophy. *308 pp.*

Bologh, R. W. Dialectical Phenomenology. *Marx's Method. 287 pp.*

Fekete, J. The Critical Twilight. *Explorations in the Ideology of Anglo-American Literary Theory from Eliot to McLuhan. 300 pp.*

Medina, A. Reflection, Time and the Novel. *Towards a Communicative Theory of Literature. 143 pp.*

International Library of Social Policy
General Editor Kathleen Jones

Bayley, M. Mental Handicap and Community Care. *426 pp.*

Bottoms, A. E. and **McClean, J. D.** Defendants in the Criminal Process. *284 pp.*

Bradshaw, J. The Family Fund. *An Initiative in Social Policy. About 224 pp.*

Butler, J. R. Family Doctors and Public Policy. *208 pp.*

Davies, Martin. Prisoners of Society. *Attitudes and Aftercare. 204 pp.*

Gittus, Elizabeth. Flats, Families and the Under-Fives. *285 pp.*

Holman, Robert. Trading in Children. *A Study of Private Fostering. 355 pp.*

Jeffs, A. Young People and the Youth Service. *160 pp.*

Jones, Howard and Cornes, Paul. Open Prisons. *288 pp.*

Jones, Kathleen. History of the Mental Health Service. *428 pp.*

Jones, Kathleen with **Brown, John, Cunningham, W. J., Roberts, Julian** and **Williams, Peter.** Opening the Door. *A Study of New Policies for the Mentally Handicapped. 278 pp.*

Karn, Valerie. Retiring to the Seaside. *400 pp. 2 maps. Numerous tables.*

King, R. D. and **Elliot, K. W.** Albany: Birth of a Prison—End of an Era. *394 pp.*

Thomas, J. E. The English Prison Officer since 1850: *A Study in Conflict. 258 pp.*

Walton, R. G. Women in Social Work. *303 pp.*

● **Woodward, J.** To Do the Sick No Harm. *A Study of the British Voluntary Hospital System to 1875. 234 pp.*

International Library of Welfare and Philosophy
General Editors Noel Timms and David Watson

● **McDermott, F. E.** (Ed.) Self-Determination in Social Work. *A Collection of Essays on Self-determination and Related Concepts by Philosophers and Social Work Theorists. Contributors: F. P. Biestek, S. Bernstein, A. Keith-Lucas, D. Sayer, H. H. Perelman, C. Whittington, R. F. Stalley, F. E. McDermott, I. Berlin, H. J. McCloskey, H. L. A. Hart, J. Wilson, A. I. Melden, S. I. Benn. 254 pp.*

● **Plant, Raymond.** Community and Ideology. *104 pp.*

Ragg, Nicholas M. People Not Cases. *A Philosophical Approach to Social Work. 168 pp.*

● **Timms, Noel** and **Watson, David.** (Eds) Talking About Welfare. *Readings in Philosophy and Social Policy. Contributors: T. H. Marshall, R. B. Brandt, G. H. von Wright, K. Nielsen, M. Cranston, R. M. Titmuss, R. S. Downie, E. Telfer, D. Donnison, J. Benson, P. Leonard, A. Keith-Lucas, D. Walsh, I. T. Ramsey. 320 pp.*

● Philosophy in Social Work. *250 pp.*

● **Weale, A.** Equality and Social Policy. *164 pp.*

Library of Social Work
General Editor Noel Timms

● **Baldock, Peter.** Community Work and Social Work. *140 pp.*

○ **Beedell, Christopher.** Residential Life with Children. *210 pp. Crown 8vo.*

● **Berry, Juliet.** Daily Experience in Residential Life. *A Study of Children and their Care-givers. 202 pp.*

○ Social Work with Children. *190 pp. Crown 8vo.*

● **Brearley, C. Paul.** Residential Work with the Elderly. *116 pp.*

● Social Work, Ageing and Society. *126 pp.*

● **Cheetham, Juliet.** Social Work with Immigrants. *240 pp. Crown 8vo.*

● **Cross, Crispin P.** (Ed.) Interviewing and Communication in Social Work. *Contributions by C. P. Cross, D. Laurenson, B. Strutt, S. Raven. 192 pp. Crown 8vo.*

● **Curnock, Kathleen** and **Hardiker, Pauline.** Towards Practice Theory. *Skills and Methods in Social Assessments. 208 pp.*

● **Davies, Bernard.** The Use of Groups in Social Work Practice. *158 pp.*

● **Davies, Martin.** Support Systems in Social Work. *144 pp.*

Ellis, June. (Ed.) West African Families in Britain. *A Meeting of Two Cultures. Contributions by Pat Stapleton, Vivien Biggs. 150 pp. 1 Map.*

● **Hart, John.** Social Work and Sexual Conduct. *230 pp.*

● **Hutten, Joan M.** Short-Term Contracts in Social Work. *Contributions by Stella M. Hall, Elsie Osborne, Mannie Sher, Eva Sternberg, Elizabeth Tuters. 134 pp.*

Jackson, Michael P. and **Valencia, B. Michael.** Financial Aid Through Social Work. *140 pp.*

● **Jones, Howard.** The Residential Community. *A Setting for Social Work. 150 pp.*

● (Ed.) Towards a New Social Work. *Contributions by Howard Jones, D. A. Fowler, J. R. Cypher, R. G. Walton, Geoffrey Mungham, Philip Priestley, Ian Shaw, M. Bartley, R. Deacon, Irwin Epstein, Geoffrey Pearson. 184 pp.*

Jones, Ray and **Pritchard, Colin.** (Eds) Social Work With Adolescents. *Contributions by Ray Jones, Colin Pritchard, Jack Dunham, Florence Rossetti, Andrew Kerslake, John Burns, William Gregory, Graham Templeman, Kenneth E. Reid, Audrey Taylor. About 170 pp.*

○ **Jordon, William.** The Social Worker in Family Situations. *160 pp. Crown 8vo.*

● **Laycock, A. L.** Adolescents and Social Work. *128 pp. Crown 8vo.*

● **Lees, Ray.** Politics and Social Work. *128 pp. Crown 8vo.*

● Research Strategies for Social Welfare. *112 pp. Tables.*

○ **McCullough, M. K.** and **Ely, Peter J.** Social Work with Groups. *127 pp. Crown 8vo.*

● **Moffett, Jonathan.** Concepts in Casework Treatment. *128 pp. Crown 8vo.*

Parsloe, Phyllida. Juvenile Justice in Britain and the United States. *The Balance of Needs and Rights. 336 pp.*

● **Plant, Raymond.** Social and Moral Theory in Casework. *112 pp. Crown 8vo.*

Priestley, Philip, Fears, Denise and **Fuller, Roger.** Justice for Juveniles. *The 1969 Children and Young Persons Act: A Case for Reform? 128 pp.*

● **Pritchard, Colin** and **Taylor, Richard.** Social Work: Reform or Revolution? *170 pp.*

○ **Pugh, Elisabeth.** Social Work in Child Care. *128 pp. Crown 8vo.*

● **Robinson, Margaret.** Schools and Social Work. *282 pp.*

○ **Ruddock, Ralph.** Roles and Relationships. *128 pp. Crown 8vo.*

● **Sainsbury, Eric.** Social Diagnosis in Casework. *118 pp. Crown 8vo.*

● Social Work with Families. *Perceptions of Social Casework among Clients of a Family Service. 188 pp.*

Seed, Philip. The Expansion of Social Work in Britain. *128 pp. Crown 8vo.*

● **Shaw, John.** The Self in Social Work. *124 pp.*

Smale, Gerald G. Prophecy, Behaviour and Change. *An Examination of Self-fulfilling Prophecies in Helping Relationships. 116 pp. Crown 8vo.*

Smith, Gilbert. Social Need. *Policy, Practice and Research. 155 pp.*

● Social Work and the Sociology of Organisations. *124 pp. Revised edition.*

● **Sutton, Carole.** Psychology for Social Workers and Counsellors. *An Introduction. 248 pp.*

● **Timms, Noel.** Language of Social Casework. *122 pp. Crown 8vo.*

● Recording in Social Work. *124 pp. Crown 8vo.*

● **Todd, F. Joan.** Social Work with the Mentally Subnormal. *96 pp. Crown 8vo.*

● **Walrond-Skinner, Sue.** Family Therapy. *The Treatment of Natural Systems. 172 pp.*

● **Warham, Joyce.** An Introduction to Administration for Social Workers. *Revised edition. 112 pp.*

● An Open Case. *The Organisational Context of Social Work. 172 pp.*

○ **Wittenberg, Isca Salzberger.** Psycho-Analytic Insight and Relationships. *A Kleinian Approach. 196 pp. Crown 8vo.*

Primary Socialization, Language and Education

General Editor Basil Bernstein

Adlam, Diana S., *with the assistance of Geoffrey Turner and Lesley Lineker.* Code in Context. *272 pp.*

Bernstein, Basil. Class, Codes and Control. *3 volumes.*
- 1. *Theoretical Studies Towards a Sociology of Language. 254 pp.*
2. *Applied Studies Towards a Sociology of Language. 377 pp.*
- 3. *Towards a Theory of Educational Transmission. 167 pp.*

Brandis, W. and **Bernstein, B.** Selection and Control. *176 pp.*

Brandis, Walter and **Henderson, Dorothy.** Social Class, Language and Communication. *288 pp.*

Cook-Gumperz, Jenny. Social Control and Socialization. *A Study of Class Differences in the Language of Maternal Control. 290 pp.*

- **Gahagan, D. M.** and **G. A.** Talk Reform. *Exploration in Language for Infant School Children. 160 pp.*

Hawkins, P. R. Social Class, the Nominal Group and Verbal Strategies. *About 220 pp.*

Robinson, W. P. and **Rackstraw, Susan D. A.** A Question of Answers. *2 volumes. 192 pp. and 180 pp.*

Turner, Geoffrey J. and **Mohan, Bernard A.** A Linguistic Description and Computer Programme for Children's Speech. *208 pp.*

Reports of the Institute of Community Studies

Baker, J. The Neighbourhood Advice Centre. *A Community Project in Camden. 320 pp.*

- **Cartwright, Ann.** Patients and their Doctors. *A Study of General Practice. 304 pp.*

Dench, Geoff. Maltese in London. *A Case-study in the Erosion of Ethnic Consciousness. 302 pp.*

Jackson, Brian and **Marsden, Dennis.** Education and the Working Class: *Some General Themes Raised by a Study of 88 Working-class Children in a Northern Industrial City. 268 pp. 2 folders.*

Marris, Peter. The Experience of Higher Education. *232 pp. 27 tables.*
- Loss and Change. *192 pp.*

Marris, Peter and **Rein, Martin.** Dilemmas of Social Reform. *Poverty and Community Action in the United States. 256 pp.*

Marris, Peter and **Somerset, Anthony.** African Businessmen. *A Study of Entrepreneurship and Development in Kenya. 256 pp.*

Mills, Richard. Young Outsiders: *a Study in Alternative Communities. 216 pp.*

Runciman, W. G. Relative Deprivation and Social Justice. *A Study of Attitudes to Social Inequality in Twentieth-Century England. 352 pp.*

Willmott, Peter. Adolescent Boys in East London. *230 pp.*

Willmott, Peter and **Young, Michael.** Family and Class in a London Suburb. *202 pp. 47 tables.*

Young, Michael and **McGeeney, Patrick.** Learning Begins at Home. *A Study of a Junior School and its Parents. 128 pp.*

Young, Michael and **Willmott, Peter.** Family and Kinship in East London. *Foreword by Richard M. Titmuss. 252 pp. 39 tables.*
The Symmetrical Family. *410 pp.*

Reports of the Institute for Social Studies in Medical Care

Cartwright, Ann, Hockey, Lisbeth and **Anderson, John J.** Life Before Death. *310 pp.*

Dunnell, Karen and **Cartwright, Ann.** Medicine Takers, Prescribers and Hoarders. *190 pp.*

Farrell, C. My Mother Said. . . *A Study of the Way Young People Learned About Sex and Birth Control. 288 pp.*

Medicine, Illness and Society
General Editor   W. M. Williams

Hall, David J. Social Relations & Innovation. *Changing the State of Play in Hospitals. 232 pp.*

Hall, David J. and **Stacey, M.** (Eds) Beyond Separation. *234 pp.*

Robinson, David. The Process of Becoming Ill. *142 pp.*

Stacey, Margaret *et al.* Hospitals, Children and Their Families. *The Report of a Pilot Study. 202 pp.*

Stimson, G. V. and **Webb, B.** Going to See the Doctor. *The Consultation Process in General Practice. 155 pp.*

Monographs in Social Theory
General Editor   Arthur Brittan

● **Barnes, B.** Scientific Knowledge and Sociological Theory. *192 pp.*

Bauman, Zygmunt. Culture as Praxis. *204 pp.*

● **Dixon, Keith.** Sociological Theory. *Pretence and Possibility. 142 pp.*
The Sociology of Belief. *Fallacy and Foundation. About 160 pp.*

Goff, T. W. Marx and Mead. *Contributions to a Sociology of Knowledge. 176 pp.*

Meltzer, B. N., Petras, J. W. and **Reynolds, L. T.** Symbolic Interactionism. *Genesis, Varieties and Criticisms. 144 pp.*

● **Smith, Anthony D.** The Concept of Social Change. *A Critique of the Functionalist Theory of Social Change. 208 pp.*

Routledge Social Science Journals

The British Journal of Sociology. *Editor – Angus Stewart; Associate Editor – Leslie Sklair. Vol. 1, No. 1 – March 1950 and Quarterly. Roy. 8vo. All back issues available. An international journal publishing original papers in the field of sociology and related areas.*

Community Work. *Edited by David Jones and Marjorie Mayo. 1973. Published annually.*

Economy and Society. *Vol. 1, No. 1. February 1972 and Quarterly. Metric Roy. 8vo. A journal for all social scientists covering sociology, philosophy, anthropology, economics and history. All back numbers available.*

14

Ethnic and Racial Studies. *Editor – John Stone. Vol. 1 – 1978. Published quarterly.*
Religion. **Journal of Religion and Religions.** *Chairman of Editorial Board, Ninian Smart. Vol. 1, No. 1, Spring 1971. A journal with an inter-disciplinary approach to the study of the phenomena of religion. All back numbers available.*
Sociology of Health and Illness. *A Journal of Medical Sociology. Editor – Alan Davies; Associate Editor – Ray Jobling. Vol. 1, Spring 1979. Published 3 times per annum.*
Year Book of Social Policy in Britain. *Edited by Kathleen Jones. 1971. Published annually.*

Social and Psychological Aspects of Medical Practice
Editor Trevor Silverstone

Lader, Malcolm. Psychophysiology of Mental Illness. *280 pp.*
● Silverstone, Trevor and Turner, Paul. Drug Treatment in Psychiatry. *Revised edition. 256 pp.*
Whiteley, J. S. and Gordon, J. Group Approaches in Psychiatry. *240 pp.*

Printed and bound in Great Britain by
Redwood Burn Limited, Trowbridge & Esher